The Concept of Race in International Criminal Law

Members of racial groups are protected under international law against genocide, persecution, and apartheid. But what is race – and why was this contentious term not discussed when drafting the Statute of the International Criminal Court? Although the law uses this term, is it legitimate to talk about race today, let alone convict anyone for committing a crime against a racial group?

This book is the first comprehensive study of the concept of race in international criminal law. It explores the theoretical underpinnings for the crimes of genocide, apartheid, and persecution, and analyses all the relevant legal instruments, case law, and scholarship. It exposes how the international criminal tribunals have largely circumvented the topic of race, and how incoherent jurisprudence has resulted in inconsistent protection. The book provides important new interpretations of a problematic concept by subjecting it to a multifaceted and interdisciplinary analysis. The study argues that race in international criminal law should be constructed according to the perpetrator's perception of the victims' ostensible racial otherness. The perpetrator's imagination as manifested through his behaviour defines the victims' racial group membership.

It will be of interest to students and practitioners of international criminal law, as well as those studying genocide, apartheid, and race in domestic and international law.

Carola Lingaas is an associate professor of law at VID Specialized University in Oslo (Norway). She holds a PhD in international criminal law from the University of Oslo. She has published within the areas of international criminal law, human rights law, and migration. In most of her research projects, Professor Lingaas draws on research from the social sciences for the interpretation of the law. Prior to joining academia, Carola Lingaas worked for several years for the Red Cross, nationally and internationally.

International and Comparative Criminal Justice

Series Editors: Mark Findlay

Law School, Singapore Management University, Singapore

Ralph Henham

Nottingham Law School, Nottingham Trent University, UK

This series explores the new and rapidly developing field of international and comparative criminal justice and engages with its most important emerging themes and debates. It focuses on three interrelated aspects of scholarship which go to the root of understanding the nature and significance of international criminal justice in the broader context of globalization and global governance. These include: the theoretical and methodological problems posed by the development of international and comparative criminal justice; comparative contextual analysis; the reciprocal relationship between comparative and international criminal justice; and contributions which endeavor to build understandings of global justice on foundations of comparative contextual analysis.

Also in the series

Developing Restorative Justice Jurisprudence
Rethinking Responses to Criminal Wrongdoing
Tony Foley

The Exclusionary Rule of Evidence
Comparative Analysis and Proposals for Reform
Kuo-hsing Hsieh

Policing Undocumented Migrants
Law, Violence and Responsibility
Louise Boon-Kuo

Principled International Criminal Justice
Lessons from Tort Law
Mark Findlay and Joanna Chuah Hui Ying

The Concept of Race in International Criminal Law
Carola Lingaas

For more information about this series, please visit: www.routledge.com/International-and-Comparative-Criminal-Justice/book-series/ICCJ

The Concept of Race in International Criminal Law

Carola Lingaas

Routledge
Taylor & Francis Group
LONDON AND NEW YORK

First published 2020
by Routledge
2 Park Square, Milton Park, Abingdon, Oxon OX14 4RN

and by Routledge
52 Vanderbilt Avenue, New York, NY 10017

Routledge is an imprint of the Taylor & Francis Group, an informa business

First issued in paperback 2021

British Library Cataloguing-in-Publication Data
A catalogue record for this book is available from the British Library

Library of Congress Cataloging-in-Publication Data
A catalog record for this book has been requested

ISBN: 978-1-138-33554-7 (hbk)
ISBN: 978-1-03-208914-0 (pbk)
ISBN: 978-0-429-44372-5 (ebk)

Typeset in Galliard
by Apex CoVantage, LLC

To Aina and Sofia

Contents

Figures

Acronyms

AAPA	American Association of Physical Anthropologists
Add.	Addendum
AJIL	American Journal of International Law
Art.	Article
Arts.	Articles
BYIL	British Yearbook of International Law
CCL	Control Council Law
CERD	Committee on the Elimination of Racial Discrimination
comp.	compiled
CPK	Communist Party of Kampuchea
CUP	Cambridge University Press
DNA	Deoxyribonucleic acid
Doc	Document
DPRK	Democratic People's Republic of Korea
DRC	Democratic Republic of the Congo
ECCC	Extraordinary Chambers in the Courts of Cambodia
ECOSOC	Economic and Social Council
ECtHR	European Court of Human Rights
ed	edition/editor
eds	editors
eg	for example (*exempli gratia*)
EJIL	European Journal of International Law
ESCWA	Economic and Social Commission for Western Asia
et al.	and others (*et alii*)
etc	and so on (*et cetera*)
ETS	European Treaty Series
et seq.	and what follows (*et sequitur*)
GA	General Assembly
GAOR	General Assembly Official Records
IACtHR	Inter-American Court of Human Rights
ibid	in the same place (*ibidem*)
ICC	International Criminal Court

ICERD	International Convention on the Elimination of all Forms of Racial Discrimination
ICJ	International Court of Justice
ICRC	International Committee of the Red Cross
ICSID	International Centre for Settlement of Investment Disputes
ICTR	International Criminal Tribunal for the Prosecution of Persons Responsible for Genocide and Other Serious Violations of International Humanitarian Law Committed in the Territory of Rwanda and Rwandan Citizens Responsible for Genocide and Other such Violations Committed in the Territory of Neighbouring States, between 1 January 1994 and 31 December 1994, established by Resolution S/RES/955 (1994) of 8 November 1994.
ICTY	International Criminal Tribunal for the Prosecution of Persons Responsible for Serious Violations of International Humanitarian Law Committed in the Territory of the Former Yugoslavia since 1991, established by Resolution S/RES/827 (1993) on 25 May 1993.
ID	identity
ie	that is (*id est*)
ILC	International Law Commission
IMT	International Military Tribunal of Nuremberg
IMTFE	International Military Tribunal for the Far East
incl.	including
JICJ	Journal of International Criminal Justice
LJIL	Leiden Journal of International Law
NMT	Nuremberg Military Tribunals
No	Number
Nos	Numbers
Nr	Nummer (number)
NSDAP	Nationalsozialistische Deutsche Arbeiterpartei (National Socialist German Workers' Party)
OPT	Occupied Palestinian Territories
OUP	Oxford University Press
para	paragraph
PCA	Permanent Court of Arbitration
pp	pages
Res.	Resolution
RTLM	Radio Télévision Libre des Mille Collines
RuSHA	Rasse- und Siedlungshauptamt (Race and Settlement Main Office)
SC	Security Council
SS	Schutzstaffel
trans	translated
UDHR	Universal Declaration of Human Rights

UK	United Kingdom
UN	United Nations
UNCHR	United Nations Commission on Human Rights
UNESCO	United Nations Educational, Scientific and Cultural Organisation
UNRIAA	United Nations Reports of International Arbitral Awards
UNTS	United Nations Treaty Series
UNWCC	United Nations War Crimes Commission
UP	University Press
US	United States
USA	United States of America
USSR	Union of Soviet Socialist Republics
VCLT	Vienna Convention on the Law of Treaties
viz	that is to say (*videlicet*)
Vol.	Volume
vs	versus
WTO	World Trade Organisation
WWII	Second World War
YBILC	Yearbook of the International Law Commission

Acknowledgements

This book is the revised version of my doctoral thesis, written at the Institute for Public and International Law at the Faculty of Law, University of Oslo. During my employment as a PhD fellow, I received invaluable support and assistance from numerous persons. My heartfelt and sincere appreciation and gratitude go to my supervisors, Ulf Stridbeck and Gentian Zyberi. I also benefited from the advice of my two previous supervisors, Jo Stigen and Øystein Rolandsen, during the initial phase of writing the thesis.

My thanks extend to my former colleagues at the Institute, at PluriCourts, and the Faculty of Law for their unfailing support through the years. A special thank you goes to the ever thought-provoking and knowledgeable William Schabas, who commented the midway examination of the thesis, and Peter Scharff-Smith, Alette Smeulers, and Caroline Fournet, who formed the committee for my defence. I could not have wished for a better committee composed of such brilliant and critical academics. I am immensely grateful for the excellent feedback and suggestions they gave to me, both in the evaluation report and during the public defence of my thesis.

The metamorphosis of the thesis into a book took place at VID Specialized University where I am currently employed as an associate professor of law. I am grateful to the dean of the faculty for giving me the space and time to write this book, and to my colleagues for cheering along the way.

While researching this book, I benefited from generous funding that enabled me to look further and investigate deeper. I am very grateful to the Royal Norwegian Society of Sciences and Letters (DKNVS), Det juridiske fakultetets reisefond av 1973, incentives funds and internationalization grants of the Department of Public and International Law for generous funding that made field and archival research and participation at conferences possible. The National Commission for the Fight Against Genocide (CNLG) and Aegis Trust, both in Rwanda, granted me status as affiliate researcher and provided me with insight into the Rwandese genocide.

Many colleagues and friends have taken time to read and reflect on my work and discuss ideas with me. I particularly wish to thank Joanna Nicholson who has read, commented, re-read, and re-commented countless drafts. Thank you for lending me a hand, time and again. My gratitude extends to Dina Townsend and Eléonore Maitre-Ekrem for their continuous support. A big thank you also to the staff of Routledge for their patience and professional assistance.

Throughout the writing of this book, I have been blessed with a circle of wonderful friends whose support I value so deeply. My profound appreciation and heartfelt gratitude, however, goes to my wonderful daughters, Aina and Sofia, for their understanding and support. I could not be more proud of you. Above all, thank you, Snorre, for your unfailing trust, faith, and confidence in me – and in your constant support and love.

1 Constructing race for international criminal law

1.1 Introduction

> If people define a situation as real, it is real in its consequences.[1]

Whenever we describe someone or name something, we impose a classification. Classification is a fundamental operation of the human mind and therefore a product of our capacity for abstraction. The problem lies not in our ability to classify, but in treating classifications as though they were real.[2] The construction of a racial identity is essentially the outcome of a number of collective experiences involving the creation of binary pairs or opposites.[3] Each epoch, each society, each nation creates and re-creates 'others'. The identification and classification of these 'others' are subject to continuous interpretation and re-interpretation of how they differ from 'us'. Their identity in this sense can therefore be wholly artificial, created solely with a view to highlighting perceived

1 So-called **Thomas Theorem**. This axiom by W. I. Thomas and Dorothy Swaine Thomas has been proclaimed one of sociology's most influential ideas: <www.encyclopedia.com/doc/1O88-ThomasTheorem.html>.

2 Rogers Brubaker, *Ethnicity Without Groups* (Harvard UP 2004) 32, 72; John Searle, *The Construction of Social Reality* (Penguin 1996) 1–9, 75, 87–88, 227–228; Gregory Stanton, 'Blue Scarves and Yellow Stars: Classification and Symbolization in the Cambodian Genocide' (1989) <www.genocidewatch.org/images/AboutGen89BlueScarvesandYellowStars.pdf>. All websites last accessed 30 April 2019.

3 Robert Wald Sussman, *The Myth of Race: The Troubling Persistence of an Unscientific Idea* (Harvard UP 2014) 1–2, 304–305; Zimitri Erasmus, 'Apartheid Race Categories', 79 *Transformation* (2012) 2–3; Thomas Hylland Eriksen, *Ethnicity and Nationalism* (Pluto Press 3rd ed 2010) 5; Stephen Cornell, Douglas Hartmann, *Ethnicity and Race: Making Identities in a Changing World* (Pine Forge Press 1998) 23; Michael Banton, *International Action Against Racial Discrimination* (Clarendon Press 1996) 76–82; Ellis Cashmore, 'Race', in Ellis Cashmore (ed), *Dictionary of Race and Ethnic Relations* (Routledge 3rd ed 1994) 267.

differences between 'us' and 'them' – and to justify discriminatory treatment.[4] The crimes of genocide, apartheid, and persecution originate at this group-level discrimination of 'others'.

In international criminal law, the provisions on the crimes of genocide, apartheid, and persecution all include references to the concept of race. In each instance, the law seeks to protect individuals recognised as belonging to a group or collectivity.[5] The perpetrator[6] targets an individual precisely because of his[7] membership of such a group, including the racial group. Race is thus one of several categories that the law puts at the disposal of the courts. For the crime of genocide, the law offers the racial, ethnical, religious, and national group. For the crime of apartheid, the law only mentions the racial group, while the crime of persecution lists political, racial, national, ethnic, cultural, religious, gender, or other grounds that are universally recognised as impermissible under international law.[8] The category 'racial group' is an analytical tool for extrapolating from individual victims the purported characteristic of the imagined archetypal 'racial' group member.[9] However, the assignment of victims to such a category does not signify its objective existence. What it does show is that the perpetrators – and consequently the judges – assume that they do.[10]

The concept of race has a physical connotation, originating in the now highly contested idea of classifying individuals according to one or more phenotypical traits. At the same time, race transcends biology and carries with it a metaphysical dimension, according to which a person's racial group membership is defined by a perception of his otherness. Despite scientific advances in genetic research overturning common beliefs of the existence of racial categories of humans, the social relevance of racial categorisation, racial discrimination, and race-thinking

4 David Livingstone Smith, *Less Than Human: Why We Demean, Enslave, and Exterminate Others* (St. Martin's Press 2011) 167; Sussman (n 3) 1; Brubaker (n 2) 72; William Schabas, *Genocide in International Law: The Crime of Crimes* (CUP 2nd ed 2009) 142; Banton (n 3) 76–82; Mark Levene, 'A Twentieth-Century Phenomenon?', in Carol Rittner, John Roth, James Smith (eds), *Will Genocide Ever End?* (Paragon 2002) 66.

5 Already in its first session in 1946, the General Assembly affirmed that 'genocide is the denial of the right of existence of entire groups' (UN Doc A/PV.55 (11 December 1946) 1134). The group notion is discussed in Chapters 3.5.2 (genocide), 4.6.2 (apartheid), 5.3.4.3 (persecution) and 5.4.3 (persecution).

6 Understood according to General Introduction to the Elements of Crimes of the Rome Statute, para 8: 'the term "perpetrator" is neutral as to guilt or innocence'.

7 For reasons of readability and simplicity, this book uses the masculine form in referring to unspecific individuals. This shall, however, have no implications as to the gender of a victim or perpetrator.

8 Art. 6 Rome Statute (genocide), Art. 7(1)(j) Rome Statute (apartheid), Art. 7(1)(h) Rome Statute (persecution).

9 Nigel Eltringham, *Accounting for Horror: Post-Genocide Debates in Rwanda* (Pluto Press 2004) 7.

10 Ibid 7–8. Furthermore: Stanton (n 2).

remains high.[11] Race-thinking is a way of imagining the distinctiveness of human groups and assigning meaning to perceivable features of the human body.[12] As such, the contours of race are inextricably linked to a mental image. So even though humans cannot be exhaustively divided into discrete biological human races, individuals are nonetheless targeted for their imagined membership of an imagined racial group. For the crimes of genocide, apartheid, and persecution, the victims' racial group membership is inherently linked to processes of discrimination, stigmatisation, inferiorisation, and what is generally known today as 'othering'. The perpetrators of these crimes interpret race as signifying their own superiority in the face of the inferiority of their victims, an idealized conception, which, in the mind of the perpetrators justifies an assault on the inferior racial group. The latter group is considered intrinsically different and alien and triggers feelings of fear. The perpetrator perceives the inferior group as a threat to the dominant group's position, resulting in prejudices as a defensive action.[13]

Much of our (legal) worldview depends on an understanding of objectivity.[14] In their search for an objective reality, courts seek to render predictable, verifiable judgments that are coherent with the principle of legality and its corollaries of specificity and foreseeability.[15] The Commission of Experts on Rwanda, for example, stated that while there is a need 'to recognise that there exists discrimination on racial or ethnic grounds, it is not necessary to presume or posit the existence of race or ethnicity itself as a scientifically objective fact'.[16] There is no legal requirement to advance or claim an objective classification of the racial group for any of the crimes examined in the framework of this study. Rather than relying on the objectivity of criminal law, courts need to see through

11 American Association of Physical Anthropologists, Statement on Race and Racism (March 2019), at: <www.physanth.org/about/position-statements/aapa-statement-race-and-racism-2019/>; Sussman (n 3) 2, 8; Smith (n 4) 164, 167; Eric Carlton, *War and Ideology* (Routledge 1990) 168.

12 Paul Taylor, *Race: A Philosophical Introduction* (Polity Press 2nd ed 2013) 20–21, 60; Brubaker (n 2) 32; Carlton (n 11) 169.

13 I. William Zartman, Mark Anstey, 'The Problem: Preventing Identity Conflicts and Genocide', in I. William Zartman, Mark Anstey, Paul Meerts (eds), *The Slippery Slope to Genocide: Reducing Identity Conflicts and Preventing Mass Murder* (OUP 2012) 3; Alette Smeulers, Fred Grünfeld, *International Crimes and other Gross Human Rights Violations: A Multi- and Interdisciplinary Textbook* (Martinus Nijhoff 2011) 249; Helen Fein, 'States of Genocide and other States', in Carol Rittner, John Roth, James Smith (eds), *Will Genocide Ever End?* (Paragon 2002) 47; Lincoln Quillian, 'Prejudice as a Response to Perceived Group Threat: Population Composition and Anti-Immigrant and Racial Prejudice in Europe', 60 *American Sociological Review* (1995) 588, with reference to Blumer's group-level theories. See Chapter 3.2 on othering.

14 Searle (n 2) 7, 150.

15 *Prosecutor v Hadžihasanović, Alagić and Kubura*, Case No IT-01–47-AR72, Decision on Interlocutory Appeal Challenging Jurisidiction in Relation to Command Responsibility (16 July 2003) para 34.

16 Final Report of the Commission of Experts Established Pursuant to Security Council Resolution 935 (1994), UN Doc S/1994/1405, para 159.

the eyes of the perpetrator. This study therefore suggests a subjective definition of the racial group, one mirrored in the perpetrator's intent and perception of his victims' otherness.

1.2 Interpreting race for international criminal law

Historically, situations of massive human rights violations have been dealt with by various means such as truth and reconciliation commissions or amnesties. Nowadays, there is an undisputable trend toward prosecuting international crimes.[17] The creation of the International Criminal Court (ICC) as the first permanent treaty-based criminal court was of major significance, despite recent criticism concerning its seemingly biased prosecutorial selection of cases.[18] The law of genocide, persecution, and apartheid in the Rome Statute of the ICC,[19] the Convention on the Prevention and Punishment of the Crime of Genocide (Genocide Convention),[20] and the International Convention on the Suppression and Punishment of the Crime of Apartheid (Apartheid Convention),[21] together with other statutes, are the focus of this study. They provide the normative foundation for the analysis of the term 'racial'. The three crimes that contain a reference to the concept of race are defined as follows: 'genocide means any of the following acts committed with intent to destroy, in whole or in part, a national, ethnical, racial or religious group, as such'.[22] The crime of apartheid means 'inhumane acts . . . committed in the context of an institutionalized regime of systematic oppression and domination by one racial group over any other racial group'.[23] Finally, persecution is a crime against humanity committed 'against any identifiable group or collectivity on political, racial, national, ethnic, cultural, religious, gender . . ., or other grounds that are universally recognised as impermissible under international law'.[24] The law of genocide, apartheid, and persecution does not define race. Yet, in penalising discriminatory treatment of a 'racial group' or 'on racial grounds', it becomes necessary to legally interpret

17 Dov Jacobs, 'Positivism and International Criminal Law: The Principle of Legality as a Rule of Conflict of Theories', in Jean d'Aspremont, Jörg Kammerhofer (eds), *International Legal Positivism in a Post-Modern World* (CUP 2014) 23; Ilias Bantekas, 'The Anthropological Dimension of International Crimes and International Criminal Justice', in Ilias Bantekas, Emmanouela Mylonaki (eds), *Criminological Approaches to International Criminal Law* (CUP 2014) 248.

18 Nicole Rafter, *The Crime of All Crimes: Toward a Criminology of Genocide* (NYUP 2016) 202.

19 UN Doc. A/CONF.183/9 (17 July 1998).

20 UN GA Res. 260 (III) ((9 December 1948), 78 UNTS 277.

21 UN GA Res. 3068, UN Doc. A/9030 (1973).

22 Art. 2 Genocide Convention, Art. 6 Rome Statute, Art. 2 ICTY Statute and Art. 4 ICTR Statute.

23 Art. 7(2)(h) Rome Statute.

24 Art. 7(1)(h) Rome Statute.

race. That interpretation may differ from related definitions suitable for biological or other purposes.[25] With each judgment, so it seems, international criminal tribunals have sought to re-define the requirements of racial group membership, resulting in inconsistent protection for the victims of international crimes. The interpretation of one single adjective – racial – can change the outcome of a trial. When, furthermore, ambiguity arises on definitions, the *in dubio pro reo* rule applies, entailing a legal interpretation in favour of the defendant.[26] In the Rwandan case, for example, there was a considerable risk that *génocidaires* would benefit from this rule and be acquitted insofar as their Tutsi victims could not be categorically said to belong to any of the four protected groups of genocide.[27]

In its attempt to define the exhaustive victim categories of genocide, the Trial Chamber of the International Criminal Tribunal for Rwanda (ICTR)[28] in the *Akayesu* judgment reverted to an objective understanding of race, 'based on the hereditary physical traits often identified with a geographical region, irrespective of linguistic, cultural, national or religious factors'.[29] Some legal scholars criticised this approach, but the majority remained silent and have done little to enlighten the issue of race for international criminal law. The number of references to the problem in the academic literature is therefore small,[30] creating a perceptible research gap this study aims to mitigate.

Albeit contained in three legal provisions, the concept of race has never been comprehensively analysed for international criminal law. Owing to its historical burden, the labelling of a group as a racial group is usually considered taboo in international law.[31] However, despite its dubious connotations, the term 'race' cannot in itself be treated as non-existent.[32] The continued use of the term is

25 Cashmore (n 3) 265. For reasons of readability, in discussing race, inverted commas will not be used.

26 Art. 22 (2) Rome Statute. See also *Prosecutor v Katanga*, Case No ICC-01/04–01/07, Judgment pursuant to Article 74 of the Statute (7 March 2014), para. 51.

27 See Chapter 3.6.5 on the legal categorisation of the Hutu and Tutsi.

28 International Criminal Tribunal for the Prosecution of Persons Responsible for Genocide and Other Serious Violations of International Humanitarian Law Committed in the Territory of Rwanda and Rwandan Citizens Responsible for Genocide and Other such Violations Committed in the Territory of Neighbouring States, between 1 January 1994 and 31 December 1994, established by Resolution S/RES/955 (1994) of 8 November 1994.

29 *Prosecutor v Akayesu*, Case No ICTR-96–4-T (2 September 1998), para. 514. See analysis of all relevant judgments of the ICTR and ICTY in Chapter 3.9.2.

30 Schabas (n 4) 140; John Jones, Steven Powles, *International Criminal Practice: The International Criminal Tribunal for the Former Yugoslavia, The International Criminal Tribunal for Rwanda, The International Criminal Court, The Special Court of Sierra Leone, The East Timor Special Panels for Serious Crimes, War Crimes Prosecutions in Kosovo* (OUP 3rd ed 2003) 172.

31 Larissa van den Herik, *The Contribution of the Rwanda Tribunal to the Development of International Law* (Martinus Nijhoff 2005) 267.

32 Gro Nystuen, *Achieving Peace or Protecting Human Rights? Conflicts Between Norms Regarding Ethnic Discrimination in the Dayton Peace Agreement* (Martinus Nijhoff 2005) 119.

not uncontroversial, not least because it perpetuates the categorisation of people and associated prejudices.[33] This study does not urge a re-negotiation of treaties such as the Genocide Convention or the Rome Statute of the ICC in order to replace or remove the word 'racial'. It also argues that replacing 'race' with 'colour'[34] will neither prevent stigmatisation for reasons of perceived racial characteristics nor assist the courts in determining the group membership of the victim. This study argues instead that, since its first appearance in positive international criminal law in context of post-WWII trials in 1945, the meaning of race has evolved. This changed understanding necessitates an evolutive interpretation of race for the crime of genocide, apartheid, and persecution to embrace socially constructed identities and the perception of an individual's belonging to a distinct racial group.[35] This study, in particular, maintains that the concept of othering is crucial not only to understand genocide, apartheid, and persecution, but essential to correctly identify and define race in international criminal law.

1.3 Structure

Each of the crimes examined in this book presents its own challenges in the analysis of the concept of race. At first sight, the crime of apartheid seems to be the most suitable to evaluate the notion of race because it protects only racial groups. However, since there has never been a criminal trial, let alone a conviction, for the crime of apartheid, its marginal role in international criminal law should be acknowledged. As to the crime of persecution, the multitude of discriminatory grounds listed in the respective provisions doubtless encourages courts to circumvent any issues of race. Indeed, judicial efforts to define racial grounds for the crime of persecution have been trivial at best. This leaves genocide as the decidedly most appropriate crime through which to examine the concept of race. It will dominate the legal analysis of this book also for other reasons. First, there is extensive case law on genocide from the international tribunals on the atrocities in Rwanda and the former Yugoslavia as well as the subsequent practices of other courts. Second, while it is contested whether apartheid constitutes a crime in a post-apartheid world, the relevance of the crime of genocide remains high, as a fairly recent arrest warrant issued by the ICC for the alleged commission of genocide and a judgment by the Trial Chamber of the Extraordinary Chambers in the Courts of Cambodia (ECCC)

33 Sharona Hoffman, 'Is There a Place for "Race" as a Legal Concept?', 36 *Arizona State Law Journal* (2004) 1098–1099, 1159; Gordon Allport, *The Nature of Prejudice* (Doubleday Anchor Books 2nd ed 1958) xii.

34 As suggested by Hoffman (n 33) 1146.

35 See Chapter 3.7.2 on evolutive interpretation.

confirms.[36] Third, the crime of genocide has a special position in international law, owing to its elevated status as a treaty and a customary crime and its *jus cogens* prohibition.[37] Lastly, the crime of genocide with its special intent to destroy a group as such is particularly well suited to revealing the interconnectedness of the perpetrator's intent and his selection of the racial victim group. Later discussions will show that the protected groups of genocide, including the racial group, are subjectively defined by means of the perpetrator's *mens rea*.[38]

This book unfolds in a sequence of six chapters, each devoted to the question: what is race in context of international criminal law? Chapter 1 contains introductory remarks, while Chapter 2 provides a historical insight into the discovery and expansion of the concept of race, with a particular focus on how the Nazis defined race and how that definition prompted its later inclusion in the Genocide Convention. Albeit not limited to legal history, these discussions create the understanding of race on which the later legal analyses will rely. Chapter 2 also deals with contemporary approaches to race, particularly in sociology and anthropology, which have proven to be of considerable value to this research. This study will limit itself to stating the findings of natural scientists in order to refute the claim that individuals can be usefully categorised into distinct racial groups on the basis of physical traits.[39] The following three chapters are the centrepiece of the study. Chapter 3 discusses the crimes of genocide, Chapter 4 examines the crime against humanity of apartheid, and Chapter 5 analyses the crime against humanity of persecution. Finally, Chapter 6 offers a final conclusion.

36 *Prosecutor v Al-Bashir*, Case No ICC-02/05-01/09-94, Second Decision on the Prosecution's Application for a Warrant of Arrest against Omar Hassan Ahmad Al Bashir (12 July 2010); *Prosecutor v Nuon Chea and Khieu Samphân*, Case No 002/19-09-2007/ECCC/TC (16 November 2018).

37 *Case Concerning Armed Activities on the Territory of the Congo* (*Democratic Republic of the Congo* v *Uganda*), Jurisdiction of the Court and Admissibility of the Application, ICJ Judgment (2006), para. 64 with reference to *Application of the Convention on the Prevention and Punishment of the Crime of Genocide (Bosnia and Herzegovina* v *Yugoslavia)*, ICJ Judgment on Preliminary Objections (1996), para. 31.

38 See foremost Chapter 3.5.3.

39 For in-depth discussions, the reader is referred to specialised scholarship.

2 Historical aspects of race

> [Some people] imagine . . . that the essential stuffing of two races may be as different as copper and quicksilver.[1]

2.1 Introduction

This chapter provides a fragmentary overview of the history of race. It starts by discussing the discovery of race, before narrowing in on the racial theories and laws of the National Socialist German Workers' Party (*Nationalsozialistische Deutsche Arbeiterpartei*, NSDAP, or in short Nazi), which ultimately led to the Holocaust. The extermination of the Jews and other groups deemed racially inferior by the Nazis is undoubtedly one of history's most atrocious genocides. The chapter concludes by exploring contemporary understandings of race and ethnicity, which create an important baseline for the later discussions on race for the crimes of genocide, apartheid, and persecution. While the focus of this chapter is primarily legal history, the non-legal parts contribute to an understanding of the dynamics of racial relations, particularly leading up to the Holocaust. The next section will identify developments that eventually enabled the establishment and enforcement of the Nazi racial theories. As such, it is not a comprehensive historical review of the concept of race. Rather, it limits itself to a few selected historical proponents dealing with race whose theories assisted the creation of the Nazi racial worldview.

2.2 The discovery of race

In the sixteenth century, Europeans colonized large parts of the world. In their encounter with new cultures and peoples, the colonialists discovered what they considered to be fundamental and symptomatic differences in appearance and behaviour, which justified and legitimized subjugation, enslavement, and

1 Gunnar Dahlberg, *Race, Reason and Rubbish: An Examination of the Biological Credentials of the Nazi Creed* (Unwin Brothers 1942) 200.

sometimes even extermination of the racially distinct 'others'.[2] Racial classification of the inferior 'other' captured the attention of scientists who attempted to establish a scientific foundation of racial differences. In discussions of race, the names of two scientists appear regularly: Carl Linnaeus and Arthur de Gobineau.[3] Their discoveries informed the scientific foundation of racial scientism of later years. In his book *Systema Naturae* (1758), the Swedish scientist Carl Linnaeus (1707–78) created a link between exterior features and inner qualities. Based on the four natural elements (air, earth, fire, and water), the four points of the compass (north, east, south, and west), the four continents (Europe, America, Asia, and Africa), and the four humours of the body (blood, phlegm, yellow and black bile), the four canonical races were defined: *Europeaeus* (white), *Asiaticus* (yellow), *Africanus* (black), and *Americanus* (red).[4] According to Linnaeus, each of the different racial groups had different characteristics, including temperament and posture.[5]

Arthur de Gobineau (1816–82), who claimed to be a descendant of the Nordic God Odin and the Norwegian pirate Ottar Jarl, exerted a strong influence on Nazi race theories.[6] In his *Essay on the Inequality of the Human Race*

2 Mark Kielsgard, *Responding to Modern Genocide: At the Confluence of Law and Politics* (Routledge 2016) 17; Alon Confino, *A World Without Jews: The Nazi Imagination from Persecution to Genocide* (Yale UP 2014) 11; Paul Taylor, *Race: A Philosophical Introduction* (Polity Press 2nd ed 2013) 39–40; David Livingstone Smith, *Less Than Human: Why We Demean, Enslave, and Exterminate Others* (St. Martin's Press 2011) 3; Jonathan Marks, 'Race: Past, Present, and Future', in Barbara Koenig, Sandra Soo-Jin Lee, Sarah Richardson (eds), *Revisiting Race in a Genomic Age* (Rutgers UP 2008) 22; Guillermo Levy, 'Considerations on the Connections between Race, Politics, Economics, and Genocide', 8 *Journal of Genocide Research* (2006) 138; Eric Weitz, *A Century of Genocide: Utopias of Race and Nation* (Princeton UP 2003) 20, 24, 27; Stephen Cornell, Douglas Hartmann, *Ethnicity and Race: Making Identities in a Changing World* (Pine Forge Press 1998) 22, 27.

3 Michael Banton, *What We Now Know About Race and Ethnicity* (Berghahn 2015) 13; Robert Wald Sussman, *The Myth of Race: The Troubling Persistence of an Unscientific Idea* (Harvard UP 2014) 15–19; Carolyn Fluehr-Lobban, *Race and Racism: An Introduction* (AltaMira Press 2006) 10; Richard Osborne, 'The History and Nature of Race Classification', in Richard Osborne (ed), *The Biological and Social Meaning of Race* (WH Freeman & Co 1971) 159–164; Lars Beckman, *Ras och Rasfördomar* (Prisma 1966) 27.

4 Jonathan Marks, 'Solving the Riddle of Race', 59 *Studies in History and Philosophy of Biological and Biomedical Sciences* (2016) 162; Michael Yudell, *Race Unmasked: Biology and Race in the Twentieth Century* (Colombia UP 2014) 26; Staffan Müller-Wille, 'Race and History: Comments from an Epistemological Point of View', 39 *Science, Technology and Human Values* (2014) 598–601; Christian Sundquist, 'The Meaning of Race in the DNA Era: Science, History and the Law', 27 *Temple Journal of Science, Technology and Environmental Law* (2008) 234–235; Fluehr-Lobban (n 3) 10–11; Loïc Wacquant, 'For an Analytic of Racial Domination', 11 *Political Power and Social Theory* (1997) 223, 231; Stephan Jay Gould, *The Mismeasure of Man* (3rd ed Penguin 1997) 403–405.

5 Müller-Wille (n 4) 601; Nystuen (n 4) 119; Wacquant (n 4) 223, 231.

6 Carole Reynaud-Paligot, 'Construction and Circulation of the Notion of "Race" in the Nineteenth Century', in Nicolas Bancel, Thomas David, Dominic Thomas (eds), *The Invention of Race: Scientific and Popular Representations* (Routledge 2014) 93; Hannah Arendt, *The Origins of Totalitarianism* (Harcourt Brace & Co 1951) 172.

Figure 2.1 Human Races. Unknown year. Engraving by John Henry Walker (1831–1899).

Photo credit: McCord Museum, M991X.5.300.

(1853–55), Gobineau concluded that mixing races led to degeneration and ultimately to a decrease in blood quality.[7] His vision was the superiority of the white race in terms of beauty, strength, and intelligence; within the white race, the Aryan-Germanic races were the most intelligent, energetic, and strongest.[8]

7 Banton (n 3) 15; Anton Weiss-Wendt, Rory Yeomans, 'The Holocaust and Historiographical Debates on Racial Science', in Anton Weiss-Wendt, Rory Yeomans (eds), *Racial Science in Hitler's New Europe, 1938–1945* (University of Nebraska Press 2013) 4; Weitz (n 2) 34, 37; Lawrence Hirschfeld, *Race in the Making: Cognition, Culture, and the Child's Construction of Human Kinds* (Massachusetts Institute of Technology 1996) 55.

8 Sussman (n 3) 37–38; Reynaud-Paligot (n 6) 93; Nigel Eltringham, '"Invaders Who Have Stolen the Country": The Hamitic Hypothesis, Race and the Rwandan Genocide', 12 *Social Identities* (2006) 437; Weitz (n 2) 35; Michael Banton, *Racial Theories* (CUP 2nd ed 1998) 63–68.

The use of Gobineau's ideas by the Nazis created the myth that his *Essay* was a major work.[9] However, his vision was in no way original; rather it popularized ideas of the intellectual community of his time.[10]

The notion of contamination of pure blood was also applied in the so-called Jim Crow legislation of the United States (US), an act that remained in force until 1965. Most Southern states adopted the 'one-drop rule', under which an individual with a traceable amount of black ancestry was considered black.[11] The strict separation of races is also illustrated in a US trial judge's statement of 1958: 'Almighty God created the races white, black, yellow, Malay and red, and he placed them on separate continents. . . . The fact that he separated the races shows that he did not intend for the races to mix'.[12] Similarly, the Prime Minister of South Africa during the apartheid era called for 'no intermixture of blood between the two colours' because the 'civilizing races [were] rapidly submerged in the quicksands of the African blood'.[13] Disturbing as these racialist and colonialist theories may appear today, they were completely in line with the public opinion of the time.[14]

In sum, the so-called races of mankind are incidental and arbitrary social designations invented during the eighteenth century to identify and organise the peoples encountered during European colonialism.[15]

2.3 Social Darwinism and eugenics

The theoretical framework of social Darwinism originates in the ideas of Charles Darwin (1809–82) and his seminal work *On the Origin of Species by Means of Natural Selection* (1859), in which he argued that the main driving force in the evolution of species was the struggle for survival and natural selection. Only the best-adapted variations within a species were transferred to the next

9 Sussman (n 3) 36–37; Reynaud-Paligot (n 6) 93–94; Arendt (n 6) 170.

10 Reynaud-Paligot (n 6) 93–94; Fluehr-Lobban (n 3) 106; Weitz (n 2) 34; Banton (n 47) 63.

11 Banton (n 3) 43–44; Yudell (n 4) 41–42; Sussman (n 3) 74; Smith (n 2) 184; Marks (n 2) 22; Fluehr-Lobban (n 3) 12–15; Cornell, Hartmann (n 2) 24; Hirschfeld (n 7) 161–162; Ian Haney López, *White by Law: The Legal Construction of Race* (NYUP 2006) 20, 83.

12 Judge Leon M. Bazile, Indictment for Felony (1958), *Loving v Virginia*, <https://lva.omeka.net/items/show/54>.

13 Quoted in John Reynolds, 'Third World Approaches to International Law and the Ghosts of Apartheid', in David Keane, Yvonne McDermott (eds), *The Challenge of Human Rights: Past, Present and Future* (Edward Elgar 2012) 197. Chapters 4.2–4.4. discuss the history of apartheid.

14 Tzvetan Todorov, 'Critical Response: "Race", Writing, and Culture' (trans Loulou Mack), 13 *Critical Inquiry* (1986) 179.

15 Richard Cooper, Jay Kaufman, Ryk Ward, 'Race and Genomics', 348 *New England Journal of Medicine* (2003) 1166; David Brion Davis, 'Constructing Race: A Reflection', 54 *The William and Mary Quarterly: A Magazine of Early American History and Culture* (1997) 7.

generation.[16] Social Darwinism accordingly offered the concept 'survival of the fittest' as a school of thought based on the laws of nature that prescribes the supremacy of the stronger and healthier over the weaker.[17] Adolf Hitler (1889–1945), as leader of the Nazi Party, Chancellor, and *Führer* of Germany from 1933 to 1945, adopted 'the crudest perversion of the familiar Darwinian view' and portrayed the Jews as enemies whose sole intention was the weakening of Aryan racial purity.[18] In his book *Mein Kampf*, Hitler stressed that there could be no intermixing with weaker races; this would cause an intellectual and physical decline of the higher Aryan race.[19] While Hitler misused social Darwinism for political purposes, it was part of the European public and scientific discourse on race long before the Nazis came to power.[20] The social Darwinist movement inspired the new science of eugenics.[21] The term 'eugenics' signifies selective breeding in order to promote favoured characteristics and eradicate features believed harmful.[22] The theory of natural selection, inheritance of physical characteristics, and the modification by interbreeding transformed the concept of race. In the view of eugenists, race became a means to enhance a group's value.[23] Notably, one of the earliest laws adopted by the Nazi government was the Eugenic Law of 1933 (*Gesetz zur Verhütung erbkranken Nachwuchses*).[24]

Francis Galton (1822–1911) and Alfred Ploetz (1860–1940) developed independently of one another policies of so-called racial hygiene. Racial hygiene had the aim of promoting superior genetic traits, thus the hereditary improvement of a population, and included stipulations on marriage in order to ensure healthy and well-educated families.[25] Ploetz represented a school of eugenics that

16 Taylor (n 2) 42; Jon Røyne Kyllingstad, *Kortskaller og Langskaller: Fysisk Antropologi i Norge og Striden om det Nordiske Herremennesket* (Scandinavian Academic Press 2004) 17; Banton (n 47) 84–86.

17 Sussman (n 3) 48; Wolfgang Bialas, 'The Eternal Violence of the Blood: Racial Science and Nazi Ethics', in Anton Weiss-Wendt, Rory Yeomans (eds), *Racial Science in Hitler's New Europe, 1938–1945* (University of Nebraska Press 2013) 358; Sundquist (n 4) 243–244; Fluehr-Lobban (n 3) 17; Arendt (n 6) 178.

18 Marius Marrus, 'Hitler's Antisemitism', in Frank Chalk, Kurt Jonassohn (eds), *The History and Sociology of Genocide* (Yale UP 1990) 331.

19 Adolf Hitler, *Mein Kampf* (Verlag Franz Eher Nachfolger 13th ed 1932) 312–314.

20 Bialas (n 17) 358; François Haas, 'German Science and Black Racism: Roots of the Nazi Holocaust', 22 *The FASEB Journal* (2008) 336.

21 Sussman (n 3) 49; Sundquist (n 4) 245; Arendt (n 6) 178.

22 Yudell (n 4) 14; Taylor (n 2) 44; Weiss-Wendt, Yeomans (n 7) 5.

23 Michael Banton, *International Action Against Racial Discrimination* (Clarendon Press 1996) 84.

24 Isabel Heinemann, 'Defining "(Un)Wanted Population Addition"', in Anton Weiss-Wendt, Rory Yeomans (eds), *Racial Science in Hitler's New Europe* (University of Nebraska Press 2013) 39.

25 Sussman (n 3) 49–51; Yudell (n 4) 16, 29; Amy Carney, 'Preserving the "Master Race"', in Anton Weiss-Wendt, Rory Yeomans (eds), *Racial Science in Hitler's New Europe* (University of Nebraska Press 2013) 62; Kyllingstad (n 16) 80; Weitz (n 2) 38–39, 41; Robert Proctor, 'Nazi Doctor, Racial Medicine, and Human Experimentation', in George Annas, Michael Grodin (eds), *The Nazi Doctors and the Nuremberg Code: Human Rights in Human Experimentation* (OUP 1992) 18.

Figure 2.2 Winderen Laboratorium: Unharmonic Racecrossings. Unknown year.

Source: Courtesy Kristiania Arbeiderakademi/ Norwegian Museum of Science and Technology.

emphasised the importance of the Nordic race, whereas Galton connected his theory of racial hygiene to the issue of good or bad hereditary characteristics.[26] Anti-Semitism was not a vital factor; Ploetz even considered the Jewish race, together with the Nordic, one of the superior races of the world.[27] Influenced by Darwinian evolutionary theory and coinciding with European imperialist expansion and colonialism of the time, Galton believed that the different races reflected a natural evolutionary hierarchy, headed by the Europeans at the top. Such views were widely held, in myriad disciplines, ranging from psychology, to anthropology, ethnography, and biology. The wide support of various disciplines, in combination with popular approval, undoubtedly contributed to legitimising scientific racism.[28]

26 Francis Galton, 'Hereditary Talent and Character', 12 *Macmillan's Magazine* (1865) 318–327. Furthermore: Sussman (n 3) 111; Kyllingstad (n 16) 80; Robert Proctor, 'From *Anthropologie* to *Rassenkunde* in the German Anthropological Tradition', in George Stocking (ed), *Bones, Bodies, Behavior: Essays on Biological Anthropology* (University of Wisconsin Press 1988) 143.

27 Kyllingstad (n 16) 80; Proctor (n 25) 18.

28 Martha Augoustinos, Katherine Reynolds, 'Prejudice, Racism, and Social Psychology', in Martha Augoustinos, Katherine Reynolds (eds), *Understanding Prejudice, Racism, and Social Conflict* (Sage Publications 2001) 5.

Not only natural and social scientists, but also international lawyers influenced the racialized thinking of the time. While many believed in a hierarchy of races, with the Europeans as the superior race, few expressed their sentiments as openly as James Lorimer (1818–90).[29] His book *The Institutes of Law* reads: 'the single life of Socrates is of greater value than the whole existence of the Negro race'.[30] According to Lorimer, statehood was a racial category, and the development of a state depended on the quality of its inhabitants' race.[31] If the power of the state fell into the hands of the inferior race, there was a risk that 'the absolute claim of the superior race itself will be cut off'.[32] According to Lorimer, the law needed to be aligned with the facts, including racial hierarchies. Since race was a scientific category and justification for generalizing the behaviour of human groups, it was a necessary aspect of international law.[33]

2.4 Nazi race theories

Germany's defeat after World War I caused humiliation, destabilization, and recession.[34] National Socialism radicalized Jewish hatred by making the Jews responsible for all the symptoms of decay of the pre- and interwar time.[35] In seizing power in 1933, the Nazis elevated the persecution of Jews to official state policy.[36] Although 'the Nazis neither invented nor monopolized [the] idea of superior peoples, . . . the consequences they wrought gave [the notion] a

29 Martti Koskenniemi, 'Race, Hierarchy and International Law: Lorimer's Legal Science', 27 *EJIL* (2016) 415–417.
30 Quoted in ibid 421.
31 Ibid 424.
32 Ibid 425.
33 Ibid 429.
34 Sussman (n 3) 110; Adam Jones, *Genocide: A Comprehensive Introduction* (Routledge 2nd ed 2011) 236; Ben Kiernan, *Blood and Soil: A World History of Genocide and Extermination From Sparta to Darfur* (Yale UP 2007) 418.
35 Internationaler Militärgerichtshof Nürnberg, Der Prozess gegen die Hauptkriegsverbrecher vor dem Internationalen Militärgerichtshof, Nürnberg 14. November 1945–1. Oktober 1946, Band I: Amtlicher Wortlaut in Deutscher Sprache (1947) 200; Werner May, *Deutscher Nationalkatechismus: Dem jungen Deutschen in Schule und Beruf* (Heinrich Handels Verlag 2nd ed 1934) 24; Hitler (n 19) 359–360.

Furthermore: Richard Heideman, 'Legalizing Hate: The Significance of the Nuremberg Laws and the Post-War Nuremberg Trials', 39 *Loyola LA International & Comparative Law Review* (2017) 12–13; Michael Bazyler, *Holocaust, Genocide, and the Law: A Quest for Justice in a Post-Holocaust World* (OUP 2016) 5; Kielsgard (n 2) 65; Confino (n 2) 14, 30, 151; Taylor (n 2) 43; Jones (n 34) 34; Marrus (n 18) 332; Yehuda Bauer, 'The Evolution of Nazi Jewish Policy, 1933–1938', in Frank Chalk, Kurt Jonassohn (eds), *The History and Sociology of Genocide* (Yale UP 1990) 338; Lucy Dawidowicz, *The War Against the Jews: 1933–1945* (Bantam 1975) 202–203, 214; Anonymous, 'Genocide: A Commentary on the Convention', 58 *Yale Law Journal* (1948–1949) 1142.
36 Internationaler Militärgerichtshof Nürnberg (n 35) 200; Proctor (n 26) 157; Michael Banton, 'Social Aspects of the Race Question', in UNESCO, *Four Statements on the Race Question* (1969) 17; Arendt (n 6) 158; Anonymous (n 35) 1142. In 1933, less than one

new and terrible meaning'.[37] Hans Friedrich Karl Günther (1891–1968), nicknamed *Rassengünther* (Race Günther) and *Rassenpapst* (Race Pope), laid the scientific foundation of Nazi Aryan racial superiority theories.[38] In his best-selling book *Eine Kleine Rassenkunde des Deutschen Volkes* (A Little Racial Lesson on the German People), Günther asserted:

> The Jews are not a religious community, because there exist Jews with different creeds and many so-called free-religious Jews, who do not belong to any certain creed. The Jews are a people and, same as any people, a mixture of different races.[39]

According to Günther, the outward appearance, genetic predisposition, and mental qualities of the group members demonstrated the higher value of the Aryan race.[40] Günther described the Jews as 'a thing of ferment and disturbance, a wedge driven by Asia into the European structure'.[41] Quite in the spirit of the time, Günther advised against racial mixing because it would lead to racial degeneration.[42] Nazi policies caused polarization in racial scholarship.[43] One scholar who openly criticised the Nazis during their ascendancy was the Swedish physician and racial biologist Gunnar Dahlberg (1893–1956). As part of a larger academic movement,[44] Dahlberg denounced Nazi anti-Semitism. The Jews, Dahlberg wrote in his work *Race, Reason, Rubbish* (1942), could not possibly

percent of Germans were practicing Jews: Bazyler (n 35) 8; Robert Gellately, 'The Third Reich, the Holocaust, and Visions of Serial Genocide', in Robert Gellately, Ben Kiernan (eds), *The Specter of Genocide: Mass Murder in Historical Perspective* (CUP 2003) 244.

37 *United States of America v Ulrich Greifelt* et al. (*RuSHA* Case), Trials of War Criminals Before the Nuremberg Military Tribunals under Control Council Law No 10, Vol. 4, Opening Statement of the Prosecution (October 1946–April 1949) 33. See also Proctor (n 26) 139–140.

38 Claus Bundgård Christensen, Niels Bo Poulsen, Peter Scharff Smith, *Waffen-SS: Europas Nazistiske Soldater* (Gyldendal 2015) 83; Sussman (n 3) 123; Terje Emberland, 'Pure-Blooded Vikings and Peasants', in Anton Weiss-Wendt, Rory Yeomans (eds), *Racial Science in Hitler's New Europe* (University of Nebraska Press 2013) 110; Sundquist (n 4) 251; Kiernan (n 34) 420–421; Proctor (n 26) 149, 157.

39 <https://archive.org/stream/Guenther-Hans-Kleine-Rassenkunde-des-deutschen-Volkes-Text/GuentherHans-KleineRassenkundeDesDeutschenVolkes193388S.Text#page/n39/mode/2up>, 39. Furthermore: Christensen, Poulsen, Smith (n 38) 83; Sussman (n 3) 124; Heinemann (n 24) 38.

40 Sussman (n 3) 124; Heinemann (n 24) 38.

41 <https://archive.org/details/Guenther-Hans-Kleine-Rassenkunde-des-deutschen-Volkes-Text>.

42 Heinemann (n 24) 38.

43 Kyllingstad (n 16) 88, 159; Proctor (n 26) 140, 164–165.

44 See for a detailed analysis: Elazar Barkan, 'Mobilizing Scientists against Nazi Racism, 1933–1939', in George Stocking (ed), *Bones, Bodies, Behavior: Essays on Biological Anthropology* (University of Wisconsin Press 1988) 180–205.

be a pure race because they varied with regard to eye and hair colour.[45] 'There will surely be few so bold as to assert than an average divergence of external appearance is of fundamental importance'[46] and he adds, '[t]here is no scientific basis for the statement that Jews are inferior'.[47]

Nazi race theories had two sides: the racial exclusion of the Jews and the unification of blood-related Germanic races.[48] It has even been asserted that the Germanic countries, namely Denmark, Norway, Belgium, and the Netherlands, were annexed and occupied principally for racial reasons and only secondarily for territorial gains.[49] In order to justify the superiority of the Germans, despite their apparent blood kinship with the other Nordics, the Nazis made use of the idea of the *Volk* (a people). Nazi propaganda claimed that while Germans and Danes were racially alike and therefore equal, this equality applied to the race only, not to the *Volk*: 'As a *Volk* we are superior to the Danes'.[50] Hitler created the concept of a homogenous German Aryan master race (*Herrenvolk* or *Herrenrasse*) as the sole rightful rulers of the world.[51] Race became the *Leitmotiv* of National Socialism; the Nazi state considered everything through the lens of race, and no characteristics of assimilation could push aside the race factor.[52] The Nazis used race as a technique of othering, which legitimised dehumanisation and ill-treatment of the racially 'others'.[53] The propaganda of the early 1930s transformed race into the leading feature of Nazi policy. The textbook *Deutscher National-Katechismus* (German National Catechism) reads: 'What is race?' and answers: 'A group of living creatures is a race when its individual members share the same appearance and genetic inheritance'.[54] This in turn

45 Dahlberg (n 1) 224. Dahlberg was involved in the elaboration of the UNESCO Statement on Race (Beckman (n 3) 58, see Chapter 2.6.
46 Dahlberg (n 1) 225–226.
47 Ibid 229–230.
48 May (n 35) 23. Furthermore: Steffen Werther, '"Nordic-Germanic" Dreams and National Realities: A Case Study of the Danish Region of Sønderylland, 1933–1945', in Anton Weiss-Wendt, Rory Yeomans (eds), *Racial Science in Hitler's New Europe, 1938–1945* (University of Nebraska Press 2013) 131; Saul Friedländer, *The Years of Extermination: Nazi Germany and the Jews, 1939–1945* (Weinfeld & Nicolson 2007) 75; Kyllingstad (n 16) 81; Bauer (n 35) 338.
49 Josef Ackermann, *Heinrich Himmler als Ideologe* (Musterschmidt 1970) 182.
50 Quoted in Werther (n 48) 137. Similar: Sussman (n 3) 108; Smith (n 2) 21.
51 Internationaler Militärgerichtshof Nürnberg (n 35), p. 200. Furthermore: Henry Jr. King, 'Genocide and Nuremberg', in Ralph Henham, Paul Behrens (eds), *The Criminal Law of Genocide* (Ashgate 2007) 30; Vivian Grosswald Curran, 'Fear of Formalism: Indications from the Fascist Period in France and Germany of Judicial Methodology's Impact on Substantive Law', 35 *Cornell International Law Journal* (2001) 124.
52 Peter Scharff Smith, 'Dehumanization, Social Contact and Techniques of Othering: Combining the Lessons from Holocaust Studies and Prison Research', in Anna Eriksson (ed), *Punishing the Other: The Social Production of Immorality Revisited* (Routledge 2016) 21; Levy (n 2) 140; Proctor (n 26) 148; Dawidowicz (n 35) 77.
53 Smith (n 52) 13, 19. See more on othering ahead, especially in Chapters 3.2 and 3.3.
54 May (n 35) 22.

Figure 2.3 Aus dem Gesicht spricht die Seele der Rasse (From the face speaks the soul of the race), 1938. Classroom chart on "German Youth, Jewish Youth", from Alfred Vogel's text *Erblehre und Rassenkunde in bildlicher Darstellung*, juxtaposing the faces of German and Jewish children for racial classification

Photo credit: United States Holocaust Memorial Museum #14945, courtesy of Library of Congress.

meant '[p]hysical characteristics that are inherited: the colour of the skin, the shape of the skull, and particularly facial features (shape of the nose, mouth, lips), etc'.[55] Race was based on heredity and physical appearance, but it was also used to tell the story of eternal origins and connections to a *Heimat*, an emotional attachment to a territory conceived as home, be it a physical locality or an abstract homeland.[56]

Nazi ideology proclaimed that the superior races not only had the right, but an obligation to subjugate and exterminate inferior races. Character, abilities, and behaviour were part of the Nazi racial theories, and racial hygienic considerations led to the exclusion of lesser-valued human beings in order to hinder their reproduction. Although the Jews were the prime targets of Nazi discrimination, marginalisation, and dehumanisation, also other groups were the victims of brutal repressions and killings: the Roma (Gypsies); Communists; mentally and physically disabled; homosexuals; 'asocial' elements like the homeless; promiscuous women; and alcoholics were not spared either.[57] The laws of life and nature were declared as the foundation of Nazi racial policy; the real barbarism consisted in the unnatural preservation of the weak.[58] At the core was the notion of a constant battle for survival of the races, in which the weak or sick were destroyed by the healthy and strong.[59] Racial purification could only be achieved if the superior and inferior races were completely separated and intermarriage prohibited.[60] Eugenics was a key element of Nazi racial policy, ranging from the preservation of German racial purity to the exclusion of Jewish impurity. It resulted in the death of six million Jews.[61]

Blood purity was one of the most important issues in defining race. In the words of Hitler: 'Race is determined exclusively through blood'.[62] In *Mein Kampf*, the importance of maintaining the purity of Aryan blood, the master blood (*Herrenblut*) as well as the blood of the enslaved race and the subjugated is mentioned again and again.[63] The mixing of blood was considered tantamount to lowering the racial level and to the death of all cultures.[64] Hitler presents

55 Ibid 22.

56 Heideman (n 35) 13; Confino (n 2) 64, 68; Ackermann (n 49) 173.

57 Jones (n 34) 238–239; Kielsgard (n 2) 62; Bialas (n 17) 355; Ben Kiernan, 'Twentieth-Century Genocides: Underlying Ideological Themes from Armenia to East Timor', in Robert Gellately, Ben Kiernan (eds), *The Specter of Genocide: Mass Murder in Historical Perspective* (CUP 2003) 31.

58 Nicole Rafter, *The Crime of All Crimes: Toward a Criminology of Genocide* (NYUP 2016) 19; Bialas (n 17) 354–355.

59 <www.rassengesetze.nuernberg.de>.

60 Bialas (n 17) 356–357.

61 Heideman (n 35) 16; Bazyler (n 35) 3; Confino (n 2) 190; Douglas Greenberg, 'Citizenship, National Identity, and Genocide', in René Provost, Payam Akhavan (eds), *Confronting Genocide* (Springer 2011) 83; Gellately (n 36) 251; Dawidowicz (n 35) 86–87.

62 Hitler (n 19) 342.

63 Ibid 319–320.

64 Ibid 324. See discussion in Mark Rapley, '"How to do X without doing Y": Accomplishing Discrimination without "Being Racist" – "Doing Equity"', in Martha Augoustinos,

the mixture of Aryan and Jewish blood as a threat to Aryan superiority. Simultaneously and paradoxically, he asserts that the Jews attached great importance to the purity of their blood too.[65] Jewish religious teaching, Hitler claims, was primarily a recipe for keeping the Jewish blood pure.[66] While apparently neither the Jews nor the Nazis wanted to mix blood, the Jews were nonetheless portrayed as a ubiquitous threat.

Hitler believed the Jews masked their existence under the cover of a religious community, which prevented them from revealing their true self.[67] The Jews were members of a *Volk*: 'Jewry has always been a people with certain racial characteristics and never a religion'.[68] While nowadays Judaism most likely would be considered a religion, the Nazis singled out and persecuted the Jews for their race, not their creed.[69] In order to dehumanise the Jews, the Nazis used epithets such as parasites, viruses, animals (rats, cockroaches, lice), and an 'eternal fungous growth', invading body and home.[70] Hitler compared Jews to syphilis, a contagious disease threatening the *Volkskörper*, the body of the German people.[71] The *Reichsführer* of the *Schutzstaffel* (SS), Heinrich Himmler (1900–45) referred to the extermination of the Jews as 'exactly the same thing as delousing. Getting rid of lice is not a question of ideology. It is a matter of cleanliness'.[72] In the view of the Nazi leadership, such a dehumanisation strategy legitimised the destruction of what they considered the 'Jewish problem'.[73] Once the victims became devoid of humanity in the perpetrator's eye, they could be annihilated.[74] *Mein Kampf* did not, however, contain an explicit plan to exterminate the Jewish people. That was not formulated until 1941.[75]

Katherine Reynolds (eds), *Understanding Prejudice, Racism, and Social Conflict* (Sage Publications 2001) 231.

65 Hitler (n 19) 342.

66 Ibid 336: 'Die jüdische Religionslehre ist in erster Linie eine Anweisung zur Reinhaltung des Blutes des Judentums'.

67 Ibid 334.

68 Ibid 335.

69 Bazyler (n 35) 9; David Moshman, 'Us and Them', 7 *Identity: An International Journal of Theory and Research* (2007) 120; Caroline Fournet, *The Crime of Destruction and the Law of Genocide: Their Impact on Collective Memory* (Ashgate 2007) 6.

70 Hitler (n 19) 135, 334; Kiernan (n 34) 440; Weitz (n 2) 47. Dawidowicz (n 35) 93 refers to a 1936 standard lecture for SS units with the passage: 'The Jew is a parasite. Where ever he flourishes, the people die'. Similar processes occurred in other genocides eg Rwanda where references to cockroaches were common (see Chapter 3.6.5).

71 Hitler (n 19) 269–270.

72 Quoted in Maureen Hiebert, *Constructing Genocide and Mass Violence: Society, Crisis, Identity* (Routledge 2017) 165.

73 Christensen, Poulsen, Smith (n 38) 85; Bantekas (n 17) 252; Bauer (n 35) 339.

74 Bazyler (n 35) 3; Bauer (n 35) 340.

75 Kielsgard (n 2) 71; Greenberg (n 61) 82–83; Paul Gilroy, *Against Race: Imagining Political Culture Beyond the Color Line* (Harvard UP 2000) 148. The 'Final Solution', viz the annihilation of the Jews, was sealed at the Wannsee conference in 1942.

2.5 The creation and application of race laws

2.5.1 The Nuremberg Laws

When he came to power in 1933, Hitler moved quickly to turn his anti-Semitic ideology into law.[76] New legislation was adopted that allowed Hitler's government to pass laws that deviated from the constitution.[77] One of the earliest decrees was the Law for the Restoration of the Professional Civil Service (*Gesetz zur Wiederherstellung des Berufsbeamtentums*) that effected the removal of non-Aryan civil servants. The law defined non-Aryans as persons with one Jewish parent or one Jewish grandparent.[78] In 1935, Jews were barred from the armed forces and their shops destroyed. Ever more anti-Jewish legislation was put in place. In the period from 31 January 1933 to 31 August 1939, the Nazis passed a total of 1,448 anti-Semitic legal measures.[79] These included the nullification of Jewish names that had been translated into German,[80] and a compulsory second first name, 'Israel' for males and 'Sara' (also spelled 'Sarah') for females, to be used at all times.[81] Furthermore, Jews were excluded from a range of professions like farming their own land, administrative services, the judiciary, and journalism.[82] One of the most fateful decrees required all passports and identity cards of Jews to be marked with a large 'J'. Another decree prohibited all Jews from appearing in public without wearing a yellow Star of David.[83]

In 1935, on the direct order of Hitler, two laws were enacted that collectively became known as the Nuremberg Laws: the Reich Citizenship Law (*Reichsbürgergesetz*) and the Law for the Protection of German Blood and German Honour (*Gesetz zum Schutze des deutschen Blutes und der deutschen Ehre*).[84] The Nuremberg Laws were part of the Nazi racial hygiene policy, which also included the Sterilisation Law (*Gesetz zur Verhütung erbkranken*

76 Greenberg (n 61) 82.

77 Heideman (n 35) 9; Bazyler (n 35) 6–7.

78 Bazyler (n 35) 8; Henry Friedlander, 'Nazi Crimes and the German Law', in Nathan Stoltzfus, Henry Friedlander (eds), *Nazi Crimes and the Law* (CUP 2008) 18–19; Bauer (n 35) 345; Proctor (n 26) 162.

79 Bazyler (n 35) 8; Confino (n 2) 51. Dawidowicz (n 35) 77 notes some four hundred laws and decrees. This high discrepancy may originate in different delimitation with regard to local, regional, and state level or within the hierarchy of laws (laws, decrees, regulations).

80 Dawidowicz (n 35) 76, 80.

81 Hiebert (n 72) 151; Bazyler (n 35) 12; Confino (n 2) 107; Friedlander (n 78) 20; Dawidowicz (n 35) 130.

82 Internationaler Militärgerichtshof Nürnberg (n 35) 200; Bazyler (2016) 12; Kielsgard (n 2) 66; Bauer (n 35) 346; Dawidowicz (n 35) 72, 77.

83 Heideman (n 35) 16; Hiebert (n 72) 151; Bazyler (n 35) 12; Friedlander (n 78) 20–21. The Poles were the first in Germany to be forced to wear a purple 'P' badge (Gellately (n 36) 254).

84 Bazyler (n 35) 9; Bauer (n 35) 347–348.

Nachwuchses) and euthanasia operations. As public health measures, the Nuremberg Laws were foremost administered by physicians.[85] During the Nazi regime, a total of 181 Genetic Health Courts and Appellate Genetic Health Courts were established to adjudicate the Sterilization Law; the courts were staffed with two physicians and one lawyer. This broadening of the judicial system indicates the magnitude to which the Nazis went to implement their sterilisation law.[86]

The Nuremberg Laws contained the legal definition of German citizen and had a devastating effect on so-called racially inferior non-Aryans.[87] Remarkably, the Nuremberg Laws did not define Aryan.[88] Art. 2(1) of the Reich Citizenship Law read: 'A Reich citizen is only that citizen of German or kindred blood who by his conduct proves that he is willing and suited to loyally serve the German people and the Reich'.[89] Only Reich citizens enjoyed full political rights (Art. 2(3)). In referring to German or kindred blood, the law in effect rendered citizenship and connected political rights impossible for Jews. It is often argued that the Reich Citizenship Law denationalised Jews, who no longer were considered German citizens. However, the law did not alter the status of Jews as citizens (*Staatsangehörige*), rather, it stigmatised Jews as citizens of lesser worth by introducing the elevated category of Reich citizen (*Reichsbürger*) reserved for citizens of German or related blood.[90]

The Law for the Protection of German Blood and Honour prohibited marriages and extramarital relations between Jews and Germans. Its preamble read: 'Imbued with the insight that the purity of German blood is a prerequisite for the continued existence of the German people'.[91] While the Blood Protection Law only expressly mentioned Jews, legal commentators expanded its scope to people with 'other racially alien blood'. The connection between blood and race is explained in the First Decree to the Reich Citizenship Law, which resolved a long internal debate within the Nazi party on the definition of a Jew:[92] 'A

85 Friedlander (n 78) 18; Gellately (n 36) 246; Proctor (n 25) 20, 23.

86 Sussman (n 3) 117; Proctor (n 25) 21. Estimates range from 300,000 to 400,000 individuals who were sterilised in Germany (ibid). Friedlander (n 78) 18, notes that appeals were not possible.

87 Heideman (n 35) 15.

88 Friedlander (n 78) 19, assumes that the drafters avoided the term because of its impreciseness; instead these laws refer to citizens with 'German or related blood'.

89 Reichsbürgergesetz vom 15. September 1935, Reichsgesetzblatt (16 September 1935), p. 1146, <http://alex.onb.ac.at/cgi-content/alex?apm=0&aid=dra&datum=19350004&seite=00001146&zoom=2>.

90 Heideman (n 35) 10; Friedlander (n 78) 19. See misinterpretation in: Hiebert (n 72) 150; Jones (n 34) 236; Greenberg (n 36) 81–82.

91 Rassentrennungsgesetz vom 15. September 1935, Reichsgesetzblatt (16 September 1935), p. 1146, <http://alex.onb.ac.at/cgi-content/alex?apm=0&aid=dra&datum=19350004&seite=00001146&zoom=2>.

92 Kielsgard (n 2) 66.

Jew is anyone descended from at least three grandparents who are fully Jewish as regards race'. It moreover read that

> [a]lso deemed a Jew is a Jewish *Mischling* [German-Jewish mix-blood] subject who is descended from two fully Jewish grandparents and
> who belonged to the Jewish religious community when the law was issued or has subsequently been admitted to it;
> who was married to a Jew when the law was issued or has subsequently married one;
> who is the offspring of a marriage with a Jew, within the meaning of Paragraph I, after the Law for the Protection of German Blood and German Honour of September 15, 1935 took effect;
> who is the offspring of extramarital intercourse with a Jew, within the meaning of Paragraph I, and was born out of wedlock after July 31, 1936.[93]

Remarkably, Jewish *Mischlinge* are defined by heredity, namely their grandparental descent and by membership of the Jewish religious community.[94] The apparent contradiction to Nazi propaganda, emphasising that the Jews were not members of a creed and Judaism was not a religion, reveals the inconsistencies of the legal definition of the Jewish race.[95] In embracing a racial definition, the Nuremberg laws also departed from Judaism's own *halakhic* definition of Jewishness based on matrilineal descent.[96]

The Nuremberg Laws stood in contrast to the earlier German Civil Code, which Hitler never repealed. Nazi judges overcame this obstacle by introducing a new legal theory: since the Civil Code attributed legal personality only to living people, the judges treated Jews as dead. The reasoning was that only members of the racially pure German *Volk* were deemed to be alive and eligible to legal benefits. The Jews, who were barred from belonging to the German *Volk* by reason of blood and race, accordingly lacked the legal capacity endowed by birth. This 'civil death' of the Jews enabled the judges to Nazify the Civil Code without revising it.[97]

This section has shown that the Nazis' racialized jurisdiction defined Jewishness arbitrarily. The Nuremberg Laws gave a detailed, but incoherent, definition of who was to be considered member of the Jewish race, based on rules of descent and heredity, irrespective of an individual's actual belief or religious practice.[98]

93 Erste Verordnung zur Ausführung des Gesetzes zum Schutze des deutschen Blutes und der deutschen Ehre vom 14. November 1935, Reichsgesetzblatt (14 November 1935), p. 1334, <http://alex.onb.ac.at/cgi-content/alex?aid=dra&datum=1935&page=1480&size=45>.
94 Also recognized by Bauer (n 35) 345.
95 Kiernan (n 34) 440 and Confino (n 2) 15. See also discussions in Chapter 2.4.
96 Maureen Hiebert, 'The Three "Switches" of Identity Construction in Genocide: The Nazi Final Solution and the Cambodian Killing Fields', 3 *Genocide Studies and Prevention* (2008) 14.
97 Vivian Grosswald Curran, 'Racism's Past and Law's Future', 28 *Vermont Law Review* (2004) 710.
98 Bazyler (n 35) 9; Fournet (n 69) 6–7.

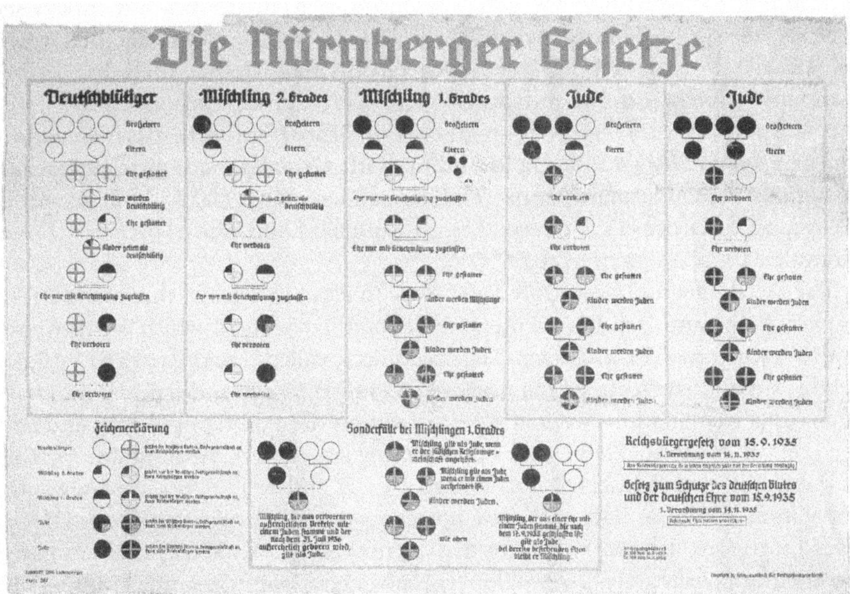

Figure 2.4 *Die Nürnberger Gesetze* (Nuremberg Race Laws). The chart has columns explaining the *Deutschblütiger* (German-bloods), *Mischling 2. Grades* (half-breeds 2. grade), *Mischling 1. Grades* (half-breeds 1. grade), and *Jude* (Jew).

Photo Credit: United States Holocaust Memorial Museum #N13862, courtesy of Hillel at Kent State.

2.5.2 *Rasse- und Siedlungshauptamt (RuSHA)*

In 1931, SS *Reichsführer* Himmler set up the *Rasse- und Siedlungshauptamt* (RuSHA, Race and Settlement Main Office) with the aim of ensuring the high racial quality of SS recruits and to lay the groundwork for Germany's racial policy.[99] The RuSHA guidelines not only contained eugenics-based rules for the marriage of SS members. They also dealt with the racial classification of large populations.[100] All the regulations had the goal of fostering racially healthy marriages that would produce many pure blooded children, who as members of the master race would perpetually serve and sustain the Nazi Thousand-Year Reich.[101] Historically speaking, however, the RuSHA is primarily known for its racial categorisations of the populations in the

99 Christensen, Poulsen, Smith (n 38) 81; Dawidowicz (n 35) 98.
100 Christensen, Poulsen, Smith (n 38) 82; Carney (n 25) 63.
101 Christensen, Poulsen, Smith (n 38) 88; Carney (n 25) 77.

occupied and annexed Eastern territories. The RuSHA set up screening procedures to determine the racial category of each person and supervised their expulsion, if deemed necessary.[102] The SS racial experts decided a person's racial worth, ranking from Race Group I or II that included 'ethnic Germans' (*Volksdeutsche*) and others who were actively pro-German before the occupation;[103] through Group III covering those fit for 're-Germanization' (*wiedereindeutschungsfähig*); and ending with Group IV comprising 'racially unsuitable' anti-German people.[104] If racial screening classified a person as belonging to Group IV, he faced forced expulsion and loss of property under Himmler's resettlement plans.[105]

The racial selection procedure took place in front of a panel that made a total of twenty-one anthropological measurements, the results of which were entered onto a race card (*Rassenkarte*). The examiners, called *Eignungsprüfer*, studied height, weight, the form of the body, skull, and face, eye and hair colour etc.[106] Such racial examinations were first performed on the Polish population and later used on other groups. Jews were never racially screened.[107] Around four percent of the Polish population fell into Group I or II and were considered a wanted population addition. The majority, however, were ascribed to Group III and forced into slave labour.[108] During the German Reich, RuSHA racial examiners screened approximately 2.7 million civilians. Jews were identified during the course of the racial examination.[109] After the war, in the so-called *RuSHA* Trial (1947–1948), the leading officials of RuSHA and its racial experts were put in the dock. 'These techniques of genocide' [ie forced Germanization through resettlement and population transfer], prosecutor James McHaney (1919–1995) said, 'while neither so quick nor perhaps so simple as outright mass extermination, are by the very nature of things far more cruel and equally effective'.[110] McHaney talks about 'techniques of genocide', but the crime of genocide did not yet exist in positive law. However, as Chapter 3.4.1 will show, Raphael Lemkin (1900–1959) had initiated the codification of the crime of genocide, which influenced the prosecution in the *RuSHA* trial.

102 Christensen, Poulsen, Smith (n 38) 102–103; Heinemann (n 24) 36; Kiernan (n 34) 445–450.
103 *United States of America v Ulrich Greifelt* et al. (*RuSHA case*), Trials of War Criminals Before the Nuremberg Military Tribunals under Control Council Law No 10, Vol. 4, Indictment, Count I (October 1946–April 1949) 615.
104 Ibid. See also Heinemann (n 24) 43–44.
105 Heinemann (n 24) 43; Dawidowicz (n 35) 150.
106 *RuSHA* case (n 103) 611–612. See also Heinemann (n 24) 44.
107 Heinemann (n 24) 44–45.
108 Ibid 44.
109 Ibid 49.
110 *RuSHA* case (n 37) 627.

Figure 2.5 Dr Hans Hilmar Staudte, a former 'race examiner' in the *Rasse- und Siedlungshauptamt*, the Race and Settlement Office, testifies as a defence witness at the RuSHA Trial.

Photo Credit: United States Holocaust Memorial Museum #43027, courtesy of National Archives and Records Administration, College Park.

2.5.3 *The* leggi razziali *in Italy*

In Italy under the Fascist dictatorship of Benito Mussolini (1883–1945), a series of laws called the *leggi razziali*, or Race Laws, were enacted. They were passed in 1938 and excluded Jews from large sections of Italian society.[111] The Race Laws do not appear to have been enacted under German pressure but grew out

111 Simon Levis Sullam, 'The Italian Executioner: Revisiting the Role of Italians in the Holocaust', 19 *Journal of Genocide Research* (2017) 22–23; Michael Livingston, *The Fascists and the Jews of Italy: Mussolini's Race Laws, 1938–1943* (CUP 2013) 1.

of the Fascist spirit of the time.[112] Other countries, like Vichy France, had also adopted anti-Semitic laws. The Italian Race Laws, however, are particularly interesting in that they distinguish between individuals on a biological and a religious basis.[113] Prior to the enactment of the Race Laws, an anti-Semitic propaganda campaign stressed the differences between the pure, superior Italian (Aryan) race (*la pura razza italiana*) and the Jews, who were not part of the Italian people (*non appartengono* or non-belonging) and therefore alien, a threat to and an enemy of the Italian race. Race was, in particular, deemed a biological concept.[114] Yet, unlike the German racial classification, the Italian system took account not only of biology, ie ancestral Jewishness, but also religious denomination, and family names.[115]

The *Leggi Razziali* did not introduce a mixed-race category, like the Nuremberg Laws' *Mischlinge*. Instead, an individual was either considered Italian (Aryan) or Jewish. The Italian racial laws were special in that they assumed the recessive character of all Judaism, thus blending race with culture (assimilation) and religion. In contested cases, the Catholic-Italian element overcame the Jewish element. The German system, in contrast, presumed contamination by Jewish blood, which could not be overcome by merely belonging to German society.[116] Italian fascists and anti-Semites were critical of the Race Laws. They considered them as insufficient and did not approve of the legal process enabling the acquisition of an Aryan identity, *arianizzazione*, either. Instead, they favoured biological racism, which marked Jews by blood and race.[117] Under pressure, the governmental Race Office disseminated racial propaganda on how to easily identify Jews amid Italians. Based on strict racial biology, the Jews were characterised by physical characteristics, their alleged congenital criminality, and predisposition to prostitution.[118] The Race Laws aimed at the gradual destruction of Jewish economic and cultural influence, yet with a relatively low level of physical violence. In this regard, the *leggi razziali* had more in common with the Jim Crow laws or South African apartheid statutes than the Nuremberg Laws.[119]

112 Sullam (n 111) 22–25; Livingston (n 111) 14–15; Elisabetta Cassina Wolff, 'Biological Racism and Antisemitism as Intellectual Constructions in Italian Fascism: The Case of *Telesio Interlandi* and *La difesa della razza*', in Anton Weiss-Wendt, Rory Yeomans (eds), *Racial Science in Hitler's New Europe, 1938–1945* (University of Nebraska Press 2013) 176.
113 Livingston (n 111) 12.
114 Sullam (n 111) 25, 28–30; Livingston (n 111) 17.
115 Livingston (n 111) 35, 66.
116 Ibid 35, 40, 43.
117 Wolff (n 112) 189.
118 Ibid 184, 188; Sullam (n 111) 25.
119 Livingston (n 111) 72. Disaccord: Sullam (n 111) 24, arguing for an inherent genocidal nature of the Italian anti-Jewish policies. See Chapter 2.2 (Jim Crow laws) and Chapter 4.3 (apartheid legislation).

The historical review of race ends with a discussion of the UNESCO program on race, which was born of a collective sense of remorse and post-war liberal optimism; it was a 'piece of mental engineering in the shadow of the Holocaust'.[120]

2.6 The UNESCO statements on race

The historiography of race began with its invention by Linnaeus in 1735. At its end stands the UNESCO Statement of Race of 1950 that dismisses race as a legitimate biological concept.[121] After WWII, the critique of race gained a stronger normative thrust and became the prevailing intellectual platform.[122] Since there was great confusion and controversy about the notion of race, UNESCO aimed at clarifying its definition in order to remove prejudice.[123] The four UNESCO Statements of 1950, 1951, 1964, and 1967 mark the largest and internationally most significant attempt to widely disseminate scientifically accurate information on racial issues.[124] UNESCO was at the heart of an international scientific dispute over the correct definition of the concept of race and invited a team of ten expert cultural anthropologists and sociologists to attempt to settle on a scientific consensus on race or, in other words, an authoritative definition of race.[125]

The first UNESCO Statement on Race (1950) was met with a great deal of criticism for relying primarily on sociological approaches to race and for effectively reinterpreting race as a social product.[126] According to the Statement, most scientists agreed that mankind is one and all men belong to the same species, *homo sapiens*, and its three major divisions: the Mongoloid, the Negroid, and the Caucasoid, subject to reservations insofar as the division is dynamic rather than static.[127] Race was still very much considered a phenotype: human races are mentioned in plural, some of which had 'a white skin in cold climates

120 Poul Duedahl, *UNESCO Man: Changing the Concept of Race, 1945–65*, p. 3: <http://vbn.aau.dk/files/61248765/UNESCO_Man_Paper_Poul_Duedahl.pdf>. Furthermore: Sundquist (n 4) 252; Michelle Brattain, 'Race, Racism, and Antiracism: UNESCO and the Politics of Presenting Science to the Postwar Public', *American Historical Review* (2007) 1386; UNESCO, *The Race Question* (1950) 1.

121 Müller-Wille (n 4) 598; Sussman (n 3) 1; Taylor (n 2) 71. See Chapter 2.2 on the Discovery of Race.

122 Marks (n 4) 163.

123 UNESCO, *The Race Concept: Results of An Inquiry* (1952) 5–6; UNESCO (n 120) 2.

124 Beckman (n 3) 83.

125 Duedahl (n 120) 1, 8.

126 Taylor (n 2) 73; Brattain (n 120) 1393; UNESCO, 'Statement on the Nature of Race and Race Differences' (1951), in *Four Statements on the Race Question* (1969) 36; Beckman (n 3) 83.

127 UNESCO, 'Statement on Race 1950', in *Four Statements on the Race Question* (1969) 30–31.

and a black in hot climates'.[128] Race, according to the UNESCO Statement, is defined as a group or population that is characterised by some 'concentrations, relative as to frequency and distribution, of hereditary particles (genes) or physical characters, which appear, fluctuate, and often disappear in the course of time by reason of geographic and/or cultural isolation'.[129] Later UN documents refer to this definition as well, noting that despite the emotional overtones that attach to the term 'race' and despite the difficulties involved in scientific racial classification, there are nevertheless certain inherited physical characteristics that differ between groups.[130] The scientists involved in the first UNESCO statement on race recognised the social importance of physical traits according to which a group was perceived, based largely on preconceptions.[131] The statement 'race is not so much a biological phenomenon as a social myth',[132] was decisively the most controversial one and bore the imprint of Ashley Montagu (1905–1999), a driving force against the anthropological treatment of race as phenotype.[133] Already in 1941, in declaring the whole concept of race 'utterly erroneous and meaningless', Montagu had shocked his physical anthropology colleagues.[134] Despite receiving positive press coverage, scholarly criticism forced UNESCO only one year later to convene a new group of scientists to rewrite the statement.[135]

In direct contradiction to the first statement that lacked authority from the fields of physical anthropology and genetics,[136] the second UNESCO Statement on the Nature of Race and Race Differences (1951) returned to a biological definition of race and divided people into 'non-literate' and 'more civilized', based on intelligence tests.[137] This connection between race and intelligence was one of the most frequently criticised points of the whole statement.[138] As such, the Second Statement was viewed as 'a retreat from the antiracist spirit of the first statement on race'.[139] Albeit more accurately reflecting the current

128 UNESCO (n 123) 22.

129 UNESCO (n 127) 30–31. Also mentioned in Nicodème Ruhashyankiko, *Study of the Question of the Prevention and Punishment of the Crime of Genocide*, UN Doc. E/CN.4/Sub. 2/416 (4 July 1978), para. 74.

130 See UNCHR, Report by the Secretary-General, Review of Studies of Problems of Race Relations and of the Creation and Maintenance of Racial Attitude, Twenty-Ninth Session, UN Doc. E/CN.4/1105 (14 November 1972) 20. Similar: Ruhashyankiko (n 129), paras. 74–76.

131 UNESCO (n 127) 31.

132 Ibid 33.

133 Sussman (n 3) 4; Brattain (n 120) 1396; Duedahl (n 120) 9.

134 Brattain (n 120) 1393.

135 Yudell (n 4) 150–153; Brattain (n 120) 1388, 1398; UNESCO (123) 6; Duedahl (n 120) 14–15.

136 UNESCO (n 127) 36; UNESCO (n 123) 6. Confirmed by Duedahl (n 120) 13.

137 UNESCO (n 126) 40. Furthermore: Yudell (n 4) 157; Brattain (n 120) 1388.

138 Yudell (n 4) 160. Duedahl (n 120) 17, analyses the statement as rejecting the notion that mental traits could be used to classify races.

139 Yudell (n 4) 157.

scientific understanding of race, the Second Statement implicitly confirmed the belief that phenotype was about an individual's biological inheritance. The scientists deliberately avoided saying that races did not exist. Rather, the statement claims that the 'physical anthropologist and the man in the street both know that races exist'.[140] Despite rejecting the social notion of race, the 1951 UNESCO Statement was understood as proof of the historical construction of race as a temporal, ephemeral phenomenon dependent on the people who invested it with authority and meaning.[141] Scientific discrepancies in the understanding of race revealed the absence of consensus beyond the agreement about the wrongfulness of Nazism.[142] Furthermore, the onset of the Cold War considerably impeded antiracist discourses and ability of the UNESCO statements to transform politics and popular beliefs.[143] Nonetheless, several cases on segregation before US courts in the 1950s mentioned the UNESCO statements as the newest available scientific evidence, thus giving them legal significance.[144]

The 1964 UNESCO Proposals on the Biological Aspects of Race were drafted with the intention to update and complete the 1951 Statement. In an obvious evasion of the term 'race', the proposals acknowledged that there are noticeable physical differences between populations. The classification of mankind into major stocks had been proposed on the basis of hereditary physical traits.[145] The proposals considered physical characters in no way a sign of 'a general inferiority or superiority of this or that race',[146] but do not quite let go of the concept of race. Despite downplaying its importance, they concluded that there 'is no national, religious, geographic, linguistic or cultural group which constitutes a race *ipso facto*; the concept of race is purely biological'.[147] In contradiction to the 1951 Statement, the 1964 Proposals rejected the significance of intelligence tests for racial determination[148] and stressed that '[r]acist theories can in no way pretend to have any scientific foundation'.[149]

The conclusions of the 1964 Proposals were largely confirmed by the 1967 UNESCO Statement on Race and Racial Prejudice. The latter opens by quoting Art. 1 Universal Declaration of Human Rights (UDHR)[150]: 'All men are born free and equal in both dignity and rights' and highlighting the obstacle that

140 UNESCO (n 126) 37.
141 Brattain (n 120) 1413.
142 Ibid 1387.
143 Ibid 1397.
144 Duedahl (n 120) 26–27.
145 UNESCO, 'Proposals on the Biological Aspects of Race 1964', in *Four Statements on the Race Question* (1969) 44.
146 Ibid 45.
147 Ibid 47.
148 Ibid 47–48.
149 Ibid 44.
150 UN GA Res. 217 A (III) (10 December 1948).

racism presented to the recognition of equal dignity.[151] In much stronger language than any previous UNESCO document, the 1967 Statement condemns racism and denies it any scientific basis: racism grossly falsified the knowledge of human biology.[152] The statement held intergroup problems – race relations – to be social rather than biological.[153] Lastly, it recognises the vicious circle that racism creates: 'Racism tends to be cumulative. Discrimination deprives a group of equal treatment and presents that group as a problem. The group then tends to be blamed for its own condition, leading to further elaboration of racist theory'.[154] More than a decade later, the UNESCO General Conference invited its Director-General to prepare, on the basis the 1967 Statement on Race and Racial Prejudice, a preliminary study on the legal technical aspects of race and racial prejudice.[155] That study resulted in the unanimously adopted non-binding 1978 Declaration on Race and Racial Prejudice.[156]

Unlike earlier statements, the UNESCO Declaration was the first comprehensive instrument to cover all aspects of race and racism. In dealing with legal, biological, sociological, cultural, economic, and political implications, it confirmed UNESCO's multi-disciplinary approach, rather than relying on expert scholarship only.[157] Art. 1 of the Declaration states that '[a]ll human beings belong to a single species and are descended from a common stock. They are born equal in dignity and rights and all form an integral part of humanity'.[158] Individuals had the right to be different and such differences ought not to serve as pretext for racial discrimination or for apartheid, which is explicitly mentioned as an extreme form of racism.[159] As Natan Lerner notes, this recognition was the first ever in an international instrument of the right of individuals and groups to be different, a right related to the right not to be forced to assimilate, which is mentioned in the preamble.[160] The protection of group identity is at the core of the law of genocide, apartheid, and to a large extent also of the law of persecution, as later parts of this study will discuss.

The Declaration confirms earlier statements that no innate intellectual differences in humans exist and rejects theories of racial superiority as lacking scientific foundation.[161] Art. 4(2) notably holds that 'one of the most serious violations

151 UNESCO, 'Statement on Race and Racial Prejudice 1967', in *Four Statements on the Race Question* (1969) 50.
152 Ibid 50–51.
153 Ibid 51.
154 Ibid 53.
155 Natan Lerner, 'New Concepts in the UNESCO Declaration on Race and Racial Prejudice', 3 *Human Rights Quarterly* (1981) 50.
156 <www.ohchr.org/Documents/ProfessionalInterest/race.pdf>.
157 Lerner (n 155) 49, 52.
158 UNESCO Declaration on Race and Racial Prejudice (1978), Art. 1(1).
159 Ibid Art. 1(2). See Chapter 4 on the crime of apartheid.
160 Lerner (n 155) 53.
161 UNESCO Declaration on Race and Racial Prejudice (1978), Arts. 1(4) and 2(1).

of the principle [of equality in dignity and rights is] represented by apartheid, which, like genocide, is a crime against humanity, and gravely disturbs international peace and security'. It thereby affirmed the criminal nature of apartheid. The fact that genocide is described as a crime against humanity might, from today's perspective, seem peculiar, considering that international criminal statutes consistently distinguish between three core international crimes: crimes against humanity, genocide, and war crimes.[162] Such a distinction, however, was not equally clear-cut in 1978. Finally, Art. 9(1) of the Declaration reads:

> The principle of the equality in dignity and rights of all human beings and all peoples, irrespective of race, colour and origin, is a generally accepted and recognised principle of international law. Consequently any form of racial discrimination practised by a State constitutes a violation of international law giving rise to its international responsibility.[163]

This statement is important for distinguishing between race and colour, thus implying that race cannot be equated with colour. Moreover, a breach of the prohibition of racial discrimination by a state is considered an act contrary to international law that entailed state responsibility.[164]

The final sections will provide an introduction to the contemporary definition of race and ethnicity. While a wide array of disciplines – anthropology, sociology, medicine, biology, history, philosophy, political science, social psychology, among others – deals with questions of race and ethnicity, this study chooses to focus on established sociological and anthropological academic literature given the thematic significance to law.

2.7 Contemporary understandings of race and ethnicity

The concept of race finds its origin in the belief that the human population can be organised into biologically distinct groups, each with unique physical, social, and intellectual characteristics.[165] Although physical appearance is biologically

162 See discussions on genocide (Chapter 3) and on crimes against humanity (Chapters 4 and 5). Nowadays, the crime of aggression has to also included to the list of core international crimes, as codified in Art. 8bis Rome Statute.

163 UNESCO Declaration on Race and Racial Prejudice (1978), Art. 9(1).

164 For more information on state responsibility, see ILC Draft Articles on Responsibility of States for Internationally Wrongful Acts, with commentaries, UN Doc. A/56/10 (2001), which is considered customary law. Note that by 1978, the ICJ had rendered two decisions on state responsibility for breach of the principle of non-discrimination: the *Case Concerning the Barcelona Traction, Light and Power Company Limited* (*Belgium v Spain*), Second Phase, ICJ Judgment (1970) and *Legal Consequences for States of the Continued Presence of South Africa in Namibia (South West Africa) Notwithstanding Security Council Resolution 276 (1970)*, ICJ Advisory Opinion (1971).

165 American Association of Physical Anthropologists (AAPA), Statement on Race and Racism (March 2019), at: <www.physanth.org/about/position-statements/aapa-statement-race-

heritable, the practical importance of race lies in the human capacity to create and assign meanings.[166] Historical research shows that race has always transcended physical differences; these differences have no meaning apart from the social values humans apply to them.[167] Race is the imposition of a group categorisation based on alleged inferiority and is therefore inseparably linked to the identity of the 'others'.[168] This recognition is also crucial for the understanding of race in the crimes of genocide, apartheid, and persecution, as later chapters will discuss.[169] Nowadays, mainstream social science understands race as a socially constructed identity in a given local setting, irrespective of whether it has a biological reality or not.[170] As a consequence, human beings cannot be divided into discrete, self-evident biological 'races'.[171] Racism builds on the assumption that personality is linked to inherent qualities between races and may assume sociological importance despite the lack of objective existence.[172] Thus, racism is prejudice intellectualized as fact whereby members of one racial group are intrinsically perceived as superior to those of other races, and discriminatory behaviour is based on hereditary physical appearance.[173] The belief in such a racial hierarchy of groups and in the biological differences between racial groups,

---

and-racism-2019/>; Yudell (n 4) 2; Stephen Cornell, Douglas Hartmann, 'Conceptual Confusions and Divides: Race, Ethnicity, and the Study of Immigration', in Nancy Foner, George Fredrickson (eds), *Not Just Black and White: Historical and Contemporary Perspectives on Immigration, Race, and Ethnicity in the United States* (Russell Sage 2004) 26; Gerd Baumann, *The Multicultural Riddle: Rethinking National, Ethnic, and Religious Identities* (Routledge 1999) 20; Hirschfeld (n 7) 1.

166 Lawrence Bobo, 'Foreword', in Koenig, Barbara, Soo-Jin Lee, Sandra, Richardson, Sarah (eds), *Revisiting Race in a Genomic Age* (Rutgers UP 2008) x; Eric Carlton, *War and Ideology* (Routledge 1990) 168.

167 Barbara Koenig, Sandra Soo-Jin Lee, Sarah Richardson, 'Introduction', in Barbara Koenig, Sandra Soo-Jin Lee, Sarah Richardson (eds), *Revisiting Race in a Genomic Age* (Rutgers UP 2008) 15; Fluehr-Lobban (n 3) 4; Cornell, Hartmann (n 2) 24; Hirschfeld (n 7) 4; Carlton (n 166) 168; AAPA (n 165).

168 Taylor (n 2) 39; Robert Jenkins, *Rethinking Ethnicity* (Sage Publications 2nd ed 2008) 23; Nigel Eltringham, *Accounting for Horror: Post-Genocide Debates in Rwanda* (Pluto Press 2004) 5–12; Jeff Spinner, *The Boundaries of Citizenship: Race, Ethnicity, and Nationality in the Liberal State* (John Hopkins UP 1994) 19; Cornell, Hartmann (n 2) 28; Hirschfeld (n 7) 28; Banton (n 23) 76.

169 See Chapter 3 (genocide), Chapter 4 (apartheid), Chapter 5 (persecution).

170 Francis Deng, 'The Challenge of Managing Identity Conflicts', in I. William Zartman, Mark Anstey, Paul Meerts (eds), *The Slippery Slope to Genocide* (OUP 2012) xi; Yudell (n 4) 2; Smith (n 2) 167; Thomas Hylland Eriksen, *Ethnicity and Nationalism* (Pluto Press 3rd ed 2010) 6; Spinner (n 168) 17–19; López (n 11) 68; Cornell, Hartmann (n 165) 26; Hirschfeld (n 7) 3.

171 Sundquist (n 4) 233; Banton (n 47) 196, 212; Cornell, Hartmann (n 2) 23; Hirschfeld (n 7) xii, 3; AAPA (n 165).

172 AAPA (n 165); Hylland Eriksen (n 170) 6; Carlton (n 166) 173.

173 AAPA (n 165); Spinner (n 178) 19; Fluehr-Lobban (n 3) 4, 20; Augoustinos, Reynolds (n 28) 3; Banton (n 47) 114; Carlton (n 166) 173. See further discussions on prejudice in Chapters 3.2 and 3.3.

implies that their variability is fundamental and fixed.[174] Even though biological terms define the construction of a race, the biological criteria that are used to identify a group as different, the significance of this difference, and the application of these criteria to selected groups, are all socially constructed.[175] More specific, the understanding that different racial groups exist, is largely based on assumptions that surface characteristics reflect deeper essential, unchangeable, features.[176] While characteristics like skin colour, hair texture or body shape are the basis of racial categorisation, these characteristics do not necessarily have an inherent significance. Rather, we give these characteristics meaning and in the process, we create races.[177] In sum, race is understood as the perception of a person's belonging to a distinct racial group.[178] The practical importance of race for international criminal law and the crimes of genocide, apartheid, and persecution lies in the reasons for targeting a victim group and whether the perpetrator perceived the victims to be members of a racially distinct group. The perception of the victims' racial group membership is connected to the assignment of identity markers and leads to their separation as 'others'. The victim group, irrespective of its real or imagined existence, gains social and legal relevance once it is effectively treated as different and real.[179]

It is difficult, if not impossible, to discuss race without also considering ethnicity. Albeit closely related, they are nevertheless two distinct concepts. The word 'ethnicity' originates in ancient Greek *ethnos*, referring to situations in which a collectivity of humans lived and acted together. Commonly, *ethnos* is translated as 'people' or 'nation'.[180] Nation was understood as people of common blood or descent, rather than a political unit.[181] The later Latin term *ethnikos* had a broader meaning in referring to the 'others'.[182] Othering, in Greek and Roman times, was limited to non-believers and had a religious connotation.[183] In a similar vein, in the Middle Ages, all non-Christians were

174 Augoustinos, Reynolds (n 28) 3.
175 Spinner (n 178) 19; AAPA (n 165).
176 Augoustinos, Reynolds (n 28) 3, also with a discussion of contemporary racism based on cultural hierarchies and on perceived differences in fundamental social values; AAPA (n 165).
177 Smith (n 2) 184; Rogers Brubaker, *Ethnicity Without Groups* (Harvard UP 2004) 84; Cornell, Hartmann (n 2) 24.
178 Brubaker (n 177) 32, 47, 72; Sundquist (n 4) 233; Banton (n 23) 52.
179 See similarly Alette Smeulers, Fred Grünfeld, *International Crimes and other Gross Human Rights Violations: A Multi- and Interdisciplinary Textbook* (Martinus Nijhoff 2011) 250.
180 Jenkins (n 168) 10; Ellis Cashmore, 'Ethnicity', in Ellis Cashmore (ed), *Dictionary of Race and Ethnic Relations* (Routledge 3rd ed 1994) 102.
181 David Berreby, *Us and Them: The Science of Identity* (University of Chicago Press 2008) 85.
182 Julia Costa Lopez, 'Beyond Eurocentrism and Orientalism: Revisiting the Othering of Jews and Muslims Through Medieval Canon Law', 42 *Review of International Studies* (2016) 458; Berreby (n 181) 17.
183 Lopez (n 182) 455, 458; Sussman (n 3) 11; Cornell, Hartmann (n 2) 16; Dahlberg (n 1) 219.

categorised as others: Jewish and Muslim identities were reduced to their inability to comprehend the Bible.[184] In removing similarities between Christians and the others, the latter's humanity was revoked. Once absolute othering is accomplished, the gateway for a dynamic of destruction stands open.[185] Chapter 3.2 analyses the process of othering and demonstrates that the creation of dichotomies – 'us' versus 'them' – is symptomatic of any genocide.

In contemporary history, ethnicity changed its meaning. Common descent lost its importance, while (self-)perception of the group became more significant.[186] The renowned Norwegian social anthropologist, Fredrik Barth (1928–2016) argued that cultural characteristics do not make social groups distinct. Rather social interactions with other groups make differences visible and meaningful. Such processes of assignment are not absolute; they are fluid and can change as forces and claims among groups shift.[187] In claiming ethnicity, a group distances itself from another group based on culture, language, religion, behaviour, and beliefs and thereby draws a boundary between 'us' and 'them'. Thus, an ethnic group cannot exist in isolation.[188]

What, then, are the differences between race and ethnicity? Ethnicity is often based on a perceived common ancestry, shared history, or shared symbols of community.[189] Race, on the other hand, is identified by perceived common physical characteristics.[190] Ethnicity and race can overlap if the identification of the group involves both appearance and ancestry.[191] Yet, unlike ethnicity, race always entails a construction of hierarchy.[192] In other words: race is typically assigned by others, while ethnicity frequently originates in a reactive and creative self-assignment by members of the group.[193] Critical voices, however, note that

184 Lopez (n 182) 454–455, 466; Sussman (n 3) 11; Taylor (n 2) 39; Berreby (n 181) 86; Sundquist (n 4) 234; Levy (n 2) 137.

185 Lopez (n 182) 467.

186 Jenkins (n 168) 24; Cornell, Hartmann (n 2) 16–17; Cashmore (n 180) 102. For a comprehensive analysis, see Eltringham (n 168) 5–12.

187 Fredrik Barth, 'Introduction', in Fredrik Barth (ed), *Ethnic Groups and Boundaries: The Social Organization of Culture Difference* (Waveland Press 1969/98) 11–15. Furthermore: Banton (n 3) 100; Rapley (n 64) 233; Cornell, Hartmann (n 2) 72.

188 Max Weber, *Grundriss der Sozialökonomik, III. Abteilung: Wirtschaft und Gesellschaft* (Verlag von JCB Mohr [Paul Siebeck] 1922) 219, 221; Cornell, Hartmann (n 2) 17, 20; Cashmore (n 180) 102–103; Anthony Smith, *The Ethnic Origins of Nations* (Blackwell 1986/93) 15.

189 Cornell, Hartmann (n 2) 32; Carlton (n 166) 168; Weber (n 188) 219.

190 Cornell, Hartmann (n 165) 26; Ellis Cashmore, 'Race', in Ellis Cashmore (ed), *Dictionary of Race and Ethnic Relations* (Routledge 3rd ed 1994) 267; AAPA (n 165).

191 Cornell, Hartmann (n 165) 29; Hylland Eriksen (n 170) 9.

192 Sussman (n 3) 2; Weitz (n 2) 21; Spinner (n 168) 25.

193 Cornell, Hartmann (n 165) 28–29; Weitz (n 2) 22; Banton (n 47) 198–199. Note that ethnicity may nevertheless be an imposed identity: Cornell, Hartmann (n 2) 29; Cashmore (n 180) 102, 105. Smith (n 188) 14–16 notes that an alteration of ethnicity only occurs in exceptional circumstances.

ethnicity was the late-twentieth-century photocopy of race, with even vaguer outlines, but just as bad a design.[194] The European Court of Human Rights (ECtHR) defined the two concepts as follows:

> Whereas the notion of race is rooted in the idea of biological classification of human being into subspecies according to morphological features such as skin colour or facial characteristics, ethnicity has its origin in the idea of societal groups marked by common nationality, tribal affiliation, religious faith, shared language, or cultural and traditional origins and backgrounds.[195]

In sum, race is defined as a social construction based on perceived differences in genes and their manifestation in human bodies, especially through skin colour and other physiological features, whereas ethnicity as a social construction focuses on descent, kinship, and homeland.[196] Common to both is that the group may have no significance to others beyond the perception of the group members themselves (ethnicity) or the others who perceive them as inferior (race).[197]

2.8 Race and genes

One might have expected that the discovery of genes, clusters, DNA, alleles, and clines[198] would have put an end to the discussions on the existence of different races. There was hope that attention would shift from 'body politics of skin colour, hair texture and eye shape to the molecular-level biopolitics of the gene'.[199] Instead, conceptions of race have reappeared and persist even though genetic milestones were reached and passed.[200] Indeed, some scientists claim that the perceptions of race, albeit socially constructed, may coincide with

194 Baumann (n 165) 20. Similarly: Taylor (n 2) 54.
195 *Timishev v Russia*, ECtHR Applications No 55762/00 and 55974/00, Judgment (13 December 2005), para. 55.
196 Taylor (n 2) 55; Smith (n 2) 165–167; Cornell, Hartmann (n 165) 28; Carlton (n 166) 168.
197 Alain Bertallo, 'Von der Ethnisierung zum Genozid: Mechanismen der Mobilisierung Unbeteiligter zu Akteuren kollektiver Gewaltexzesse', in Dominik Schaller et al. (eds), *Enteignet – Vertrieben – Ermordet: Beiträge zur Genozidforschung* (Chronos 2004) 67; Barth (n 187) 14; Cashmore (n 180) 104.
198 For their definition, please refer to <www.merriam-webster.com/>. See also Sussman (n 3) 4–5.
199 Koenig, Lee, Richardson (n 167) 1.
200 Jonathan Kahn, 'The Troubling Persistence of Race in Pharmagenomics', 40 *Journal of Law, Medicine and Ethics* (2012) 873. Furthermore: Müller-Wille (n 4) 599; Jennifer Hamilton, 'Revitalizing Difference in the HapMap: Race and Contemporary Human Genetic Variation Research', 36 *Journal of Law, Medicine and Ethics* (2008) 471; Brattain (n 120) 1413; AAPA (n 165).

genetically distinct biological races.[201] The purpose of this section is to provide insight into the complex issues of race and genes based on some leading research in the field of the sociology of science, genetic anthropology, and evolutionary and molecular genetics. Genetic research does not provide evidence for the existence of genetically distinct racial or ethnical groups.[202] As a matter of fact, biological features that are usually considered to delineate racial groups, like skin or hair colour, hair texture, or facial features, vary across space and time, irrespective of racial groups.[203] There is overwhelming evidence that racial and ethnic categories are socially and historically constructed. They change over time and differ according to location.[204] Because of such variation, the human species is not subdivided into discrete, genetically distinct, and biologically homogeneous racial or continental groups.[205] Geographic distance and other environmental factors have limited the gene flow between populations and a genetic cluster is therefore usually comprised of people who live geographically close together.[206] On a general level, humans share 99.9 percent of their DNA with each other. Human genomes vary only by 0.1 percent.[207] Within this genetic variation, 85 percent is due to individual differences within populations and only 15 percent between populations.[208] Phenotypic features that individuals code as race do not correlate with genes: pigmentation phenotypes are complex, and there is no single gene for skin colour. Dozens of genes, together with environmental influences, can influence skin colour.[209] DNA sequence merely assists in producing a final phenotype. It is therefore too simplistic to rely on DNA alone in

201 Shiao et al., 'The Genomic Challenge to the Social Construction of Race' 30 *Sociological Theory* (2012) 67–88, cited in Joan Fujimura et al., 'Clines Without Classes: How to Make Sense of Human Variation', 32 *Sociological Theory* (2014) 209; Hua Tang et al., 'Genetic Structure, Self-Identified Race/Ethnicity, and Confounding in Case-Control Association Studies', 76 *American Journal of Human Genetics* (2005) 274.

202 Fujimura (n 201) 209; Kahn (n 200) 873–885; Sundquist (n 4) 232; Tang (n 201) 273 (arguing for a correspondence between genetic clusters and race); Cooper, Kaufman, Ward (n 15) 1168; Leda Cosmides, John Tooby, Robert Kurzban, 'Perceptions of Race', 7 *Trends in Cognitive Sciences* (2003) 173.

203 Fujimura (n 202) 209–210.

204 AAPA (n 165); Sussman (n 3) 305; Fujimura (n 202) 209; Smith (n 2) 167; Hylland Eriksen (n 170) 5; Howard (2008) 10; López (n 11) 78; Banton (n 47) 196; Davis (n 15) 7.

205 Fujimura (n 202) 210.

206 Ibid 211; Tang (n 201) 268; Michael Bamshad et al., 'Human Population Genetic Structure and Inference of Group Membership', 72 *American Journal of Human Genetics* (2003) 579, 587.

207 AAPA (n 165); Koenig, Lee, Richardson (n 167) 1; Hamilton (n 200) 471.

208 Banton (n 3) 22; Fujimura (n 202) 217 with reference to Richard Lewontin, 'The Appointment of Human Diversity' 6 *Evolutionary Biology* (1972) 381–98; Bamshad (n 206) 578. Furthermore: Hylland Eriksen (n 170) 6; Cornell, Hartmann (n 2) 22–23; Hirschfeld (n 7) 4.

209 Fujimura (n 202) 218; Bobo (n 166) x; Fluehr-Lobban (n 3) 50–54; Cosmides, Tooby, Kurzban (n 202) 173; Gilroy (n 75) 49; Cashmore (n 190) 267.

determining our physical characteristics.[210] In sum, researchers in social sciences understand race as a reflection of social hierarchies rather than biological or genetic differences. Visible differences like skin colour, while clearly biological, cannot explain the meaning of race in social life and how it functions as an identity marker. Genetic scientists, on the other hand, disagree on the usefulness of racial classification and chose to leave unanswered the question of biological determinants between races.[211]

2.9 Interim conclusion

This chapter has shown how the concept of race has changed throughout history. 'We can see a direct linear relationship of racist ideology through the centuries', Robert Wald Sussman writes, 'and we can follow a historical pattern of racial prejudice and hatred'.[212] Originating in the designation and inferiorisation of other people in colonial times, the concept of race gradually emerged in science that tried to explain the superiority of the Europeans. Belief in the purity of blood and alleged dangers of racial intermixing eventually yielded social Darwinism and eugenics. These studies of natural selection and inheritance attracted the attention of the scientific community. The step from racial hygiene to Nazi racial policies and their idea of Aryan superiority was predictable. Nazi racism homed in on anti-Semitism. Yet the definition of Jews was not as straightforward as might have been expected. Rather it was a combination of different concepts, primarily related to blood, but also to ancestry and membership to a *Volk*. The Nuremberg Laws, as measures of racial hygiene, provided the legal basis for the definition of the Jewish race, with fatal consequences for the Jewish population in the German Reich. The Italian Race Laws, in contrast, defined Jews according to their assimilation, their names, and religion and considered Jewishness recessive.

Contemporary approaches to race and ethnicity in social and natural sciences have concluded that there is no gene for race and that race is a social rather than a biological concept. The UNESCO Statements on Race confirmed that humans cannot be categorised into distinct racial groups. Race is based on perceived physical characteristics, irrespective of their actual existence, and fuelled by prejudice and an underlying theory that human variation can be racially categorised.[213] Following this historical introduction to race, it is now time to analyse the concept of race for the crimes of genocide, apartheid, and persecution, respectively.

210 Fujimura (n 202) 219; Sundquist (n 4) 262.
211 Smith (n 2) 164, 174, 183–184; Koenig, Lee, Richardson (n 167) 15.
212 Sussman (n 3) 304.
213 Ibid.

3 The concept of race in the law of genocide

It was left to the twentieth century to produce so extraordinary a killing that even a new word had to be created to define it.[1]

3.1 Introduction

This chapter provides a comprehensive analysis of the racial group in the law of genocide, as well as its application by courts. The social sciences have long advocated a subjective definition of the victim groups of genocide,[2] and jurisprudence and legal scholarship are slow to follow suit. This chapter will argue for the adoption of such a subjective approach in jurisprudence by translating the notion of othering into international criminal law and by explaining the *dolus specialis* of destroying a racial group by a genocidal process. This study thereby connects legal and extralegal doctrine on genocide. The legal analysis of the racial group 'has been subject of little attempt at detailed analysis'[3] and this study aims at contributing research to this commonly underresearched area of international criminal law.

Genocide has been labelled as the 'crime of crimes',[4] situated at the apex of the pyramid of crimes, suggesting thereby a hierarchy within the system of

1 *United States of America v Otto Ohlendorf* et al. (*Einsatzgruppen* Case), Trials of War Criminals Before the Nuremberg Military Tribunals under Control Council Law No 10, Vol. 4, Opinion and Judgment (October 1946–April 1949), US Government Printing Office (1950).

2 Francis Deng, 'The Challenge of Managing Identity Conflicts', in I. William Zartman, Mark Anstey, Paul Meerts (eds), *The Slippery Slope to Genocide* (OUP 2012) xi; Martin Shaw, 'Sociology and Genocide', in Donald Bloxham, Dirk Moses (eds), *The Oxford Handbook of Genocide Studies* (OUP 2010/2013) 150.

3 See John RWD Jones, Steven Powles, *International Criminal Practice* (OUP 3rd ed 2003) 156. Similarly: William Schabas, *Genocide in International Law: The Crime of Crimes* (CUP 2nd ed 2009) 172.

4 *Prosecutor v Al Bashir*, Case No ICC-02/05-01/09-3, Decision on the Prosecution's Application for a Warrant of Arrest Against Omar Hassan Al Bashir (4 March 2009), para. 133; *Prosecutor v Kayishema and Ruzindana*, Case No ICTR-95-1-T, Sentence (21 May 1999), para. 9; *Prosecutor v Kambanda*, Case No ICTR-97-23-S, Trial Judgment and

international criminal justice,[5] a notion that this study rejects. The crime of genocide carries an unmatched rhetorical power and moral stigma, setting it apart from crimes against humanity and war crimes.[6] Genocide is described as the 'ultimate crime and the gravest violation of human rights it is possible to commit',[7] owing mostly to its mental element that not only includes the commission of enumerated genocidal acts, but also the destruction of a protected group as such.[8] Although the horrendousness of the crime of genocide is not reflected in higher sentences that would justify its reputation as the 'crime of crimes', it does have a qualitatively different character than most other international crimes in that it must be directed at individuals because of their membership of a group.[9] Random killings are not the core; it is the intent to eliminate a group for its existence and its character as a coherent community that defines genocide.[10]

Sentence (4 September 1998), para. 16; *Prosecutor v Akayesu*, Case No ICTR-96-4-T, Statement by President Kama (2 September 1998). Furthermore: William Schabas, *The International Criminal Court: A Commentary on the Rome Statute* (OUP 2nd ed 2016) 124; Roger O'Keefe, *International Criminal Law* (OUP 2015) 160.

5 Disaccord: *Prosecutor v Kayishema*, Case No ICTR-95-1-A (1 June 2001), para. 367; *Prosecutor v Bikindi*, Case No ICTR-01-72-A (18 March 2010), para. 145; *Prosecutor v Mrkšić and Šljivančanin*, Case No IT-95-13/1-A (5 May 2009), para. 375; *Prosecutor v Nahimana* et al., Case No ICTR-99-52-A (28 November 2007), para. 1060; *Prosecutor v Trbić*, Case No IT-05-88/1-PT, Decision on Referral of Case Under Rule 11bis with Confidential Annex (27 April 2007), para. 19; *Prosecutor v Stakić*, Case No IT-97-24-A (22 March 2006), para. 375; *Prosecutor v Krstić*, Case No IT-98-33-T (2 August 2001), paras. 699–700; *Prosecutor v Blaškić*, Case No IT-95-14-T (3 March 2000), paras. 801–802. Scholarship: Eyal Mayroz, 'Genocide: To Prevent and Punish "Radical Evil"', in Philipp Kastner (ed) *International Criminal Law in Context* (Routledge 2018) 71; Nasour Koursami, *The 'Contextual Elements' of the Crime of Genocide* (Springer 2018) 175; Payam Akhavan, *Reducing Genocide to Law: Definition, Meaning, and the Ultimate Crime* (CUP 2012) 67–81; Richard May, Marieke Wierda, 'Is There a Hierarchy of Crimes in International Law?', in Lal Chand Vohrah et al. (eds), *Man's Inhumanity to Man: Essays on International Law in Honour of Antonio Cassese* (Kluwer Law International 2003) 512–514.

6 William Schabas, 'Atrocity Crimes', in William Schabas (ed), *The Cambridge Companion to International Criminal Law* (CUP 2016) 207; Stefan Kirsch, 'The Social and the Legal Concept of Genocide', in Paul Behrens, Ralph Henham (eds), *Elements of Genocide* (Routledge 2013) 8; Patricia Wald, 'Genocide and Crimes Against Humanity', 6 *Washington University Global Studies Law Review* (2007) 629.

7 Benjamin Whitaker, Revised and Updated Report on the Question of the Prevention and Punishment of the Crime of Genocide, UN Doc. E/CN.4/Sub.2/1985/6, para. 14.

8 Robert Cryer et al., *An Introduction to International Criminal Law and Procedure* (CUP 2nd ed 2010) 203.

9 Richard Ashby Wilson, 'Crimes against Humanity and the Conundrum of Race and Ethnicity at the International Criminal Tribunal for Rwanda', in Ilana Feldman, Miriam Ticktin (eds), *In the Name of Humanity: The Government of Threat and Care* (Duke UP 2010) 31. Note that the crimes against humanity of persecution and apartheid also contain the group notion.

10 Malcolm Shaw, 'Genocide in International Law', in Yoram Dinstein, Mala Tabory (eds), *International Law at a Time of Perplexity: Essay in Honour of Shabtai Rosenne* (Martinus Nijhoff 1989) 805.

The crux of this study, in the words of Richard Ashby Wilson, is the following:

> There appears to be an intrinsic paradox: while the international court administering humanitarian law is highly uncomfortable with collective categories and any suggestion that it might be reproducing the categorisations of the *génocidaires*, it requires these very categories to secure convictions for the crime of genocide.[11]

This chapter endeavours to offer a clear, specific, and contemporary legal definition of the concept of race for the crime of genocide because, while the Genocide Convention remained textually static – and has survived intact in all the statutes of international and hybrid courts, notwithstanding a slight modification in the Rome Statute – , its interpretative evolution has been fluid.[12] In recognising that race is a generic term that is difficult to define and susceptible to change over time, an evolutive interpretation leads to a subjective definition of race, based on the perception of the perpetrator.[13] Such a subjective approach to race may result in an expansion of the protection offered by the law of genocide to include any victim perceived as racially different, yet bearing in mind the principle of legality. Adherence to a strict definition of genocide was stressed as early as the drafting process; without it, the idea of genocide would risk indefinite expansion.[14]

The following two sections (3.2. and 3.3.) will explain the dynamics of genocide as a criminal process, based on social science research. Such a discussion is not only important for a general understanding of genocide, but crucial for later suggestions of the subjective approach as the preferable legal interpretation of the racial group.

3.2 Perception of 'Otherness'

The perception of otherness, or, as it commonly is known, 'othering', is about marginalisation and creating a hierarchy around notions of difference.[15] Othering has been defined as a 'set of dynamics, processes, and structures that engender

11 Wilson (n 9) 31.

12 Wald (n 6) 621, 623. Similarly: Judith Derenzo, Michael Garcia, 'Genocide: Legal Precedent Surrounding the Definition of the Crime', *Congressional Research Service Report for Congress* (2004) 1.

13 See Chapter 3.7.2 on evolutive interpretation. Furthermore: Tarcisio Gazzini, *Interpretation of International Investment Treaties* (Hart 2016) 105; Julian Arato, 'Subsequent Practice and Evolutive Interpretation: Techniques of Treaty Interpretation Over Time and Their Diverse Consequences', 9 *The Law and Practice of International Courts and Tribunals* (2010) 468–470 on generic terms.

14 Draft Convention on the Crime of Genocide, UN Doc. E/447 (1947), p. 16. See Chapter 3.4.4 on the codification of the crime of genocide.

15 Anthony Amatrudo, Leslie William Blake, *Human Rights and the Criminal Justice System* (Routledge 2015) 75–76; Larry May, 'Identifying Groups in Genocide Cases',

marginality and persistent inequality across any of the full range of human differences based on group identities'.[16] The process of othering encompasses expressions of prejudice and provides a set of common conditions that assist in the construction of images and identities.[17] Individuals perceive each other as similar, as belonging to a likeminded group, while simultaneously perceiving others outside of their own group as different. Virtually all genocidal situations are characterised by the division of society between the dominant in-group and the inferior and stigmatised out-group.[18] In such situations, dichotomies between the groups are continuously and increasingly reinforced until they reach the destruction of identities and ultimately the destruction of the out-group itself.[19] These processes explain group-based inequality, first of the 'others' as distinct and inferior, but also of 'us' as a group deserving of its socially superior rank and with a duty to defend its position against the menace of the others.[20]

---

in Larry May, Zachary Hoskins (eds), *International Criminal Law and Philosophy* (CUP 2010) 92.

16 John Powell, Stephen Menendian, 'The Problem of Othering: Towards Inclusiveness and Belonging', 1 *Othering & Belonging* (2016) 17.

17 Rowan Savage, 'Modern Genocidal Dehumanization: A New Model', 47 *Patterns of Prejudice* (2013) 155; Herbert Blumer, 'Race Prejudice as a Sense of Group Position', 1 *Pacific Sociological Review* (1958) 4; Gordon Allport, *The Nature of Prejudice* (Doubleday Anchor Books 2nd ed 1958) 30, 42.

18 Julie Bernath, 'The Politics of Difference in Transitional Justice: Genocide and the Construction of Victimhood at the Khmer Rouge Tribunal', 12 *Journal of Intervention and Statebuilding* (2018) 370; Alette Smeulers, Fred Grünfeld, *International Crimes and other Gross Human Rights Violations: A Multi- and Interdisciplinary Textbook* (Martinus Nijhoff 2011) 248–251; Deng (n 2) x; Alexander Laban Hinton, 'The Dark Side of Modernity: Toward an Anthropology of Genocide', in Alexander Laban Hinton (ed), *Annihilating Difference: The Anthropology of Genocide* (University of California Press 2002) 6; Frank Chalk, Kurt Jonassohn, *The History and Sociology of Genocide: Analyses and Case Studies* (Yale UP 1990) 28.

19 Deng (n 2) xi; Anthonie Holslag, 'The Process of Othering from the "Social Imaginaire" to Physical Acts: An Anthropological Approach', 9 *Genocide Studies and Prevention: An International Journal* (2015) 96; Adil Ahmad Haque, 'Group Violence and Group Vengeance: Toward a Retributive Theory of International Criminal Law', 9 *Buffalo Criminal Law Review* (2005) 309; Hinton (n 18) 6.

20 Mark Kielsgard, *Responding to Modern Genocide: At the Confluence of Law and Politic* (Routledge 2016) 126; Powell, Menendian (n 16) 17; Amatrudo, Blake (n 15) 75–76; Holslag (n 19) 96, 102; Smeulers, Grünfeld (n 18) 249; Cherif M. Bassiouni, *Crimes Against Humanity: Historical Evolution and Contemporary Application* (CUP 2011) 63; Maureen Hiebert, 'The Three "Switches" of Identity Construction in Genocide: The Nazi Final Solution and the Cambodian Killing Fields', 3 *Genocide Studies and Prevention: An International Journal* (2008) 6, 8; Winston Nagan, Vivile Rodin, 'Racism, Genocide, and Mass Murder: Towards a Legal Theory about Group Deprivations', 17 *National Black Law Journal* (2004) 174; Carmen Luke, Vicki Carrington, 'Race Matters', 21 *Journal of Intercultural Studies* (2000) 22; Jack Nusan Porter, 'What is Genocide? Notes Towards a Definition', in Jack Nusan Porter (ed), *Genocide and Human Rights: A Global Anthology* (University Press of America 1982) 12; Kurt Glaser, Stefan Possony, *Victims of Politics: The State of Human Rights* (Columbia UP 1979) 56, 88.

Characterising another racial group is to define one's own group and as such inevitably a collective social process.[21] Social science research has convincingly demonstrated that the construction of differences are always influenced by the perpetrator's perspective and do not rely on scientifically provable objective criteria. Moreover, group categories such as race are mobilised in pre-genocidal contexts in order to produce rigid and impermeable identities of the opposing groups.[22] Race, a group identity constructed as dangerous, deep-seated, and inassimilable, is really a metaphor for otherness.[23]

Only once the 'others' are perceived as a threat to the exclusive position of the dominant in-group is racial prejudice established.[24] For the crime of genocide this signifies that the *génocidaire* targets individual group members because they represent the victim group, whose destruction is his ultimate goal.[25] There might be some factual basis for the negative image of the out-group, yet once it is formed, it tends to be exaggerated.[26] Ideas of enmity necessarily reduce the out-group to a common and, in the eyes of the in-group, unifying identity marker.[27] While the social sciences have recognised othering as a critical element of genocide, the legal significance of the process remains largely undiscussed. This study argues that othering is not only part of any genocide, but can moreover assist in the legal analysis of the crime of genocide. As such, othering will translate into law in that the perpetrator perceives the others as different, a threat to his own group, and therefore aims at destroying them. The perception of 'otherness' becomes part of the definition of a racial group and the intent to destroy it. Thereby othering offers not only descriptive or explanatory value to understanding genocide, but also possesses legal value. Naturally, othering occurs in other settings too and does not necessarily lead to genocide. A contemporary biologist even considers the group-versus-group position to be the principal driving force that makes us what we are.[28] Any division of people into

21 Powell, Menendian (n 16) 23–24; Lincoln Quillian, 'Prejudice as a Response to Perceived Group Threat: Population Composition and Anti-Immigrant and Racial Prejudice in Europe', 60 *American Sociological Review* (1995) 592; Blumer (n 17) 3–4.

22 Bernath (n 18) 370; Shaw (n 2) 150.

23 Daniel Feierstein, *Genocide as Social Practice: Reorganizing Society Under the Nazis and Argentina's Military Juntas* (Rutgers UP 2014) 20.

24 Blumer (n 17) 4, 6. Holslag (n 19) 96; Eric Carlton, *War and Ideology* (Routledge 1990) 170.

25 See discussion on group membership in Chapter 3.5.2.

26 Deng (n 2) xi; I. William Zartman, Mark Anstey, 'The Problem: Preventing Identity Conflicts and Genocide', in I. William Zartman, Mark Anstey, Paul Meerts (eds), *The Slippery Slope to Genocide: Reducing Identity Conflicts and Preventing Mass Murder* (OUP 2012) 9; Henri Tajfel, *Human Groups and Social Categories: Studies in Social Psychology* (CUP 1981) 133; Smeulers, Grünfeld (n 18) 251; Glaser, Possony (n 20) 56; Rogers Brubaker, *Ethnicity Without Groups* (Harvard UP 2004) 74.

27 Powell, Menendian (n 16) 24; Zartman, Anstey (n 26) 12, Smeulers, Grünfeld (n 18) 248; Holslag (n 19) 107; Tajfel (n 26) 132; Blumer (n 17) 6.

28 Edward Wilson, *The Social Conquest of Earth* (Liveright Publishing Corporation 2012) 62.

groups will, according to social psychological experiments, result in identification of individuals with their group (even if it is arbitrarily composed). Thereafter, bias and prejudice are quickly established, favouring one's own in-group and judging the members of the out-group as less likable, less fair, and less trustworthy.[29]

It is not uncommon for groups to identify as different those individuals who act, speak, dress, and especially, look different. They are recognised as not being one of 'us'. It does not matter whether these differences are genuine, as long as 'we' want to see 'them' as different.[30] Othering occurs in the clash between civilizations, but also between groups that have closely lived together for a long time, as in Rwanda, Bosnia, or Germany before WWII.[31] Individuals tend to ascribe more human qualities to the members of their in-group than to those of the out-group, which is seen as lacking aspects of humanness. The dehumanisation partially or fully removes the 'other's' humanness, which is a fundamental aspect of social perception, and, as such, an inherently subjective notion. Importantly, the out-group and its members are denied their human uniqueness because of their perceived lack of rationality, refinement, and civility, all attributes that the in-group considers innate and part of an essence of its being.[32] Individuals of a racially 'other' group are seen as unintelligent, immoral, and bestial. In the eyes of the dominant in-group, they lack the human essence and are therefore animal-like. Recent research has shown that people who are socially excluded feel they are lacking in human nature and, conversely, perceive that the person who excluded them also lacks in human nature.[33] Othering and dehumanisation of a group that is considered racially inferior is thus linked to essential dimensions of social perception, whereby the racial 'others' are perceived as missing humanness.[34]

Almost every violent social interaction is characterised by the objectivising and dehumanising of the others.[35] Such techniques are, according to M. Cherif

29 Ibid 59; Tajfel (n 26) 137.

30 Carlton (n 24) 169; Tajfel (n 26) 241–243.

31 Kate Temoney, 'The 1994 Rwandan Genocide: The Religion/Genocide Nexus, Sexual Violence, and the Future of Genocide Studies', 10 *Genocide Studies and Prevention* (2016) 6; Anton Blok, *Honour and Violence* (Polity Press 2001) 125–128; Luke, Carrington (n 20) 22. See more in Chapter 2.4 (on WWII and Nazi conceptions), Chapter 3.6.5 (Rwanda), 3.3.3, 3.3.5, and 5.3.4.4 (Bosnia).

32 Savage (n 17) 143; Nick Haslam et al., 'Humanness, Dehumanization, and Moral Psychology', in Mario Mikulincer and Phillip Shaver (eds), *The Social Psychology of Morality: Exploring the Causes of Good and Evil* (American Psychological Association 2012) 205.

33 Ibid, 206.

34 See Chapter 3.3.5. on dehumanisation.

35 Bassiouni (n 20) 63; Daniela Demko, 'Die von der Genozidkonvention geschützten "Gruppen" als Regelungsgegenstand des "Specific Intent"', 2 *Schweizerische Zeitschrift für Internationales und Europäisches Recht* (2009) 235. Similarly: Gerd Baumann, *The Multicultural Riddle: Rethinking National, Ethnic, and Religious Identities* (Routledge 1999) 62–63; Carlton (n 24) 169; Tajfel (n 26) 241.

Bassiouni, necessary in order to 'circumvent human inhibitory mechanisms [that] would prevent from engaging in violence against people of the same objectivised category that the perpetrator belongs to'.[36] The members of the out-group are not considered as fully human and are therefore not afforded moral recognition. Objectified and dehumanised 'others' are denied moral patiency and the capacity for suffering, which facilitates immoral conduct, aggression, violence, and extreme situations like genocide.[37] Dehumanisation is a development by which victims are excluded from the moral universe of the perpetrators. It is this moral disengagement that ultimately legitimises attacks and killings that would otherwise be immoral and objectionable. As a consequence, ordinary standards of behaviour and morality no longer apply: othering becomes a socially accepted way of perceiving outsiders to one's own group.[38] 'The existence of these "others"', Alexander Laban Hinton writes,

> provides a sort of moral glue that binds the members of a given social group together. Moreover, 'others' may serve as objects of projection onto whom negative feelings and ideas may be transferred, thereby inflating one's own sense of self-worth and moral superiority.[39]

The process of othering can lead to genocide when the other group is seen as a threat to the values, ideas, and the identity of a self-declared superior group. Any genocidal ideology combines extreme polarization of the victim group (the dehumanisation) with a survival discourse, whereby the survival of the in-group and all its members is threatened by the enemy out-group.[40] In the eyes of the perpetrators, the other group needs to be destroyed as a way of self-defence, while the victims may not even be aware of being part of a group, which may indeed be purely artificial.[41] Ultimately, the process that identifies, creates, and

36 Bassiouni (n 20) 63.

37 Haslam (n 32) 204, 213.

38 Savage (n 17) 144, 151, 155; Ervin Staub, 'The Roots and Prevention of Genocide and Related Mass Violence', in I. William Zartman, Mark Anstey, Paul Meerts (eds), *The Slippery Slope to Genocide: Reducing Identity Conflict and Preventing Mass Murder* (OUP 2012) 39; Helen Fein, 'States of Genocide and other States', in Carol Rittner, John Roth, James Smith (eds), *Will Genocide Ever End?* (Paragon 2002) 47; Zartman, Anstey (n 26) 9; Amatrudo, Blake (n 15) 76; Russell Hardin, *One for All: The Logic of Group Conflict* (Princeton UP 1995) 145–147.

39 Alexander Laban Hinton, 'Genocide and Anthropology: Introduction', in Alexander Laban Hinton (ed), *Genocide: An Anthropological Reader* (Blackwell Publishers 2002) 9.

40 Nicole Rafter, *The Crime of All Crimes: Toward a Criminology of Genocide* (NYUP 2016) 84–85, 127–128, Zartman, Anstey (n 26) 3, 5, 7–9; Smeulers, Grünfeld (n 18) 249–251; Hiebert (n 20), p. 12; Jeremy Gunn, 'The Complexity of Religion and the Definition of "Religion" in International Law', 16 *Harvard Human Rights Journal* (2003) 203; Chalk, Jonassohn (n 18) 28; Porter (n 20) 12.

41 Savage (n 17) 151; Maureen Hiebert, *Constructing Genocide and Mass Violence: Society, Crisis, Identity* (Routledge 2017) 141–142; Holslag (n 19) 96; Scott Straus, *The Order*

stigmatises the victim group leads to a dehumanisation of the victims. The perpetrator redefines the identity of the victims as aliens who deserve to be eliminated.[42]

3.3 The stages of genocide

3.3.1 Introduction

At the heart of any genocide lies the element of identity, which is crucial to explain the crime.[43] Therefore, genocide is not so much a crime of hate as a crime of identity.[44] Identity refers to the absence of difference in dimensions that are used to define a social category. The collective identity of one group only exists in opposition to another collective identity, which is either created by means of self-identification or ascription.[45] The fact that the crime of genocide is rooted in identity enables us to recognise how the perpetrator categorises his victims by creating dichotomies, and then stigmatises them to the point of dehumanisation, leading ultimately to their destruction, a process he then denies.[46]

Several academics have, independently of one another, identified these stages, steps, preconditions, or common warning signs as characteristic of any genocide. They vary in the number of genocidal phases from between three and twelve.[47] Also the UN Secretary-General and the UN Office of the Special Advisor on the Prevention of Genocide acknowledged certain stages inherent to any genocide, including the identity-based nature of genocide, its group-level discrimination, and real or perceived differences between the groups.[48] These phases may

---

of Genocide: Race, Power, and War in Rwanda (Cornell UP 2006) 241; Henry Huttenbach, 'Locating the Holocaust on the Genocide Spectrum', 3 *Holocaust & Genocide Studies* (1988) 299.

42 Zartman, Anstey (n 26) 8; Rafter (n 40) 28, 96; Nagan, Rodin (n 20) 137.

43 Rafter (n 40) 95; David Moshman, 'Us and Them: Identity and Genocide', 7 *Identity: An International Journal of Theory and Research* (2007) 116.

44 This study will, apart from analysing specific genocide trials that marginally dealt with propaganda, not further discuss hate propaganda or incitement to genocide.

45 Smeulers, Grünfeld (n 18) 248; Rafter (n 40) 96; Zartman, Anstey (n 26) 14; Holslag (n 19) 98; Hiebert (n 20) 9; Moshman (n 43) 116.

46 Moshman (n 43) 132.

47 Professor Stanton first presented a matrix consisting of eight, later ten, stages. See Gregory Stanton, 'Countries at Risk Report', *Genocide Watch* (2012); Gregory Stanton, 'Could the Rwandan Genocide Have Been Prevented?', 6 *Journal of Genocide Research* (2004); <www.genocidewatch.org/aboutgenocide/8stagesofgenocide.html>; <www.genocidewatch.org/genocide/tenstagesofgenocide.html>. Others: Hiebert (n 41) 141; Moshman (n 43) 116, 131; Fein (n 38) 47–48.

48 Report of the Secretary-General on the Implementation of the Five Point Action Plan and the Activities of the Special Adviser on the Prevention of Genocide, UN Doc. E/CN.4/2006/84 (9 March 2006), p. 11 (Annex); UN Office of the Special Advisor on

occur simultaneously and are not necessarily linear; but they all continue to operate throughout a genocidal process.[49] For the purpose of this study and its focus on the definition of the racial victim group in genocide, not all stages are equally relevant. The discussion will therefore limit itself to the stages of classification, symbolisation, discrimination, and dehumanisation as identified by Gregory Stanton in his matrix of genocidal stages and complemented by related research. These selected stages help explain how the perpetrator constructs the identity of his victim in a manner that renders, in his eyes, their destruction the only viable option.[50] This study argues that an understanding of the genocidal stages will be particularly helpful in analysing the construction of the *génocidaire*'s special intent to destroy a group. As such, the definition of the victim group is linked to the perpetrator's intent, which becomes apparent in the description of the different stages of genocide, connecting the proof of the *mens rea* with evidentiary matters of the crime.[51]

3.3.2 *Classification*

The process of classifying and identifying the others, the aliens, is a precondition of genocide. Prejudices reverse the position of 'us and them' into an 'us versus them'.[52] The classification with its associated discrimination, segregation, or even genocide, depends on the availability of signs by which the victims can be identified as belonging to a particular group.[53] For example, under the Khmer Rouge in Cambodia, pre-prepared statistical lists were used to single out Vietnamese.[54] In Rwanda in 1994, control of identity (ID) cards at roadblocks established the ethnicity of an individual.[55] But also physical differences were employed: the perpetrators interpreted skin colour or other phenotypical features as signs of group membership. As Michael Banton emphasises, although such

the Prevention of Genocide, Framework of Analysis for Atrocity Crimes: a Tool for Prevention (3 October 2014), <www.un.org/en/preventgenocide/adviser/pdf/framework%20of%20analysis%20for%20atrocity%20crimes_en.pdf>; Deng (n 2) xii.

49 Stanton (n 47) 4; Hiebert (n 20) 11.

50 Kielsgard (n 20) 87; Hiebert (n 20) 7.

51 See Chapter 3.5.3.2 on the proof of the genocidal intent. Similar argument in Shaw (n 2) 150.

52 Brubaker (n 26) 82; Stanton (n 47) 213; Baumann (n 35) 62.

53 Michael Banton, *Racial Theories* (CUP 2nd ed 1998) 211.

54 *Prosecutor v Nuon Chea, Ieng Sary, Khieu Samphan, Ieng Thirith*, Case No 002/19-09-2007-ECCC-OCIJ, Closing Order (Indictment), (15 September 2010), para. 1344.

55 René Degni-Ségui, Special Rapporteur of the UNCHR, Report on the Situation of Human Rights in Rwanda, UN Doc. E/CN.4/1995/71 (17 January 1995) 4–5, also noting that roadblocks were set up within 30–45 minutes after the assassinations of President Habyarimana of Rwanda on 6 April 1994, proving that the massacres were planned. See more in Chapters 3.6.2 and 3.6.5.

identity signs or markers may be called racial, they are not. They designate rather an assignment to a social category. 'Race is a second-order abstraction' that identifies an outsider to one's own group.[56]

The group labels of race, ethnicity, religion, or nationality, if applied by the dominant in-group, can point to the manner by which 'they' are distinguished from 'us'. Such dichotomization usually accentuates one particular dimension of the victims' identity, rendering other dimensions of their identity marginal.[57] The victim is reduced to one aspect of his identity and stigmatised because of it. Such a process occurred, for example, in Germany under Hitler. The Nazi ideology determined that the Jews were a distinct racial group and could no longer be part of the Aryan German nation. Their Jewishness became the defining identity marker, regardless of assimilation, citizenship, beliefs, or professions.[58]

In sum, genocide is perpetrated by individuals acting collectively on behalf of what they perceive to be their own group against what they perceive to be a different group.[59] This is valid for the lone *génocidaire* as much as for a state-directed genocidal campaign involving many actors, because even an individual with a twisted mindset will still believe that he is acting in defence of 'our' group. The perception of the perpetrator of the differentness becomes the point of departure for the analysis of any genocide, even if that perception of the victim group is 'wildly inaccurate'.[60]

3.3.3 Symbolisation

Following its identification, the victim group's symbolisation occurs, in which its members are given names or required to wear distinctive signs of identification.[61] The yellow Star of David, which the Nazis made all Jews sew onto their outer garments, is most probably *the* archetypal symbol, with corresponding grave consequences for its bearers. In Cambodia, blue scarves were forced upon the inhabitants of the Eastern zone, singled out for destruction by the Khmer Rouge leadership.[62] A different type of symbol was applied to the Muslim

56 Banton (n 53) 212. Similar discussion Brubaker (n 26) 82; Baumann (n 35) 62–63.

57 Deng (n 2) xi; Demko (n 35) 234; Moshman (n 43) 118–119. Similar discussion: David Livingstone Smith, *Less Than Human: Why We Demean, Enslave, and Exterminate Others* (St. Martin's Press 2011) 185; Brubaker (n 26) 74.

58 Hiebert (n 41) 151; Moshman (n 43) 120. See also Chapters 2.4, 3.8.3 and 3.9.3.

59 Bassiouni (n 20) 63; Moshman (n 43) 116; Haque (n 19) 319; Mark Drumbl, *Atrocity, Punishment, and International Law* (CUP 2007) 30; Alette Smeulers, Lotte Hoex, 'Studying Microdynamics of the Rwandan Genocide', 50 *British Journal of Criminology* (2010) 435–454; George Fletscher, Jens David Ohlin, 'Reclaiming Fundamental Principles of Criminal Law in the Darfur Case', 3 *JICJ* (2005) 545.

60 Moshman (n 43) 116.

61 Stanton (n 47) 213.

62 Stanton (n 2). The ID cards introduced by the Belgium colonisers in Rwanda are another example of symbols that reified and solidified the group identity, making any change difficult (Moshman (n 43) 119).

internees in the Bosnian war: their foreheads were engraved with (Christian) crosses.[63] While classification and symbolisation are universally human, they can result in genocide if they lead to the next two stages: discrimination and dehumanisation.[64]

3.3.4 *Discrimination*

Processes of categorising, identifying and defining in- and out-groups translate into systems of discrimination.[65] Discrimination is the behavioural aspect of prejudice; it results from the rejection of others due to negative attitudes or preconception.[66] Prejudice emanates from a person's capacity to categorise and then rationalise categories – stereotypes – through emotive reasoning; it is characterised by irrationality and emotional evaluation, namely antipathy.[67] Importantly, prejudice impedes receptiveness to counter-arguments or reverse evidence; prejudicial people are considered virtually immune to reasoned opinions discrediting their beliefs.[68] Social science research has demonstrated that racial prejudice is the result of a collective threat, whereby the dominant group develops a social position relative to the racially 'other' group. The in-group's prejudice is underpinned by feelings of superiority, feelings that the subordinate race is alien and intrinsically different, feelings of deserving certain privileges and advantages, and, lastly, feelings of fear and suspicion. More specifically, the in-group has a collective feeling of being threatened, which leads to prejudice against the out-group. Thus, the racial group is a primary social identity through which prejudices against (racial) outsiders are formed.[69]

According to Stanton, the stage of discrimination is reached when the dominant group uses law, custom, and political power to deny the rights of other groups, for example by stripping them of certain civil rights or citizenship.[70] Examples of formalised discrimination include the Nuremberg Laws of 1935, but also the present-day denial of citizenship to the Rohingya Muslim minority

63 Lori Lyman Bruun, 'Beyond the 1948 Convention: Emerging Principles of Genocide in Customary International Law', 17 *Maryland Journal of International Law and Trade* (1993) 202.

64 Stanton (n 47) 4.

65 Zartman, Anstey (n 26) 7.

66 Nagan, Rodin (n 20) 156; Brubaker (n 26) 74; Martha Augoustinos, Katherine Reynolds, 'Prejudice, Racism, and Social Psychology', in Martha Augoustinos, Katherine Reynolds (eds), *Understanding Prejudice, Racism, and Social Conflict* (Sage Publications 2001) 2.

67 Tajfel (n 26) 132–134, 143–146; Augoustinos, Reynolds (n 66) 2; Quillian (n 21) 587.

68 Gerald Jaynes, 'Immigration and the Social Construction of Otherness: "Underclass" Stigma and Intergroup Relations', in Nancy Foner, George Fredrickson (eds), *Not Just Black and White* (Russell Sage 2004) 101; Brubaker (n 26) 73; Carolyn Fluehr-Lobban, *Race and Racism: An Introduction* (AltaMira Press 2006) 24; Glaser, Possony (n 20) 85.

69 Quillian (n 21) 588 and 592.

70 Stanton (n 47).

in Myanmar.[71] Discrimination and group dominance are considered necessary, albeit not in themselves sufficient, conditions for genocide.[72] The discrimination need not be formalized, but may nevertheless be apparent in the perpetrator's acts. In separating members of a protected group from other persons, the perpetrator manifestly engages in an act of discrimination. The discriminatory singling-out of Tutsi at check-points, at roadblocks, on football fields, in churches, in hospitals and other places of refuge, is a strong (evidentiary) indicator of a genocidal intent.[73] Conversely, if the perpetrator has unimpeded access to logistical or structural resources with which to effectuate the destruction of a group and he nonetheless omits to do so, his omission could serve as probative evidence of a lack of genocidal intent.[74]

3.3.5 Dehumanisation

Dehumanisation is inherent to any genocidal process and removes all humanness from the victims, who therefore are not one of 'us'.[75] Dehumanisation is a belief, a way of thinking, that some beings only appear human, but actually, beneath the surface, are not human after all.[76] Although dehumanisation is a necessary part of a genocidal process, it is not a sufficient one.[77] The victim group's dehumanisation alone will not lead to genocide. Rather, the mortal threat that the out-group allegedly presents to the perpetrator's in-group is what ultimately distinguishes genocide from other discrimination or inhumane treatment.[78] Individuals, including friends, neighbours, colleagues, even relatives, are replaced by a collective categorisation of the 'others', resonating in declarations such as '*Umwanzi ni umwe ni umutusi*' ('The enemy is one, it is the Tutsi').[79] The perpetrator essentialises the identity of the members of the dehumanised group, in that he considers this identity inherent to the group. In doing so, dehumanisation concerns the group as a group.[80] The dehumanisation

71 Ibid 4; Nagan, Rodin (n 20) 137; Fein (n 38) 47. See Chapter 2.5.1 on the Nuremberg Laws.

72 Nagan, Rodin (n 20) 144.

73 Paul Behrens, 'A Moment of Kindness? Consistency and Genocidal Intent', in Ralph Henham, Paul Behrens (eds), *The Criminal Law of Genocide: International, Comparative and Contextual Aspects* (Ashgate 2007) 136–137. For example: *Prosecutor v Ntawukulilyayo*, Case No ICTR-05–82-T (3 August 2010), paras. 328–329; *Prosecutor v Rukundo*, Case No ICTR-2001–70-T (27 February 2009), para. 567.

See Temoney (n 31) 9 for a discussion of the symbolic meaning of the excessive number of roadblocks.

74 Behrens (n 73) 137. See Chapter 3.5.3.2. on the proof of genocidal intent.

75 Savage (n 17) 142; Temoney (n 31) 7; Moshman (n 43) 123, 131; Fein (n 38) 47.

76 Smith (n 57) 5, 13.

77 Savage (n 17) 147.

78 Hiebert (n 41) 142; Savage (n 17) 157–158.

79 Savage (n 17) 143; Straus (n 41) 173.

80 Savage (n 17) 143.

of a victim group, perceived as belonging to another race, satisfies this empirically proven requirement of an essentialised and inherent identity: the concept of race, in the eyes of the perpetrator, is inherent to all members of the victim group. Furthermore, the group is defined as unworthy of the moral considerations afforded to members of the perpetrator's in-group.[81] Dehumanisation and the construction of a racial identity have in common the creation of a binary, vested with innate characteristics and therefore perceived as being of a lesser value.

Often the perpetrators distinguish their victims by some stigma or myth and refer to them by humiliating metaphors, a treatment they believe to be fully justified. Such ideology is then spread by propaganda that defines the victim as outside the pale of human existence and therefore susceptible to attack.[82] The vital communication aspect by which 'the others' are first identified, portrayed as a ubiquitous threat and then targeted as victims of genocide, is acknowledged by several scholars.[83] Communication is here understood broadly to include any kind of utterances by the perpetrator that reveal his perception of the victim group: 'if you are not with us, you are against us'. Propaganda becomes the best predictor of imminent violence.[84] Degrading epithets like cockroach, maggot, pagan, savages, unbelievers, vermin, and disease (cancer, plague) deny the victims' humanity. Usually, the dehumanisation of the victim group is necessary for the perpetrator to overcome the typical human disgust against the violence.[85] In a genocide trial, dehumanising communication in the shape of speeches, statements, utterances, (written) orders, texts and publications can all become proof of the genocidal intent.[86]

81 Ibid 144, 151, 159; Mark Rapley, '"How to do X without doing Y": Accomplishing Discrimination without "Being Racist" – "Doing Equity"', in Martha Augoustinos, Katherine Reynolds (eds), *Understanding Prejudice, Racism, and Social Conflict* (Sage Publications 2001) 233.

82 Jesús Romero-Trillo, 'The Identity Narratives', in I. William Zartman, Mark Anstey, Paul Meerts, *The Slippery Slope to Genocide* (OUP 2012) 74; Smith (n 57) 21; Smeulers, Grünfeld (n 18) 101, 249–251; Alain Bertallo, 'Von der Ethnisierung zum Genozid: Mechanismen der Mobilisierung Unbeteiligter zu Akteuren kollektiver Gewaltexzesse', in Dominik Schaller et al. (eds), *Enteignet – Vertrieben – Ermordet: Beiträge zur Genozidforschung* (Chronos Verlag 2004) 72; Porter (n 20) 12.

83 Savage (n 17) 149, 158–159; Romero-Trillo (n 82) 80; Zartman, Anstey (n 26) 9–10; Rapley (n 81) 237; Smeulers, Grünfeld (n 18) 251; Rafter (n 40) 44; Smith (n 57) 21–25; Hiebert (n 20) 6; Moshman (n 43) 121; Behrens (n 73) 137; Nagan, Rodin (n 20) 169; Hardin (n 38) 147; Fein (n 38) 47.

84 Bassiouni (n 20) 63; Stanton (n 47) 215.

85 *Prosecutor v Ruggiu*, Case No ICTR-97-23-I, Trial Judgment (1 June 2000), para. 22. Furthermore: Hiebert (n 41) 142; Kielsgard (n 20) 83; Stanton (n 47) 4; Bassiouni (n 20) 63; Drumbl (n 59) 41.

86 The relevance of acts and statements of the accused for the determination of his underlying intent was already recognised in the first genocide trial in *Prosecutor v Akayesu*, Case No ICTR-96-4-T (2 September 1998), para. 728. See further discussion on the trial in Chapter 3.6 and on the importance of communication for the proof of the genocidal intent in Chapter 3.5.3.2.

Dehumanisation took place, for instance, during the Holocaust. Within the Nazi-constructed racial hierarchy of inferiors, the Jews embodied the absolute evil and were subhumans to be annihilated first and immediately.[87] The manufacturing of a common enemy, the Jews, that present a threat to the in-group, legitimised the (state) violence used against them. The Jews were seen as one, a group, an objectivised mass, whose destruction was considered necessary for the survival of the Aryan in-group. As Chapter 2.4 discussed, the Jews were exposed to decades of degrading and inferiorating rhetoric before Hitler and the Nazis rose to power. Yet, the manner by which the Nazis used stigmatising and dehumanising rhetoric in order to construct the Jews not as individuals, but as representatives of an objectified out-group that shared collective characteristics, legitimised their later destruction.[88]

Further back in time, accounts of the 1915 mass atrocities by the Young Turk movement against the Armenian population in the Ottoman Empire illustrate dehumanisation in practice: 'On the question, how I, as a doctor, could have murdered, I can answer as follows: the Armenians had become hazardous microbes in the body of this country. Well, isn't it a doctor's duty to kill microbes?'[89] The Armenians' humanity was removed by depicting them as disease-causing microbes that had to be exterminated. Later sections will show that dehumanisation processes were also in evidence in Rwanda where Hutu extremist propaganda described the Tutsi in dysphemisms: 'a Tutsi is called a cockroach because he takes advantage of the night, he conceals himself in order to achieve his objectives'.[90] The clearing of 'tall trees', playing on the stereotype of Tutsi height, or the pulling of 'weeds' or 'bush clearing', were other metaphors.[91] Dehumanisation also happened in Bosnia where the Serbian militia members commonly referred to Muslims as 'filth'.[92]

87 *United States of America v Ulrich Greifelt* et al. (*RuSHA* case), Trials of War Criminals Before the Nuremberg Military Tribunals under Control Council Law No 10, Vol. 4, Opening Statement of the Prosecution (October 1946–April 1949) 33. Furthermore: Richard Heideman, 'Legalizing Hate: The Significance of the Nuremberg Laws and the Post-War Nuremberg Trials', 39 *Loyola of Los Angeles International and Comparative Law Review* (2017) 16; David Deutsch, Niza Yanay, 'The Politics of Intimacy: Nazi and Hutu Propaganda as Case Studies', 18 *Journal of Genocide Research* (2016) 26; Smith (n 57) 15.

88 Savage (n 17) 156; Rapley (n 81) 233.

89 Quote by Mehmed Reshid, Governor of Diyarbekir. Exhibited in the Armenian Genocide Museum in Yerevan (10 July 2015). Photographic evidence in file with the author.

90 Richard Ashby Wilson, 'Propaganda and History in International Criminal Trials', 14 *JICJ* (2016) 534; Nigel Eltringham, '"Invaders Who Have Stolen the Country": The Hamitic Hypothesis, Race and the Rwandan Genocide', 12 *Social Identities* (2006) 437.

91 Temoney (n 31) 11; Cori Wielenga, 'Genocide and Identity: Stereotyping, "Othering" and Violence in Rwanda' (2011) <www.genocidescholars.org/sites/default/files/document%09%5Bcurrent-page%3A1%5D/documents/IAGS%202011%20CORI%20Wielenga.pdf> 5; Moshman (n 43) 121; Christopher Taylor, *Sacrifice as Terror: The Rwandan Genocide of 1994* (Berg 1999) 141–142; Gérard Prunier, *The Rwandan Crisis: History of a Genocide* (Hurst & Company 1997) 248.

92 Bruun (n 63) 202. See Chapter 5.3.4.4 on inferiorisation and dehumanisation in the context of the Bosnian war.

This section has sketched the common characteristics of genocide. Later discussions on the legal elements of the crime of genocide will make use of these stages and the process of othering. For now, attention will be directed at the creation of the crime of genocide.

3.4 The origins of the crime of genocide

3.4.1 Lemkin and the creation of the term 'genocide'

Lemkin coined the term genocide in 1944 in reference to the crimes committed by the Nazi regime against Jews and other minorities during the then still ongoing WWII.[93] The word 'genocide' is a neologism that combines the ancient Greek word *genos* ('race' or 'tribe', thus kinship-based groups) with the Latin suffix *cide* (from *caedere* for 'to kill').[94] By 1933, Lemkin was already engaged in defining a new international crime, which was 'conceived as oppressive and destructive actions directed against individuals as members of a national, religious, or racial group',[95] delineating an early version of the crime of genocide. Lemkin originally formulated the crime of barbarity as a crime directed against '*les collectivités ethniques, confessionelles ou sociales*',[96] thus omitting race. In an article of 1947, however, Lemkin describes this very proposal of the crime of barbarity as 'extermination of racial, religious or social collectivities'.[97] This statement could give the impression that Lemkin used the terms 'racial' and 'ethnical' interchangeably. However, later in that same article he refers to 'disputes with underlying ethnical, racial, and religious tensions',[98] hence distinguishing between the two notions.

Lemkin focused on actions that were directed against victims not in their individual capacity, but as members of a national group, with nationality embracing a broader notion than citizenship.[99] The protection of collective identities

93 Carsten Stahn, *A Critical Introduction to International Criminal Law* (CUP 2018) 33; Cryer (n 8) 205; John Quigley, *The Genocide Convention: An International Law Analysis* (Ashgate 2006) 4–5.

94 Raphael Lemkin, *Axis Rule in Occupied Europe: Laws of Occupation, Analysis of Government, Proposals for Redress* (Carnegie Endowment for International Peace 1944) 79, also holding that 'ethnocide' would express the same idea, consisting of the Greek 'ethnos' (nation) and the Latin 'cide' (kill). Furthermore: Michael Bazyler, *Holocaust, Genocide, and the Law: A Quest for Justice in a Post-Holocaust World* (OUP 2016) xxiii; Henry Jr King, 'Genocide and Nuremberg', in Ralph Henham, Paul Behrens (eds), *The Criminal Law of Genocide: International, Comparative and Contextual Aspects* (Ashgate 2007) 29.

95 Lemkin (n 94) 91. This is the only version that included the national group.

96 <www.preventgenocide.org/fr/lemkin/madrid1933.htm>.

97 Raphael Lemkin, 'Genocide as a Crime under International Law', 41 *AJIL* (1947) 146.

98 Ibid 151.

99 Lemkin (n 94) 79–91.

was central to Lemkin.[100] As an advocate for the creation of an international multilateral treaty to protect 'minority groups from oppression because of their nationhood, religion, or race',[101] Lemkin introduced minority groups into the equation.[102] Lemkin's book was published in 1944, and he advocated the application of the crime of genocide in the trials of the Nazi leadership.

3.4.2 *The Nuremberg Trials*

WWII and the Nazi regime's aspiration of an Aryan State ended in May 1945 with the unconditional surrender of the German *Reich*. The Allied Forces decided to prosecute the major war criminals of the European Axis and to that end established the International Military Tribunal (IMT) in Nuremberg. The Allied Powers had actually set up a War Crimes Commission (UNWCC) even before the end of WWII, in 1943, in order to hold perpetrators of crimes committed on the territories controlled by the Axis forces to account. The UNWCC's statute was influenced by the inter-war focus on minority protection, which targeted policies aiming at the destruction of collective identities as well as the imposition of the perpetrator's identity through assimilatory practices.[103] The UNWCC's mandate was to consider 'atrocities which were committed by the Nazis against German Jews and Catholics, as well as other offences perpetrated on religious or racial grounds in pursuance of Nazi ideology'.[104] In this sense, the UNWCC was concerned with crimes that today would be situated at the intersection between persecution and genocide.[105] The UNWCC was superseded by the Nuremberg Trials.

Much to Lemkin's dismay, the Nuremberg Charter did not include the crime of genocide, although its Art. 6(c) regulated the crime against humanity of persecution of racial, religious, and cultural groups.[106] Because of British

100 Philippe Sands, *East West Street: On the Origins of Genocide and Crimes against Humanity* (Weidenfeld & Nicolson 2016) 291; Ernesto Verdeja, 'Genocide: Debating Definitions', in Adam Lupel, Ernesto Verdeja (eds), *Responding to Genocide: The Politics of International Action* (Lynne Rienner Publishers 2013) 22–23; Stahn (n 93) 33.

101 Lemkin (n 94) 93.

102 Also in a later article, minorities are mentioned: 'right of intervention on behalf of minorities lates for destruction' (Lemkin (n 97) 150).

103 Ana Filipa Vrdoljak, 'Genocide and Restitution: Ensuring Each Group's Contribution to Humanity', 22 *EJIL* (2011) 23; Angela Paul, *Kritische Analyse und Reformvorschlag zu Art. II Genozidkonvention* (Springer Verlag 2008) 21–22.

104 History of the United Nations War Crimes Commission and the Development of the Laws of War (1948) 175, <www.unwcc.org/documents/>.

105 See Chapter 5.3.2.1 discussing the intersection between persecution and genocide.

106 Charter of the International Military Tribunal <http://avalon.law.yale.edu/imt/imtconst.asp>; London Agreement by the Governments of the UK, USA, the Provisional Government of the French Republic and the USSR for the Prosecution and Punishment of the Major War Criminals of the European Axis (8 August 1945), <http://avalon.law.yale.edu/imt/imtchart.asp>.

objections, the indictment against the Nazi leadership did not contain the charge of genocide as a separate international crime.[107] The indictment nonetheless included genocide in count 3, on war crimes:

> They conducted deliberate and systematic genocide, viz., the extermination of racial and national groups, against the civilian population of certain occupied territories in order to destroy particular races and classes of people and national, racial, or religious groups, particularly Jews, Poles and Gypsies and others.[108]

It is notable that the indictment only refers to the extermination of racial and national groups, but then uses the term 'classes' (in German: *Volksklasse*), as well as the now well-established national, racial, and religious categories. Although genocide was mentioned in the indictment, it was not perceived as a crime in its own right.[109] All the same, the prosecution repeatedly used the term 'genocide,' albeit often in a rhetorical rather than a legal sense.[110] 'Genocide', the British prosecutor in the *Göring* case emphasised, 'was not restricted to extermination of the Jewish people or the gypsies. It was applied . . . to Yugoslavia, to the non-German inhabitants of Alsace-Lorraine, to the people of the Low Countries and of Norway'.[111] Similarly, in his final statement, the French prosecutor stressed how

> the defendants engaged in the . . . extermination of . . . groups whose existence hampered the hegemony of the German race. This is a crime so monstrous, so undreamt of in history . . . that the term "genocide" has had to be coined to define it.[112]

107 Trial of the Major War Criminals before the IMT, Vol. 1 (1947) 43–44; Sands (n 100) 186; David Crowe, *War Crimes, Genocide, and Justice* (Palgrave Macmillan 2014) 287.

108 Trial of the Major War Criminals before the IMT, Vol. 1 (1947) 43–44.

109 Crowe (n 107) 287; Vrdoljak (n 103) 24; Fanny Martin, 'The Notion of "Protected Group" in the Genocide Convention and Its Application', in Paola Gaeta (ed), *The UN Genocide Convention: A Commentary* (OUP 2009) 115; William Schabas, 'National Courts Finally Begin to Prosecute Genocide', 1 *JICJ* (2003) 41; Johan van der Vyver, 'Prosecution and Punishment of the Crime of Genocide', 23 *Fordham International Law Journal* (2000) 286.

110 Martin (n 109) 115; Hilary Earl, *The Nuremberg SS-Einsatzgruppen Trial, 1945–1958: Atrocity, Law, and History* (CUP 2009) 93; David Nersessian, 'Comparative Approaches to Punishing Hate: The Intersection of Genocide and Crimes Against Humanity', 43 *Stanford Journal of International Law* (2007) 244; Peter Quayle, 'Unimaginable Evil: The Legislative Limitations of the Genocide Convention', 5 *International Criminal Law Review* (2005) 370.

111 *Prosecutor v Hermann Göring* et al., Trial of the Major War Criminals Before the International Military Tribunal, Vol. XIX, Proceedings (14 November 1945–1 October 1946), p. 497.

112 Ibid 531.

These frequent references to the term genocide are quite remarkable, considering Lemkin had only published his book one year prior to the IMT.

The yet-to-be legally codified crime of genocide was tested not only in the indictment of the IMT, but also in several national trials by the US Nuremberg Military Tribunals (NMT). The *Einsatzgruppen* trial dealt with mass killings of Soviet Jews by the *Einsatzgruppen* units in 1941; in his opening statement, Prosecutor Ferencz declared: 'This trial deals with the crime of genocide'.[113] The judgment equally noted that 'the annihilation of the Jews had nothing to do with the defense of Germany [and] the genocide program was in no way connected with the protection of the *Vaterland*'.[114] The *Einsatzgruppen* case was the only trial to deal exclusively with crimes against Jews, and although a thorough description of genocide was given at trial, the prosecutors missed an early opportunity to develop the legal concept into positive law.[115] Furthermore, no effort was made to explicate the group nature of the crime.[116]

Genocide was also mentioned in the trial against members of the Race and Resettlement Office (*Rasse- und Siedlungshauptamt*, the so-called *RuSHA*-trial). Defendant Brückner expressly objected to the prosecution's use of the word 'genocide'. The application of such a new concept was, he claimed, incoherent with the principle of justice *nullum crimen sine lege* and therefore violated rules of international law.[117] According to Brückner, even Lemkin referred to genocide as a '*new* expression and a *new* conception for the extermination of nations', revealing that genocide was not yet acknowledged in international law.[118]

In the *RuSHA*-trial, count one of the indictment alleged the creation and operation of a 'systematic program of genocide, aimed at the destruction of foreign nations and ethnic groups'.[119] While all fourteen defendants were charged on count one, only eight were found guilty of it, thus indirectly of

113 *United States of America v Otto Ohlendorf* et al. (*Einsatzgruppen* Case), Trials of War Criminals Before the Nuremberg Military Tribunals under Control Council Law No 10, Vol. 4, Opening Statement of the Prosecution (October 1946–April 1949), p. 32.

114 *United States of America v Otto Ohlendorf* et al., Vol. 4, Opinion and Judgment, pp. 469–470.

115 Earl (n 110) 95. Earl assumes it was due to the high burden of proof that the crime of genocide requires with its intention to destroy the group that made it 'next to impossible' to secure a conviction for genocide (ibid). See also Hilary Earl, 'Legacies of the Nuremberg SS-Einsatzgruppen Trial After 70 Years', 39 *Loyola Los Angeles International and Comparative Law Review* (2017) 106–107.

116 Earl (n 115) 107.

117 *United States of America v Ulrich Greifelt* et al. (*RuSHA* Case), Trials of War Criminals Before the Nuremberg Military Tribunals under Control Council Law No 10, Vol. 5, General Defenses and Special Issues (October 1946–April 1949), p. 5.

118 Ibid 4, emphasis in original.

119 *United States of America v Ulrich Greifelt* et al. (*RuSHA* Case), Trials of War Criminals Before the Nuremberg Military Tribunals under Control Council Law No 10, Vol. 4, Indictment (October 1946–April 1949), p. 609.

genocide.[120] But the conviction was not based on a violation of the Genocide Convention which, at the time, was neither adopted nor ratified. Instead, count 1 was listed under the heading of crimes against humanity. Since WWII, the introduction to the *RuSHA*-trial proceedings states, 'genocide has become the widely used term to describe the systematic persecution and elimination of ethnic or religious groups'.[121] Although relegated to a footnote, this statement limits the protection from genocide to the ethnic and religious group only. This is all the more peculiar considering that the NMT trials dealt with the extermination of Jews and the persecution of other so-called inferior groups, which at the time were considered either 'racial' or 'national' groups. That Jews were construed as a racial group is apparent in several passages of the Nuremberg judgments, with the following as a characteristic example: The German defendant claimed the Russian Jews were victims of a military attack during the ongoing war in Russia. The judges quashed this objection:

> It was claimed that the killing of the Jews was predicated on the circumstances of the German-Russian War, but in point of fact Jews were oppressed in Germany and German-occupied territory long prior to that war. . . . The circumstance that Jews were living in Russia when the German forces invaded Russia was simply a coincidence which did not call for their annihilation. If merely being an inhabitant of Russia made that inhabitant a threat to Germany then the Einsatzgruppen would have had to kill every Russian, regardless of race.[122]

Also the US Chief Prosecutor, Robert Jackson, referred to Jews as a race. Aware of his duty to confront race-specific-crimes, he did not want 'to exaggerate racial tensions [in countries where Jews still existed]' and, indeed, wished to 'get away from the racial aspects of the situation'.[123] Moreover, Jackson described the crime of genocide in a report as the destruction of racial minorities and subjugated populations.[124] This link between race and minorities will be discussed in Chapter 3.5.2.2.

120 The judgment reproduced a slightly shortened version of count 1 of the indictment: *United States of America v Ulrich Greifelt* et al. (*RuSHA* Case), Trials of War Criminals Before the Nuremberg Military Tribunals Under Control Council Law No 10, Vol. 5, Judgment (October 1946–April 1949), p. 88. See the fourteen convictions: ibid 154–163.

121 *United States of America v Ulrich Greifelt* et al. (*RuSHA* Case), Trials of War Criminals Before the Nuremberg Military Tribunals under Control Council Law No 10, Vol. 4, Introduction (October 1946–April 1949), p. 599.

122 *United States of America v Otto Ohlendorf* et al., Vol. 4, Opinion and Judgment, p. 464.

123 Quoted in Donald Bloxham, 'The Holocaust on Trial: Crimes Against Humanity, Justice, and the Writing of the Historical Record', in Dominik Schaller, et al. (eds), *Enteignet – Vertrieben – Ermordet: Beiträge zur Genozidforschung* (Chronos 2004) 298.

124 Sands (n 100) 184.

In several trials, the German defendants repeatedly tabled the objection that the Jews had to be exterminated because they were bearers of Bolshevism and hence a threat to the competing Nazi *Weltanschauung*.[125] Their criminal acts, the Nazis argued, were politically rather than racially motivated by defending the German nation against the 'red menace'. In consequence, the Genocide Convention was drafted so as to prevent defendants from defining their acts as politically motivated homicide rather than as genocide by requiring a broad criminal intent, the *dolus specialis*, discussed in Chapter 3.5.3.[126]

3.4.3 *The meaning of race at the time of drafting the Genocide Convention*

Chapter 2 dealt with the historiography of race. This section examines the understanding of race when Lemkin wrote his book *Axis Rule in Occupied Europe* where he formulated the crime of genocide upon which the Genocide Convention was drafted. At the time, the concept of race contained two distinct notions: one of national subgroups, another on heredity biology. The first component embraced the notion of nation states and subgroups of people.[127] Lemkin's study showed that different European subgroups like Germans, Poles, and Jews were understood as distinct racial groups.[128] This conception was not uncommon at the time.[129] Linguistically, the English 'race' was used interchangeably with English 'nation'.[130] An example of the use of the term 'race' in connection with an earlier case of mass violence, in Armenia in 1915, confirms this understanding. The deportation and killing of the predominantly Christian Armenian population by the Ottoman Empire was nothing less, the American consul in Aleppo, Jesse B. Jackson, noted 'than the extermination of the

125 *United States of America v Otto Ohlendorf* et al., Vol. 4, Opinion and Judgment, p. 476.

126 *Application of the Convention on the Prevention and Punishment of the Crime of Genocide (Serbia and Montenegro v Bosnia and Herzegovina)*, Supplement to the Application and to the Second Request for the Indication of Provisional Measures of Protection submitted by the Government of the Republic of Bosnia and Herzegovina, ICJ (1993), p. 13. See discussion of the alleged legal defense of pre-emptive strike against the Judeo-Boshevism in the Soviet Union: Bloxham (n 123) 309.

127 In a section titled 'Racial Differentiation', Lemkin discusses differences of wages paid to German construction workers compared to Eastern workers or Jews, implying that Germans, Poles, Ukrainians and Jews were races [Lemkin (n 94) 70–71].

128 Lemkin (n 94) 87–88; Diane Marie Amann, 'Group Mentality, Expressivism, and Genocide', 2 *International Criminal Law Review* (2002) 98.

129 Confirmed and further examples in Richard Falk, Virginia Tilley, *Israeli Practices towards the Palestinian People and the Question of Apartheid: Palestine and the Israeli Occupation, Issue No 1*, Economic and Social Commission for Western Asia, UN Doc. E/ESCWA/ECRI/2017/1 (2017) 23.

130 Anton Weiss-Wendt, Rory Yeomans, 'The Holocaust and Historiographical Debates on Racial Science', in Anton Weiss-Wendt, Rory Yeomans (eds), *Racial Science in Hitler's New Europe, 1938–1945* (University of Nebraska Press 2013) 9; Ellis Cashmore, 'Race', in Ellis Cashmore (ed), *Dictionary of Race and Ethnic Relations* (Routledge 3rd ed 1994) 267.

Armenian race'.[131] With regard to the Armenian atrocities, Winston Churchill wrote, 'the clearance of the race [of Armenians] from Asia Minor was about as complete as such an act, on a scale so great, could well be' with its aim of 'clearing Turkish soil of a Christian race'.[132] The Armenian Christians were thereby described as a distinct race. Equally, the international lawyer Egon Schwelb referred to these atrocities committed 'on Turkish territory . . . against persons of Turkish citizenship though Armenian or Greek race'.[133]

The second conception of race was founded in biology and heredity. Chapter 2 described the proliferation of race theories in Europe long before the Nazis seized power and imposed their racial views and legislation on everyone under their control. When Lemkin published his book in 1944, the Holocaust was still occurring, and the concept of race was therefore undoubtedly influenced by the Nazis' complex system of racial classification.[134] According to Nazi ideology, the concept of race was an amalgam of national origin, biology, and heredity.[135] The Nazis considered, for example, the Norwegians and Dutch as related by blood to the Aryan race and hence worthy of life, whereas the Jewish race was to be destroyed in its entirety.[136] The following section will show how this understanding influenced the codification of the crime of genocide.

131 Jesse Jackson, Deportation of Armenians, Letter to Henry Morgenthau, American Ambassador in Constantinople, Document No Aleppo 333 (3 August 1915), US State Department Index No 867.4016/126, in Ara Sarafian (comp), *United States Official Documents on the Armenian Genocide, Vol I: The Lower Euphrates* (Armenian Review 1993) 41. A similar statement was made by the German Ambassador to the Ottoman Empire, von Wangenheim: 'the government is indeed pursuing its goal of exterminating the Armenian race in the Ottoman Empire' (quoted in Whitaker (n 7), para. 24, footnote 13). For an analysis of the Armenian genocide, see Rafter (n 40) 92, 132–137.

132 Winston Churchill, *The World Crisis: The Aftermath* (Thornton Butterworth 1929) 405.

133 Egon Schwelb, 'Crimes against Humanity', in Hersch Lauterpacht (ed), *BYIL* (1946) 182. With regard to the Nazi atrocities, Schwelb talks about 'crimes committed against persons of Jewish race' (ibid 184).

134 Also recognised by EW Vierdag, *The Concept of Discrimination in International Law: With Special Reference to Human Rights* (Martinus Nijhoff 1973) 89 with regard to the UN Charter: 'it can readily be assumed that . . . the term "race" is used in the same biological sense as it was in the National-Socialistic ideology before and during the war'. Straus affirms that Lemkin grounded his work in the Nazis commission of genocide based on their preoccupation with biology; see Scott Straus, 'Contested Meanings and Conflicting Imperatives: a Conceptual Analysis of Genocide', 3 *Journal of Genocide Research* (2001) 365. Similarly King (n 94) 30. See also Chapter 2.4.

135 Confirmed by Amann (n 128) 98; William Schabas, 'The Crime of Genocide in the Jurisprudence of the International Criminal Tribunals', in Horst Fischer, Claus Kress, Sascha Rolf Lüder (eds), *International and National Prosecution of Crimes Under International Law* (Berliner Verlag 2001) 453–454; William Schabas, 'Groups Protected by the Genocide Convention: Conflicting Interpretations from the International Criminal Tribunal for Rwanda', 6 *International Law Students Association Journal of International and Comparative Law* (2000) 381; Porter (n 20) 13, 56. See Chapter 2.5.1 on the Nuremberg Racial Laws.

136 Lemkin (n 94) 81, 86–87.

3.4.4 *The codification of the crime of genocide*

While the Genocide Convention owes its existence to Lemkin's relentless efforts and lobbying, in the view of Ernesto Verdeja, however, it misses many of his careful sociological insights about the nature of genocide.[137] Lemkin's understanding of genocide was slightly different than the crime codified in the Genocide Convention.[138] He understood genocide as occurring in two different phases: the destruction of the national particularities of a suppressed group, followed by the imposition of the national pattern of the oppressors.[139] In drafting the Genocide Convention, however, the policy of compulsory assimilation of a national element was excluded from the notion of genocide.[140] Lemkin linked genocide to the Holocaust. The Holocaust was the archetypal genocide, and the universal moral revulsion against it provided the catalyst for the adoption of the Genocide Convention.[141] The Genocide Convention and its definition of the crime of genocide are therefore a reaction, a legal answer, to the Holocaust and, as such, heavily influenced by historical events.[142] In 1946, the General Assembly Resolution 96 (I) declared genocide an international crime, whether 'committed on religious, racial, political or any other grounds'.[143] In noting that '[g]enocide is a denial of the right to existence of entire human groups', the Resolution's preamble recognises the importance to protect certain groups.

137 Verdeja (n 100) 22.

138 Ibid; Stahn (n 93) 33–34; Ben Kiernan, *Blood and Soil: A World History of Genocide and Extermination from Sparta to Darfur* (Yale UP 2007) 10.

139 Lemkin (n 94) 79.

140 UN Secretary-General, Draft Convention on the Crime of Genocide and Comments, UN Doc. E/447 (26 June 1947), p. 23. Assimilation is understood as an attempt to erase the differences that define group boundaries and is inherently hierarchical in that group-based identities and differences are submerged and repressed [Powell, Menendian (n 16) 31–32].

141 Payam Akhavan, 'Enforcement of the Genocide Convention: A Challenge to Civilization', 8 *Harvard Human Rights Journal* (1995) 229.

142 Lemkin acknowledges that 'Germany's practices actually provided the basis for developing the concept of genocide' [Lemkin (n 97) 151]. Accord: *Prosecutor v Jelisić*, Case No IT-95-10-T (14 December 1999), para. 60: 'The concepts of genocide and crimes against humanity came about as a reaction to the horrors committed by the Nazis during the Second World War – genocide being more particularly associated with the holocaust'. Furthermore: Stahn (n 93) 34; Daniel Rothenberg, '"Let Justice Judge": An Interview with Judge Baltasar Garzón and Analysis of His Ideas', 24 *Human Rights Quarterly* (2002) 948; Marjolein Cupido, 'The Contextual Embedding of Genocide: A Casuistic Analysis of the Interplay Between Law and Facts', 15 *Melbourne Journal of International Law* (2014) 409; Gerhard Werle, Florian Jessberger, *Principles of International Criminal Law* (OUP 3rd ed 2014) 290; Cryer (n 8) 205; Steven Ratner, Jason Abrams, James Bischoff, *Accountability for Human Rights Atrocities in International Law: Beyond the Nuremberg Legacy* (OUP 3rd ed 2009) 44; Paul (n 103) 3; Kiernan (n 138) 11; Matthew Lippman, 'A Road Map to the 1948 Convention on the Prevention and Punishment of the Crime of Genocide', 4 *Journal of Genocide Research* (2002) 179; Vierdag (n 134) 89.

143 UN GA Res. 96 (I) (11 December 1946).

In its first Draft Convention, the UN Secretariat expanded such protection to 'racial, national, linguistic, religious or political groups of human beings', thereby offering the widest possible protection for the enumerated groups.[144] Also an amendment proposed by France in 1948 referred to a non-exclusive list of groups: 'particularly by reason of his nationality, race, religion or opinions'.[145] Subsequently, however, the Ad Hoc Committee on Genocide prepared a second Draft Convention that limited protection to national, racial, religious, and political groups only.[146] Crimes of this kind (ie genocide), the Committee's vice-chairman noted, 'were by their nature organically connected with fascism, Nazism and other racial "theories" which preached hatred of races and nationalities as well as the ascendancy of so-called "superior" races and the extermination of so-called "inferior" races'.[147] His statement confirms the connection of the recent experiences of the Holocaust with theories of racial superiority.[148] There is no doubt that this understanding of race was closely linked to the Nazi pogrom against the Jews and other groups. Formulated differently: because Jews were considered a race, it was completely uncontroversial to include racial groups in the draft article.[149] This understanding is also reflected in the *Eichmann* trial, the single most important genocide trial prior to the creation of the International Criminal Tribunal for the Former Yugoslavia (ICTY) and the ICTR, before the District Court of Jerusalem. During the Nazi regime, Adolf Eichmann was leader of the department of Emigration and Evacuation (*Auswanderung und Räumung*) in the Reich Security Main Office (*Reichssicherheitshauptamt*). In this position, he oversaw the deportation of over four million Jews to ghettos and concentration camps. Eichmann was charged under the 'Nazis and Nazi Collaborators Law' and convicted of 'crimes against the Jewish People'.[150] While this domestic law was modelled after Art. 2 Genocide Convention, it

144 UN Secretary-General, Draft Convention on the Crime of Gencoide and Comments (26 June 1947), UN Doc. E/447, Art. I (I).

145 France: Art. 1 Draft Convention on Genocide, UN Doc. A/C.6/211 (1 October 1948).

146 Karim Azkoul, Rapporteur of the Ad Hoc Committee on Genocide, *Report of the Committee and Draft Convention drawn up by the Committee*, UN Doc. E/794 (24 May 1948), p. 13: 'The Committee was unanimously in favour of protecting national, racial and religious groups'.

147 ECOSOC, Ad Hoc Committee on Genocide, Summary Record of the Third Meeting, UN Doc. E/AC.25/SR.3 (1948), p. 2.

148 Matthew Lippman, 'Genocide: The Crime of the Century: The Jurisprudence of Death at the Dawn of the New Millennium', 23 *Houston Journal of International Law* (2000–2001) 527, 530.

149 Schabas confirms that there were hardly any discussions of the term 'racial' during the negotiations, suggesting that the term was very close to the core of what the Genocide Convention was intended to protect [Schabas (n 135) 377–378]. He assumes that Jews, Gypsies, and Armenians might all have been qualified as 'racial group' by many of the delegates attending the General Assembly session of 1948 (ibid 385). Accord: Amann (n 128) 98; Vierdag (n 134) 89.

150 Paul (n 103) 53; Quigley (n 93) 24. Arendt remarks that the counts five through twelve of the indictment against Eichmann also dealt with crimes against humanity; they included

nevertheless contained a substantial deviation in limiting the protection to the Jewish people only.[151] The Israeli court viewed the Jewish people as a national and racial group rather than a religious group. The crime of genocide, it held,

> is intended to exterminate the nation as a group. According to Hitler's murderous racialism, the Nazis singled out Jews from all other citizens in all the countries of their domination, and carried the Jews to their death solely because of their racial affiliation.[152]

The Court sentenced Eichmann for his crimes against the Jewish people, based on Hitler's racialism and the racial affiliation of the Jews. Today, in the context of the Genocide Convention, Jews would most likely be considered a religious group, possibly an ethnic group, but probably not a racial group.[153] This change in denomination demonstrates the volatility of group characterisations.

Unlike the uncontroversial inclusion of racial groups into the Draft Genocide Convention, political groups were inserted following a tight vote of four to three.[154] The category was criticised for not being stable and permanent and being 'based on a body of theoretical concepts whereas sentiment or tradition bound the members of a national, racial or religious group'.[155] The Sixth

genocide against non-Jewish people and all other crimes, committed against Jews or non-Jews [Hannah Arendt, *Eichmann in Jerusalem: A Report on the Banality of Evil* (Penguin Books, 1963/1987) 244].

151 William Schabas, 'Judicial Activism and the Crime of Genocide', in Shane Darcy, Joseph Powderly (eds), *Judicial Creativity at the International Criminal Tribunal* (OUP 2010) 64; Paul (n 103) 53. The law reads: 'A person who has committed one of the following acts: (1) done, during the period of the Nazi regime in an enemy country, an act constituting a crime against the Jewish people; . . . is liable to death penalty" (ibid).

152 *The Attorney-General of Israel v Eichmann*, Criminal, Case No 40/61, District Court of Jerusalem (11 December 1961), para. 38: <www.asser.nl/upload/documents/DomCLIC/Docs/NLP/Israel/Eichmann_Judgement_11-12-1961.pdf>.

153 Falk, Tilley (n 129) 23, considers Jewishness 'certainly as a religious identity' because Judaism is a religious faith. Note that the report concludes that Jews and Palestinians are racial groups for the purpose of International Convention on the Elimination of All Forms Racial Discrimination (ICERD) and the Apartheid Convention (ibid 25). See Chapter 4.5.5 for an in-depth discussion.

154 ECOSOC, Ad Hoc Committee on Genocide, Summary Record of the Thirteenth Meeting, UN Doc. E/AC.25/SR.13 (1948), p. 4. General discussion on which groups should be protected: ECOSOC, Ad Hoc Committee on Genocide, Summary Record of the Third Meeting, UN Doc. E/AC.25/SR.3 (1948), pp. 10–12.

155 ECOSOC, Ad Hoc Committee on Genocide, Summary Record of the Thirteenth Meeting, UN Doc. E/AC.25/SR.13 (1948), p. 2. See Report of the Seventy-Fifth meeting of 15 October 1948 on the discussion of the protection of political groups, UN Doc. A/C.6/SR.75 (1948); Draft Code of Crimes Against the Peace and Security of Mankind, UN Doc. A/51/10 (1996), Art. 17, Commentary No 9.

Furthermore: David Shea Bettwy, 'The Genocide Convention and Unprotected Groups: Is the Scope of Protection Expanding under Customary International Law?', 2 *Notre Dame Journal of International and Comparative Law* (2011) 175; Schabas (n 4) 117, 151. See Chapter 3.6.3 on permanence and stability.

Committee thereafter chose to exclude political groups from the protection of the Genocide Convention, a limitation imposed by powerful states that appeared to be contrary to Lemkin's wishes.[156] The lack of protection for political groups is notably one of the most contentious issues in the law of genocide.[157] Politically motivated mass crimes that were not afforded protection occurred, for example, in Cambodia under the Khmer Rouge regime in 1975–1979[158] or in Indonesia in 1965–1966 and demonstrate the weakness of the exhaustive list of protected groups.[159] Nonetheless, the acts remain prohibited, albeit under other provisions.[160]

According to a UN report, it was argued during debates in the Sixth Committee 'that an exhaustive enumeration was necessitated by the principle *nulla poena sine lege* . . . and that it would be impossible to provide for the punishment of crimes not specified in the criminal code'.[161] The protected national, ethnic, racial, and religious groups were understood as an exclusive list, a *numerus clausus*, and the drafters purposely limited the protection to these four specific groups.[162] Fifty years after the drafting of the Genocide Convention, the States

156 Kielsgard (n 20) 49; Adam Jones, *The Scourge of Genocide* (Routledge 2013) 60 and 230; Claus Kress, 'The Crime of Genocide Under International Law', 6 *International Criminal Law Review* (2006) 473–474; John Ciorciari, '"Auto-Genocide" and the Cambodian Reign of Terror', in Dominik Schaller et al. (eds), *Enteignet – Vertrieben – Ermordet: Beiträge zur Genozidforschung* (Chronos 2004) 421; Barbara Lüders, *Die Strafbarkeit von Völkermord nach dem Römischen Statut für den Internationalen Strafgerichtshof* (Berliner Wissenschafts-Verlag 2004) 67; Jones, Powles (n 3) 166; Bruun (n 63) 206; Shaw (n 10) 808; Whitaker (n 7) para. 35.

157 Nersessian (n 110) 223; Straus (n 134) 361–362; Bruun (n 63) 204. Academia is split as to whether the crime of genocide under customary law protects political groups. Vest rejects this assumption since all newer international legislations incorporate the traditional narrow wording of the Genocide Convention [Hans Vest, *Genozid durch organisatorische Machtapparate* (Nomos Verlagsgesellschaft 2002) 130]. Note, however, that on a domestic level a significant number of states included political groups into their national laws [Jan Wouters, Sten Verhoeven, 'The Domestic Prosecution of Genocide', in Paul Behrens, Ralph Henham (eds), *Elements of Genocide* (Routledge, 2013) 181].

158 See Chapter 3.12 on the ECCC and the *prima facie* assumption of genocide against the ethnic Vietnamese and Muslim Cham, possibly also the Buddhist monks.

159 Rafter (n 40) 80–105; Eric Weitz, *A Century of Genocide: Utopias of Race and Nation* (Princeton UP 2003) 9.

160 Ronald Slye, Beth van Schaack, *International Criminal Law: The Essentials* (Wolters Kluwer 2009) 224; Guglielmo Verdirame, 'The Genocide Definition in the Jurisprudence of the Ad Hoc Tribunals', 49 *International and Comparative Law Quarterly* (2000) 581. *Prosecutor v Nchamihigo*, Case No ICTR-01-63-T (12 November 2008), para. 337 and *Prosecutor v Nahimana* et al., Case No ICTR-99-52-A (28 November 2007), para. 496, both dealt with cases of killings of Hutu political opponents. Being members of a political rather than an ethnical group, their killing was not considered genocide.

161 Nicodème Ruhashyankiko, *Study of the Question of the Prevention and Punishment of the Crime of Genocide*, UN Doc. E/CN.4/Sub. 2/416 (4 July 1978), para. 48.

162 *Prosecutor v Krstić*, Case No IT-98-33-T (2 August 2001), para. 554; *Application of the Convention on the Prevention and Punishment of Genocide (Bosnia and Herzegovina v*

Parties to the Rome Statute again discussed widening the definition of genocide to encompass social and political groups in order to fill 'any gap in the definition'.[163] This suggestion was rejected since Art. 2 Genocide Convention has an authoritative definition, which is widely accepted by states.[164]

In returning to 1948, the *procès-verbaux* of the Sixth Committee reveal how certain state delegates understood race. For instance, Manfred Lachs of Poland emphasised: 'The convention on genocide must seek to protect human beings whatever the colour of their skin, the god they worshipped and the national groups to which they belonged. Those who needed protection most were those who could not alter their status'.[165] Lachs equated race with a person's skin colour and religion with the worship of a god. The categories of racial, national, and religious groups were, according to the delegate, immutable.[166] Such individual statements on the meaning of certain provisions in a drafting process do, however, have no binding effect; they merely reflect a certain interpretation of a particular text.[167]

There was only a very limited debate on the racial and national group in the drafting of the Genocide Convention. Both categories were included at an early stage, and apparently their meaning was self-evident to the drafters who endorsed Art. 2 without a vote.[168] Claus Kress confirms the scarcity of discussions on the definition of the four protected groups; there was a discernible tendency to refrain from any delimitation efforts.[169] The drafters deliberately decided to enumerate the protected groups, leaving a more detailed definition to the implementing legislation as foreseen in Art. 5 Genocide Convention.[170]

Serbia and Montenegro), ICJ Public Sitting, Document No CR/2006/43 (8 May 2006), p. 31. Confirmed by: Werle, Jessberger (n 142) 295; Kress (n 156) 473; David Nersessian, 'The Razor's Edge: Defining and Protecting Human Groups Under the Genocide Convention', 36 *Cornell International Law Journal* (2003) 299, 306; Emanuela Fronza, 'Genocide in the Rome Statute', in Flavia Lattanzi, William Schabas (eds), *Essays on the Rome Statute of the International Criminal Court* (il Sirente 1992) 133. Szpak does not consider the four categories a *numerus clausus* [Agnieszka Szpak, 'National, Ethnic, Racial, and Religious Groups Protected Against Genocide in the Jurisprudence of the Ad Hoc International Criminal Tribunals', 23 *EJIL* (2012) 160–161]. Similarly: van der Vyver (n 109) 304.

163 Report of the *Ad Hoc* Committee on the Establishment of an International Criminal Court, UN Doc. A/50/22 (1995), paras. 60–61.

164 Ibid. See Chapter 3.11.1 on the drafting history of genocide in the Rome Statute.

165 UN Doc. A/C.6/SR.75 (1948) 111.

166 See Chapter 3.6.3 on the immutability of the protected groups.

167 UN Doc. A/C.6/SR.132 (1948) 700; David Nersessian, 'The Contours of Genocidal Intent: Troubling Jurisprudence from the International Criminal Tribunals', 37 *Texas International Law Journal* (2002) 244.

168 Martin (n 109) 114–115.

169 Kress (n 156) 475.

170 Corsin Bisaz, *The Concept of Group Rights in International Law: Groups as Contested Right-Holders, Subjects and Legal Persons* (Martinus Nijhoff 2012) 92; William Schabas,

The fifty-six participants at the General Assembly approved the Genocide Convention by unanimous vote on 9 December 1948, only one day before the adoption of the UDHR.[171] The Convention entered into force in January 1951 with its twentieth ratification. To date, 150 States have ratified the Convention, whereas forty-one are signatories.[172] Together with the UDHR, the Genocide Convention 'marked a dramatic shift from a "state-centric" to a "human-centric" conception of international law' and was revolutionary by the standards of the time.[173] It was and remains, despite incongruities on several elements, such as the definition of the victim groups, the benchmark for genocide scholars from all sciences.[174]

While in 1948 the concept of race was not perceived as problematic and therefore not further elaborated, nowadays the notion is highly controversial. Nearly seventy years later and with significant achievements in DNA coding, we know now that there are no biologically distinct human races.[175] The preparatory works to the Genocide Convention as a historical supplementary source of interpretation are not able to illuminate the meaning of race without leading to an offensive result for contemporary trials. This conclusion agrees to a point with the Dissenting Opinion of Judge Alvarez in the ICJ Advisory Opinion *Reservations to the Genocide Convention*. He warned of the dangers of excessive reference to the preparatory works of the Genocide Convention. Such treaties had 'acquired a life of their own', he said; it was necessary to look ahead, not back to the *travaux préparatoires*, but have regard to new conditions.[176] Conventions 'can be compared to ships which leave the yards in which they have

'The "Odious Scourge": Evolving Interpretations of the Crime of Genocide', 1 *Genocide Studies and Prevention* (2006) 99; Lawrence LeBlanc, 'The United Nations Genocide Convention and Political Groups: Should the United States Propose an Amendment?', 13 *Yale Journal of International Law* (1988) 271–273. This important fact will be dealt with in Chapter 3.7.2 on the evolutive interpretation of the treaty.

171 UN GA Res. 260 B (III) of 9 December 1948.
According to the UN library of international law, 56 representatives were present <http://legal.un.org/avl/ha/cppcg/cppcg.html>.

172 <https://treaties.un.org> for the ratification status.

173 Payam Akhavan, 'Genocide', in Ann-Marie de Brouwer, Alette Smeulers (eds), *The Elgar Companion to the International Criminal Tribunal for Rwanda* (Edward Elgar 2016) 80; Payam Akhavan, 'Balkanizing Jurisdiction: Reflections on Article IX of the Genocide Convention in *Croatia v Serbia*', 28 *LJIL* (2015) 893.

174 Straus (n 134) 361.

175 See Chapter 2.8.

176 *Reservations to the Genocide Convention*, Dissenting Opinion of Judge Alvarez, ICJ Advisory Opinion (1951), p. 53. Note a similar argumentation by the ICERD, considering that the CERD 'as a living instrument, must be interpreted and applied taking into [account] the circumstances of contemporary society' and recalling 'the increased sensitivities in respect of words such as the offending term appertaining today' [*Hagan v Australia*, No 26/2002, Communication, UN Doc. CERD/C/62/D/26/2002 (20 March 2003), para. 7.3].

been built, and sail away independently, no longer attached to the past, and only with regard to the future'.[177] His argument reinforces the call for an evolutive interpretation of the Genocide Convention in that new developments have to be taken into account.[178]

Precisely half a century after the Nuremberg Trials began, the 1996 International Law Commission (ILC) Draft Code of Crimes Against the Peace and Security of Mankind (Draft Code of Crimes) referred to the Charter of the Nuremberg Tribunal. Its commentary on the crime of genocide reads:

> Racial and religious groups are covered by the Charter of the Nürnberg Tribunal and the [Genocide] Convention. In addition, the Convention also covers national or ethnical groups. Article 17 [of the Draft Code] recognises the same categories of protected groups as the Convention. The word 'ethnical' used in the Convention has been replaced by the word 'ethnic' in article 17 to reflect modern English usage without in any way affecting the substance of the provision.[179]

In effect, the ILC does not provide any guidance to the interpretation of racial, religious, national, or ethnic groups, but merely refers to the substantive law.[180] Thus far, no conclusion as to the interpretation of race can be reached.

3.5 The legal elements of the crime of genocide

3.5.1 The definition of the crime of genocide: introductory remarks

Art. 6 Rome Statute, Art. 2 ICTY Statute and Art. 4 ICTR Statute reproduce verbatim the elements of the crime of genocide as set forth in Arts. 2 (and 3) of the Genocide Convention. As such, the Genocide Convention becomes central to the interpretation of the respective statutes.[181] Each one encounters

177 *Reservations to the Genocide Convention*, Dissenting Opinion (n 176), p. 53.

178 See for further analysis Chapter 3.7.2 (on evolutive interpretation). Similar discussion in *Case Concerning the Gabčikovo-Nagymaros Project (Hungary vs Slovakia)*, ICJ Judgment (1997), para. 112: 'the Treaty is not static, and is open to adapt to emerging norms of international law'.

179 Draft Code of Crimes Against the Peace and Security of Mankind, UN Doc. A/51/10 (1996), Art. 17, Commentary No 9. Note that the 1991 ILC Draft Code of Crimes did not discuss the protected groups of genocide (UN Doc. A/CN.4/L.459 (1991), pp. 214–216).

180 Also recognised by Gideon Boas, James Bischoff, Natalie Reid, *Elements of Crimes Under International Law: International Criminal Law Practitioners Library Series* (CUP 2008) 152.

181 Bassiouni even terms genocide a 'single instrument crime', see M. Cherif Bassiouni, *Introduction to International Criminal Law* (Martinus Nijhoff 2nd ed 2013) 154; Dapo Akande, 'Sources of International Criminal Law', in Antonio Cassese (ed), *The Oxford Companion to International Criminal Justice* (OUP 2009) 48.

the same difficulties associated with defining the members of the protected victim groups, in particular the racial group. At the same time, any interpretation of an analogous instrument is also 'persuasive evidence of a plausible interpretation of the Genocide Convention', albeit not *ipso facto* decisive for the meaning of the Convention.[182] The definition of genocide in Art. 2 Genocide Convention, the 1996 ILC Draft Code of Crimes emphasised, is widely accepted and generally recognised as the authoritative definition of the crime.[183] Art. 2 reads:

> In the present Convention, genocide means any of the following acts committed with intent to destroy, in whole or in part, a national, ethnical, racial or religious group, as such:
>
> (a) Killing members of the group;
> (b) Causing serious bodily or mental harm to members of the group;
> (c) Deliberately inflicting on the group conditions of life calculated to bring about its physical destruction in whole or in part;
> (d) Imposing measures intended to prevent births within the group;
> (e) Forcibly transferring children of the group to another group.

Legislative specificity demands that each offense must consist of a material (objective) element, the *actus reus*, and a mental (subjective) element, the *mens rea*.[184] In order to reach a conviction for genocide, a court has to demonstrate the following three elements: 1) an underlying act of the offence that consists of one of the enumerated *actus rei*; 2) the intent to commit the underlying act (*mens rea*); and 3) the specific intent to destroy a human group (*dolus specialis* or special/specific/genocidal intent).[185] These elements, though

182 Nersessian (n 167) 242. Similarly: Boas, Bischoff, Reid (n 180) 151.

183 Draft Code of Crimes against the Peace and Security of Mankind. Titles and texts of articles adopted by the Commission at its forty-eighth session, UN Doc. A/CN.4/L.532 (1996), Commentary 3 to Art. 17 (genocide), p. 44. *Prosecutor v Furundžija*, Case No IT-95-17/1-T (10 December 1998), para. 227 held that the Draft Code was an 'authoritative international instrument'.

184 James Taulbee, *International Crime and Punishment: A Guide to the Issues* (ABC Clio 2009) 43; Gerhard Werle, 'General Principles of International Criminal Law', in Antonio Cassese (ed), *The Oxford Companion to International Criminal Justice* (OUP 2009) 56; John Jones, '"Whose Intent is it Anyway?" Genocide and the Intent to Destroy a Group', in Lal Chand Vohrah et al. (eds), *Man's Inhumanity to Man: Essays on International Law in Honour of Antonio Cassese* (Kluwer Law International 2003) 470.

185 *Prosecutor v Brđanin*, Case No IT-99-36-T (1 September 2004), para. 695. David Nersessian, *Genocide and Political Groups* (OUP 2010) 13; Payam Akhavan, 'The Crime of Genocide in the ICTR Jurisprudence', 3 *JICJ* (2005) 991–992; Derenzo, Garcia (n 12) 10; Roberta Arnold, 'The *Mens Rea* of Genocide under the Statute of the International Criminal Court', 14 *Criminal Law Forum* (2003) 128–129; Cécile Aptel, 'The Intent to Commit Genocide in the Case Law of the International Criminal Tribunal for Rwanda', 13 *Criminal Law Forum* (2002) 275.

analytically distinct, are linked.[186] In aiming at the whole or partial destruction of a group, the group dimension of the perpetrator's *dolus specialis* is central to the crime.[187]

3.5.2 The group as object of protection

3.5.2.1 Group membership and group identity

The perpetrator commits the prohibited acts of genocide against individuals for reason of their group membership.[188] The traditional view is that the victim of the crime of genocide is not only the individual, but also the group itself.[189] In fact, the Genocide Convention was intended to protect the 'fundamental right of a human group to exist as a group',[190] and accordingly, genocide is a deprivation of a group's right to exist.[191] The 1996 ILC Draft Code of Crimes equally emphasises the importance of the group victimhood:

> It is the membership of the individual in a particular group rather than the identity of the individual that is the decisive criterion in determining the immediate victims of the crime of genocide. The group itself is the ultimate target or intended victim of this type of massive criminal conduct.

186 *Application of the Convention on the Prevention and Punishment of the Crime of Genocide (Croatia v Serbia)*, ICJ Summary Judgment (15 February 2015) 10.

187 The *dolus specialis* applies to all material acts of genocide (Draft Code of Crimes Against the Peace and Security of Mankind: UN Doc. A/51/10 (1996), Art. 17, Commentary No 5); *Prosecutor v Musema*, Case No ICTR-96–13-A, Trial Judgment (27 January 2000), paras. 164, 166. Furthermore: O'Keefe (n 4) 146; Devrim Aydin, 'The Interpretation of Genocidal Intent under the Genocide Convention and the Jurisprudence of International Courts', 78 *Journal of Criminal Law* (2014) 430, 432; Nersessian (n 185) 174; Demko (n 35) 225; Akhavan (n 185) 992.

188 Caroline Fournet, *Genocide and Crimes Against Humanity: Misconceptions and Confusion in French Law and Practice* (Hart 2013) 105; Bisaz (n 170) 85; Wilson (n 9) 51; Demko (n 35) 226–227; Aptel (n 185) 279; David Alonzo-Maizlish, 'In Whole or in Part: Group Rights, The Intent Element of Genocide, and the "Qualitative Criterion"', 77 *New York University Law Review* (2002) 1399; Chalk, Jonassohn (n 18) 31; Alexander Greenawalt, 'Rethinking Genocidal Intent: The Case for a Knowledge-Based Interpretation', 99 *Columbia Law Review* (1999) 2265.

189 Widely acknowledged: *Prosecutor v Popović* et al., Case No IT-05–88-T (10 June 2010), para. 821; *Prosecutor v Milosević*, Case No IT-02–54-T, Decision on Motion for Judgment of Acquittal (16 June 2004), para. 123; *Prosecutor v Sikirica*, Case No IT-95–8-T, Judgment on Defence Motions to Acquit (3 September 2001), para. 34; *Prosecutor v Musema*, Case No ICTR- 96–13-A, Trial Judgment (27 January 2000), para. 165; *Prosecutor v Akayesu*, Case No ICTR-96–4-T (2 September 1998), para. 521. See also Kai Ambos, *Treatise on International Criminal Law, Vol. II: The Crimes and Sentencing* (OUP 2014) 44; Nina Jørgensen, 'The Definition of Genocide: Joining the Dots in the Light of Recent Practice', 1 *International Criminal Law Review* (2001) 304.

190 UN Doc. A/PV.179 (1948), p. 852.

191 UN GA Res. 96 (I) (1946).

> The action taken against the individual members of the group is the means used to achieve the ultimate criminal objective with respect to the group.[192]

The perpetrator considers the individual victim 'a means to an end: a step further along the path of destroying the group'.[193] While it is uncontested that the victims have to be members of a group protected within the ambit of the Genocide Convention, there has been scholarly debate as to whether the group itself should have a legal value of its own.[194] The law of genocide does not define the protected victim groups. This lack of definition has led to inconsistent approaches in the jurisprudence of international criminal tribunals.[195] Even during the drafting of the Genocide Convention it was repeatedly pointed out that its definitions were too vague.[196] In addition, confining protection to only national, ethnic, racial, and religious groups has been criticised for seemingly assigning greater value to some groups than to others.[197]

In a rather recent appeals judgment, the ICTY confirmed that the 'identification of one of these protected groups as the victim of the proscribed acts is . . . one of the required components of establishing the crime of genocide'.[198] The threshold question for any prosecution for genocide is thus whether the targeted group falls within one of the protected categories.[199] But case law manifests a distinct unease in assigning victims to a specific group, particularly

192 Draft Code of Crimes Against the Peace and Security of Mankind, UN Doc. A/51/10 (1996), Art. 17, Commentary No 6.

193 Ibid.

194 For further reading: Bisaz (n 170) 96; May (n 15) 91–107; Nersessian (n 185) 68; David Luban, 'Calling Genocide by Its Rightful Name: Lemkin's Word, Darfur, and the UN Report', 7 *Chicago Journal of International Law* (2007) 309; Alonzo-Maizlish (n 188) 1369–1403.

195 See Chapter 3.9.2 for more information. Furthermore: Akhavan 2016 (n 173) 96; Kielsgard (n 20) 49; Fournet (n 188) 105; Bisaz (n 170) 88; Mark Drumbl, 'The Crime of Genocide', in: Bartram Brown (ed), *Research Handbook on International Criminal Law* (Edward Elgar 2011) 44; Christoph Safferling, 'The Special Intent Requirement in the Crime of Genocide', in Christoph Safferling, Eckart Conze (eds), *The Genocide Convention Sixty Years After Its Adoption* (TMC Asser Press 2010) 167; David Lisson, 'Defining "National Group" in the Genocide Convention: A Case Study of Timor-Leste', 60 *Stanford Law Review* (2008) 1462; Antonio Cassese, *International Criminal Law* (OUP 2nd ed 2008) 138; Akhavan (n 185) 1005; Amann (n 128) 133; Straus (n 134) 365.

196 See eg the statement by Mr Bartos (Yugoslavia) who noted that neither the preamble nor Art. 1 Draft Convention defined the group of human beings, the *genus* (UN Doc. A/C.6/SR.63, 30 September 1948, p. 9) or Mr Manini y Rios (Urgugay) who said that the word 'group' should be defined more precisely [UN Doc. A/C.6/SR.64 (1 October 1948), p. 16]. Also discussed in Boas, Bischoff, Reid (n 180) 147; Bruun (n 63) 197.

197 Wouters, Verhoeven (n 157) 186.

198 *Prosecutor v Tolimir*, Case No IT-05–88/2-A (8 April 2015), para. 182.

199 Nersessian (n 185) 21; Lisson (n 195) 1460. Behrens considers the 'true threshold criterion for genocide' to be on the 'subjective side of the crime' [Paul Behrens, 'Between Abstract Event and Individualized Crime: Genocidal Intent in the Case of Croatia', 28 *LJIL* (2015) 925]. Kai Ambos, 'Some Preliminary Reflections on the *Mens Rea* Requirements of the

to the racial group.[200] The existence of a group is the protected value that justifies the criminalisation of genocide and makes it a crime with a *dolus specialis.* As a consequence, the establishment of a perpetrator's special intent can only take place in conjunction with the identification of a protected group, at which his conduct is aimed.[201] Art. 2 Genocide Convention refers to the groups in the *dolus specialis* of the crime as well as in paragraphs (a)–(e) that list the individual genocidal acts (the *actus rei*). The groups therefore have to exist in the mind of the perpetrator, and he must in fact target members of one of the protected groups.[202] This study suggests that the racial group ought to be identified by means of the perpetrator's *dolus specialis* alone, viz. his perception of the victims' otherness. Importantly, this suggestion of a subjective definition of the racial group is coherent with an evolutive interpretation of race.[203] The next section will discuss whether the four protected groups should be understood as four corner posts delimiting an area of group protection – and whether the protection is limited to minority groups only.

3.5.2.2 *The four corner posts*

In *Krstić*, which dealt with the killing of men (civilian and soldiers) of military age in Srebrenica, the ICTY Trial Chamber held:

> National, ethnical, racial or religious group [sic] are not clearly defined in the [Genocide] Convention or elsewhere. In contrast, the preparatory work on the Convention . . . show[s] that the concepts of protected groups and national minorities partially overlap and are on occasion synonymous.[204]

Crimes of the ICC Statute and of the Elements of Crimes', in Lal Chand Vohrah et al. (eds), *Man's Inhumanity to Man: Essays on International Law in Honour of Antonio Cassese* (Kluwer Law International 2003) 16–17 considers the victim group, as an object of the perpetrator's action, a factual circumstance as defined by Art. 30(3) Rome Statute.

200 Hassan Bubacar Jallow, 'The ICTR's Elaboration of the Core International Crimes of Genocide, Crimes against Humanity and War Crimes and Modes of Liability', in Ann-Marie de Brouwer, Alette Smeulers (eds), *The Elgar Companion to the International Criminal Tribunal for Rwanda* (Edward Elgar 2016) 453; Wouters, Verhoeven (n 157) 185. See Chapter 3.9.2 on the *ad hoc* tribunals' case law, Chapter 3.11 on the ICC's case law on genocide, Chapters 3.12 on ECCC's jurisprudence.

201 Martin (n 109) 112–113; Demko (n 35) 224–226; Wilson (n 9) 51.

202 *Prosecutor v Kaing Guek Eav alias Duch*, Case No 001/18-07-2007/ECCC/SC, Appeal Judgment (3 February 2012), para. 268; *Prosecutor v Tolimir*, Case No IT-05-88/2-T (12 December 2012), para. 735; *Prosecutor v Brđanin*, Case No IT-99-36-T (1 September 2004), para. 684. Furthermore: Monika Ambrus, 'Genocide and Discrimination: Lessons to Be Learnt from Discrimination Law', 25 *LJIL* (2012) 946; Kai Ambos, 'What Does 'Intent to Destroy' in Genocide Mean?', 91 *International Review of the Red Cross* (2009) 834; Nersessian (n 167) 256; William Schabas, *Genocide in International Law* (CUP 1st ed 2000) 110–111 (omitted in 2nd ed 2009).

203 See Chapter 3.7.2 on evolutive interpretation.

204 *Prosecutor v Krstić*, Case No IT-98-33-T (2 August 2001), para. 555.

Furthermore,

> The preparatory work of the Convention shows that setting out such a list was designed more to describe a single phenomenon, roughly corresponding to what was recognised, before the second world war, as 'national minorities', rather than to refer to several distinct prototypes of human groups. To attempt to differentiate each of the named groups on the basis of scientifically objective criteria would thus be inconsistent with the object and purpose of the Convention.[205]

This judgment prompts several comments, particularly with regard to national minorities and the description of the list of protected groups as a single phenomenon. Even though the drafters initially had national minorities in mind, this idea is not translated into the wording of the Genocide Convention.[206] Rather, its *travaux préparatoires* reveal that genocide was defined as the deliberate destruction of a group, not only minorities.[207] In the course of drafting, the link to minority protection was removed because it could result in 'an undue extension of the notion of genocide and amounted to reconstituting the former protection of minorities (which was based on other conceptions)'.[208] Undoubtedly, the national, religious, racial, and ethnic groups of the Genocide Convention are not clear-cut and often overlap.[209] In suggesting that the list of these four groups describes a single phenomenon, *Krstić* embraces what could be termed a four-corner-approach, delimiting 'an area within which a [sic] myriad of groups covered by the Convention find protection'.[210]

205 ibid para. 556. Accord: *Prosecutor v Brđanin*, Case No IT-99–36-T (1 September 2004), para. 682.

206 Bisaz (n 170) 87–88; William Schabas, 'Genocide Law in a Time of Transition: Recent Developments in the Law of Genocide', 61 *Rutgers Law Review* (2008–2009) 190; Luban (n 194) 317; Larissa van den Herik, 'The Schism Between the Legal and the Social Concept of Genocide in Light of the Responsibility to Protect', in Ralph Henham, Paul Behrens (eds), *The Criminal Law of Genocide: International, Comparative and Contextual Aspects* (Ashgate 2007) 87; Ciorciari (n 156) 428; Schabas (n 109) 41; Pieter Drost, *The Crime of the State: Penal Protection for Fundamental Freedoms of Persons and Peoples, Book II: Genocide: United Nations Legislation on International Criminal Law* (AW Sythoff 1959) 122.

207 Quigley (n 93) 149; UN Secretary-General, Draft Convention on the Crime of Genocide and Comments, UN Doc. E/447 (26 June 1947), p. 16.

208 Ibid 27.

209 Werle, Jessberger (n 142) 296; Ambos (n 189) 5; Schabas (n 4) 129; Paul (n 103) 106; Nersessian (n 162) 303; Daniel Ntanda Nsereko, 'Genocide: A Crime against Mankind', in Gabrielle Kirk McDonald, Olivia Swaak-Goldman (eds), *Substantive and Procedural Aspects of International Criminal Law: The Experience of International and National Courts* (Kluwer Law International 2000) 131.

210 Schabas (n 4) 129; Schabas (n 206) 167; Schabas 2000 (n 135) 385. Furthermore: Darryl Robinson, Gillian MacNeil, 'The Tribunals and the Renaissance of International Criminal Law: Three Themes', 110 *AJIL* (2016) 5.

William Schabas considers that within the four corner posts, the protected groups are in a dynamic and synergistic relationship, where each group contributes to the construction of the other.[211] This approach, which recognises that the groups are hard to separate and form one larger whole, has also been termed an ensemble or holistic approach.[212] In possessing the characteristics of several groups, the need to definitively assign the victim to one particular group is seemingly eliminated.[213] While *Krstić* to a large degree endorsed this ensemble approach, *Stakić* later rejected it and held that, although a victim group may be distinguishable on more than one basis, the elements of genocide must be considered in relation to each group separately.[214] The ICTY's last judgment, however, seems to reverse the *Stakić* approach in favour of the ensemble approach. In the *Mladić* judgment, the Trial Chamber concludes that the victims were members of a 'national, ethnical, and/or religious' group.[215] In their historical analysis, the judges discuss how Maršal Tito discouraged ethnic division and nationalism. Nonetheless, the various groups remained conscious of their separate identities. The judgment mentions Bosnia-Herzegovina with Serbs, Muslims, and Croats as 'the predominant nationalities', but then concludes that the victims 'are protected groups within the meaning . . . of the Statute'.[216] Albeit laying clear the facts that the involved groups had distinct (national) identities, the judges avoid a categorisation of the victim groups, notably because the defence did not dispute the group status. In dealing with the four protected groups as one, in the manner of the four-corner approach, the judgment circumvents defining each individual victim group. In a similar vein, Chapter 3.12 will show that the most recent judgment of the Extraordinary Chambers in the Courts of Cambodia (ECCC) concluded that certain victims were members of a national, ethnic, and/or a racial group.

Diane Amann favours an ensemble approach because '[t]o probe whether victims belonged to an enumerated group and thus suffered genocide may seem to exalt legal nicety over societal necessity'.[217] Nevertheless, she acknowledges that an absolute refusal to differentiate among the adjectives in the Convention would violate a basic canon of construction, namely the principle

211 Schabas (n 4) 129; Schabas 2000 (n 135) 385. Similarly: Allard K. Lowenstein International Human Rights Clinic, Yale Law School, *Persecution of the Rohingya Muslims: Is Genocide Occurring in Myanmar's Rakhine State? A Legal Analysis* (2015) 41. For a critique: May (n 15) 100–102.

212 Bisaz (n 170) 93; Amann (n 128) 109–113.

213 Werle, Jessberger (n 142) 296; Paul (n 103) 107.

214 *Prosecutor v Stakić*, Case No IT-97–24-T (31 July 2003), para. 512.

215 *Prosecutor v Mladić*, Case No IT-09–92-T (22 November 2017), para. 3442.

216 Ibid.

217 Amann (n 128) 113.

of effectiveness.[218] The *Akayesu* appeals judgment articulated the principle as follows:

> [O]ne of the basic rules of interpretation requires that a provision or part thereof should not be interpreted in a manner to render it redundant or bereft of any object, unless such a conclusion is inevitable. One must proceed from the assumption that the lawmakers intended to give some effect to each of the words used.[219]

Formulated differently: the ensemble approach contradicts the principle of effectiveness, whereby each word in a legal text carries its distinct meaning.[220] The principle of effectiveness or in its Latin rendition, *ut res magis valeat quam pereat*, has been recognised by the ICJ as 'one of the fundamental principles of interpretation of treaties'[221] and is part of an interpretation according to Art. 31(1) Vienna Convention on the Law of Treaties (VCLT) that realizes the aims of a treaty.[222] Christian Tams and co-authors point out that merging the categories, in effect, leads to deleting the four group elements and replacing them with an unspecified category. This result is irreconcilable not only with the principle of effectiveness, but also with *nullum crimen sine lege stricta*, whereby a crime shall be strictly construed and not extended by analogy.[223]

218 Ibid 138.

219 *Prosecutor v Akayesu*, Case No ICTR-96-4-A (1 June 2001), para. 468.

220 *Prosecutor v Galić*, Case No IT-98-29-T (5 December 2003), para. 91; Kress (n 156) 475.

221 *Case Concerning the Territorial Dispute (Libyan Arab Jamahiriya v Chad)*, ICJ Judgment (1994), para. 51. For an extensive analysis of ICJ jurisprudence until 1967 on the principle of effectiveness, see Myres McDougal, Harold Lasswell, James Miller, *The Interpretation of Agreements and World Public Order: Principles of Content and Procedure* (Yale UP 1967) 156–186.

222 The principle of effectiveness is not explicitly included in the VCLT, but has been applied in treaty interpretation in national, regional, and international jurisprudence. See Leena Grover, *Interpreting Crimes in the Rome Statute of the International Criminal Court* (CUP 2014) 55, 198–199; Richard Gardiner, *Treaty Interpretation* (OUP 2008) 159–160; Hersch Lauterpacht, 'Restrictive Interpretation and the Principle of Effectiveness in the Interpretation of Treaties', *British Year Book of International Law* (1949) 68.

223 Christian Tams, Lars Berster, Björn Schiffbauer, *Convention on the Prevention and Punishment of the Crime of Genocide: A Commentary* (CH Beck 2014) 102. Furthermore: Quigley (n 93) 149; Akhavan (n 187) 999.

In *Vasiliauskas v Lithuania*, ECtHR Application No 35343/05, Dissenting Opinion of Judges Villiger, Power-Forde, Pinto de Albuquerque, and Kūris, Grand Chamber Judgment (20 October 2015), para. 11, the minority judges appealed to refraining from too 'formalistic reasoning' in the fight of impunity. Rather the ECtHR has a role as the 'conscience of Europe' (ibid para. 18). Such expansive view puts at risk the fundamental principles of international criminal law, including the principles of legality and fairness [Kai Ambos, 'The Crime of Genocide and the Principle of Legality Under Article 7 of the European Convention on Human Rights', 17 *Human Rights Law Review* (2017) 185–186].

In contradiction to the four-corner-approach, this study argues that each protected group, including the racial group, should be defined individually, in accordance with the principle of effectiveness. In addition, the ensemble approach disregards the nature of any pre-genocidal process, typically characterised by the creation of and designation to a victim category, in which the perpetrator defines his victims according to the characteristics emphasised and highlighted by himself.[224] Whether they reflect a reality is irrelevant, because the perpetrator treats them as real and acts upon such belief. The perpetrator selects his victims for reasons of their – alleged or real – membership of a group or for reasons of identity, against which the perpetrator defines himself as different. He holds the definitional power (*Definitionsmacht*) over the collective identity of the victim group.[225] As a rule, the perpetrator reduces the victim's identity to a single marker, which is quite the opposite of the ensemble approach.[226] Lastly, the parameters of the four corners can only be set if each individual group that marks one of the four boundaries is defined. This will logically result in an individual definition of the national, racial, religious, and ethnic group.

3.5.3 *The intent to destroy*

Genocide, in the words of *Krstić*, is 'one of the worst crimes known to humankind, and its gravity is reflected in the stringent requirement of specific intent'.[227] The intent to destroy, in whole or in part, one of the four groups, is the key element that distinguishes genocide from other international crimes. It is characterised by a psychological relationship between the physical result and the mental state of the perpetrator.[228] The crime of genocide consists of two distinct subjective elements that need to be proven in order to establish criminal liability: a *mens rea* to commit one of the underlying genocidal acts and a *dolus specialis* to destroy the group as such.[229] The *dolus specialis* is, as such, not merely a

224 Recognised by Mark Levene, 'A Twentieth-Century Phenomenon?', in Carol Rittner, John Roth, James Smith (eds), *Will Genocide Ever End?* (Paragon 2002) 65; Huttenbach (n 41) 295.

225 Mayroz (n 5) 79; Rafter (n 40) 95; Zartman, Anstey (n 26) 8; Smeulers, Grünfeld (n 18) 249–251.

226 Also recognised by Paul Behrens, 'Genocide and the Question of Motives', 10 *JICJ* (2012) 513; Hiebert (n 20) 10; Haque (n 19) 320. See Chapters 2.7, 3.2 and 5.3.1 on identity markers.

227 *Prosecutor v Krstić*, Case No IT-98–33-A (19 April 2004), para. 134.

228 *Prosecutor v Akayesu*, Case No ICTR-96–4-T (2 September 1998), para. 518. Confirmed by: *Prosecutor v Musema*, Case No ICTR-96–13-A, Trial Judgment (27 January 2000), para. 166. Paul Behrens, 'The Crime of Genocide and the Problem of Subjective Substantiality', 59 *German Yearbook of International Law* (2016) 325.

229 Geert-Jan Alexander Knoops, Mens Rea *at the International Criminal Court* (Brill Nijhoff 2017) 95; Akhavan 2016 (n 173) 83; Behrens (n 199) 923; Safferling (n 195) 170; Otto Triffterer, 'Genocide, Its Particular Intent to Destroy in Whole or in Part the Group as Such', 14 *LJIL* (2001) 400.

counterpart to an existing *actus reus*, but exists outside the latter. The crime of genocide is thus distinguished by a 'surplus of intent'.[230] It is the perpetrator's intention to destroy individuals because of their (perceived) membership of a group that distinguishes genocide from other crimes, irrespective of what his underlying motive may have been.[231] Accordingly, proof of a motive is not required for a conviction of genocide, which is widely recognised both in case law and in academia.[232] In the words of the *Stakić* Appeals Chamber, 'in genocide cases, the reason why the accused sought to destroy the victim group has no bearing on guilt'.[233] The difficulties of separating intent from motive have led several scholars to call for a determination of intent based on the perpetrator's knowledge.[234] The knowledge-based approach lowers the standard for genocidal intent to one wherein the prosecution must prove that the perpetrator had knowledge of a genocidal campaign that would result in the destruction of a group.[235]

230 *Prosecutor v Stakić*, Case No IT-97–24-T (31 July 2003), para. 520. Furthermore: Paul Behrens, 'Art. 6: Genocide', in Mark Klamberg (ed), *Commentary on the Law of the International Criminal Court* (TOAEP 2017) 20.

231 *Prosecutor v Rukundo,* Case No ICTR-2001–70-T (27 February 2009), para. 557; *Prosecutor v Brđanin*, Case No IT-99–36-T (1 September 2004), para. 695; *Prosecutor v Kayishema and Ruzindana*, Case No ICTR-95–1-T (21 May 1999), para. 91; *Prosecutor v Kambanda*, Case No ICTR-97–23-S, Judgment and Sentence (4 September 1998), para. 16.

232 Eg *Prosecutor v Bagosora* et al., Case No ICTR-98-41-T (18 December 2008), para. 2115; *Prosecutor v Ntakirutimana and Ntakirutimana*, Case Nos. ICTR-96–10-A and ICTR-96–17-A (13 December 2004), para. 304; *Prosecutor v Jelisić*, Case No IT-95–10-A (5 July 2001), paras. 49, 71; *Prosecutor v Tadić,* Case No IT-95–1-A (15 July 1999), para. 269. Some scholars advocate recognition of the motive as an element to prove the required mental element: Behrens (n 199) 932; Behrens (n 226) 501–523; Safferling (n 195) 164. Also discussed in: *Prosecutor v Jelisić and Češić*, Prosecutor's Pre-Trial Brief, Case No IT-95–10-PT (19 November 1998), para. 3.5. On the legal irrelevance of motive for the crime of genocide: Michelle Jarvis, Alan Tieger, 'Applying the Genocide Convention at the ICTY: The Influence of Paradigms Past', 14 *JICJ* (2016) 863; O'Keefe (n 4) 151; Aydin (n 187) 431; Verdeja (n 100) 32; Cryer (n 8) 223; Nersessian (n 185) 39; Schabas (n 4) 302; Taulbee (n 184) 123; Boas, Bischoff, Reid (n 180) 162, 308; Jones, Powles (n 3) 156; Arnold (n 185) 136; Jones (n 184) 468; Amann (n 128) 93; Machteld Boot, *Genocide, Crimes Against Humanity, War Crimes:* Nullum Crimen Sine Lege *and the Subject Matter Jurisdiction of the International Criminal Court* (Intersentia 2002) 386; Nersessian (n 167) 267–268.

233 *Prosecutor v Stakić*, Case No IT-97–24-A (22 March 2006), para. 45.

234 Stahn (n 93) 43–44; Janine Natalya Clark, 'Elucidating the *Dolus Specialis*: An Analysis of ICTY Jurisprudence on Genocidal Intent', 26 *Criminal Law Forum* (2015) 516–525; Larry May, *Genocide: A Normative Account* (CUP 2010) 121–131; Ambos (n 202) 839 et seq; Hans Vest, 'A Structure-Based Concept of Genocidal Intent', 5 *JICJ* (2007) 786 et seq; Claus Kress, 'The Darfur Report and Genocidal Intent', 3 *JICJ* (2005) 562 et seq; Greenawalt (n 188) 2265–2270, 2288–2294.

235 Stahn (n 93) 44; Claus Kress, 'The ICC's First Encounter with the Crime of Genocide: The Case against Al Bashir', in Carsten Stahn (ed), *The Law and Practice of the International Criminal Court* (OUP 2015) 695–700; Greenawalt (n 188) 2265. Furthermore: Safferling (n 195) 171–173; Schabas (n 4) 242–243.

Yet the international criminal judiciary has consistently rejected such a knowledge-standard for genocide.[236]

Distinct from the Genocide Convention, Art. 30(1) Rome Statute requires the *actus reus* to have been committed 'with intent and knowledge'. As such, the Rome Statute requires volitional (intent) as well as a cognitive (knowledge) element.[237] However, as a default rule, Art. 30(1) Rome Statute applies only when the intent element of a crime is not 'otherwise provided' for in the relevant criminal provision.[238] While the Elements of Crimes leave unanswered whether Art. 30 applies to acts of genocide,[239] and the Chambers of the ICC have yet to deal with the matter, it can be anticipated that such application is unlikely, since Art. 6 Rome Statute specifically provides for the *dolus specialis* of the crime of genocide.[240] Notably, element (c) in the Introduction to Art. 6 of the Elements of Crimes reads:

> Notwithstanding the normal requirement for a mental element provided for in article 30, and recognizing that knowledge of the circumstances will usually be addressed in proving genocidal intent, the appropriate requirement, if any, for a mental element regarding this circumstance will need to be decided by the Court on a case-by-case basis.

Also the 1996 ILC Draft Code of Crimes held that the perpetrator could not commit acts of genocide without knowledge of their consequences, since the acts were by their very nature conscious, intentional, or volitional.[241] Thus, the crime of genocide cannot be committed as a result of negligence or accident, since the perpetrator clearly seeks the result of the offence.[242]

3.5.3.1 'As Such'

The destruction of the group must be intended 'as such' and reinforces the fact that the victims are chosen due to their membership of a group.[243] The 1996

236 *Prosecutor v Akayesu*, Case No ICTR-96–4-T (2 September 1998), paras. 521 and 544; *Prosecutor v Jelisić*, Case No IT-95–10-T (14 December 1999), para. 86; *Prosecutor v Jelisić*, Case No IT-95–10-A (5 July 2001), para. 46; *Prosecutor v Krstić*, Case No IT-98–33-T (2 August 2001), para. 561.

237 Schabas (n 4) 133; Ambos (n 202) 834.

238 Arnold (n 185) 132.

239 Nersessian (n 167) 265.

240 Accord: Knoops (n 229) 93–94; Safferling (n 195) 170.

241 ILC Report on the work of its forty-eighth session, UN Doc. A/51/10 (1996), Comment No 5 to Art. 17.

242 Safferling (n 195) 164.

243 Derenzo, Garcia (n 12) 17; Jones, Powles (n 3) 155; Aptel (n 185) 280; Whitaker (n 7) para. 38; Drost (n 206) 83. Note that *Prosecutor v Niyitegeka*, Case No ICTR-96–14-A (9 July 2004), para. 49 concluded that 'as such' expressed the concept of motives. Accord: Schabas (n 4) 294.

ILC Draft Code of Crimes confirmed that the 'intention must be to destroy the group "as such", meaning as a separate and distinct entity'.[244] Similarly, in the opinion of the ICTY Appeals Chamber, the term 'as such' has great significance, for it shows that the offence requires intent to destroy a collection of people who have a particular group identity.[245] An important aspect of the intent element concerns the question of whether the perpetrator sought the destruction of a group because of its national, racial, ethnic, or religious characteristics. The wording of the Genocide Convention does indeed suggest so. The *travaux préparatoires* confirm that the crime must be committed 'on grounds of national or racial origin',[246] while the Special Rapporteur on the 1986 ILC Draft Code of Crimes declared that genocide presents 'the intention to harm a person or group of persons because of their race, nationality, religion or political opinions'.[247] Additionally, the intent to destroy a group as such refers to its existence as a separate and distinct entity, not just as individuals because of their membership of a particular group.[248] Several judgments by the *ad hoc* tribunals held that the *dolus specialis* presupposes that the perpetrator selects his victims because they are part of a group which he seeks to destroy.[249] In doing so, the tribunals recognise that the crime of genocide is an attack on a group for reasons of the group's very existence.[250]

3.5.3.2 *Proof of the genocidal intent*

Academics have described the *actus reus* as the objective appearance – the mirror – of the *mens rea*, whereas the specific intent lacks such a corresponding pendant.[251] The successful prosecution of the crime of genocide requires not only the proof of intent to commit one of the underlying genocidal acts,

244 ILC Draft Code of Crimes (1996), UN Doc. A/CN.4/L.532, p. 45.

245 *Prosecutor v Stakić*, Case No IT-97–24-A (22 March 2006), para. 20. Confirmed in *Prosecutor v Sikirica*, Case No IT-95–8-T, Judgment on Defence Motions to Acquit (3 September 2001), para. 89.

246 Hirad Abtahi, Philippa Webb, *The Genocide Convention: The Travaux Préparatoires* (Martinus Nijhoff 2008) 1124.

247 Doudou Thiam, Fourth Report on the Draft Code of Offences Against the Peace and Security of Mankind, UN Doc. A/CN.4/398 (1986), para. 25. The crime of genocide is listed under the heading 'Crimes against Humanity'.

248 Ibid para. 30.

249 *Prosecutor v Krstić*, Case No IT-98–33-T (2 August 2001), para. 561; *Prosecutor v Kupreškić* et al., Case No IT-95–16-T (14 January 2000), para. 636; *Prosecutor v Jelisić*, Case No IT-95–10-T (14 December 1999), para. 67.

250 *Prosecutor v Niyitegeka*, Case No ICTR-96–14-T (16 May 2003), para. 410 with reference to *Prosecutor v Akayesu*, Case No ICTR-96–4-T (2 September 1998), para. 521. Confirmed by *Prosecutor v Niyitegeka*, Case No ICTR-96–14-A (9 July 2004), para. 53.

251 Behrens (n 199) 924, 933; Clark (n 234) 500; Behrens (n 226) 504, 506; Safferling (n 195) 164; Werle (n 184); Ambos (n 202) 835; Arnold (n 185) 127 et seq; Triffterer (n 229) 401.

but also the proof of intent to destroy the targeted group. Due to the principle of *nullum crimen sine lege*, in proving the facts relevant to the case, Otto Triffterer suggests a strict separation of the two different intents, the *dolus specialis* and the *mens rea* of each genocidal act.[252] Indeed, the proof of an overarching special intent to destroy a group is not inherently linked with the intent to, for example, kill members of the group. Triffterer's approach provides a practical method for determining each of the elements of the *mens rea* in a manner that avoids potential conflation and is therefore a useful approach to adopt. A compartmentalisation of the intent requirements was, however, rejected by the *Stakić* Appeals Chamber. It held that, rather than considering separately whether the intent to destroy the victim group was given for each of the genocidal acts, all the available evidence should be taken together and assessed whether it demonstrated a genocidal mental state.[253]

The perpetrator's intent includes the racial group, and the proof of this intent, interconnected with the racial group, is one of the most difficult issues for a court of law.[254] It has even been suggested that the crime of genocide is redundant due to the obstacles the intent requirement has created for the prosecution.[255] Indications of such intent are rarely overt; often only indirect or circumstantial evidence is available.[256] An empirical assessment of all evidence is needed to ascertain whether the specific intent required by the law of genocide is established.[257]

252 Triffterer (n 229) 401.

253 *Prosecutor v Stakić*, Case No 97–24-A (22 March 2006), para. 55. The *Karadžić* trial judgment followed this approach (*Prosecutor v Karadžić*, Case No 95–5/18-T (24 March 2016), para. 550.

254 *Prosecutor v Musema*, Case No ICTR-96-13-A, Trial Judgment (27 January 2000), para. 166. Furthermore: Stahn (n 93) 37, 41; Kielsgard (n 20) 85; Evelyne Schmid, *Taking Economic, Social and Cultural Rights Seriously in International Criminal Law* (CUP 2015) 209; Clark (n 234) 501; Werle, Jessberger (n 142) 320; Boas, Bischoff, Reid (n 180) 160; Paul (n 103) 79; Behrens (n 73) 125; Vest (n 234) 781; Paul Roth, 'The Politics of Definition', in Carol Rittner, John Roth, James Smith (eds), *Will Genocide Ever End?* (Paragon 2002) 26; William Schabas, 'Was Genocide Committed in Bosnia and Herzegovina?', 25 *Fordham International Law Journal* (2001) 36.

255 Alexander Murray, 'Does International Criminal Law Still Require a 'Crime of Crimes'? A Comparative Review of Genocide and Crimes Against Humanity', 3 *Goettingen Journal of International Law* (2011) 590. Similarly: Bisaz (n 170) 89.

256 *Prosecutor v Tolimir*, Case No IT-05–88/2-T (12 December 2012), para. 745; *Application of the Convention on the Prevention and Punishment of the Crime of Genocide (Croatia v Serbia)*, ICJ Judgment (2015), para. 143. Mayroz (n 5) 75; O'Keefe (n 4) 152–153; Cupido (n 142) 384; Cryer (n 8) 225; Ratner, Abrams, Bischoff (n 142) 37; Boas, Bischoff, Reid (n 180) 160; van den Herik (n 206) 89; Akhavan (n 185) 997; Nersessian (n 167) 266; Aptel (n 185) 276; Vladimir Tochilovsky, *Jurisprudence of the International Criminal Courts and the European Court of Human Rights: Procedure and Evidence* (Martinus Nijhoff 2008) 25.

257 *Prosecutor v Sikirica*, Case No IT-95–8-T, Judgment on Defence Motions to Acquit (3 September 2001), para. 59.

Concerning the proof of *dolus specialis*, the ICTR *Akayesu* Trial Chamber held intent to be:

> a mental factor which is difficult, even impossible, to determine. . . . [I]t is possible to deduce the genocidal intent . . . from the general context of the perpetration . . . . Other factors, such as the scale of atrocities committed, . . . the fact of deliberately and systematically targeting victims on account of their membership of a particular group, while excluding the members of other groups, can enable the Chamber to infer the genocidal intent of a particular act.[258]

So in addition to the actual behaviour of the accused, contextual elements are relevant in proving genocidal intent.[259] The use of such circumstantial evidence is, however, not uncontested.[260] For reasons of due process, any circumstantial evidence has to be connected to the perpetrator's intent to destroy a particular victim group. This study does not consider sufficient the mere presence of a perpetrator at or participation in a mass killing, even if committed against a clearly defined or selected group. Rather, before a criminal tribunal, the proof of the perpetrator's specific intent to kill the individual victims for reason of their group membership with the intention to destroy the group, for being the group it is, has to be proven beyond reasonable doubt. Courts should revert to contextual elements to prove the perpetrator's genocidal intent, but they cannot be taken to replace an individual examination of a perpetrator's intent to destroy a specific group. Unless this mental element can be proven, the respective court ought to rather prosecute the perpetrator for the crime against humanity of extermination or murder. In the *Application of the Convention on the Prevention and Punishment of the Crime of Genocide*, the ICJ held that great care must be taken in evaluating the facts that demonstrate the necessary intent.[261] The *dolus specialis* had 'to be convincingly shown by reference to particular circumstances, unless a general plan to that end can be convincingly demonstrated

258 *Prosecutor v Akayesu*, Case No ICTR-96–4-T (2 September 1998), para. 523. Confirmed in: *Prosecutor v Rukundo,* Case No ICTR-2001–70-T (27 February 2009), para. 557; *Prosecutor v Musema*, Case No ICTR-96–13-A, Trial Judgment (27 January 2000), para. 166; *Prosecutor v Rutaganda*, Case No ICTR-96–3-T (6 December 1999), para. 63.

259 *Prosecutor v Jelisić*, Case No IT-95–10-A (5 July 2001), paras. 46–47. Similarly: *Prosecutor v Ntagerura, Bagambiki, Imanishimwe* (*Cyangugu* case), Case No ICTR-99–46-T (25 February 2004), para. 663; Stahn (n 93) 41; Koursami (n 5) 178–182; Stefan Kirsch, 'The Two Notions of Genocide: Distinguishing Macro Phenomena and Individual Misconduct', 42 *Creighton Law Review* (2008–2009) 357.

260 For an in-depth discussion: Koursami (n 5).

261 *Application of the Convention on the Prevention and Punishment of the Crime of Genocide (Bosnia and Herzegovina v Serbia and Montenegro)*, ICJ Judgment (2007), para. 189. The ICJ was equally reluctant in *Application of the Convention on the Prevention and Punishment of the Crime of Genocide* (*Croatia v Serbia*), ICJ Judgment (2015), para. 438. See criticism in Behrens (n 199) 931–932.

to exist'.[262] With this statement, the ICJ approved of a two-step approach, whereby either the perpetrator's individual intent to destroy a protected group has to be proven, or, alternatively, that his act was committed with the intention of participating in a genocidal plan.[263]

In adjudicating acts committed in the past, criminal law is, per definition, applied retrospectively. The judicial system responds to earlier conflicts or criminal acts or omissions and constructs the required elements from the collected evidence. Judges therefore need to take an *ex post facto* perspective on the facts of the case. While this applies equally to all international crimes, the intent to commit genocide is so hard to prove that it becomes unmistakable only once a group is virtually annihilated. At this point, any prevention or intervention *ex ante* is probably pointless, given that the destruction is already too advanced. It is too late for the victims of the genocide; not, however, for the prosecution.[264] The prosecution needs to establish the perpetrator's genocidal intent based on evidence that can identify the victim group as it appears in the eyes of the perpetrator.[265] The perpetrator's pre-genocidal oral or written statements or other acts that reveal his perception of the victims can therefore be of evidentiary value. Although rarely discussed in academic literature, also archival documents can become important in constructing the *dolus specialis.* Already *Akayesu*, the first-ever verdict on the crime of genocide, recognised that the selection of victims can assist in the assessment of the genocidal intent.[266] Typically, the victims – in our case, members of the racial group – become discernible by means of othering. Originating in the discrimination and stigmatisation of the 'others' who are considered different, inferior, and a threat to the in-group, an imaginary victim group in itself is not protected by the law of genocide. The law limits its protection to four enumerated human groups: the national, ethnic, racial, and religious group. Increasingly, criminal courts and academics have become aware that 'the alleged stability and integrity of these groups is very much open to question – not least because group identity is often imposed (even imagined) by perpetrators'.[267] Hence, the process of othering has to be fuelled by what the perpetrator perceives to be racial, ethnical, national, or religious characteristics of the victim group. A number of judgments describe othering, namely the setting apart of the out-group, which could be indicative

262 *Application of the Convention on the Prevention and Punishment of the Crime of Genocide (Bosnia and Herzegovina v Serbia and Montenegro)*, ICJ Judgment (2007), para. 373.

263 See discussion in Schabas (n 4) 157–163; Jones, Powles (n 3) 156.

264 Roth (n 254) 26.

265 Nigel Eltringham, 'Illuminating the Broader Context': Anthropological and Historical Knowledge at the International Criminal Tribunal for Rwanda, 19 *Journal of the Royal Anthropological Institute* (2013) 342; Nersessian (n 185) 31.

266 *Prosecutor v Akayesu*, Case No ICTR-96-4-T (2 September 1998), para. 523; Behrens (n 73) 136.

267 Adam Jones, *Genocide: A Comprehensive Introduction* (Routledge 2nd ed 2011) 34. See also Shaw (n 2) 150.

of the genocidal intent. In the *Cyangugu* case, on the eve of the atrocities in Rwanda in April 1994, soldiers came to a football field and 'determine[d] whether the refugees entirely were Tutsi'.[268] In *Semanza*, the accused 'instructed soldiers to separate Hutu from Tutsi, who were then killed by gunfire and grenades'.[269] Similarly, in *Muhimana*, '[b]efore the attacks on Mubuga Church commenced, Hutu refugees, who were intermingled with the Tutsi, were instructed to come out of the church'.[270]

The prosecution, and to a lesser degree, the judges of the ECCC equally recognised the importance of othering in determining the genocidal intent: 'the deliberate and systematic identifying, targeting, gathering and killing of people due to their membership of the Vietnamese group . . . often identified through the use of pre-prepared statistical lists'.[271] The indiscriminate mass killings of women, children, young and old alike, particularly if targeted in places of refuge, can be a strong indication of the process of othering, with the ultimate goal of destroying members of a protected group.[272]

Othering is continuous and happens through complex processes of communication and interaction between the members of the in-group in a public arena by means of 'talk, tales, stories, gossip, anecdotes, messages, pronouncements, news accounts, orations, sermons, preachments and the like'.[273] Courts have increasingly come to recognise the importance of such communication for the proof of genocidal intent. Several judgments by both *ad hoc* tribunals concluded that, although challenging for the prosecution, genocidal intent can be

268 *Prosecutor v Ntagerura, Bagambiki, Imanishimwe* (*Cyangugu* case), Case No ICTR-99–46-T (25 February 2004), para. 654.

269 *Prosecutor v Semanza*, Case No ICTR-97–20-T (15 May 2003), para. 429.

270 *Prosecutor v Muhimana*, Case No ICTR-95–1B-T (28 April 2005), para. 515, emphasis omitted.

271 *Prosecutor v Nuon Chea, Ieng Sary, Khieu Samphan, Ieng Thirith*, Case No 002/19–09–2007-ECCC-OCIJ, Closing Order (Indictment), (15 September 2010), para. 1344. Partially confirmed in *Prosecutor v Nuon Chea and Khieu Samphân*, Case No 002/19–09–2007/ECCC/TC (16 November 2018), paras. 3421, 3500, 3503, 3508, 3513, etc.

272 Similar arguments were made in the *Einsatzgruppen* trial. The prosecution held that 'there was absolutely no rational basis for killing children except genocide and the killing of races' (*United States of America v Otto Ohlendorf* et al. (*Einsatzgruppen* Case), Opinion and Judgment (October 1946–April 1949), p. 356). See also *The Attorney-General of Israel v Eichmann*, Case No 40/61, Judgment (11 December 1961), para. 182. See discussion in Stahn (n 93) 41; Kielsgard (n 20) 127; Mélanie Vianney-Liaud, 'Legal Constraints in the Interpretation of Genocide', in Simon Meisenberg, Ignaz Stegmiller (eds), *The Extraordinary Chambers in the Courts of Cambodia: Assessing Their Contribution to International Criminal Law* (TMC Asser 2016) 281; Schabas (n 4) 164; Jones, Powles (n 3) 156. Furthermore: *Prosecutor v Krstić*, Case No IT-98–33-T (2 August 2001), para. 595; *Prosecutor v Krstić*, Case No IT-98–33-A (19 April 2004), para. 37; *Prosecutor v Serushago*, Case No ICTR-98–03-S (5 February 1999), para. 25(i); *Prosecutor v Kayishema and Ruzindana*, Case No ICTR-95-1-T (21 May 1999), para. 532.

273 Blumer (n 17) 5. See also Powell, Menendian (n 16) 24.

determined by reference to the othering expressed by the perpetrator in derogatory language rather than physical acts.[274] The *Ntakirutimana* case illustrates what is probably the exception rather than the rule in terms of available evidence: the case discloses that the attackers chased Tutsi refugees while singing: 'Exterminate them; look for them everywhere; kill them; and get it over with, in all the forests'.[275] In *Karadžić and Mladić*, the ICTY Trial Chamber held that the genocidal special intent

> derives from the combined effect of speeches or projects laying the groundwork for and justifying the acts, from the massive scale of their destructive effect and from their specific nature, which aims at undermining what is considered to be the foundation of the group.[276]

The judges acknowledged here the evidentiary importance of the perpetrator's behaviour, which found expression in, among other things, his speeches. Although the Trial Chamber referred to Karadžić's statements and speeches containing rhetorical warnings of annihilation, it ultimately concluded that there was no evidence from which to infer genocidal intent.[277] The Appeals Chamber, in obvious recognition of the evidentiary value of utterances, overturned this decision and found the Trial Chamber should have taken into consideration Karadžić's oral declarations in deciding his intent.[278] The trial judgment against Karadžić reiterated the significance of 'highly inflammatory speeches and statements' as evidence of genocidal intent. However, the Chamber considered these speeches as having the effect of identifying the historic enemies of the Bosnian Serbs and furthering the objective of ethnic separation; they did not demonstrate intent to destroy the Bosnian Muslim and/or

274 *Prosecutor v Krajišnik*, Case No IT-00–39-T (27 September 2006), para. 869; *Prosecutor v Mpambara*, Case No ICTR-01–65-T (11 September 2006), para. 8; *Prosecutor v Kamuhanda*, Case No ICTR-99–54A-T (22 January 2004), para. 625; *Prosecutor v Gacumbitsi*, Case No 01–64-T (17 June 2004), paras. 252–253; *Prosecutor v Ndindabahizi*, Case No ICTR-2001–71-I, Trial Judgment (15 July 2004), para. 454; *Prosecutor v Kajelijeli*, Case No ICTR-98–44A-T (1 December 2003), para. 806; *Prosecutor v Bagilishema*, Case No ICTR-95–1A-T (7 June 2001), para. 63; *Prosecutor v Musema*, Case No ICTR-96–13-A, Trial Judgment (27 January 2000), paras. 932–933; *Prosecutor v Kayishema and Ruzindana*, Case No ICTR-95–1-T (21 May 1999), para. 93.

275 *Prosecutor v Ntakirutimana and Ntakirutimana*, Case Nos ICTR-96–10-T and ICTR-96–17-T (21 February 2003), para. 828. Also discussed in Behrens (n 73) 128.

276 *Prosecutor v Karadžić and Mladić*, Cases Nos IT-95–5-R61 and IT-95–18-R61, Review of the Indictments Pursuant to Rule 61 of the Rules of Procedure and Evidence (11 July 1996), para. 95.

277 *Prosecutor v Karadžić*, Case No 95–5/18-T, Rule 98bis Judgment (28 June 2012), Transcript p. 28769, lines 8–11, 16–21.

278 *Prosecutor v Karadžić*, Case No IT-95–5/18-AR98bis.l, Appeals Judgment (11 July 2013), paras. 97–101. Discussed in Jarvis, Tieger (n 232) 869; Cupido (n 142) 395.

Bosnian Croats.[279] This conclusion was reached notwithstanding that evidence was introduced with statements of the accused using words such as 'annihilation', 'vanish[ing]', 'elimination', and 'extinction' of Bosnian Muslims.[280] The Trial Chamber even admitted into evidence the diary of co-perpetrator Mladić in assessing Karadžić's genocidal intent.[281]

The ECCC also stressed the importance of speeches, statements, and written evidence for establishing the *dolus specialis* of genocide, albeit mindful of the fact that numerous publications contained propaganda. The judges also considered evidence such as meeting minutes, notebooks, policy documents and telegrams, and Ieng Sary's diary.[282] The Khmer Rouge published a call to kill all Vietnamese civilians in Cambodia in the *Revolutionary Flag* magazine, and the 'policy to destroy the Vietnamese group was taught to cadres, as reflected in cadre notebooks and witness evidence'.[283] An infamous slogan of the Khmer Rouge cadre, which illustrates the dehumanisation of their victims, was: 'To keep you is no gain, to lose you is no loss'.[284]

It is, however, important to distinguish between contextual evidence and the behaviour of the perpetrator.[285] In this regard, *Bagilishema* recognised that 'the use of context to determine the intent of an accused must be counterbalanced with the actual conduct of the accused' and held that the intent had to be established above all by relying on the accused's own behaviour.[286] This study therefore suggests that when attempting to prove intent to destroy a certain group, the prosecution should begin by examining the perpetrator's behaviour, also beyond the actual *actus reus*, especially with regard to labelling a group as an enemy or a threat, and othering expressed in pamphlets or public statements. Contextual factors like the number of victims, level of planning, or systematic

279 *Prosecutor v Karadžić*, Case No IT-95–5–18-T (25 March 2016), paras. 2598–2599. The appeals judgment of the International Residual Mechanism for Criminal Tribunals discusses the significance of his inflammatory speeches in the context of various crimes and modes of liabilities. See for instance *Prosecutor v Karadžić*, Case No MICT-13-55-A (20 March 2019), paras. 679 or 742. It did not overturn the conviction of genocide (committed as part of a joint criminal enterprise in Srebrenica), but did increase the sentence from forty years to lifetime.

280 Ibid para. 2599.

281 Ibid para. 2604.

282 *Prosecutor v Nuon Chea and Khieu Samphân*, Case No 002/19–09–2007/ECCC/TC, Judgment (16 November 2018), paras. 3745–3747.

283 *Prosecutor v Nuon Chea, Ieng Sary, Khieu Samphan, Ieng Thirith*, Case No 002/19–09–2007-ECCC-OCIJ, Closing Order (Indictment) (15 September 2010), para. 1346.

284 Also quoted as 'keeping you is no gain, taking you away, no loss' (Sixth Investigative Request of Co-Lawyers for Civil Parties Concerning the Charge of Genocide Against the Khmer Nationals, Case No 002/19–09–2007-ECCC/OCIJ (4 February 2010), para. 23). Similarly Rafter (n 40) 125; Stanton (n 2).

285 Cupido (n 142) 388, 391, 397.

286 *Prosecutor v Bagilishema*, Case No ICTR-95–1A-T (7 June 2001), para. 63.

and destructive patterns of behaviour toward a particular group further assist in establishing the genocidal intent.[287]

In the choice between genocide and crimes against humanity, prosecutors have often chosen the latter over the former, precisely because of the evidentiary restraints associated with proving genocidal intent.[288] In holding that 'a perpetrator's statements must be understood in their proper context', the ICTY Appeals Chamber in *Stakić* refused to accept evidence of derogatory statements as proof of genocidal intent.[289] Also in *Brđanin*, the Trial Chamber agreed that some of the accused's 'utterances are openly nasty, hateful, intolerable, repulsive and disgraceful', but while they strongly suggested discriminatory intent, the judges could not conclude that he had an intent to destroy the Bosnian Muslims and Bosnian Croats.[290] By contrast, the ICTR Trial Chamber convicted Kayishema for genocide partly based on evidence of incriminating utterances such as 'Tutsi dogs', 'Tutsi sons of bitches' and commanding people to 'get to work', ie to begin to kill Tutsi.[291]

The ICTY Trial Chamber moreover dismissed genocide charges against Jelisić who had called himself 'the Serb Adolf' and sworn to rid the world of Muslims.[292] The accused was acquitted for genocide despite keeping a tally of the Muslims he had killed and wanting to sterilise Muslim women in order to prevent an increase of the Muslim population. He even declared that he had to execute twenty to thirty persons before he could drink his coffee each morning.[293] Commentators have criticised the ICTY for not charging Jelisić with genocide because there could hardly be clearer evidence of his intent to destroy the Bosnian Muslims, notwithstanding the fact that he could realistically not have achieved his goals single-handedly.[294] Although the Appeals Chamber concluded that the Trial Chamber had erred in dismissing the genocide charge, it did not overrule the trial judgment, because it considered Jelisić sufficiently punished for the other counts.[295]

The *dolus specialis* and the definition of the protected (racial) group remain the focus of the following part, which discusses the first genocide trial judgment in history. After examining the *Akayesu* case, the core of this chapter is reached: the analysis of the jurisprudence of the international criminal tribunals to define

287 Drumbl (n 195) 52; Ratner, Abrams, Bischoff (n 142) 38; Behrens (n 73) 127, 136; Aptel (n 185) 288. See also Report of the Group of Experts for Cambodia established pursuant to General Assembly resolution 52/135 (15 March 1999), para. 64.

288 Wald (n 6) 626.

289 *Prosecutor v Stakić*, Case No IT-97–24-A (22 March 2006), para. 52.

290 *Prosecutor v Brđanin*, Case No IT-99–36-T (1 September 2004), paras. 986–987.

291 *Prosecutor v Kayishema and Ruzindana*, Case No ICTR-95–1-T (21 May 1999), paras. 538–539. Also discussed in Temoney (n 31) 11; Cupido (n 142) 390.

292 *Prosecutor v Jelisić*, Case No IT-95–10-T (19 December 1999), para. 102.

293 Ibid paras. 102–103. See similar discussion in Jarvis, Tieger (n 232) 867.

294 Jarvis, Tieger (n 232) 867; Cassese (2010) 138; Behrens (n 73) 138; Stahn (n 93) 38–39.

295 *Prosecutor v Jelisić*, Case No IT-95–10-A (5 July 2001), paras. 68, 74–77.

the group membership of the victims of genocide. The chapter ends by suggesting a perpetrator-based subjective approach that reflects the process of othering and which in turn is mirrored in the *dolus specialis*, the intent to destroy, in whole or in part, a racial group, as such.

3.6 *Akayesu* and the interpretative revolution

3.6.1 *Introduction*

Akayesu was the first individual to stand trial for genocide before an international tribunal.[296] The *Akayesu* judgment set a number of important legal precedents and marked the start of a jurisprudential revolution in the application and interpretation of genocide.[297] Even today, nearly two decades later, the judgment remains a yardstick for the definition of genocide. As this was the first genocide trial, the ICTR Trial Chamber had to discuss all the legal elements of the crime. The Chamber reasoned that since the special intent to commit genocide lay in the intent to destroy, in whole or in part, a national, ethnical, racial, or religious group, it was necessary to objectively determine the meaning of these social categories.[298] *Akayesu* provided a dual conceptualisation: it defined each of the protected groups and formulated overarching, common criteria that applied to all four groups, ie permanence and stability.[299] Since determined by birth, membership of the groups was considered continuous and often irremediable.[300]

3.6.2 *Rwanda and the creation of the ICTR*

On 6 April 1994, a plane carrying President Juvénal Habyarimana of Rwanda and President Cyprien Ntaryamira of Burundi was shot down by a surface-to-air missile as it approached Kigali airport. All passengers were killed. The deaths of these two presidents triggered widespread violence, initially in Kigali but rapidly spreading to other parts of Rwanda.[301] In the aftermath of the events

296 *Prosecutor v Akayesu*, Case No ICTR-96-4-T (2 September 1998).

297 See Boas, Bischoff, Reid (n 180) 143. Similarly: Jallow (n 200) 449; Lennart Aspegren, Jamie Williamson, 'The Rwanda Tribunal and Genocide', in Emmanuel Decaux, Adama Dieng, Malick Sow (eds), *From Human Rights to International Criminal Law: Studies in Honour of an African Jurist, the Late Judge Laïty Kama* (Martinus Nijhoff 2007) 221.

298 *Prosecutor v Akayesu*, Case No ICTR-96-4-T (2 September 1998), para. 510.

299 Ibid. It remains unclear whether the ICTR considered the Tutsi an ethnic, stable, and permanent group – or as a group protected by reason of its stability and permanency, regardless of its qualification under Art. 2 [Martin (n 109) 118–119]. See discussion in Chapter 3.6.3.

300 *Prosecutor v Akayesu*, Case No ICTR-96-4-T (2 September 1998), para. 511.

301 Barbora Holá, Alette Smeulers, 'Rwanda and the ICTR: Facts and Figures', in Ann-Marie de Brouwer, Alette Smeulers (eds), *The Elgar Companion to the International Criminal Tribunal for Rwanda* (Edward Elgar 2016) 45; Smeulers, Hoex (n 59) 435; Taulbee (n 184) 62; Prunier (n 91) 211–212.

in Rwanda in 1994, during which more than 800,000 civilians, or ten percent of the total Rwandan population and approximately 75 to 85 percent of the Tutsi population, were killed,[302] the UN Security Council adopted Resolution 935. It requested the Secretary-General to establish an impartial Commission of Experts with the mandate to determine whether serious breaches of humanitarian law, including genocide, had been committed in Rwanda.[303] The Commission submitted a preliminary report, stipulating that

> [o]verwhelming evidence indicates that the extermination of Tutsi by Hutu had been planned months in advance of its actual execution. The mass exterminations of Tutsi were . . . motivated out of ethnic hatred. These mass exterminations were clearly 'committed with intent to destroy, in whole or in part, a national, ethnic, racial, or religious group, as such' within the meaning of [Art. 2 Genocide Convention].[304]

While the Commission suggested placing the Rwandan cases under the competence of the already established ICTY in order to provide for consistency in the legal interpretation and application of international law,[305] the Security Council, acting under Chapter VII of the UN Charter, decided to establish yet another *ad hoc* criminal tribunal as a measure to restore international peace and security.[306] The state of Rwanda was at the time a member of the Security Council and pressed for the creation of the tribunal.[307] Eventually, however, Rwanda voted against the enabling resolution to establish the tribunal because it considered it inadequate.[308] The *International Criminal Tribunal for the Prosecution of Persons Responsible for Genocide and Other Serious Violations of International Humanitarian Law Committed in the Territory of Rwanda and Rwandan Citizens Responsible for Genocide and Other Such Violations Committed*

302 Degni-Ségui (n 55) 4, estimates that up to 1 million people were killed. See also Holá, Smeulers (2016) 46; Wilson (n 9) 35; Aspegren, Williamson (n 297) 203. Eltringham (n 265) 340 refers to 937,000 deaths.

303 UN Doc. S/RES/935 (1 July 1994).

304 Letter Dated 1 October 1994 from the Secretary-General to the President of the Security Council, UN Doc. S/1994/1125, Annex: Preliminary Report of the Independent Commission of Experts Established in Accordance with Security Council Resolution 935 (1994), para. 44. See also Degni-Ségui (n 55) 4–5.

305 Preliminary Report (n 304), para. 139.

306 UN Doc. S/RES/955 (1994).

307 Taulbee (n 184) 63; Eltringham (n 265) 340.

308 The negativity stemmed from different factors: the inability of the ICTR to prosecute the thousands of suspects detained in Rwandan prisons, the limitation of the temporal jurisdiction to events in 1994, the location of the tribunal in Tanzania instead of in Rwanda, the shared Appeals Chamber with the ICTY, and the prohibition of capital punishment. See Taulbee (n 184) 63; Larissa van den Herik, *The Contribution of the Rwanda Tribunal to the Development of International Law* (Martinus Nijhoff Publishers 2005) 43.

in the Territory of Neighboring States Between 1 January and 31 December 1994 (ICTR) was confronted with two groups whose ID cards labelled them as distinct ethnicities. This classification originated in German and Belgian colonialism: the Germans, later succeeded by the Belgians, perceived the Tutsi to be more like them in height and colour and designated them as the indigenous elite.[309] 'Certain physical traits have commonly been attributed to the Tutsi population that are taken to distinguish them from Hutu', the Final Report of the Commission of Experts reads. 'Tutsi are described as being taller than Hutu, with more aquiline noses, thinner ankles, longer fingers and longer gums'.[310] A Belgian law of 1931 created a wealth-based system of division according to which everyone who owned more than ten cows was a Tutsi.[311] ID cards were introduced in 1933 and indicated an individual's ethnicity, depending on a classification of names by census.[312] Their introduction consolidated the affiliation to the Tutsi, Hutu, or Twa group and simultaneously entrenched the notion of Tutsi superiority.[313] During the killings that began on 7 April 1994, census lists were used and anyone with 'Tutsi' marked on his ID card was immediately killed.[314]

309 *Prosecutor v Akayesu*, Case No ICTR-96–4-T (2 September 1998), para. 82. Furthermore: Wielenga (n 91) 2; Aspegren, Williamson (n 297) 216; Eltringham (n 90) 432 with several examples; Akhavan (n 185) 1000; Beth van Schaack, 'Darfur and the Rhetoric of Genocide', 26 *Whittier Law Review* (2005) 1120; Amann (n 128) 103; Stephen Cornell, Douglas Hartmann, *Ethnicity and Race: Making Identities in a Changing World* (Pine Forge Press 1998) 40.

310 Preliminary Report (n 304), para. 46. Importantly, the report refers to what was commonly *attributed* to the Tutsi, thus not claiming any objective facts.

311 Shivon Byamukama, John Kapranos Huntley, 'Criminal Justice in the Aftermath of the 1994 Rwanda Genocide', in Ralph Henham, Paul Behrens (eds), *The Criminal Law of Genocide* (Ashgate 2007) 234; Paul Magnarella, 'Recent Developments in the International Law of Genocide', in Alexander Laban Hinton (ed), *Annihilating Difference: The Anthropology of Genocide* (University of California Press 2002) 317 and 321. According to Alex de Waal, 'Genocide in Rwanda, 10 *Anthropology Today* (1994) 2, the law was introduced in 1926.

312 Helen Hintjens, 'When Identity Becomes a Knife: Reflecting on the Genocide in Rwanda',1 *Ethnicities* (2001) 29.

313 Wielenga (n 91) 3; Smeulers, Hoex (n 59) 438; Kiernan (n 138) 555; Nigel Eltringham, *Accounting for Horror: Post-Genocide Debates in Rwanda* (Pluto Press 2004) 18; Lüders (n 156) 87; Verdirame (n 160) 589; Schabas 2000 (n 135) 379; Diane Amann, 'Prosecutor v Akayesu', 93 *AJIL* (1999) 195; John Bowen, 'The Myth of Global Ethnic Conflict', in Alexander Laban Hinton (ed), *Genocide: An Anthropological Reader* (Blackwell Publishers 2002) 336–337; Philip Gourevitch, *We Wish To Inform You that Tomorrow We Will Be Killed With Our Families: Stories From Rwanda* (Picador 1998) 57. Straus (n 41) 19 estimates the proportions in the population as 84–90% Hutu, 9–15% Tutsi, 1% Twa.

314 *Prosecutor v Nchamihigo,* Case No ICTR-01–63-T (12 November 2008), para. 341; *Prosecutor v Rukundo,* Case No ICTR-2001–70-T (27 February 2009), para. 567; *Prosecutor v Bagosora* et al., Case No ICTR-98–41, Amended Indictment (12 August 1999), para. 6.31; Preliminary Report (n 304), para. 47. Kapranos Huntley Byamukama (n 311) 234; Aspegren, Williamson (n 297) 204; Prunier (n 91) 222, 249.

The Hutu/Tutsi dichotomy was a colonially implanted racialist myth that gradually became a socially constructed reality and ultimately defined the population fated for extermination.[315] In pre-colonial times, the line separating the Hutu from the Tutsi was permeable because their distinction was class-based.[316] The Tutsi and Hutu spoke the same language, had the same nationality and often the same religion. Essentially they had the same culture as well, thus preventing clear distinctions based on ethnicity that use – among other things – language, religion, and culture as distinctive criteria.[317] By 1994, the groups perceived each other as separate, hostile ethnical groups.[318] As the genocidal Hutu power ideology took hold, the abyss between Hutu and Tutsi grew larger, leading to a collapse of the middle ground and forcing anyone to stand on one side or the other.[319]

The ICTR's jurisprudence has been analysed as reflecting a 'prevalent angst at characterising the extermination of almost a million Tutsi as something other than the "crime of crimes"',[320] which could only be achieved by concluding that the Tutsi were one of four exclusive protected groups. The following section shows how *Akayesu* ended up assigning protection to the Tutsi victims as a stable and permanent group.

3.6.3 Stability and permanence

The *travaux préparatoires* to the Genocide Convention reveal that membership of a racial, religious, or national group was seen as a permanent and inevitable feature, the destruction of which 'appeared most heinous in the light of the conscience of humanity, since it was directed against human beings whom chance

315 *Prosecutor v Kayishema and Ruzindana*, Case No ICTR-95–1-T (21 May 1999), paras. 34–35. Furthermore: Wielenga (n 91) 2; Byamukama, Kapranos Huntley (n 311) 233; George William Mugwanya, *The Crime of Genocide in International Law: Appraising the Contribution of the UN Tribunal for Rwanda* (Cameron May 2007) 33–34; Akhavan (n 185) 1000; Gourevitch (n 313) 165; Prunier (n 91) 9, 38, 46, 249; 347; Hardin (n 38) 169. A wealthy Hutu could become a Tutsi through a process of *Kwihutura* (cleansing oneself of Hutuness) as much as a Tutsi could become a Hutu if he lost his cattle (Byamukama, Kapranos Huntley (n 311) 234; Prunier (n 91) 13–14). Nersessian talks about the *Ubuhake* ritual contract whereby cattle was transferred, giving a Hutu a new social position and ownership rights as a Tutsi [Nersessian (n 185) 53].

316 *Prosecutor v Kayishema and Ruzindana*, Case No ICTR-95-1-T (21 May 1999), para. 34. Confirmed by Mugwanya (n 315) 34, emphasising that the distinction was based on lineage or kinship rather than ethnicity; Amann (n 128) 103; Gourevitch (n 313) 47.

317 *Prosecutor v Akayesu*, Case No 96–4-T (2 September 1998), para. 170. Furthermore: Ratner, Abrams, Bischoff (n 142) 35; Caroline Fournet, *The Crime of Destruction and the Law of Genocide: Their Impact on Collective Memory* (Ashgate 2007) 47; Magnarella (n 311) 313, 317; Hintjens (n 312) 43; Banton (n 53) 210. See more in Chapter 3.6.5.

318 Bowen (n 313) 337; Amann (n 314) 195–196; Alex de Waal, 'Group Identity, Rationality, and the State', 11 *Critical Review* (1997) 287; Prunier (n 91) 347.

319 Moshman (n 43) 119; Smeulers, Hoex (n 59) 439; Zartman, Anstey (n 26) 9.

320 Akhavan (n 185) 103.

alone had grouped together'.[321] Since the group members were products of circumstances beyond their control, it was odious to destroy them when they had no choice but to belong to the group.[322] The drafters acknowledged that people could change their nationality or religion, but it was assumed that those born into religious groups could not easily abandon or alter their faith.[323] In his *Study on the Crime of Genocide* (1978), the UN Special Rapporteur Nicodème Ruhashyankiko observed that genocide should be regarded as a crime committed against a group of individuals permanently possessing certain common features.[324] Often, but not always, the protected groups are of a permanent and stable nature.[325] These characteristics are contested, because voluntary groups can also be stable and permanent, while, for example, religious and national groups often have flexible membership criteria that enable entry to and exit from the group.[326]

In most cases of group confrontation between 'us' and 'them', the ascriptive (and for the case of genocide: pejorative) status is, according to Kurt Glaser and Stefan Possony's analysis, allocated at the birth of a child, hence setting in motion his socialisation and group membership. If such characteristics are present and observable at this early stage in life, they cannot wilfully be changed.[327] Seen from this perspective, one could indeed argue that group membership is indelible.[328] Nonetheless, for the crime of genocide such victim categorisation can, but does not have to, occur at the birth of an individual. Rather, the perpetrator often ascribes to a victim a group membership irrespective of any birth-determined cohesion. As such, he creates the group from members not previously connected, while leaving out others with identical (observable) characteristics.

Akayesu (mis)used the criteria of permanence and stability in order to expand the protection of the Genocide Convention.[329] The Tribunal considered the

321 UN Doc. A/C.6/SR.74 (1948), p. 99.

322 Szpak (n 162) 159; Ntanda Nsereko (n 209) 130.

323 UN Doc. A/C.6/SR.74 (1948), p. 99; Werle, Jessberger (n 142) 295; Gunn (n 40) 201; Ntanda Nsereko (n 209) 130; Schabas 2000 (n 135) 378.

324 Ruhashyankiko (n 161), para. 56.

325 Werle, Jessberger (n 142) 295; Lyal Sunga, *The Emerging System of International Criminal Law: Developments in Codification and Implementation* (Kluwer Law International 1997) 112.

326 Nersessian (n 185) 53; Sonali Shah, 'The Oversight of the Last Great International Institutions of the Twentieth Century: The International Criminal Court's Definition of Genocide', 16 *Emory International Law Review* (2002) 384.

327 Glaser, Possony (n 20) 89.

328 Mayroz (n 5) 76; Paul Boghossian, 'The Concept of Genocide', 12 *Journal of Genocide Research* (2010) 74.

329 Matthias Schuster, 'The Crime of Genocide Applied in Practice: Selected Aspects of the Jurisprudence of the *ad hoc* Tribunals' Appeals Chambers', in Christoph Safferling, Eckart Conze (eds), *The Genocide Convention Sixty Years After Its Adoption* (TMC Asser Press 2010) 216–217; Schabas (n 170) 98; Eltringham (n 313) 29; Jones, Powles (n 3) 167.

enumeration of the four protected groups in the Genocide Convention as too restrictive and held that any similarly stable and permanent group should be embraced by the Convention:

> the Chamber considered whether the protected groups should be limited to only the four groups specifically mentioned or whether any group, similar to the four groups in terms of its stability and permanence, should also be included. The Chamber found that it was necessary . . . to respect the intent of the drafters of the Genocide Convention which . . . was clearly to protect any stable and permanent group.[330]

Commentators have pointed out that if any permanent and stable group were to be included within the definition of genocide, then unisexual/gender groups, homosexuals, or persons permanently mentally or physically impaired at birth might constitute protected groups too.[331] This was clearly not the intention of the Genocide Convention's drafters.[332] *Akayesu* created a 'stable and permanent'-threshold in an attempt to assign the group objective contours.[333] The judgment has been heavily criticised for breaching the principle of *nullum crimen sine lege*.[334] In adopting the permanent and stable approach, the ICTR clearly stretched the boundaries of legal interpretation into the controversial area of judicial lawmaking.[335] Had the drafters wanted a reference to stable groups, wording to that effect could have been included in the Convention.[336]

Only very few judgments have followed the *Akayesu* approach, thereby limiting the effect of the residual category of non-enumerated 'stable and permanent'

330 *Prosecutor v Akayesu*, Case No ICTR-96–4-T (2 September 1998), para. 701.

331 Katy Grady, 'The Genocide Convention's Protected Groups: A Place for Gender?', in Chile Eboe-Osuji (ed), *Protecting Humanity: Essays in International Law and Policy in Honour of Navanethem Pillay* (Martinus Nijhoff 2010) 165–184; Demko (n 35) 241; Magnarella (n 311) 318; van der Vyver (n 109) 306.

332 Martin (n 109) 115; Akhavan (n 185) 1001; Quayle (n 110) 367; Jørgensen (n 189) 288.

333 Gaetano Pentassuglia, *Minority Groups and Judicial Discourse in International Law: A Comparative Perspective* (Martinus Nijhoff 2009) 30; Eltringham (n 313) 29; Lüders (n 156) 53; William Schabas, 'Commentary on *Prosecutor v Akayesu*', in André Klip, Göran Sluiter (eds), *Annotated Leading Cases of International Criminal Tribunals: The International Criminal Tribunal for Rwanda 1994–1999* (Intersentia 1999) 543.

334 Akhavan 2016 (n 173) 98; Jallow (n 200) 451; Fournet (n 188) 106; Werle, Jessberger (n 142) 297; Schuster (n 329) 217; Akhavan (n 185) 1001; Lüders (n 156) 284; Boot (n 232) 431; Schabas 2001 (n 135) 451–452.

335 William Schabas, 'Genocide', in Otto Triffterer, Kai Ambos (eds), *The Rome Statute of the International Criminal Court: A Commentary* (CH Beck 3rd ed 2016) 135; Schabas (n 151) 70–72; Schabas (n 4) 136; Guénaël Mettraux, *International Crimes and the* ad hoc *Tribunals* (OUP 2005) 230; Jones, Powles (n 3) 168; Jørgensen (n 189) 288.

336 Markus Wagner, 'The ICC and its Jurisdiction: Myths, Misperceptions and Realities', in Armin von Bogdandy, Rüdiger Wolfrum (eds), 7 *Max Planck Yearbook of United Nations Law* (Martinus Nijhoff 2003) 423; Schabas 2001 (n 135) 451.

groups. The international case law on the point in question appears to be settled.[337] The Darfur Commission's Report was one of the few that held *Akayesu*'s interpretative expansion to be in line with the object and scope of the provision on genocide.[338] Chapter 3.10 will discuss how innovative and ground-breaking the Darfur report was in many aspects, yet remarkably outdated in referring to the permanent and stable approach. The Commission's allegation that states had not challenged the approach, which therefore had become part of customary law,[339] is unquestionably wrong, considering that hardly any judgments followed the approach to begin with.[340]

The preparatory work shows the intention of the drafters to limit the protection of the Genocide Convention to stable groups objectively defined and to which individuals belong regardless of their own desires. The criteria of stability and permanence were considered, but never used in an expansive manner. Rather, they served as a justification for the inclusion of particular types of groups.[341] It can therefore be concluded that not every group with a certain degree of stability is considered a protected group. Such reading would lead to an expansion of the protection unintended by the drafters.[342]

3.6.4 *The racial group*

'The conventional definition of racial group', *Akayesu* held, 'is based on the hereditary physical traits often identified with a geographical region, irrespective of linguistic, cultural, national or religious factors'.[343] The ICTR Trial Chamber did not provide any supporting evidence, legal or extra-legal, to substantiate

337 *Prosecutor v Rutaganda*, Case No ICTR-96-3-T (6 December 1999), paras. 56–57; *Prosecutor v Muhimana*, Case No ICTR-95-1B-T (28 April 2005), para. 510. Furthermore Kress (n 235) 683; Alexander Zahar, Göran Sluiter, *International Criminal Law: A Critical Introduction* (OUP 2008) 161; Lisson (n 195) 1465; William Schabas, 'Interpreting the Statutes of the *ad hoc* Tribunals', in Lal Chand Vohrah et al. (eds), *Man's Inhumanity to Man: Essays on International Law in Honour of Antonio Cassese* (Kluwer Law International 2003) 168. See discussion of ECCC jurisprudence in Chapter 3.12 that reverted to the stable and permanent approach.

338 Report of the International Commission of Inquiry on Darfur, UN Doc. S/2005/60 (25 January 2005), para. 501.

339 Ibid.

340 Accord: Kress (n 235) 683; Cryer (n 8) 209; Schabas (n 151) 73; William Schabas, 'Genocide, Crimes against Humanity, and Darfur: The Commission of Inquiry's Findings on Genocide', 27 *Cardozo Law Review* (2006) 1713.

341 See eg UN Doc. A/C.6/SR.64 (1 October 1948), in Abtahi, Webb (n 246) 1309; *Prosecutor v Jelisić*, Case No IT-95-10-T (14 December 1999), para. 69. Furthermore: Schabas (n 151) 72; Quigley (n 93) 150.

342 Nersessian (n 185) 54; William Schabas, *The UN International Criminal Tribunals: The Former Yugoslavia, Rwanda and Sierra Leone* (CUP 2006) 168; Kress (n 156) 474–475.

343 *Prosecutor v Akayesu*, Case No ICTR-96-4-T (2 September 1998), para. 514.

this definition.[344] The reference to 'hereditary physical traits' implies an objective approach to a scientifically highly disputed method, namely the identification of people by means of their physical appearance, such as their skin colour. According to an English dictionary, hereditary signifies 'genetically transmitted or transmittable from parent to offspring'.[345] Defining race as the genetic transmission of physical traits is not only scientifically wrong, it also preserves outdated and contentious methods of classifying people.[346] Or in the words of Nigel Eltringham: 'To suggest, even in passing, that racial groups are defined by "hereditary physical traits" . . . flies in the face of empirical evidence regarding phenotype'.[347] The Trial Chamber weakens its statement by referring to 'the conventional definition of racial group', hence leaving undiscussed its accuracy or contemporaneity. The term 'identified with a geographical region' seems to point to the perpetrator's perception of the groups' racial affiliation according to their geographical origin or location. This subjectivity is further emphasised by the clarification that racial membership is irrespective of linguistic, cultural, national, or religious factors, thereby delimiting it from the other protected groups. In sum, the Tribunal took a primarily objective approach with due consideration of certain subjective elements.[348]

Justice Hassan Bubacar Jallow is one of few to suggest crediting the ICTR for its pioneering attempt to identify the objective criteria of the victim groups of genocide.[349] The majority of scholars, however, criticise *Akayesu*'s objective definition of the racial group by employing physical and biological criteria instead of taking into account the broader social and historical context of the group.[350] Schabas agrees: 'Although modern science now rejects the whole notion of the objective existence of "races", for the purposes of the Convention the term ought to be construed not only to reflect the intent of the drafters but to ensure as large a protection of vulnerable groups as possible'.[351] In doing so, Schabas

344 Also recognised by Schuster (n 329) 216.

345 <www.merriam-webster.com/dictionary/hereditary>.

346 Also recognised by Smith (n 57) 164–165.

347 Eltringham (n 313) 29.

348 Scholars who conclude that *Akayesu* took a purely objective approach: Werle, Jessberger (n 142) 296; Szpak (n 162) 162; Schuster (n 329) 216; Pentassuglia (n 333) 30; Boas, Bischoff, Reid (n 180) 174; van den Herik (n 309) 129; Verdirame (n 160) 592. Rebecca Young, 'How Do We Know Them When We See Them? The Subjective Evolution in the Identification of Victim Groups for the Purpose of Genocide', 10 *International Criminal Law Review* (2010) 11, notes that the ICTR relied on objective and subjective evidence of group identification. Few commentators classify *Akayesu* as taking a subjective approach: Derenzo, Garcia (n 12) 18; Paul Magnarella, 'Some Milestones and Achievements at the International Criminal Tribunal for Rwanda: The 1998 *Kambanda* and *Akayesu* Cases', 11 *Florida Journal of International Law* (1997) 531.

349 Jallow (n 200) 452.

350 Eg Verdeja (n 100) 29; Bisaz (n 170) 93; Schuster (n 329) 217; Wilson (n 9) 33–34, 37; Eltringham (n 313) 29.

351 Schabas (n 334) 541.

apparently proposes an evolutive interpretation of race to cover more individuals, not fewer. This study equally argues that the concept and understanding of race has evolved and cannot be interpreted as in 1948. The discussion will return to such evolutive interpretation in Chapter 3.7.2.

When the Genocide Convention was drafted, race was an unproblematic and undisputed concept, but mutated to becoming the most troublesome group category to interpret and apply.[352] 'International jurists have struggled with how to adapt the 1948 notion of "racial group" to contemporary notions of race and biological descent', a report concludes.[353] Moreover, the concept of race has changed over time and is now a social construct that differs from society to society.[354] Despite the fact that the biological notion of race has been scientifically discredited, genocide can still be committed against a racial group. In defining race as a fluid category where 'groups define one another's social position in terms of certain physical or other characteristics which are believed to be genetically determined',[355] the emphasis shifts from objective, biological facts to subjective, perceived beliefs.

The problems created by *Akayesu*'s classification of the Tutsi victims are summed up by Eltringham who asks why the ICTR did not avoid

> these problems and take a perpetrator-oriented approach and ask the simple question 'How did the perpetrators define their targets'? Did the ICTR fear, that by defining the Tutsi as a *race* (in accordance with how they were defined by the perpetrators) they would be accused of endorsing this view? In the end, the ICTR did not really deal with how Tutsi were targeted: the perception of racial distinction. This was unfortunate given that race . . . has no empirical basis . . . . By failing to underline this point, the ICTR missed the opportunity to reveal the wholly ideational nature of the genocidal mentality.[356]

In its conclusion, this study endorses Eltringham's proposal that the victim groups of genocide should be defined subjectively, based on the perpetrator's perception, which reflects the genocidal nature of othering best. For now, however, the focus remains on the Rwandan genocide and whether the Tutsi can be considered a racial or ethnic group in the ambit of the law of genocide.

3.6.5 *Tutsi: a race or ethnicity?*

The classification of the Tutsi victims as members of an ethnical, racial, national, or religious group was one of the main challenges for the ICTR. Due to the high

352 Schabas (n 4) 139; Cornell, Hartmann (n 309) 21. See also Chapters 3.4.3 and 3.4.4.

353 Lowenstein (n 211) 40.

354 Ibid. Also recognized by Ambrus (n 202) 953; Baumann (n 35) 58. See Chapter 2.7 for a discussion of the contemporary understanding of race.

355 Glaser, Possony (n 20) 67.

356 Eltringham (n 313) 30, emphasis in original.

rate of intermarriage, common language, religion, cultural practices, and geographic area of settlement, the Hutu and Tutsi are neither distinct tribes nor distinct ethnic groups.[357] Notwithstanding commonalities, every Rwandan had a strong personal identification with one of the three groups of Hutu, Tutsi, and Twa; there was a clear difference of identity.[358] From an international criminal law point of view, Schabas suggests that while the racial group category in the crime of genocide might have seemed the best choice, the ICTR judges were probably uncomfortable with the notion itself and its whiff of racism.[359] Undeniably, the Belgian Hutu/Tutsi conception was largely built on racial stereotypes: the Tutsi were perceived as taller, finer featured, and lighter skinned, while the Hutu were seen as short, stocky, and dark. As elsewhere at the time, racially obsessed anthropologists conducted scientific measurements of phenotypic differences also in Rwanda.[360] External characteristics were coupled with moral qualities: the Tutsi were considered intelligent, refined, and courageous, whereas the Hutu were extroverted, unmannerly, but hardworking and obedient. The Hutu's allegedly smaller stature signalled to the Belgians their lower position on the evolutionary ladder.[361] In assigning fixed and unchangeable physical and moral qualities, one could indeed argue that the Hutu/Tutsi dichotomy was racial.

The role of racism in the mass killings, originating in the implanted vision of the Tutsi's racial superiority and the interconnected inferiority complex among the Hutu, is widely acknowledged.[362] The Hutu perpetrators themselves used racial language in describing the conflict: 'The Tutsis don't want to share this country with another race',[363] or the headlines of a magazine that read:

357 *Prosecutor v Akayesu*, Case No ICTR-96-4-T (2 September 1998), para. 516. Furthermore: Stahn (n 93) 36; Temoney (n 31) 6–7; Douglas Greenberg, 'Citizenship, National Identity, and Genocide', in René Provost, Payam Akhavan (eds), *Confronting Genocide* (Springer 2011) 87; Helen Klann, Phillipa McKenzie, 'Judge Laïty Kama: Five Cases to Develop International Criminal Law', in Emmanuel Decaux, Adama Dieng, Malick Sow (eds), *From Human Rights to International Criminal Law: Studies in Honour of an African Jurist, the Late Judge Laïty Kama* (Martinus Nijhoff 2007) 26; Schabas (n 151) 70–71; Grady (n 331) 177; Ratner, Abrams, Bischoff (n 142) 35; Fournet (n 318) 47; Kiernan (n 138) 555; Straus (n 41) 9, 18–22; Amann (n 128) 94; Gourevitch (n 313) 48; Banton (n 53) 210; Prunier (n 91) 5. Disaccord: Hardin (n 38) 169.

358 Staub (n 38) 38; Wilson (n 9) 47; Byamukama, Kapranos Huntley (n 311) 234; Prunier (n 91) 23–40.

359 Schabas (n 151) 71. Furthermore: Wilson (n 9) 31, 54; Zahar, Sluiter (n 337) 160; Schabas (n 334) 542.

360 See Chapters 2.3 and 2.5.2 on anthropological measurements in Europe.

361 Wielenga (n 91) 3; Straus (n 41) 21; Hintjens (n 312) 29; Taylor (n 91) 60; Cornell, Hartmann (n 309) 40; Gourevitch (n 313) 52; Prunier (n 91) 6.

362 Rafter (n 40) 155; Rapley (n 81) 232; Wielenga (n 91) 2–3; Wilson (n 9) 54; Kiernan (n 138) 563; Straus (n 41) 20–21; van den Herik (n 309) 129; Eltringham (n 313) 19ff; Nagan, Rodin (n 20) 216; Cornell, Hartmann (n 309) 70; Prunier (n 91) 9, 37–39, 347.

363 Straus (n 41) 129–130 and Eltringham (n 313) 18–19; Cornell, Hartmann (n 309) 40; Gourevitch (n 313) 50.

'By the way, the Tutsi race could be extinguished'.[364] The Hutu power ideology drew from a myth according to which the Tutsi were foreigners from Ethiopia who had invaded and stolen the country from the indigenous Hutu Bantus.[365] Perceived as a threat, as the enemy from within, the Tutsi had to be pre-emptively eliminated before they could 'swallow' the suppressed Hutu culture.[366] This understanding corresponds to social science research whereas, in (pre-)genocidal situations, the in-group considers itself as superior to the out-group, which, albeit inferior and subhuman, nonetheless is portrayed as an ubiquitous threat.[367] Hutu extremist propaganda was dominated by feelings of inferiority and found its release in reversing positions: the Tutsi were inferiorated by means of hate speech, dehumanised by epithets like 'cockroaches' (*inyenzi*), and ultimately exterminated.[368] Interestingly, the derogatory term of *inyenzi* was originally chosen by the Tutsi themselves. In wake of the massacres of Hutus in neighbouring Burundi in 1972–93, Tutsi fighters fled into exile. They crossed the Rwandan borders at night, calling themselves *inyenzi* to accentuate their stealth.[369] Gradually, however, the appellation acquired first a condescending and then a dehumanising meaning.[370] In the *Akayesu* trial, the expert witness on linguistics, Dr Mathias Ruzindana, testified that the incitement to destroy the *inyenzi* was a call to kill the Tutsi.[371] This interpretation later became a cornerstone of the prosecution case in the ICTR *Media* trial proceedings.[372] The trial judgment discusses a Hutu propaganda article published in February 1993 in the magazine *Kangura* (Kinyarwanda for 'wake

364 *La Médaille Nyiramacibiri* (February 1994) cited in Prunier (n 91) 222. See also Eltringham (n 313) 21.
365 In reference to the Hamitic thesis or myth: Akhavan 2016 (n 173) 96; Temoney (n 31) 5–6; Rafter (n 40) 157; Wilson (n 9) 47; Kiernan (n 138) 560; Moshman (n 43) 119; Eltringham (n 313) 21–22; Hardin (n 38) 57, 169; Hintjens (n 312) 26; Taylor (n 91) 55–97; Prunier (n 91) 8, 11, 80.
366 *Prosecutor v Nahimana* et al., Case No ICTR-99–52-T (3 December 2003), paras. 179–180. See also *Prosecutor v Ruggiu*, Case No ICTR-97–32-I, Trial Judgment (1 June 2000), para. 44(i). Furthermore: Temoney (n 31) 7–8; Holslag (n 19) 102; Kiernan (n 138) 559; Straus (n 41) 158; Hinton (n 18) 16, 20; Hintjens (n 312) 37, 42; Gourevitch (n 313) 88, 157; Prunier (n 91) 226–227.
367 See Chapter 3.3.
368 Deutsch, Yanay (n 87) 22; Rafter (n 40) 93–94; Drumbl (n 59) 41; Straus (n 41) 158; Hintjens (n 312) 43. See also *Prosecutor v Kayishema and Ruzindana*, Case No ICTR-95–1-T (21 May 1999), para. 538; *Prosecutor v Ruggiu*, Case No ICTR-97–32, Amended Indictment (18 December 1998) 6–7; *Prosecutor v Nahimana* et al., Case No ICTR-99–52-T (3 December 2003) 45–51 on the Hutu *Ten Commandments*.
369 Wilson (n 90) 534; Hintjens (n 312) 33; Gourevitch (n 313) 64.
370 *Prosecutor v Akayesu*, Case No ICTR-96–4-T (2 September 1998), para. 149.
371 Ibid paras. 146, 148, 340, 361. Discussed in: Richard Ashby Wilson, 'Expert Evidence on Trial: Social Researchers in the International Criminal Courtroom', 43 *American Ethnologist* (2016) 734.
372 Ibid 736; Wilson (n 90) 534. See Chapter 3.9.4 on the *Media* trial.

others up'). The article was titled *A Cockroach Cannot Give Birth to a Butterfly* and ends with these words:

> In our language a Tutsi is called cockroach because he takes advantage of the night to achieve his objectives. The word *Inyenzi* is a reminder of the redoubtable snake whose venom is extremely poisonous. The fact that the Tutsi chose such names is very significant to those who want to understand.[373]

The article furthermore refers to a genetic difference between the groups: 'Experts on human genetics inform us that the demographic weakness of Tutsis is due to the fact that they marry among themselves'.[374] Likewise, the Hutu extremist private radio station, *Radio Télévision Libre des Mille Collines* (RTLM), which also Chapter 5.3.4.4 discusses, broadcasted the same statement several times: 'The *inyenzi* have always been Tutsi. We will exterminate them. One can identify them because they are of one race. You can identify them by their height and their small nose. When you see that small nose, break it'.[375] There appears to have been, at least in Hutu propaganda, an understanding of biological differences.[376] Although Kinyarwanda does not have a word for race,[377] the Hutu extremists conceived the Tutsi as a racially distinct group. Thus, even if the victims are not labeled or called a race, they are nonetheless believed to be racially distinct.[378]

The *Akayesu* Trial Chamber was pressed to find objective criteria to match the Tutsi with one of the protected groups of the Genocide Convention: '[T]he Chamber finds that there are a number of objective indicators of the group as a group with a distinct identity',[379] including ID cards and Rwanda's Constitution and Civil Code that contained references to a person's identification by ethnicity.[380] Although the perpetrators did use the ID cards to confirm their victims' group membership, the larger understanding of the Tutsi victim group, however, involved considerable, if not predominant, elements of racial identification. In noting that the Tutsi did not have a language or distinct culture separate from the rest of the Rwandan population, the Trial Chamber rendered the definition of the Tutsi as a distinct ethnic group difficult.[381]

373 *Prosecutor v Nahimana* et al., Case No ICTR-99–52-T (3 December 2003), para. 179.
374 Ibid.
375 Kiernan (n 138) 567.
376 Confirmed by Rafter (n 40) 155; Kiernan (n 138) 558; Eltringham (n 313) 21–24.
377 The Kinyarwandan word *ubwoko* describes ethnic groups, clans, tribes, thus categories. See Straus (n 41) 129–130.
378 Smith (n 57) 185.
379 *Prosecutor v Akayesu*, Case No ICTR-96–4-T (2 September 1998), para 170.
380 Ibid; Drumbl (n 195) 45.
381 *Prosecutor v Akayesu*, Case No ICTR-96–4-T (2 September 1998), para 170. Similarly: *Prosecutor v Kayishema and Ruzindana*, Case No ICTR-95–1-T (21 May 1999), para. 34.

The ambiguity regarding the delicate issue of race or ethnicity surfaced in *Niyitegeka*. In holding that the accused targeted the 'Tutsi population with the intent to destroy, in whole or in part, a racial or ethnic group',[382] the ICTR left unanswered the Tutsi's group membership. Only a few paragraphs later and without any further discussion, the Trial Chamber concluded that 'the Accused perpetrated these acts with the requisite intent to destroy . . . the Tutsi ethnic group'.[383] Similarly, in the *Kambanda* case, the Trial Chamber did not elaborate on the protected groups, but simply concluded that the accused targeted members of the Tutsi population with the 'intent to destroy, in whole or in part, an ethnic or racial group, as such'.[384] The Tribunal assumed that the Tutsi were either an ethnic or a racial group, but refrained from defining them. Such legal definition became redundant when the ICTR declared the 1994 genocide in Rwanda and the victims' Tutsi ethnicity facts of common knowledge.[385]

3.7 Interpreting race for the crime of genocide

3.7.1 The 'Object and Purpose' of the genocide convention

Akayesu's inept and unsubstantiated definition of racial group *per se* shows the need for a more comprehensive interpretation of race for the crime of genocide. According to Arts. 31 and 32 VCLT, treaties shall 'be interpreted in good faith in accordance with the ordinary meaning to be given to the terms of the treaty in their context and in the light of its object and purpose'.[386] The analysis of the Genocide Convention's object and purpose addresses the overarching question: was the Convention drafted as a human rights treaty or as an international criminal law treaty with a punitive purpose? The underlying values of the Convention can be significant for the determination of whether an expansive interpretation of race was intended by the drafters. There might, however, be no conclusive answer to this question, since the treaty appears to contain distinct strands of human rights law and of international criminal law. While human

382 *Prosecutor v Niyitegeka*, Case No ICTR-96–14-T (16 May 2003), para. 408.

383 Ibid para. 419.

384 *Prosecutor v Kambanda*, Case No ICTR-97–23-S, Judgment and Sentence (4 September 1998), para. 40(1).

385 *Prosecutor v Karemera* et al., Case No ICTR-98–44-AR73(C), Decision on Prosecutor's Interlocutory Appeal of Decision on Judicial Notice (16 June 2006), paras. 29, 31, 35.

386 Strictly speaking, the VCLT (adopted 1969) is not applicable to the Genocide Convention (adopted 1948) because Art. 4 VCLT bars a retroactive application. However, the ICJ has repeatedly confirmed that Arts. 31–33 VCLT articulate the general principles of interpretation in the international legal system and form part of customary law: *Case concerning the Territorial Dispute (Libyan Arab Jamahiriya v Chad)*, ICJ Judgment (1994), para. 41; *Arbitral Award of 31 July 1989 (Guinea Bissau v Senegal)*, ICJ Judgment (1991), p. 70; *Competence of the General Assembly for the Admission of a State to the United Nations*, ICJ Advisory Opinion (1950), p. 8. Accord: *Prosecutor v Tadić*, Case No IT-94–1-A (15 July 1999), para. 303.

rights law provides the normative foundation for international criminal law, different obligations arise from each field of law: whereas human rights law imposes obligations on states, international criminal law addresses the criminal liability of individuals. These two areas of law are not informed by and do not promote identical principles and definitions.[387] Rather each branch has a distinct subject matter and its specific modalities of enforcement.[388] Particularly because of the far-reaching consequences for individuals, international criminal law favours a strict construction of statutes and their narrow interpretation in order to comply with the principle of legality, while international human rights law generally justifies a broad, dynamic interpretation to enhance the rights of the victims against interference from a state.[389]

The magnitude of the crime itself may call for a broad interpretation of the law. Such is the suggestion of four judges in the dissenting opinion of the 1951 ICJ Advisory Opinion *Reservations to the Genocide Convention* who held that 'the enormity of the crime of genocide can hardly be exaggerated, and any treaty for its repression deserves the most generous interpretation'.[390] The ICJ equally highlighted that the Genocide Convention was 'adopted for a purely humanitarian and civilizing purpose', and its object was 'confirm and endorse the most elementary principles of morality'.[391] This statement could indicate acceptance of an expansive approach for humanitarian purposes and for reasons of morality.[392] But the Genocide Convention was also created with the clear intention of holding responsible individuals who committed genocide. In 1946, the UN General Assembly Resolution 96 (I) explicitly declared genocide an international crime, whether committed on religious, racial, political or any other grounds.[393] During the drafting of the Convention in 1948, the Pakistani

387 Noora Arajärvi, *The Changing Nature of Customary International Law* (Routledge 2014) 70.

388 M. Cherif Bassiouni, 'The Protection of "Collective Victims" in International Law', in M. Cherif Bassiouni (ed), *International Protection of Victims* (Association International de Droit Pénal, Editions Érès 1988) 189.

389 Annika Jones, 'Insight into an Emerging Relationship: Use of Human Rights Jurisprudence at the International Criminal Court', 16 *Human Rights Law Review* (2016) 708; Walter Kälin, Jörg Künzli, *The Law of International Human Rights Protection* (OUP 2009) 38; Darryl Robinson, 'The Identity Crisis of International Criminal Law', 21 *LJIL* (2008) 946. Arguably, also international criminal law can justify a broad interpretation to include more victim groups. Such interpretation cannot, however, compromise the rights of the accused.

390 *Reservations to the Convention on the Prevention and Punishment of the Crime of Genocide*, Dissenting Opinion of Judges Guerrero, McNari, Read and Hsu Mo, ICJ Advisory Opinion (1951), p. 47.

391 *Reservations to the Convention on the Prevention and Punishment of the Crime of Genocide*, ICJ Advisory Opinion (1951), p. 23. Confirmed by: *Application of the Convention on the Prevention and Punishment of the Crime of Genocide (Bosnia and Herzegovina v Serbia and Montenegro)*, ICJ Judgment (2007), para. 194.

392 Also recognised by Akhavan 2015 (n 173) 894.

393 UN GA Res. 96 (I) (11 December 1946).

delegate accused of the 'complete failure to understand the real aim of the convention on genocide . . . [that] was not designed to proclaim rights but to punish certain crimes'.[394] She obviously understood the Convention as an instrument of international criminal law, which warranted narrow interpretation. Moreover, the Judges Shi and Vereshchetin in the 1996 ICJ Judgment on the *Application of the Genocide Convention* (*Bosnia and Herzegovina v Yugoslavia*) emphasise that the Convention 'is essentially and primarily directed towards the punishment of persons committing genocide' and it 'remains an instrument relating to the criminal responsibility of individuals'.[395] The judges thereby focused on the punitive purpose of the treaty. The Genocide Convention's preamble does not make any explicit reference to human rights or the protection of different groups, whereas it makes clear that 'genocide is a crime under international law'. In the ICTY, ICTR, ECCC, and ICC Statutes and their respective provisions on genocide the penal aspect is clearly foregrounded. In sum, no conclusive answer can be offered, but it appears as though the punitive aspect slightly outweighs the humanitarian aspect of the law of genocide, which would suggest a narrow interpretation in order to cohere with the principle of legality.

In returning to Arts. 31 and 32 VCLT, the next section focuses on the ordinary meaning of race for international criminal law. This study argues that 'race' is a generic term, the ordinary meaning of which has changed, thereby obliging an evolutive interpretation of the term for the crime of genocide.

3.7.2 Evolutive interpretation of race and the principle of effectiveness

The Genocide Convention was drafted with the clear intention to protect four exclusive groups only. The precise definition of the ethnic and national group was not quite settled yet, while the racial group was not subject to any discussion.[396] Moreover, the drafters left the definition of the protected groups open for the courts to settle.[397] In concluding a treaty of perpetual duration that contains four generic terms relating to or descriptive of a whole group, the drafters chose terms that are not static, but rather evolutive, and therefore susceptible to change.[398] The ICJ set up two conditions for where such an

394 UN Doc. A/PV.178 (9 December 1948), in Abtahi, Webb (n 246) 2051.

395 *Application of the Convention on the Prevention and Punishment of the Crime of Genocide (Bosnia and Herzegovina v Yugoslavia)*, Preliminary Objections, Joint Declaration of Judge Shi and Judge Vereshchetin, ICJ Judgment (1996), p. 631.

396 UN Doc. A/C.6/SR.69 (statement by Shawcross) in Abtahi, Webb (n 246) 1359–1360. Furthermore: Schabas (n 4) 121. See Chapter 3.4.4 on the drafting history of the Genocide Convention.

397 Bisaz (n 170) 92; Schabas (n 170) 99; LeBlanc (n 170) 271–273.

398 Judge Higgins defined "generic" as 'a known legal term, whose content the parties expected would change through time' [*Case Concerning Kasikili/ Sedudu Island* (*Botswana*

evolutive interpretation must be presupposed. The first is that 'generic terms' are used, whose meaning the parties necessarily were aware of could evolve over time. The second condition is that the treaty was entered into for a very long time or was of undetermined duration.[399] The Genocide Convention and the Rome Statute were both entered into for an indeterminate time and are of continuous duration. Additionally, in relating to an indeterminate class of referents, race should be considered a generic term.[400] Therefore, the generic term 'racial group' has to be interpreted evolutively. An interpretation is evolutive if the words in a treaty stay the same, but their ordinary meaning is altered.[401] Importantly, an evolutive interpretation is the result, not the means of interpretation: the meaning attached to the text of a treaty is changed through interpretation.[402] Although Arts. 31 and 32 VCLT do not expressly mention evolutive interpretation, it is nonetheless coherent with Art. 31(1) VCLT, because the 'ordinary meaning' of a term may change over time. The VCLT does not determine whether it is the ordinary meaning at the time of the treaty conclusion or at the time of the treaty's interpretation that should prevail.[403] Generic terms 'must be understood to have the meaning they bear on each occasion on which the Treaty is to be applied', the ICJ clarified, 'and not necessarily their original meaning'.[404] Similarly, in the *South West Africa* Advisory Opinion, the ICJ declared:

> that the concepts embodied in [the treaty] . . . were not static, but were by definition evolutionary. The parties . . . must consequently be deemed

---

v *Namibia*), ICJ Judgment (1999), Declaration of Judge Higgins, para. 2]. Furthermore Gazzini (n 13) 105; Panos Merkouris, *Article 31(3)(c) VCLT and the Principle of Systemic Integration: Normative Shadows in Plato's Cave* (Brill Nijhoff 2015) 141–142; Arato (n 13) 468–469.

399 *Dispute regarding Navigational and Related Rights* (*Costa Rica v Nicaragua*), ICJ Judgment (2009), para. 66. See discussion in Christian Djeffal, *Static and Evolutive Treaty Interpretation: A Functional Reconstruction* (CUP 2016) 29, 33; Merkouris (n 398) 150–151; Sondre Torp Helmersen, 'Evolutive Treaty Interpretation: Legality, Semantics and Distinctions', 6 *European Journal of Legal Studies* (2013) 136.

400 The ILC Study Group on Fragmentation also suggests an evolutive interpretation of a treaty, if a) there are subsequent technical, economic or legal developments; b) the concept set up an obligation for further progressive development for the parties; or c) the concept – in our case: race – has a very general nature or is expressed in general terms that demand to take into account changing circumstances (Report of the Study Group of the ILC, Fragmentation of International Law: Difficulties Arising from the Diversification and Expansion of International Law, UN Doc. A/CN.4/L.682 (13 April 2006), pp. 242–243).

401 *Dispute regarding Navigational and Related Rights* (*Costa Rica v Nicaragua*), ICJ Judgment (2009), paras. 63–66. Furthermore Djeffal (n 399) 19; Arato (n 13) 465; Gardiner (n 222) 242–243.

402 Djeffal (n 399) 22–24; Merkouris (n 398) 141–143; Gardiner (n 222) 242–243.

403 Merkouris (n 398) 125; Helmersen (n 399) 131.

404 *Dispute regarding Navigational and Related Rights (Costa Rica v Nicaragua)*, ICJ Judgment (2009), para. 70. Similarly *Aegean Sea Continental Shelf (Greece v Turkey)*,

> to have accepted them as such. That is why . . . the Court must take into consideration the changes which have occurred in the supervening half-century, and its interpretation cannot remain unaffected by the subsequent development of law.[405]

More than half a century has passed since the Genocide Convention, as the legal response to the Holocaust, was created. The meaning of race has changed drastically since 1948, not least due to scientific and social developments, making an evolutive interpretation of Art. 2 Genocide Convention imperative. Indeed, historical research has shown that the meaning of race has never stopped changing: before the eighteenth century, for example, it was rarely used and then only with reference to a group of people with a common line of descent.[406] Nowadays, race is about being or claiming an identity as well as having a historically and socially constructed – and often externally imposed – identity.[407] In interpreting a treaty, 'we must have regard to the exigencies of contemporary life', Judge Alvarez in the ICJ case *Competence of the General Assembly for the Admission of a State to the United Nations* noted, 'rather than to the intentions of those who framed it'.[408] The changed meaning that results from an evolutionary interpretation of treaties should be understood as evolution intended,[409] thus linked to the state parties' intent. The judicial interpreter is given the task of respecting the drafters' intent, while taking account of the normative, societal, technological, and linguistic developments that have occurred afterwards.[410] Tipping the balance toward an evolutive interpretation could contradict the principle of contemporaneity, whereas the terms of a treaty must be interpreted according to the meaning that was attributed to them at the time of the treaty's

---

ICJ Judgment (1978), para. 77; *US – Import Prohibition of Certain Shrimp and Shrimp Products (US-Shrimp)*, WTO Appellate Body Report, Case No WT/DS58/AB/R (12 October 1998), paras. 129–130. Furthermore Arato (n 13) 471; Gardiner (n 222) 172–173; Chester Brown, *A Common Law of International Adjudication* (OUP 2007) 47.

405 *Legal Consequences for States of the Continued Presence of South Africa in Namibia (South West Africa) notwithstanding Security Council Resolution 276* (1970), ICJ Advisory Opinion (1971), para. 53.

406 Erica Howard, 'Race and Racism – Why Does European Law Have Difficulties With Definitions?', 24 *International Journal of Comparative Labour Law and Industrial Relations* (2008) 9; Michael Banton, 'Race: As Classification', in Ellis Cashmore (ed), *Encyclopedia of Race and Ethnic Studies* (Routledge 2004) 333. See also Chapter 2 on the History of Race.

407 Luke, Carrington (n 20) 5–6, 22.

408 *Competence of the General Assembly for the Admission of a State to the United Nations*, ICJ Judgment (1950), Dissenting Opinion of Judge Alvarez, p. 18. Similarly: JG Merrills 'Two Approaches to Treaty Interpretation', *Australian Yearbook of International Law* (1969) 70.

409 Eirik Bjørge, *The Evolutionary Interpretation of Treaties* (OUP 2014) 188.

410 Gazzini (n 13) 106; Arato (n 13) 465, 470. Similarly: Rothenberg (n 142) 948–951.

conclusion.[411] An interpretation of race according to the meaning it possessed in 1948 will, however, lead to a manifestly outdated, absurd, and unreasonable result. In their jurisprudence, the international criminal tribunals have without doubt moved away from the principle of contemporaneity, stripping it of its 'temporal straitjacket' whereby anachronistic interpretations may ultimately frustrate the achievement of the objects of the treaty.[412] Importantly, any evolutive interpretation has to be performed with the goal to give effect rather than depart from the intention of the parties.[413] As such, an evolutive interpretation is inherently linked to the principle of effectiveness.[414] Treaties, the ILC writes in recognition of the principle of effectiveness,

> are to be interpreted with reference to their . . . objects and purposes; and particular provisions are to be interpreted so as to give them their fullest weight and effect consistent with the normal sense of the words . . ., and in such a way that a reason and a meaning can be attributed to every part of the text.[415]

Accordingly, the terms of a treaty are ensured effectiveness in consideration of its object and purpose together with good faith, the so-called *effet utile*.[416] There is no apparent reason why race should be disregarded, since the law that contains the term remains valid. Rather, as Tams et al. contend, 'each individual word employed in a legal document implies and contributes an autonomous meaning and must hence be interpreted as a stand-alone component within the norm's substance'.[417] Thus, the interpretation of a legal text should attribute a reason and

411 Humphrey Waldock, ILC Special Rapporteur, Third Report on the Law of Treaties, 16 YBILC, UN Doc. A/CN.4/SER.A/1964/Add.1 (1964), p. 56; *Wintershall Aktiengesellschaft v Argentine Republic*, ICSID Case No ARB/04/14, Award (8 December 2008), para. 129.

412 See Gazzini (n 13) 106.

413 *Dispute regarding Navigational and Related Rights* (*Costa Rica* v *Nicaragua*), ICJ Judgment (2009), para. 64; Gazzini (n 13) 108; Merkouris (n 398) 142; Bjørge (n 409) 8.

414 Confirmed in *Award in the Arbitration Regarding the Iron Rhine ("Ijzeren Rijn") Railway Between the Kingdom of Belgium and the Kingdom of the Netherlands (Iron Rhine case)*, PCA, UNRIAA Vol. XXVII (24 May 2005), para. 80; *US – Import Prohibition of Certain Shrimp and Shrimp Products (US-Shrimp)*, WTO Appellate Body Report, Case No WT/DS58/AB/R (12 October 1998), para. 131.

415 Waldock (n 411) 55.

416 *The Right to Information on Consular Assistance in the Framework of the Guarantees of the Due Process of Law*, Case No OC-16/99, IACtHR Advisory Opinion (1999), para. 58. On the principle of effectiveness: *Prosecutor v Jelisić*, Case No IT-95-10-A, Separate Opinion of Judge Nieto-Navia (5 July 2001), para. 12. Furthermore Mark Villiger, *Commentary on the 1969 Vienna Convention on the Law of Treaties* (Martinus Nijhoff 2009) 428; Gardiner (n 222) 60–61 and 200–202; Hersch Lauterpacht, 'Restrictive Interpretation and the Principle of Effectiveness in the Interpretation of Treaties', *British Yearbook of International Law* (1949) 68.

417 Tams, Berster, Schiffbauer (n 223) 103.

meaning to every word, also to the term 'race'.[418] In general, international criminal tribunals and courts appear to have an affinity for the principle of effectiveness, as frequent references to it show.[419] The ICTY Appeals Chamber in *Tadić*, for instance, considered the principle of effectiveness to be an elementary rule of interpretation. It held the presumption warranted that lawmakers enact or agree upon rules that are well thought out and meaningful in all their elements.[420]

By interpreting the element of race in a contemporary and legally correct manner based on the perception of a group's differentness, the effectiveness of the law of genocide will be increased. The application of the principle of effectiveness will thereby prevent redundancy in giving race a meaningful content. It is, however, important to remember, as ICJ Judges Spender and Fitzmaurice have emphasised, that this 'principle of interpretation directed to giving provisions their maximum effect cannot legitimately be employed in order to introduce what would amount to a revision of these provisions'.[421] The concept of race for international criminal law must therefore be interpreted evolutively and effectively, yet without such interpretation leading to a change of the substance of the law containing the term.

The consequences of such an effective interpretation have been discussed by the ICTY and ICTR in their judgments. For instance, in the case against *Milutinović* et al., the ICTY stated that in order to give full effect to the object and purpose of customary international law, it is necessary to adopt a broad definition of the key terms that extends as much protection as possible.[422] Thus, the application of the principle of effectiveness led to a broad interpretation in order to include more victims. A comparable line of argumentation was used in *Kupreškić* et al., according to which the rules prohibiting crimes against humanity were 'intended to safeguard basic human values by banning atrocities directed against human dignity', hence suggesting an expansive interpretation.[423]

418 *Anglo-Iranian Oil Co. Case* (*United Kingdom v Iran*), Preliminary Objection, ICJ Judgment (1952), p. 105. See for a detailed discussion Carola Lingaas, 'Enhancing the Effectiveness of the Law of Genocide', in Joanna Nicholson (ed), *Strengthening the Validity of International Criminal Tribunals* (Brill Nijhoff 2018) 126–151.

419 *Prosecutor v Katanga*, Case No ICC-01/04–01/07, Trial Judgment (7 March 2014), para. 46; *Prosecutor v Akayesu*, Case No ICTR-96–4-A (7 June 2001), para. 468; *Prosecutor v Blaškić*, Case No IT-95–14-AR108bis, Judgment on the Request of the Republic of Croatia for Review of the Decision of Trial Chamber II of 18 July 1997 (29 October 1997), para. 21; *Prosecutor v Erdemović*, Case No IT-96–22-T, Trial and Sentencing Judgment (29 November 1996), para. 38.

420 *Prosecutor v Tadić*, Case No IT-94–1-A (15 July 1999), para. 284. Similarly *Prosecutor v Galić*, Case No IT-98–29-T (5 December 2003), para. 91.

421 *South West Africa* cases (*Ethiopia v South Africa; Liberia v South Africa*), Preliminary Objections, Joint Dissenting Opinion of Judges Spender and Fitzmaurice, ICJ Judgment (1962), p. 468. Similarly: *Prosecutor v Barayagwiza*, Case No ICTR-97–19-AR72, Decision, Separate Opinion of Judge Shahabuddeen (3 November 1999); *Award in the Arbitration Regarding the Iron Rhine ("Ijzeren Rijn") Railway Between the Kingdom of Belgium and the Kingdom of the Netherlands*, PCA, UNRIAA Vol. XXVII (24 May 2005), para. 49.

422 *Prosecutor v Milutinović* et al., Case No IT-05–87-T (26 February 2009), para. 147.

423 *Prosecutor v Kupreškić* et al., Case No IT-95–16-T (14 January 2000), para. 547. See also *Prosecutor v Furundžija*, Case No IT-95–17/1-T (10 December 1998), para. 183.

While this study is not recommending a broad definition of race *per se* – on the contrary, it argues for a narrow interpretation within the boundaries of the law – an evolutive interpretation of race will in effect lead to precisely that result, namely a broad interpretation that potentially embraces more victims than the drafters originally had envisaged. Two consequences follow: due to the principle of effectiveness, the element of race cannot be disregarded for the crimes of genocide, apartheid, and persecution. Yet, in arguing that the term 'race' is a generic term that has changed its meaning, and by interpreting it evolutively, the scope of the protection might be broadened to include more victims. Simultaneously, owing to the principle of legality, the law cannot be expanded beyond its (reasonable) foreseeability and specificity.

The meaning and use of the term 'race' have undoubtedly changed. The deployment of race 'in an unproblematized way in the Genocide Convention seems much less persuasive to contemporary observers than it did to Lemkin and the Convention's framer', Adam Jones remarks.[424] He acknowledges doubts as to whether race exists other than how people describe or perceive others. Yet, race could be used in a meaningful way, Jones suggests, for example to understand the mindset of a fanatic.[425] This study agrees that the concept of race can be used meaningfully, but not in reference to objectively distinct human races. Instead, the perpetrator's perception of the victim group's racial otherness will allow for the continued use of the category 'racial group', without having to revert to scientifically and morally doubtful human categories.[426] In the past two decades, the *ad hoc* tribunals and other courts have gradually adopted a partially subjective approach, while never completely letting go of certain, yet generally undefined, objective indicators of group membership.[427] The following discussion of the relevant jurisprudence reveals significant analytical confusion with regard to the subjective and objective approach.

3.8 The objective and subjective approach in defining the protected groups

3.8.1 Introduction

The drafters of the Genocide Convention certainly underestimated the complexity involved in the identification of a victim group for the crime of genocide. In omitting the definition of the four protected groups of Art. 2 Genocide

424 Jones (n 156) 58.
425 Ibid.
426 Similar conclusion by Eltringham (n 313) 31.
427 Stahn (n 93) 36; Tams, Berster, Schiffbauer (n 223) 103; Nersessian (n 185) 28; Schabas (n 4) 125; Werle, Jessberger (n 142) 297; Verdirame (n 160) 589; Vest (n 157) 131; Demko (n 35) 230; Jones, Powles (n 3) 68; Fronza (n 162) 132. The interpretation of genocide, in the view of Judge Garzón, has not always been sufficiently progressive, see Rothenberg (n 142) 949.

Convention, they opened the floodgates to controversy and criticism. Indeed, it has become an important defence strategy in international criminal trials to question the very existence of the victim group specified in the indictment.[428] In explaining the different approaches to defining the protected groups of genocide, the following analysis will canvas the advantages and disadvantages of each approach. Lastly, it will synthesize the preferred approach by tribunals and suggest the way forward. Unlike Gideon Boas and co-authors who consider the distinction between the different approaches 'largely academic',[429] the discussions will demonstrate the practical significance of the approaches to past, current, and future cases of genocide.

3.8.2 *Outlining the different approaches*

Historically, membership of one of the four protected groups was considered an objective element of the crime. From a legal point of view, the Soviet Union's delegate said during the negotiations of the Genocide Convention, the determination of an individual's group membership has to be of an objective character. He considered the racial and national groups as easily distinguishable; both constituted clearly classifiable communities.[430] The wording of Art. 2 Genocide Convention suggests that if the victim lacks membership of one of the four exclusive groups; genocide cannot be established by law. Yet at this point, as Robert Cryer and co-authors point out, the complex question arises of who ought to be able to make that determination.[431] There are two principal approaches to ascertaining membership of a group: an objective and a subjective approach. First, an objective approach assumes that groups are a social reality with a permanent and factual existence autonomous of perception.[432] The group and membership of it are considered a matter free of feelings, thoughts, or perceptions, with a reality independent of the mind.[433] In a legal analysis of the crime of genocide, the objective existence of the group would have to precede an assessment of the individual victim's membership of the group.[434] On the other hand, however, membership can be established on the basis of a subjective identification, in which the group exists to the extent that its members perceive themselves as belonging to that group (self-identification) or are perceived as doing so by the perpetrators (identification by others), or a combination of both.[435]

428 Bisaz (n 170) 92; Quigley (n 93) 146.
429 Boas, Bischoff, Reid (n 180) 176.
430 UN Doc. A/C.6/SR.74, p. 105.
431 Cryer (n 8) 211. Similarly Jones, Powles (n 3) 167.
432 Verdeja (n 100) 30; Ambrus (n 202) 943; van den Herik (n 206) 87; Aptel (n 185) 284.
433 <www.merriam-webster.com/dictionary/objective>; Demko (n 35) 229.
434 Paul (n 103) 80; Boas, Bischoff, Reid (n 180) 201; Boot (n 232) 428.
435 Werle, Jessberger (n 142) 296; Szpak (n 162) 162–163; Demko (n 35) 229; Nersessian (n 162) 307; Jones, Powles (n 3) 167; Aptel (n 185) 284; Fronza (n 162) 133.

The analysis of this study suggests that there are four different schools of thought that the subjective approach can be divided into. In the first, it is the perpetrator's perception that is foregrounded (perpetrator-based subjective approach). In the second, it is the victims' self-perception of their group membership (victim-based subjective approach). Third, it is the perceptions of the perpetrator and the victim that together determine the contours of the protected group (cumulative or double-subjective approach). Finally, the fourth approach is a so-called objectivised subjective approach, in which an initially subjective approach gradually and over time becomes objectivised, in that the perpetrator and victim believe such distinctions among their groups to have always existed. Before analysing genocide judgments in order to demonstrate the incoherence of case law to date, the conceptual challenges of the different approaches will be considered.

3.8.3 Conceptual challenges of the objective and the subjective approach

The Jewish persecution during the Holocaust illustrates the (theoretical) problems created in relying either on a purely objective or a purely subjective approach. Recall that the Jewish group was to some extent a fictional group created by the Nazis in order to promote the so-called Nordic master race.[436] The Nuremberg racial laws did not find their foundation in objective, *halakhic* rules of Judaism, but in an individual's ancestry and bloodline. Personal faith or individual observance of religious custom was mostly ignored.[437] Even Jews who had converted to Christianity, or whose Jewish grandparents had converted, were targeted.[438] The Nazis created their own objective reality as defined by the Nuremberg Laws. Thus, they characterised their Jewish victims according to an objectivised subjective approach to Judaism.[439]

It has been suggested that before pursuing any inquiry into the mind of the perpetrator, the objective existence of the group should be determined. Here, the group is expected to exist in reality and be verifiable according to some objective criterion.[440] But what would such objective test of race assess? Skin colour, head shape, hair colour or body size? Would such objective classification resort to outdated and contentious methods? Scholars have come

436 Fein (n 38) 47. See Chapter 2.4.

437 Heideman (n 87) 10; Deutsch, Yanay (n 87) 23; Bazyler (n 94) 9; Nersessian (n 185) 30; Schabas (n 206) 164; Vest (n 157) 131; Chalk, Jonassohn (n 18) 25; Huttenbach (n 41) 299. See Chapter 2.5.1.

438 Bazyler (n 94) 9; <www.ushmm.org/outreach/en/article.php?ModuleId=10007695>; Huttenbach (n 41) 299.

439 Similar conclusion in William Schabas, 'The Law and Genocide', in Donald Bloxham, Dirk Moses (eds), *The Oxford Handbook of Genocide Studies* (OUP 2010/13) 133; Nersessian (n 185) 158.

440 Kress (n 235) 685; Cryer (n 8) 213; Mugwanya (n 315) 77; Drumbl (n 195) 45.

to acknowledge the inherent difficulty of objectively characterising groups with reliability and consistency.[441] An objective approach moreover fails to recognise the perpetrator's definitional power.[442] Since the victim group's identity depends on variable and random perceptions, any genocide is inadvertently subjective.[443] This insight has led to a departure from a purely objective approach.

The teleology of the law of genocide precludes the possibility that a protected group might exist in the perpetrator's mind only, says Claus Kress. Rather, in his view, the law aims at preventing conduct that results in great losses to humanity in the form of cultural and other contributions represented by these groups.[444] This study argues that the destruction of a group perceived by the perpetrator as racially distinct, irrespective of its actual existence, would equally result in a loss to humanity. Unlike Kress' apprehension,[445] the perpetrator's perception is not necessarily incompatible with the exhaustiveness of the protected groups. Rather, as long as his perception is linked to a belief of a distinct race, ethnicity, religion, or nationality, there is hardly a risk of trivialising the crime of genocide.[446] Yet the expansion of the protection beyond these four exhaustive groups to any group defined as 'others' would be inadmissible judicial lawmaking.[447]

3.9 Post-*Akayesu*: the *ad hoc* tribunals' jurisprudence

3.9.1 Introduction

Akayesu was the first genocide trial and, in many senses, functioned as a catalyst for the interpretation of the crime of genocide inasmuch as it determined the framework for future interpretations of the crime. One area where its interpretation has changed most is the question of whether the individual victim must be a member of a protected group, or whether the subjective perception of

441 John Dugard, John Reynolds, 'Apartheid, International Law, and the Occupied Palestinian Territories', 24 *EJIL* (2013) 887; Levene (n 224) 65.

442 Paul (n 103) 161. Accord: Demko (n 35) 232–233; Mugwanya (n 315) 92; Eltringham (n 313) 31–32.

443 Ambos (n 189) 8; Fournet (n 188) 107–109; Antonio Cassese et al., *Cassese's International Criminal Law* (OUP 3rd ed 2013) 121; Verdeja (n 100) 30 ; Levene (n 224) 65; Ambrus (n 202) 935, 953; Demko (n 35) 232, 234–235; Paul (n 103) 157, 163; Fournet (n 318) 6, 57; Mugwanya (n 315) 63, 122; Eltringham (n 313) 31; Nagan, Rodin (n 20) 187; Straus (n 134) 366; Jean-Michel Chaumont, *Die Konkurrenz der Opfer: Genozid, Identität und Anerkennung* (Klampen Verlag 2001) 181–182; Chalk (1997) 52; Chalk, Jonassohn (n 18) 23. See Chapter 3.5.3.2 on the proof of intent.

444 Kress (n 235) 685 with reference to UN GA Res. 96 (I) of 1948. Accord: Safferling (n 195) 166.

445 Kress (n 235) 685.

446 As feared by Kress (n 156) 461, 464, 474.

447 See similar discussion in Verdeja (n 100) 31; May (n 15) 92–93; van den Herik (n 206) 90.

such membership is sufficient.[448] While *Akayesu* opted for a primarily objective approach, subsequent judgments have moved toward a subjective approach to defining the protected groups of genocide despite the conventional silence on the matter.[449] Nonetheless, in the overwhelming majority of contemporary genocide cases, the *ad hoc* tribunals have not exclusively relied on a subjective approach, but instead on generally undisclosed objective elements too. These approaches turn out to be neither fish nor fowl in that they do not characterise accurately the victim group and do not adequately reflect the genocidal stages of othering.

3.9.2 *Case law by the* ad hoc *tribunals*

As the first international war crimes tribunal since the Nuremberg and Tokyo Tribunal, the ICTY was established by the Security Council acting under Chapter VII of the UN Charter.[450] Its establishment was decided after a commission of experts that had investigated war crimes in the former Yugoslavia documented grave breaches of the Geneva Conventions and other violations of international humanitarian law.[451] The ICTY's mandate was not to legislate new law, but rather to apply existing customary law in such a manner as to avoid violating the principle of legality.[452] The drafting of Art. 4 ICTY Statute on the crime of genocide, which is identical to Art. 2 Genocide Convention, posed no difficulty, since the crime as defined in the Genocide Convention was considered 'beyond any doubt part of customary law'.[453] In the early case against *Nikolić* in 1995, the ICTY seemingly managed to get a head start on the ICTR by applying a

448 Boas, Bischoff, Reid (n 180) 173.

449 Ibid 174; Ambrus (n 202) 945; Paul (n 103) 105; Mugwanya (n 315) 107; Fournet (n 318) 58; Schabas (n 343) 169; Jones, Powles (n 3) 168; Aptel (n 185) 283; Verdirame (n 160) 594.

450 Established by Security Council Resolution UN Doc. S/RES/827 (25 May 1993). Furthermore: Leila Nadya Sadat, 'Crimes Against Humanity in the Modern Age', 107 *AJIL* (2013) 342.

451 Interim Report of the Commission of Experts Established Pursuant to Security Council Resolution 780 (1992), UN Doc. S/25274 (9 February 1993); Letter Dated 5 October 1993 from the Secretary-General to the President of the Security Council, UN Doc. S/26545, Annex: Second Interim Report of the Commission of Experts Established Pursuant to Security Council Resolution 780 (1992); Letter Dated 24 May 1994 from the Secretary-General to the President of the Security Council, UN Doc. S/1994/674, Annex: Final Report of the Commission of Experts Established Pursuant to Security Council Resolution 780 (1992).

452 Report of the Secretary-General Pursuant to Paragraph 2 of Security Council Resolution 808, UN Doc. S/25704 (3 May 1993), paras. 29, 34–35. Furthermore Larissa van den Herik, 'Using Custom to Reconceptualize Crimes Against Humanity', in Shane Darcy, Joseph Powderly (eds), *Judicial Creativity at the International Criminal Tribunal* (OUP 2010) 98; Nersessian (n 167) 239.

453 Report of the Secretary-General (n 452), para. 35. Confirmed by: *Prosecutor v Jelisić*, Case No IT-95-10-T (14 December 1999), para. 60.

subjective approach, though for the crime of persecution rather than genocide.[454] The Trial Chamber held that 'the civilian population subjected to such discrimination was identified by the perpetrators of the discriminatory measures'.[455] In 1999, the ICTR pronounced two judgments that gradually distanced themselves from *Akayesu*, but did not dare follow the innovative approach of *Nikolić*. The first judgment was the *Rutaganda* case that highlighted

> the concepts of national, ethnical, racial and religious groups have been researched extensively and that, at present, there are no generally and internationally accepted precise definitions thereof. Each of these concepts must be assessed in the light of a particular political, social and cultural context.[456]

The Trial Chamber held that 'membership of a group is, in essence, a subjective rather than an objective concept'.[457] Importantly, the judges did not refer to group membership of an ethnic group only, but extended their analysis to all four protected groups. The Tribunal went on to note: 'The victim is perceived by the perpetrator of genocide as belonging to a group slated for destruction. In some instances, the victim may perceive himself/herself as belonging to the said group'.[458] In requiring the groups to be relatively stable and permanent, *Rutaganda* in part followed *Akayesu*.[459] But it also took a cautious step toward a (partially) subjective approach. In advocating a perpetrator-based subjective approach, alternatively also a victim-based approach, with due consideration of contextual (objective) elements, the judgment set aside some important precedents.[460] The reactions of academia to the judgment were varied.[461] Boas and co-authors deplore the 'vague, fact-dependent formulation that [unfortunately] has been adopted by most of the judgments to date'.[462] According to the authors, *Rutaganda* echoed the subjective perception branch of the law on persecution as a crime against humanity.[463] However, Chapter 5 on the crime of persecution

454 See Chapter 5 on the crime of persecution.

455 *Prosecutor v Nikolić*, Case No IT-94–2-R61, Review of Indictment Pursuant to Rule 61 of the Rules of Procedure and Evidence (20 October 1995), para. 27.

456 *Prosecutor v Rutaganda*, Case No ICTR-96–3-T (6 December 1999), para. 56.

457 Ibid.

458 Ibid.

459 Ibid para. 57. *Prosecutor v Musema*, Case No ICTR-96–13-A, Trial Judgment (27 January 2000), paras. 161–163 applied the exact same elements. See Chapter 3.6.3 for discussion of the permanent and stable requirement.

460 *Prosecutor v Rutaganda*, Case No ICTR-96–3-T (6 December 1999), para. 57. The *Rutaganda* judgment was rendered by the same bench of judges who decided *Akayesu*, which explains their cautiousness in applying a progressive approach. See also Lisson (n 195) 1465; Amann (n 128) 107; Verdirame (n 160) 592 and 594.

461 Akhavan (n 185) 1002; Young (n 348) 12; Klann, McKenzie (n 357) 28.

462 Ibid 175.

463 Boas, Bischoff, Reid (n 180) 174.

will demonstrate that the perception-based approach developed independently for the crime of persecution and took a slightly different direction than for the crime of genocide.[464]

The other judgment of 1999, in the case of *Kayishema and Ruzindana*, presented an alternative approach:

> An ethnic group is one whose members share a common language and culture; or, a group which distinguishes itself, as such (self identification); or, a group identified as such by others, including perpetrators of the crimes (identification of others). A racial group is based on hereditary physical traits often identified with geography. A religious group includes denomination or mode of worship or a group sharing common beliefs.[465]

The clear separation by semicolons and the word 'or' confirms that the Trial Chamber was willing to apply three alternative methods of identifying an ethnical group: an objective approach to ethnicity; the perpetrator's perception of the victims; or their own self-perception.[466] The fact that the racial (and religious) group is listed later in the text and without any alternatives for its identification should not impede the application of these three possibilities for its identification. The judgment for no apparent reason omits to define the national group. A possible explanation might be the Trial Chamber's assumption that the Hutu and Tutsi could not possibly be two distinct national groups.[467]

Kayishema and Ruzindana was of major significance in the further development of the group membership concept. According to Verdirame, this judgment acknowledged that collective identities are social constructs, so-called 'imagined identities', that depend entirely on variable and contingent perceptions rather than on verifiable social facts.[468] Nevertheless, despite innovatively applying a subjective approach, the Trial Chamber in defining a racial group 'based on hereditary physical traits often identified with geography' reverts to what appears to be an objective approach. As such, it largely

464 See particularly Chapter 5.3.4.

465 *Prosecutor v Kayishema and Ruzindana*, Case No ICTR-95-1-T (21 May 1999), para. 98.

466 Ibid para. 291.

467 For a discussion of 'national group' see Carola Lingaas, 'Defining the Protected Groups of Genocide Through the Case Law of International Courts', *International Crimes Database Brief* (2015) <www.internationalcrimesdatabase.org/upload/documents/20151217T122733-Lingaas%20Final%20ICD%20Format.pdf>, pp. 5–6.

468 Verdirame (n 160) 592 with reference to Benedict Anderson, *Imagined Communities: Reflections on the Origin and Spread of Nationalism* (Verso 3rd revised ed 2006). Nersessian categorises *Kayishema* as taking an objective approach because it focused on an objective determination of the group's status, rather than linking it to the perpetrator's perception [Nersessian (n 162) 308]. However, the later reference to the *Kayishema* case in *Jelisić* shows that the ICTY understood it to take a subjective approach [*Prosecutor v Jelisić*, Case No IT-95-10-T (14 December 1999), para. 70, footnote 95].

adhered to *Akayesu*'s definition.[469] Some commentators were quick to register their disapproval of *Kayishema and Ruzindana*'s approach for allowing the perpetrator's intent to define the crime of genocide.[470] Payam Akhavan worried that such a purely subjective test could lead to a theoretical absurdity, whereby a perpetrator could define virtually any group as ethnic or racial, irrespective of its objective attributes.[471] He called some kind of objective contours of the group's existence in order to coincide with the purpose of the Genocide Convention.[472] Now while the objective recognisability of the protected group is certainly preferable in matters of proof in a trial, it ought not, nevertheless, be legally required since it disregards the fact that the victim group is ultimately created in the mind of the perpetrator and mirrored in his *dolus specialis.* Akhavan furthermore perceives the self-identification by the victims as problematic, since it could 'trump the intention of the perpetrator'.[473] Indeed, past genocides have forcefully demonstrated that perpetrators did not respect the victim's self-identification. During the Nazi regime, for example, even nonbelieving Jews were targeted, based entirely on the Nazis' own definition of racially inferior groups.[474]

In *Jelisić*, the ICTY Trial Chamber expressly chose to follow in part the subjective approach taken by the ICTR in *Kayishema and Ruzindana*.[475] 'It is the stigmatisation of a group as a distinct national, ethnical or racial unit by the community which allows it to be determined whether a targeted population constitutes a national, ethnical or racial group in the eyes of the alleged perpetrators', the Chamber emphasised.[476] For no apparent reason this statement omits the religious group, only to reintroduce it in the following paragraph of the judgment.[477] The judges then go on to make the following important statement:

> [T]o attempt to define a . . . racial group today using objective and scientifically irreproachable criteria would be a perilous exercise whose result would not necessarily correspond to the perception of the persons concerned

469 Also recognised by Boot (n 232) 432; Verdirame (n 160) 593. See Chapter 3.6 on the *Akayesu* judgment.

470 Zahar, Sluiter (n 337) 162; Kress (n 156) 461, 474–475.

471 Akhavan 2016 (n 173) 99; Akhavan (n 185) 1002.

472 Akhavan (n 185) 1002. Similarly Schabas (n 254) 39; Schabas 2001 (n 135) 455–456; Demko (n 35) 231.

473 Akhavan 2016 (n 173) 99; Akhavan (n 185) 1002. Accord: Demko (n 35) 237–238. Disaccord: May (n 15) 97.

474 See Chapters 2.4 and 2.5. Discussed in Verdeja (n 100) 31; Fournet (n 188) 109; Verdirame (n 160) 589.

475 *Prosecutor v Jelisić*, Case No IT-95–10-T (14 December 1999), para. 70, footnote 95.

476 ibid para. 70. *Prosecutor v Sikirica*, Case No IT-95–8-T, Judgment on Defence Motions to Acquit (3 September 2001), para. 88, also refers to this statement.

477 *Prosecutor v Jelisić*, Case No IT-95–10-T (14 December 1999), para. 71.

> by such categorisation. Therefore, it is more appropriate to evaluate the status of a . . . racial group from the point of view of those persons who wish to single that group out from the rest of the community. The Trial Chamber consequently elects to evaluate membership in a . . . racial group using a subjective criterion.[478]

Although it refers to *Kayishema and Ruzindana*, the *Jelisić* trial judgment strictly speaking took a different approach. The former applied a subjective approach to defining group membership and refers to either the perpetrator's or the victims' perception. *Jelisić*, however, relied exclusively on the 'eyes of the alleged perpetrators'. While both take a subjective approach, they vary as to the source of perception. As the judgment states, its position corresponds to that of *Nikolić*, according to which the population was identified by the perpetrators.[479] Albeit innovatively taking a subjective approach, the *Jelisić* judgment cites an academic work from 1959 that describes the protected groups as containing

> externally perceptible quality or characteristic which the victim has in common with the other members of the group, which makes him distinct from the rest of the society in the criminal mind of his attacker and which for that very reason causes the attacker to commit the crime against such marked and indicated individual.[480]

'Externally perceptible quality' indicates an objective approach to identifying a group member by means of visible characteristics. The reference to the perpetrator's criminal mind, however, weakens such objectivity. While the Trial Chamber in *Jelisić* indeed did take a subjective approach, it did not follow the prosecutor's suggestion in the pre-trial brief: 'Ethnicity as a distinctive identity is a subjective concept determined primarily by self-identification and community acceptance rather than by objective factors'.[481] The prosecutor suggests a victim-based subjective approach, determined by the victims' self-identification (and community acceptance). As the following analysis shows, not a single judgment ever took a purely victim-based approach, arguably because this approach does not reflect the genocidal process of othering. In 2004, the ICTY Trial Chamber in *Brđanin* confirmed the *Jelisić* approach, but went further by stating that the relevant protected group

478 Ibid para. 70. Discussed in Slye, van Schaack (n 160) 226; Lippman (n 148) 506.

479 *Prosecutor v Jelisić*, Case No IT-95–10-T (14 December 1999), para. 70, footnote 96 with reference to *Prosecutor v Nikolić*, Case No IT- 94–2-R61, Review of Indictment Pursuant to Rule 61 of the Rules of Procedure and Evidence (20 October 1995), para. 27.

480 *Prosecutor v Jelisić*, Case No IT-95–10-T (14 December 1999), para. 67, footnote 88 (emphasis omitted) with reference to Drost (n 206) 124.

481 *Prosecutor v Jelisić and Češić*, Case No IT-95–10-PT, Prosecutor's Pre-Trial Brief (19 November 1998), p. 16, para. 4.7.

> may be identified by means of the subjective criterion of the stigmatisation of the group, notably by the perpetrators of the crime, on the basis of its perceived . . . racial . . . characteristics. In some instances, the victim may perceive himself . . . to belong to the aforesaid group.[482]

The Tribunal thereby approached the *Kayishema and Ruzindana* judgment, accentuating the perpetrator's stigmatisation, but also permitting the victim's own group identification. Nonetheless, *Brđanin* demanded objective criteria in defining the protected group: 'The correct determination of the relevant protected group has to be made on a case-by-case basis, consulting both objective and subjective criteria. This is so because subjective criteria alone may not be sufficient to determine the group'.[483] In a footnote, the judges conclude: 'The Trial Chamber finds that the concept of "race" includes "ethnicity", which it finds more appropriate to refer to in the context of the present case'.[484]

The ICTY *Blagojević and Jokić* trial judgment for most of its reasoning followed *Brđanin* and found 'that the correct determination of the relevant protected group has to be made on a case-by-case basis, consulting both objective and subjective criteria'.[485] It too considered essential the criterion of stigmatisation of the group, notably by the perpetrators of the crime, on the basis of its perceived national, ethnical, racial, or religious characteristics.[486] The *Tolimir* judgment of 2012 referred to both *Brđanin* and *Jelisić* and confirmed that the group must have a particular, distinct identity and be defined by its common characteristics rather than a lack thereof.[487] It failed to specify whether 'the common characteristics' are objectively determinable or could be perceived as such. In referring to *Brđanin* that relied on the perpetrator's group identification,[488] it can be assumed that *Tolimir* also took a perpetrator-based subjective approach, but with due consideration of objective criteria, because it held that 'the determination of the group is to be made on a case-by-case basis, using both objective and subjective criteria'.[489]

The 2001 *Bagilishema* judgment confirmed the difficulties of an objective group definition. According to the ICTR Trial Chamber, the concept of racial group, *inter alia*, must be assessed in the light of a particular political, social, historical, and cultural context.[490] While the 'membership of the targeted group

482 *Prosecutor v Brđanin*, Case No IT-99–36-T (1 September 2004), para. 683; Schabas (n 4) 127.
483 *Prosecutor v Brđanin*, Case No IT-99–36-T (1 September 2004), para. 684.
484 Ibid para. 992, footnote 2484.
485 *Prosecutor v Blagojević and Jokić*, Case No IT-02–60-T (17 January 2005), para. 667.
486 Ibid.
487 *Prosecutor v Tolimir*, Case No IT-05–88/2-T (12 December 2012), para. 735. The judgment referred to the case of *Prosecutor v Stakić*, Case No IT-97–24-A (22 March 2006), paras. 19–21. See discussion on positive and negative definitions in Chapter 3.9.3.
488 *Prosecutor v Tolimir*, Case No IT-05–88/2-T (12 December 2012), para. 735, footnote 3095.
489 Ibid para. 735.
490 *Prosecutor v Bagilishema*, Case No ICTR-95–1A-T (7 June 2001), para. 65.

must be an objective feature of the society in question, there is also a subjective dimension'.[491] With regard to such subjective approach, 'the perpetrators of genocide', the Chamber emphasised, 'may characterise the targeted group in ways that do not fully correspond to conceptions of the group shared generally . . . . In such a case . . . the victim could be considered . . . as a member of the protected group'.[492] In *Bagilishema*, the Trial Chamber demands ('must be') that the group is an objective feature of society.[493] In doing so, the judgment seemingly excludes groups that are racial (or national, ethnical, or religious) in the mind of the perpetrator only. Alternatively, this statement could also be read to refer to the group's pre-genocidal existence. However, the judgment cautiously opens the door slightly to a perpetrator-based approach: the victims 'could be considered' protected members of a victim group even if they or society did not share such conception. In sum, *Bagilishema* largely built on an objective approach with due consideration of the perpetrator-based subjective approach.[494] In the view of Lüders, the *Bagilishema* trial judgment was a turning point in the ICTR's jurisprudence from an objective to a subjective approach.[495] This study, however, considers earlier judgments, in particular *Jelisić*, as more progressive for recognising the significance of the perpetrator's perception of the group and his acts of singling it out for destruction. In reference to *Bagilishema*, the *Ndindabahizi* trial judgment held that 'the subjective intentions (perceptions) of the perpetrators are of primary importance'.[496] At first sight, the Trial Chamber seemed to take a subjective perpetrator-based approach. However, it then held that physical traits were an important, if not decisive, indicator of ethnic identity in Rwanda in 1994.[497] More precisely, the judgment describes the victim Nors, who had a Rwandan mother and German father, as having 'the physical traits of a Tutsi, suggesting that he was perceived to be part-Tutsi'[498] and 'was targeted because he was understood to be, at least in part, Tutsi'.[499] Albeit relating to physical appearances, the judgment refrains from anthropologically verifying such claims. Instead, the judges rely fully on the perpetrator's understanding.

491 Ibid.
492 Ibid. The Appeals Chamber did not reverse these issues in its judgment. Similarly: *Prosecutor v Nahimana* et al., Case No ICTR-99–52-A (28 November 2007), para 496.
493 *Prosecutor v Rutaganda*, Case No ICTR-96–3-T (6 December 1999), para. 55 did also note the political, social, and cultural context, thereby being the real turning point in the ICTR's jurisdiction.
494 Discussed in the ICJ *Application of Genocide Convention* (*Bosnia and Herzegovina* v *Serbia and Montenegro*), Document Nr. CR 2006/43, Public sitting (8 May 2006), pp. 36–37.
495 Lüders (n 156) 57.
496 *Prosecutor v Ndindabahizi*, Case No ICTR-01–71-I, Trial Judgment (15 July 2004), para. 468.
497 Ibid paras. 468–469.
498 Ibid para. 467.
499 Ibid para. 469. See also discussion in Chapter 3.9.4.

The *Kajelijeli* trial judgment of 2003 acknowledged the problems of an objective group definition:

> [T]he said concept [of national, religious, racial, or ethnical groups] enjoys no generally or internationally accepted definition, rather each concept must be assessed in the light of a particular political, social, historical and cultural context. . . . [M]embership of a group is, in essence, a subjective rather than an objective concept [where] the victim is perceived by the perpetrator of genocide as belonging to a group slated for destruction. A determination of the categorised groups should be made on a case-by-case basis, by reference to both objective and subjective criteria.[500]

The Tribunal relied primarily on a subjective approach building on the perpetrator's perception. It nevertheless demanded a categorisation on a case-by-case basis, with reference to objective as well as subjective elements. It remains unclear whether the judgment considers the political, social, historical, and cultural context the required objective criteria – or whether other elements would have to be present. In the case against *Semanza*, the ICTR Trial Chamber acknowledged a certain degree of incoherence in its jurisprudence on the protected groups of genocide:

> The Statute of the Tribunal does not provide any insight into whether the group that is the target of an accused's genocidal intent is to be determined by objective or subjective criteria or by some hybrid formulation. The various Trial Chambers of this Tribunal have found that the determination . . . ought to be assessed on a case-by-case basis by reference to the *objective* particulars of a given social or historical context, and by the *subjective* perceptions of the perpetrators.[501]

It thereby endorsed earlier decisions that applied a mixed objective-subjective approach. Cryer and co-authors consider *Semanza* as illustrative of a settled practice by the Tribunals in identifying the group.[502] Whether or not the determination of a group depends on objective and subjective elements can, at this point, be left unanswered. It is, however, doubtful that a settled practice has in fact emerged, considering the inconsistent case law on the matter. The trial judgment against Seromba, a Roman Catholic priest who allowed his church to be bulldozed with 1,500 Tutsi refugees inside, concluded that case-law,

500 *Prosecutor v Kajelijeli*, Case No ICTR-98–44A-T (1. December 2003), para. 811. The *Kamuhanda* judgment uses nearly the exact same wording [*Prosecutor v Kamuhanda*, Case No ICTR-95–54A-T (22 January 2004), para. 630].

501 *Prosecutor v Semanza*, Case No ICTR-97–20-T (15 May 2003), para. 317 (emphasis in original).

502 Cryer (n 8) 213.

particularly *Semanza*, *Rutaganda*, and *Musema*, favoured a subjective standpoint, a conclusion that this study is unable to agree with.[503] Nonetheless, *Seromba* recognised that the perpetrator of the crime perceives his victim as belonging to the group targeted for destruction, but the determination of the targeted group had to be made on a case-by-case basis.[504] In wording resemblant of *Semanza*, the ICTR Trial Chamber in *Gacumbitsi* held:

> Membership of a group is a subjective rather than an objective concept. The victim is perceived by the perpetrator of genocide as belonging to a group slated for destruction, but the determination of a targeted group must be made on a case-by-case basis, consulting both objective and subjective criteria. Indeed, in a given situation, the perpetrator, just like the victim, may believe that there is an objective criterion for determining membership of an ethnic group on the basis of an administrative mechanism for the identification of an individual's ethnic group.[505]

As in earlier cases, the *Gacumbitsi* trial judgment recognised the perpetrator's identification and stigmatisation of the victims and required both objective and subjective criteria. The judges referred to what could be considered an objectivised subjective approach, in that 'administrative mechanism for the identification' (eg Rwandan ID cards designating the individual's ethnicity) become significant in determining group membership, even if such determination was not grounded in factual differences between the groups.[506] 'Evidence must also be tendered', the judgment continues, 'to show either that the victim belonged to the targeted ethnical, racial, national or religious group or that the perpetrator of the crime believed that the victim belonged to the said group'.[507] This statement links group determination to proof of the *dolus specialis*. Apparently, the prosecution is left with two options: either prove the existence of an ethnic, racial, national, or religious group or alternatively prove the perpetrator's belief that such a group did exist. This was confirmed in *Muhimana*: 'The Prosecution also has the burden of proving either that the victim belongs to the targeted . . . group or that the perpetrator of the crime believed that the victim belonged to the group'.[508]

Krstić was different from any other ICTR or ICTY judgment in that it applied an ensemble (or four corner) approach, where the four protected groups are

503 *Prosecutor v Seromba*, Case No ICTR-2001–66-T (13 December 2006), paras. 210–285.
504 Ibid para. 318.
505 *Prosecutor v Gacumbitsi*, Case No ICTR-2001–64-T (17 June 2004), para. 254.
506 See more on the objectivised subjective approach in Chapter 5.11. Furthermore Young (n 348) 16; Eltringham (n 313) 31, confirming that the ID cards' objectivity proceeded solely from subjective racism.
507 *Prosecutor v Gacumbitsi*, Case No ICTR-2001–64-T (17 June 2004), para. 255.
508 *Prosecutor v Muhimana*, Case No ICTR-95–1B-T (28 April 2005), para. 500.

construed as a single entity. Chapter 3.5.2.2 has critically discussed this approach, the content of which need not be repeated here. The *Krstić* Trial Chamber acknowledged that the differentiation of the protected groups of genocide on the basis of scientifically objective criteria would be inconsistent with the object and purpose of the Genocide Convention.[509] In considering an objective determination as incoherent with the Convention's object and purpose, the judgment seemingly *a contrario* advocated a subjective approach. Indeed, it identified 'the relevant group by using as a criterion the stigmatisation of the group, notably by the perpetrators of the crime, on the basis of its perceived national, ethnical, racial or religious characteristics'.[510] In appreciating the perpetrator's stigmatisation of perceived characteristics of the victim group, *Krstić* applies a perpetrator-based subjective approach. It is remarkable that *Krstić*, albeit advocating for an ensemble approach by which the four adjectives describe the same phenomenon, nonetheless concludes that the Bosnian Muslims constituted a national group.[511] In doing so, the judgment assigns the Bosnian Muslims to one of the four exhaustive victim group categories.

In 2006, the ICTY Appeals Chamber in *Stakić* provided an overview of earlier judgments. It asserted that *Krstić* and *Rutaganda* did not define the target groups subjectively only. Rather, according to the Appeals Chamber, *Krstić* concluded that the stigmatisation by the perpetrators could be used as 'a criterion' when defining target groups.[512] Furthermore, *Stakić* argued that, according to *Rutaganda*, national, ethnical, racial, and religious identities were largely subjective concepts. Genocide could therefore occur if the perpetrator perceived the victim as belonging to the targeted group.[513] Nonetheless, *Rutaganda* also required objective elements, as did other ICTR trial judgments.[514] It is the view of this study that the analysis in *Stakić* of the *Krstić* judgment should be challenged. In *Krstić*, the ICTY Trial Chamber was very articulate in rejecting scientific, objective criteria. It is correct that *Krstić* decided that the perpetrator's stigmatisation could be used as a criterion in identifying the protected group. But it also held that the stigmatisation of the group was decisive, 'notably by the perpetrators of the crime, on the basis of . . . perceived . . . characteristics'.[515] The words 'notably' and 'perceived' both point to the perpetrator. It would therefore seem more appropriate to acknowledge the stigmatisation by the perpetrator as *the* – and not only *a* – defining criterion. For the sake of this overall analysis, *Stakić* appears to have endorsed a mixed subjective-objective

509 *Prosecutor v Krstić*, Case No IT-98–33-T (2 August 2001), paras. 541 and 556.

510 Ibid para. 557. *Prosecutor v Blagojević and Jokić*, Case No IT-02–60-T (17 January 2005), para. 667 refers to this statement.

511 *Prosecutor v Krstić*, Case No IT-98–33-T (2 August 2001), paras. 559–560.

512 *Prosecutor v Stakić*, Case No IT-97–24-A (22 March 2006), para. 25.

513 Ibid.

514 Ibid.

515 *Prosecutor v Krstić*, Case No IT-98–33-T (2 August 2001), para. 557.

approach. Finally, this analysis ends with the *Muvunyi* trial judgment of 2006. The Trial Chamber II then held that since the ICTR Statute did not

> clearly establish the criteria for determining protected groups . . . , the Trial Chambers have tended to decide the matter on a case-by-case basis, taking into consideration both the objective and subjective particulars, including the historical context and the perpetrator's intent.[516]

The judgment appears to take a mixed objective-subjective approach. Two years later, the Appeals Chamber annulled the sentence against *Muvunyi*. The re-trial did not discuss group identification.[517] Although the annulled judgment strictly speaking is no longer legally valid, it nevertheless gives an insight into the methods of determining the protected groups. Since later cases, like *Tolimir*,[518] referred to the 2006 judgment, it continues to be legally relevant.

The analysis of the case law of the *ad hoc* tribunals has revealed three issues: while the various chambers quite obviously have moved in the direction of a more subjective approach and made an effort to develop international criminal jurisprudence accordingly, they nevertheless continue to require proof of objective elements. Although there is a preponderance of judgments applying a mixed approach, the jurisprudence is far from consistent.[519] Furthermore, the judgments, apart from isolated exceptions, did not identify the legal sources in support of the subjective approach in defining the victim groups of genocide.[520] A further contentious issue is the positive or negative definition of the protected groups, which the next section will discuss.

3.9.3 Positive and negative definition of a protected group

The question of what constitutes a protected group and who its members are can be answered positively or negatively. The *Jelisić* Trial Chamber explains:

> A group may be stigmatised . . . by way of positive or negative criteria. A 'positive approach' would consist of the perpetrators of the crime distinguishing a group by the characteristics which they deem to be particular to a national, ethnical, racial or religious group. A 'negative approach' would consist of identifying individuals as not being part of the group to which the perpetrators of the crime consider that they themselves belong and which to them displays specific national, ethnical, racial or religious

516 *Prosecutor v Muvunyi*, Case No ICTR-00–55A-T (12 September 2006), para 484.
517 *Prosecutor v Muvunyi*, Case No ICTR-00–55A-T (11 February 2010).
518 *Prosecutor v Tolimir*, Case No IT-05–88/2-T (12 December 2012), para. 735.
519 See Chapter 3.13.2 with a graphical illustration.
520 Mugwanya (n 315) 275. Exception: *Prosecutor v Bagilishema*, Case No 95–1A-T (7 June 2001), para. 65 with reference to the Report of the Commission of Experts.

> characteristics. Thereby, all individuals thus rejected would, by exclusion, make up a distinct group.[521]

In a nutshell: a positive approach describes a group by way of its characteristics and a negative approach by what it is not. In the example of the conflict in Bosnia and Herzegovina, the description of a group as 'non-Serbs' would be a negative approach. Despite conceptual challenges to it, courts have consistently rejected the negative approach. For instance, the 1996 Review of the Indictments against Karadžić and Mladić considered whether the accused had a genocidal intent to destroy one of the protected groups. The judges assumed that the intent was given with respect to the non-Serbian groups, especially the Bosnian Muslims,[522] thereby negatively defining the victims. The trial judgment against Karadžić, however, then positively defined the protected group as 'Bosnian Muslim' and 'Bosnian Croats',[523] as did the trial judgment against Mladić, explicitly stating that the 'protected group must be defined positively'.[524]

In *Brđanin*, the ICTY Trial Chamber rejected group identification by exclusion, ie by negative criteria.[525] In doing so, the Tribunal reversed the *Krnojelac* approach that understood the term 'non-Serb' to connote both religious and political distinctions, 'but does not proceed upon the basis that different ethnicities within the former Yugoslavia constitute different races'.[526] Despite not providing reasons for barring a negative group definition, the *Brđanin* judgment was later confirmed by the ICJ in the *Application of the Genocide Convention* (*Bosnia and Herzegovina v Serbia and Montenegro*):[527]

> It is a group which must have particular positive characteristics – national, ethnical, racial or religious – and not the lack of them . . . . [T]he crime requires an intent to destroy a collection of people who have a particular group identity. It is a matter of who those people are, not who they are not.[528]

Not only did the ICJ confirm the positive identification of the four protected groups and recognise the significance of the victim's group identity, it also

521 *Prosecutor v Jelisić*, Case No IT-95–10-T (14 December 1999), para. 71. This holding was not challenged on appeal.

522 *Prosecutor v Karadžić and Mladić*, Case No IT-95–5-R61 and IT-95–18-R61, Review of the Indictments Pursuant to Rule 61 of the Rules of Procedure and Evidence (11 July 1996), para. 94.

523 *Prosecutor v Karadžić,* Case No IT-95–5–18-T (25 March 2016), paras. 2573–2574. In discussing the evidence of genocidal intent, the Trial Chamber, however, refers to 'non-Serbs' (ibid para. 2596).

524 *Prosecutor v. Mladić*, Case No IT-09–92-T (22 November 2017), para. 3436.

525 *Prosecutor v Brđanin*, Case No IT-99–36-T (1 September 2004), para. 685.

526 *Prosecutor v Krnojelac*, Case No IT-97–25-T (15 March 2002), p. 11, footnote 56.

527 *Application of the Genocide Convention* (*Bosnia and Herzegovina v Serbia and Montenegro*), ICJ Judgment (2007), paras. 191–196.

528 Ibid para. 193.

referred to its own precedent, the 1951 *Advisory Opinion on the Reservations to the Genocide Convention*, where it had declared the Convention's objective to be the safeguarding of the very existence of certain human groups.[529] Such an understanding of genocide required a positive identification of the group.[530] The ICJ remarked that the ICTY Appeals Chamber in *Stakić* had reached the same conclusion for the same reasons. Indeed, *Stakić* decided that the term

> "as such" has great significance, for it shows that the offence requires intent to destroy a collection of people who have a particular group identity. Yet when a person targets individuals because they lack a particular national, ethnical, racial, or religious characteristic, the intent is not to destroy particular groups with particular identities as such, but simply to destroy individuals because they lack certain national, ethnical, racial or religious characteristics.[531]

The Appeals Chamber concluded that a negative group definition would be incompatible with the drafting history of the Genocide Convention.[532] Similarly, the majority in the ICC Pre-Trial Chamber in *Al Bashir* opined that the targeted group of genocide had to have particular (national, ethnic, racial, or religious) characteristics and not a lack thereof. Again, the judges referred to the drafting history of the Genocide Convention where 'close attention to the positive identification of groups with specific distinguishing well-established, some said immutable, characteristics' was given.[533] The rejection of the negative definition has been held objectionable in that it overlooks the social realities on the ground, such as the identification and targeting methodologies employed by the perpetrator.[534] Indeed, a perpetrator could collectively define his victims as not belonging to his own group. Such has been pointed out by Judge Shahabuddeen in a partially dissenting opinion to the *Stakić* appeals judgment. In rejecting a purely perpetrator-based subjective approach, Shahabuddeen holds that members of a victim group could be defined positively as, for example Croats, while they simultaneously saw themselves as part of a larger non-Serb group collectively targeted for belonging to a group other than the perpetrator's. Shahabuddeen

529 *Reservations to the Genocide Convention*, ICJ Advisory Opinion (1951), p. 23.
530 *Application of the Genocide Convention* (*Bosnia and Herzegovina v Serbia and Montenegro*), ICJ Judgment (2007), para. 194.
531 *Prosecutor v Stakić*, Case No IT-97–24-A (22 March 2006), para. 20.
532 Ibid, para. 22. Confirmed in: *Prosecutor v Tolimir*, Case No IT-05–88/2-T (12 December 2012), para. 735.
533 *Prosecutor v Al Bashir*, ICC-02/05–01/09, Decision on the Prosecution's Application for a Warrant of Arrest against Omar Hassan Ahmad Al Bashir (4 March 2009), para. 135.
534 Mugwanya (n 315) 99.

recognises that the existence of a non-Serb group, although negatively defined, was an evidentiary, objective fact.[535] He remarks:

> Victims may belong to different component groups. However, it would be natural for the perpetrators to say, if that is their subjective perception, that such component groups have the common characteristic of belonging to a larger 'group' defined as being *other than* the group of the perpetrators; the victims themselves may share that view.[536]

Albeit earlier rejecting a perpetrator-based definition of the victim group, the judge precisely suggests such. His wording 'subjective perception' shows that the perpetrator alone can negatively define his victims. In reference to the Final Report of the Commission of Experts established pursuant to Security Council Resolution 780 (1992),[537] Shahabuddeen asserts that nothing prevented several different victim groups from being collectively defined as 'other' than that of the perpetrator.[538] With this argument, the judge recognises the importance of othering for the legal definition of the victim groups of the crime of genocide.

The negative definition of the victims as not belonging to the perpetrator's group should, despite contrary argumentation by the drafters of the Genocide Convention,[539] not be ignored. Undeniably, specific positively identified groups were what the drafters envisaged: during the Holocaust, the Jews were targeted based upon the Nazis' own 'imagined' definition.[540] Although the Jews were positively identifiable due to the Nuremberg racial laws, they could also be negatively defined as non-Aryans. There are numerous genocidal cases in which the perpetrator singled out his victims for being 'other' than his own group, such as in Armenia, Cambodia, and Guatemala. Some of these cases will be discussed later. Despite weighty arguments to the contrary, it can be concluded, in accordance with prevailing jurisprudence, that the protected groups of genocide ought to be positively defined: they are protected for their identity, not for their lack of characteristics.

535 *Prosecutor v Stakić*, Case No IT-97–24-A, Partly Dissenting Opinion of Judge Shahabuddeen (22 March 2006), paras. 11 and 17. See also Mohamed Shahabuddeen, ***International Criminal Justice at the Yugoslav Tribunal: A Judge's Recollection*** (OUP 2012) 194–195.

536 *Prosecutor v Stakić*, Case No IT-97–24-A, Partly Dissenting Opinion of Judge Shahabuddeen (22 March 2006), para. 17, emphasis in original. Confirmed in Shahabuddeen (n 535) 195.

537 Letter dated 24 May 1994 from the Secretary-General to the President of the Security Council, UN Doc. S/1994/674 (27 May 1994), Annex, Final Report of the Commission of Experts Established Pursuant to Security Council Resolution 780 (1992), para. 96.

538 Shahabuddeen (n 535) 194.

539 *Prosecutor v Stakić*, Case No IT-97–24-A (22 March 2006), paras. 20–22.

540 Rapley (n 81) 233; Schabas (n 439) 133. See Chapter 2.5.1 on the Nuremberg laws and Chapter 3.8.3 on *halakhic* definitions.

3.9.4 *Mistake of fact*

A perpetrator can be mistaken about a victim's group membership. Such a mistake is known as *error in persona* and negates the mental element since the legal correlation between the injured object of the act as imagined by the perpetrator and the one actually injured is lacking.[541] In this regard, Art. 32(1) Rome Statute states: 'A mistake of fact shall be a ground for excluding criminal responsibility only if it negates the mental element required by the crime'. If the perpetrator perceives his victims as members of a racial group and targets them for reasons of their group membership with the intent to destroy, he becomes criminally liable for genocide of a racial group. With the intent given, there is no case for negating the mental element. As a result, the misconception of a victim's objective group membership would therefore not be a mistake of fact. Rather, the acceptance of a subjective approach to defining the protected groups of genocide leads to the conclusion that attacks against people erroneously taken to be members of a group also amount to genocide, provided the special intent is given.[542] Seemingly, the subjective approach and the mistake of fact argument are mutually exclusive.[543]

The issue can be illustrated by way of an example: Perpetrator A attacks victim B whom he perceives to be member of a racial group. Objectively, however, there are no different racial groups, and A and B arguably belong to the same group. Since the group membership is created in the mind of the perpetrator, and he identifies his victims as another race, there is no mistake as to B's group affiliation. Rather, A targets B for what he believes to be racial group membership. In other words, if the perpetrator's intent is linked to his perception of a victim as a member of a racial group, there can be no *error in persona*. For a mistake-of-fact to occur, the law has to provide some category with which the victim can objectively be compared. George William Mugwanya asks whether the issue of mistakes in defining the group really is a question of definition or rather an issue of an attempt to commit the crime.[544] The two issues are interrelated and easily confusable. Art. 25(3)(f) Rome Statute, which is applicable to all crimes within the ICC's jurisdiction, including genocide, holds that an attempt is given when the crime does not occur because of circumstances independent of the perpetrator's intention. Again, an example can illustrate the issue: Perpetrator A has acquired weapons of mass destruction in anticipation of a genocidal massacre the next day. His intent is set to destroying group B, which he considers a race distinct from his own. In the evening, however, the

541 Mohamed Elewa Badar, *The Concept of Mens Rea in International Criminal Law: The Case for a Unified Approach* (Hart Publishing 2013) 295; Karin Calvo-Goller, *The Trial Proceedings of the International Criminal Court: ICTY and ICTR Precedents* (Martinus Nijhoff 2006) 199.

542 Ambrus (n 202) 945.

543 Ibid 948.

544 Mugwanya (n 315) 100 and 103. Similarly: Safferling (n 195) 166 and 169.

warehouse in which his weapons are stored burns down and A cannot execute his plan. This example shows that the perpetrator's intent remains intact, ie the destruction of a racial group. This legal construct is thus independent of the manner in which the perpetrator defines his victim group and cannot be confused with a mistake of fact.

International criminal tribunals have occasionally adjudicated cases of mistake of fact, not least the ICTR that dealt with attacks against Hutu who either opposed the killing spree or were wrongfully identified as Tutsi. The case against *Nahimana, Barayagwiza and Ngeze* (also known as the *Media* case) discusses genocidal acts committed against Hutu who were politically opposed to the regime. These Hutu were targeted because they sided with the persecuted Tutsi, hence for taking a political stance. The Trial Chamber concluded that acts committed against these victims were genocidal acts in furtherance of the killings of the Tutsi, which the defendants Nahimana and Ngeze in return considered to be an unlawful expansion of the protected groups.[545] The prosecutor argued that the Trial Chamber relied not only on the attacks perpetrated against Hutu; he considered the Trial Chamber's approach to be 'in line with established jurisprudence that groups targeted for genocide may be defined subjectively, on the basis of a variety of criteria, including the perception of the perpetrators themselves'.[546] The trial judgment concluded that the individual is the personification of the group: 'The Chamber considers that acts committed against Hutu opponents were committed on account of their support of the Tutsi ethnic group and in furtherance of the intent to destroy the Tutsi ethnic group'.[547]

The Appeals Chamber overturned the Trial Chamber decision, arguing that acts committed against Hutu political opponents did not constitute acts of genocide

> because the victim of an act of genocide must have been targeted by reason of the fact that he or she belong to a protected group' and 'the group of "Hutu political opponents" or the group of "Tutsi individuals and Hutu political opponents" does not constitute a "national, ethnical, racial or religious group".[548]

In other words: had the perpetrator perceived a Hutu as a Tutsi and killed him for this reason, the act would be genocide, even though the victim 'objectively'

545 *Prosecutor v Nahimana* et al., Case No ICTR-99–52-A (28 November 2007), para. 493, quoting Nahimana Appellant's Brief, paras. 564–566 and Ngeze Appellant's Brief, paras. 337–338.

546 *Prosecutor v Nahimana* et al., Case No ICTR-99–52-A (28 November 2007), para 494, quoting Respondent's Brief, paras. 447–449.

547 *Prosecutor v Nahimana* et al., Case No ICTR-99–52-T (3 December 2003), para. 948.

548 *Prosecutor v Nahimana* et al., Case No ICTR-99–52-A (28 November 2007), para. 496. The ICTR Trial Chamber III concluded similarly in *Prosecutor v Nchamihigo*, Case No ICTR-01–63-T (12 November 2008), paras. 337–338.

was not Tutsi and therefore lacked membership of the targeted group.[549] The Hutu who sympathised with Tutsi were not targeted for being members of a racial, ethnical, national, or religious group; their elimination was deemed necessary for the successful execution of the genocide of the Tutsi population.[550] There was no genocidal intent to exterminate Hutu assisting the Tutsi, thereby falling short of the required *dolus specialis*.[551]

In *Ndindabahizi*, discussed in Chapter 3.9.2, the ICTR Trial Chamber was faced with the murder of Nors, the son of a Rwandan mother and a German father, who witnesses described as having 'the physical traits of a Tutsi, suggesting that he was perceived to be part-Tutsi'.[552] Nors' identity was complex, since ethnicity in Rwanda was usually transmitted from the father to offspring.[553] In addition to being described as part-Tutsi, other witnesses testified that Nors was killed because he was white or half-caste.[554] In its assessment, the Chamber placed full weight on the subjective intentions of the perpetrator, who was found guilty of genocide notwithstanding the 'wrong' characterisation of the victim.[555] The killing of Nors occurred as a consequence of the accused's instigation that all Tutsis be killed, thereby providing circumstantial support for the inference that he was, in fact, killed for that reason.[556]

This discussion on mistake of fact concludes the overall analysis of the *ad hoc* tribunals' jurisprudence. The following section will move out of the strictly legal hemisphere into the quasi-legal jurisprudence of the Commission of Inquiry on Darfur and its cutting-edge definition of the victim group of genocide.

3.10 Darfur Commission: imagined group identities

An insurgency against the government of Sudan began in Darfur in late 2002, leading to retaliations by the government and its allied forces, mostly proxy militias, in 2003. Government planes bombed villages in Darfur, followed by Janjaweed militias entering the targeted villages, looting, raping, and killing the villagers, as well as poisoning their water supplies before burning the villages to the ground.[557] Acting under Chapter VII of the UN Charter, the

549 See Chapter 3.6.5 on discussion on Hutu and Tutsi ethnicity.

550 *Prosecutor v Nchamihigo*, Case No ICTR-01–63-T (12 November 2008), para. 338; *Prosecutor v Serushago*, Case No ICTR-98–03-S (5 February 1999), p. 10, para. xxii.

551 Confirmed by Degni-Ségui (n 55) 5.

552 *Prosecutor v Ndindabahizi*, Case No ICTR-01–71-I, Trial Judgment (15 July 2004), para. 467.

553 Ibid.

554 Ibid paras. 467–469.

555 Ibid. Accord: Jallow (n 200) 454.

556 *Prosecutor v Ndindabahizi*, Case No ICTR-01–71-I, Trial Judgment (15 July 2004), para. 469. See Chapter 3.5.3.2 on issues of proof.

557 Report of the International Commission of Inquiry on Darfur, UN Doc. S/2005/60 (25 January 2005), pp. 3, 20–21, 24–25. For background information: Alex de Waal, 'Reflections on the Difficulties of Defining Darfur's Crisis as Genocide', 20 *Harvard Human Rights Journal* (2007) 27–29; van Schaack (n 309) 1104–1106.

Security Council adopted Resolution 1564 and requested the Secretary-General to inquire into the atrocities, especially to determine whether acts of genocide had occurred.[558] The Commission of Inquiry on Violations of International Humanitarian Law and Human Rights Law in Darfur (Darfur Commission) was chaired by the renowned legal scholar and former ICTY President Antonio Cassese. The Security Council later used the Commission's findings to refer the Darfur situation to the ICC.[559] In its conclusion, the Commission held that no genocide had occurred because the intent to destroy a group could not be proven.[560]

As soft law mechanisms, commissions of inquiry issue legally non-binding reports. Such reports of inquiry generally establish a set of facts, many of which are not directly tied up to legal categories. Their methodology does furthermore not follow strict rules of procedure and evidence.[561] In the execution of their respective mandate, however, the commissions have often gone beyond mere fact-finding and engaged profoundly with international criminal law.[562] In this regard, the Darfur Commission emphasised that, while not producing a legally binding report, it nonetheless adopted an approach proper to a judicial body.[563] The Commission noted that the international law of genocide contained a 'broad and loose terminology when indicating the various groups against which one can engage in acts of genocide, including references to notions that may overlap'.[564] However, the principle of effectiveness dictates that international rules are to be given maximum effect, hence suggesting that the provisions on genocide should be construed such as to render them as effective as possible in light of their object and purpose.[565] Paradoxically, the Commission acknowledges that the terminology of race is criticised as being universally outmoded or even fallacious,[566] but then proceeds to define racial groups in precisely such an outdated manner as 'sets of individuals sharing some hereditary physical traits or characteristics'.[567]

558 UN Doc. S/RES/1564 (18 September 2004); Report of the Darfur Commission (n 557), p. 2. See discussion in William Schabas, 'Has Genocide Been Committed in Darfur? The State Plan or Policy Element in the Crime of Genocide', in Ralph Henham, Paul Behrens (eds), *The Criminal Law of Genocide: International, Comparative and Contextual Aspects* (Ashgate 2007) 39; van Schaack (n 309) 1106–1110.

559 UN Doc. S/RES/1593 (31 March 2005). See Chapter 3.11.2 on the jurisprudence of the ICC.

560 Report of the Darfur Commission (n 557), paras. 514–515.

561 Larissa van den Herik, 'Accountability Through Fact-Finding: Appraising Inquiry in the Context of Srebrenica', 62 *Netherlands International Law Review* (2015) 297, 309–310.

562 Ibid 297.

563 Report of the Darfur Commission (n 557), para. 14.

564 Ibid para. 494.

565 Ibid. See Chapters 3.5.2.2 and 3.7.2 on the principle of effectiveness.

566 Report of the Darfur Commission (n 557), para 494.

567 Ibid. See discussion in van Schaack (n 309) 1115; de Waal (n 557) 28.

The Commission was confronted with atrocities that had been committed between tribal groups, which were challenging to categorise within the Genocide Convention's framework of protected groups. Not unlike the Hutu and Tutsi of the Rwandan genocide, the rival Darfuri groups shared certain characteristics and exhibited few objective differences.[568] The Commission referred to the ILC's Draft Code of Crimes of 1996 that considered tribal groups to fall within the scope of the definition of genocide.[569] Yet, in direct contradiction to the ILC, the Darfur Commission then held that tribes were not a protected group unless they also constituted a distinct racial, national, ethnical, or religious group.[570] The law extends its protection to four exclusive groups only and international criminal law should be narrowly interpreted due to the principle of legality. In respecting this limitation, the Darfur Commission's approach appears to be the more legally sound. In the opinion of the Commission, the purely objective 'stable and permanent' approach, as introduced by *Akayesu*, is rather questionable.[571] However, later in its report the Commission notes 'the object and scope . . . to protect from deliberate annihilation essentially stable and permanent human groups',[572] hence referring to stability and permanence nonetheless. The Commission concluded, when in doubt, one should also establish whether 1) a set of persons is perceived and in fact treated as belonging to one of the protected groups; and in addition 2) whether they consider themselves as belonging to one of those groups.[573] In adopting here a double-subjective approach, based on the perception of the perpetrators and the victims, the Commission analysed a gradual consolidation of the contrast between the groups.[574] The report recognises the importance of identity: the rebels were identified as 'African', whereas their opponents were seen as 'Arabs', although there were no objective grounds for such a distinction.[575] Indeed, the two groups shared the Islamic faith and Arabic language, and there was a high level of intermarriages, which blurred the differences between them.[576] Despite seemingly pledging a subjective approach, the Commission nevertheless

568 Ratner, Abrams, Bischoff (n 142) 35; van Schaack (n 309) 1116. See Chapters 3.6.2 and 3.6.5 on the classification of Tutsi.

569 ILC Draft Code of Crimes (1996), UN Doc. A/51/10, Commentary No 9 to Art. 17, p. 45.

570 Report of the Darfur Commission (n 557), paras. 496–497. In *Stakić*, the ICTY Appeals Chamber established that 'genocide was originally conceived of as the destruction of a race, tribe, nation or other group with a particular positive identity', which might indicate that tribes are protected under the law of genocide (*Prosecutor v Stakić*, Case No IT-97–24-A (22 March 2006), para. 21). See discussion in Schabas (n 4) 130.

571 Report of the Darfur Commission (n 557), para. 498. See Chapter 5.6.3 for a discussion of the stable and permanent requirement.

572 Report of the Darfur Commission (n 557), para. 501.

573 Ibid para. 498.

574 Ibid para. 510.

575 Ibid para. 509.

576 Ibid para. 508.

discussed the tribes' 'outward physical appearance'.[577] In doing so, it reverted to objective criteria it had earlier termed 'questionable'. Researchers have also recorded degradation and dehumanisation in Darfur, where witnesses testified that perpetrators shouted racial epithets such as 'all the people in the village are slaves, you make this area dirty, we are here to clean the area'.[578] The use of dehumanising language was extensively commented by the Darfur Commission too. It confirmed that the Janjaweed attackers called the 'African' villagers slaves, poison, *Zurga* (pejoratively for 'blacks'), threatening that they 'will not stay in this country'.[579]

The Darfur Commission implicitly refers to the ensemble approach, in considering that the Genocide Convention hinges 'on four categories of groups which, however, are no longer identified only by their objective connotations but also on the basis of the subjective perceptions of members of groups'.[580] Since unchallenged by states, the Commission declared this subjective interpretative expansion part of customary international law.[581] While there is an undisputable trend toward a subjective approach in defining the protected groups of genocide, there remains a large discrepancy in its judicial application.[582] Drawing a conclusion regarding the existence a new rule of customary law appears as premature today as it did in 2005, considering the lack of a uniform legal practice and an established *opinio juris* among the relevant actors.[583] Albeit not customary law (as yet), the Darfur Commission's analysis of the process of formation of perception and self-perception is appealing. It held that the creation of a subjective view generally found its origin in historical and social grounds: the 'other' group was seen as different and therefore opposed to one's own group. Gradually the process hardened and crystallised into a real and factual opposition, thereby leading to an objective contrast. The subjective standard merged with an objective reality and formed two objectively conflicting groups, one of which had the intention of destroying the other.[584] In addition to the two primary objective and subjective methods of determining group membership for the crime of genocide, the Darfur Commission seemingly added yet another category: the objectivised subjective approach. An initially subjective view of a group's differentness can, in the course of time, become objectivised if transferred from one generation to the next.[585] Eventually, the differentness

577 Ibid.
578 John Hagan, Wenona Rymond-Richmond, *Darfur and the Crime of Genocide* (CUP 2009) xxi–xxii, 8–9; van Schaack (n 309) 1116.
579 Report of the Darfur Commission (n 557), para. 511 and corresponding footnote 189.
580 Ibid para 501. See Chapter 3.5.2.2 on the ensemble approach.
581 Report of the Darfur Commission (n 557) para 501.
582 See Chapter 3.9.2 on the jurisprudence.
583 Accord: Schabas (n 151) 73.
584 Report of the Darfur Commission (n 557), para. 500.
585 ibid. Furthermore: Holslag (n 19) 99; Hiebert (n 20) 10; Anderson (n 468) 204–205; Nagan, Rodin (n 20) 137.

is considered a given fact, despite lacking a historically objective foundation. The timeframe required for such transition, however, remains unclear. Although the creation of the objectivised subjective approach is laudable for realising sociological processes in law,[586] the greatest innovation of the Darfur Commission was doubtless its recognition of imagined identities:

> [T]he approach taken to determine whether a group is a (fully) protected one has evolved from an objective to a subjective standard to take into account that "collective identities, and in particular ethnicity, are by their very nature social constructs, 'imagined' identities entirely dependent on variable and contingent perceptions, and not social facts, which are verifiable in the same manner as natural phenomena or physical facts".[587]

The importance of the concept of imagined identities lies in the acknowledgement that the victim groups of genocide, by their very nature, are phantasies, created in the mind of the perpetrator, and therefore not objectively definable. Moreover, the statement recognises the significance of identity for the crime of genocide. The future will tell whether other judgments apply the Darfur Commission's concept of imagined identities to cases of genocide. This book urges its full endorsement when the next judicial opportunity arises.

3.11 The jurisprudence of the ICC

3.11.1 The inclusion of the crime of genocide into the Rome Statute

Most delegations at the Rome Diplomatic Conference considered Arts. 2 (and 3) Genocide Convention to be an expression of customary law containing a generally acceptable definition.[588] Indeed, genocide was the only crime about which a quick and unanimous consensus was achieved.[589] The Cuban proposal to expand the protection to political and social groups led to some discussion,

586 Young (n 348) 21.

587 Report of the Darfur Commission (n 557), para. 499 (references omitted). For a discussion see Carola Lingaas, 'Imagined Identities: Defining the Racial Group in the Crime of Genocide', 10 *Genocide Studies and Prevention: An International Journal* (2016) 79–106.

588 UN Doc. A/CONF.183/C.1/SR.3 (17 June 1998), paras. 2, 20. Confirmed by Schabas (n 336) 129; Grover (n 222) 274; Boas, Bischoff, Reid (n 180) 198.

589 Mahnoush Arsanjani, 'The Rome Statute of the International Criminal Court', 93 *AJIL* (1999) 30; Wagner (n 336) 419; Herman von Hebel, Darryl Robinson, 'Crimes Within the Jurisdiction of the Court', in Roy Lee (ed), *The International Criminal Court – The Making of the Rome Statute* (Kluwer Law International 1999) 89; Beth van Schaack, 'The Definition of Crimes Against Humanity: Resolving the Incoherence', 37 *Columbia Journal of Transnational Law* (1999) 844.

but most delegations preferred to stick to the narrow definition.[590] In fact, a resumption of the historical debate on the exclusion of certain groups was perceived as putting consensus at risk.[591] The word 'racial' was never even discussed. In the end, Art. 6 Rome Statute was adopted with the support of virtually every state present at the Rome Conference.[592] Thus far, the ICC has indicted one person for the crime of genocide, for three counts of genocide, originating in the Darfur situation in Sudan. The crime of genocide has therefore only been of marginal importance in the ICC's jurisprudence.

3.11.2 The situation in Darfur

In March 2005, the Security Council referred the situation in Darfur by Resolution 1593 to the prosecutor of the ICC and determined that the situation continued to constitute a threat to international peace and security.[593] The referral was largely based on the findings of the Darfur Commission,[594] which the Resolution expressly mentions. Subsequently, the prosecutor opened an investigation against the sitting President of Sudan and Commander-in-Chief of the Sudanese Armed Forces, Omar Hassan Ahmad Al Bashir. In March 2009, Pre-Trial Chamber I found that the evidence provided by the prosecution had failed to give reasonable grounds to believe that Al Bashir had committed genocide.[595] This decision is the so far most important engagement of an ICC Chamber with the definition of the crime of genocide.[596] It was reversed by the Appeals Chamber in a judgment of February 2010 on the ground that the Pre-Trial Chamber had erred in its standard of proof.[597] In July 2010, the Pre-Trial

590 UN Doc. A/CONF.183/C.1/SR.3 (17 June 1998), para. 100. The Bureau (UN Doc. A/CONF.183/C.1/L.53 (6 July 1998), p. 1), the Drafting Committee (UN Doc. A/CONF.183/C.1/L.58 (9 July 1998), p. 9) and the Committee of the Whole (UN Doc. A/CONF.183/C.1/L.91 (16 July 1998), p. 2) suggested a provision without modifications to the Genocide Convention. Furthermore: Stahn (n 93) 35; Schabas (n 4) 127, 136; Schabas (n 206) 162; Shah (n 326) 377; Lippman (n 148) 521.

591 Shah (n 326) 377.

592 William Schabas, 'Defining Genocide', in Aristotle Constantinides, Nikos Zaikos (eds), *The Diversity of International Law: Essays in Honour of Professor Kalliopi K. Koufa* (Martinus Nijhoff 2009) 542; Lippman (n 148) 521. Jones, Powles (n 3) 167, are surprised that 'given the complexity of this question', the ICC Elements of Crimes made no attempt of clarifying the meaning of the four groups.

593 UN Doc. S/RES/1593 (2005), 31 March 2005.

594 Report of the Darfur Commission (n 557).

595 *Prosecutor v Al Bashir*, Case No ICC-02/05–01/09, Decision on the Prosecution's Application for a Warrant of Arrest Against Omar Hassan Ahmad Al Bashir (4 March 2009), para. 206.

596 Kress (n 235) 669. Similarly: Schabas (n 336) 128.

597 *Prosecutor v Al Bashir*, Case No ICC-02/05–01/09-OA, Judgment on the Appeal of the Prosecutor against the 'Decision on the Prosecution's Application for a Warrant of Arrest Against Omar Hassan Ahmad Al Bashir' (3 February 2010), paras. 41–42.

Chamber issued a second warrant of arrest that included genocide.[598] To date, Al Bashir remains at large.

The judges of the Pre-Trial Chamber found that the three targeted tribes, the Fur, the Masalit, and the Zaghawa, appeared all to have 'Sudanese nationality, similar racial features, and a shared Muslim religion',[599] and could therefore not be qualified as distinct national, racial, or religious groups. The judges answered the question whether the three tribes had distinct ethnicities affirmatively, 'as there are reasonable grounds to believe that each of the groups . . . has its own language, its own tribal customs and its own traditional links to its lands'.[600] The Pre-Trial Chamber held – albeit in a footnote only – that neither the Rome Statute nor the rules nor international criminal law in general provided for a clear definition of ethnic group.[601] With reference to the ICJ *Advisory Opinion on the Crime of Genocide*, the judges refrained from further exploring the issue of 'whether a wholly objective (based on anthropological considerations), a wholly subjective (based only upon the perception of the perpetrators), or a combined objective/subjective approach' ought to be adopted.[602] Interestingly, the presented distinction could lead to an identical result with regard to the racial group: a contemporary social anthropological understanding of race builds on the perception of differentness, thus exactly what the wholly subjective approach describes.[603]

Despite the majority's reluctance to clarify the appropriate legal approach for the definition of the victim groups, the dissenting opinion of Judge Anita Ušacka promises further debate on their contours.[604] With reference to the *ad hoc* jurisprudence, she notes that subjective criteria, like stigmatisation of the group by the perpetrators, as well as objective criteria, such as the particulars of a given social or historical context, ought to be considered.[605] Ušacka dissented on the classification of the targeted groups as three distinct ethnicities. They should

598 *Prosecutor v Al Bashir*, Case No ICC-02/05-01/09-94, Second Decision on the Prosecution's Application for a Warrant of Arrest Against Omar Hassan Ahmad Al Bashir (12 July 2010).

599 *Prosecutor v Al Bashir*, Case No ICC-02/05-01/09, Decision on the Prosecution's Application for a Warrant of Arrest Against Al Bashir (4 March 2009), para. 136.

600 Ibid para. 137.

601 Ibid footnote 152. Although unclear from the wording, it should be assumed that 'the rules' are the Elements of Crimes.

602 Ibid.

603 An approach based on physical/biological anthropology will assumingly lead to a different result.

604 *Prosecutor v Al Bashir*, Case No ICC-02/05-01/09, Decision on the Prosecution's Application for a Warrant of Arrest Against Al Bashir, Separate and Partly Dissenting Opinion of Judge Anita Ušacka (4 March 2009), paras. 24–26. Also recognised by Kress (n 235) 685.

605 *Prosecutor v Al Bashir*, Case No ICC-02/05-01/09, Decision on the Prosecution's Application for a Warrant of Arrest Against Al Bashir, Separate and Partly Dissenting Opinion of Judge Anita Ušacka (4 March 2009), para. 23.

rather be defined as a single ethnic group: the 'African tribes'. All three groups were a 'perceived unitary entity, which is in turn comprised of smaller groups, including the Fur, Masalit and Zaghawa'.[606] In embracing all non-Arab groups, Ušacka is strictly speaking suggesting a negative approach (albeit positively formulated), which jurisprudence uniformly has rejected.[607] However, her suggestion recognises that a genocidal process builds on stigmatisation and discrimination and, as such, includes an element of negative group identification, due to the phenomenon of othering. This was ultimately also the argument of Judge Shahabuddeen in his dissenting opinion in the *Stakić* appeals judgment.[608] The arguments by Judges Ušacka and Shahabuddeen reinforce the call for a negative definition of a protected victim group. Furthermore, Judge Ušacka argues that, in the context of Darfur, the ethnic faultline was considered to fall along the grounds of 'Arab' and 'African'. The perceived African-Arab polarization lead to the persons most affected perceiving themselves as either 'Arab' or 'African', the latter encompassing all three groups of the Fur, Masalit, and Zaghawa. This finding is interesting for taking into account societal structures and intergroup relations on the ground, describing the imagined abyss between 'us' and 'them'.[609]

The following section will analyse the ECCC's jurisprudence on genocide. The case law of other internationalised courts like the Iraqi High Tribunal did not contribute to the definition of the racial group for the crime of genocide and will therefore not be considered.[610] The Special Panels for Serious Crimes in East Timor and the Extraordinary African Chambers in the Senegalese courts did not indict anyone for genocide despite jurisdiction over the crime, while the Special Court for Sierra Leone or the Special Tribunal for Lebanon lack jurisdiction over genocide.

3.12 Jurisprudence of the extraordinary chambers in the courts of Cambodia

The ECCC is a hybrid court established by an agreement between the State of Cambodia and the UN.[611] Its mandate is the prosecution of the senior leaders of Democratic Kampuchea (Khmer Rouge regime), who are the most responsible

606 Ibid paras. 25–26.

607 See Chapter 3.9.3.

608 *Prosecutor v Stakić*, Case No IT-97–24-A, Partly Dissenting Opinion of Judge Shahabuddeen (22 March 2006), para. 17. See discussion in Chapter 3.9.3.

609 *Prosecutor v Al Bashir*, Case No ICC-02/05–01/09, Decision on the Prosecution's Application for a Warrant of Arrest Against Al Bashir, Separate and Partly Dissenting Opinion of Judge Anita Ušacka (4 March 2009), para. 25.

610 For a discussion of the case law: Carola Lingaas, *The Concept of Race* (PhD thesis, University of Oslo 2017) 254–255.

611 Helen Jarvis, 'Trials and Tribulations: The Long Quest for Justice for the Cambodian Genocide', in Simon Meisenberg, Ignaz Stegmiller (eds), *The Extraordinary Chambers in the Courts of Cambodia: Assessing Their Contribution to International Criminal Law* (TMC Asser 2016) 21–25.

for grave violations of national and international law on a massive scale in the period of 1975–79, leading to the death of approximately 1.7 million people.[612] In 1979, the Chairman of the UN Sub-Commission on Prevention of Discrimination and Protection of Minorities concluded that the atrocities in Cambodia were 'the most serious that had occurred anywhere in the world since [N]azism'.[613] The same year, the Khmer Rouge leaders Pol Pot and Ieng Sary were tried before the so-called People's Revolutionary Tribunal. However, this trial is considered a show trial for, among other reasons, creating a custom-made crime resembling genocide and for violating fair trial standards.[614]

The law on the establishment of the ECCC confers on it the power to try individuals suspected of committing the crime of genocide as defined in the Genocide Convention.[615] Yet, Art. 4 ECCC Law provides an altered definition of genocide: 'destroy, in whole or in part, a national, ethnical, racial or religious group, such as killing members of the group'. The law's terminology 'such as' (instead of 'as such') suggests a broader reading allowing for an open-ended list of genocidal acts. The ECCC found the terminology in the ECCC Law to be inconsistent with the definition of genocide under international law. In order not to breach the principle of legality, the ECCC therefore relates to customary law as contained in Art. 2 Genocide Convention rather than Art. 4 ECCC Law.[616] The ECCC has also stated that 'such as' was a typographical error.[617] The perpetrators declared as enemies anyone oppositional to the revolutionary Cambodia. Intellectuals, bourgeoisie, and city-dwellers were seen as suspect 'new people', a hidden class of 'enemies within', who were unable to overcome their counterrevolutionary identity.[618] The atrocities committed by the Khmer

612 <www.eccc.gov.kh/en/about-eccc/introduction>.

613 ECOSOC, UNCHR, Summary Record of the First Part (Public) of the 1510th Meeting, UN Doc. E/CN.4/SR.1510 (1979), para. 24.

614 For detail, see Frank Selbmann, 'The 1979 Trial of the People's Revolutionary Tribunal and Implications for ECCC', in Simon Meisenberg, Ignaz Stegmiller (eds), *The Extraordinary Chambers in the Courts of Cambodia: Assessing Their Contribution to International Criminal Law* (TMC Asser 2016) 77–201; Vianney-Liaud (n 272) 265; Bettwy (n 155) 188–189.

615 Law on the Establishment of Extraordinary Chambers in the Courts of Cambodia for the Prosecution of Crimes Committed During the Period of Democratic Kampuchea, with inclusion of amendments as promulgated on 27 October 2004 (NS/RKM/1004/006), Art. 4.

616 *Prosecutor v Nuon Chea* et al., Case No 002/19–09–2007-ECCC-OCIJ, Ieng Sary's Supplemental Alternative Submission to His Motion Against the Applicability of Genocide at the ECCC (21 December 2009), paras. 12–13. Confirmed in *Prosecutor v Nuon Chea and Khieu Samphân*, Case No 002/19–09–2007/ECCC/TC, Judgment (16 November 2018), paras. 783–789.

617 Ibid para. 798, footnote 2375.

618 *Prosecutor v Kaing Guek Eav alias Duch*, Case No 001/18–07–2007/ECCC/TC (26 July 2010), paras. 382–388, naming party opponents, intellectuals, students and diplomatic staff, foreigners, including Vietnamese nationals, Buddhist monks, and members

Rouge are commonly termed 'auto-genocide', since most victims belonged to the same group as the perpetrators.[619] For the crime of genocide, there is no legal requirement that the perpetrator belongs to a group other than the victims', because his intent to destroy can extend to parts of the group only ('in whole or in part').[620] As such, many victims of the Khmer Rouge regime were not targeted for their membership of the Khmer nation, but of economic, social or political groupings, none of which are protected by the Genocide Convention.[621]

The Khmer Rouge regime perceived its victims as a threat to its revolutionary ideologies and ideals of racial purity. This perception, Maureen Hiebert points out, was based on an understanding that each category of classes (revolutionary or counterrevolutionary) maintained its own essence or composition, characterised by certain elemental traits.[622] The 'new people' identified as outside of and hostile to the Khmer Rouge revolution were held to be biologically 'other' and not of the same race as the Khmer Rouge. Therefore, they had to be preemptively neutralised. In a 1978 issue of the *Revolutionary Flag*, a Communist Party of Kampuchea (CPK) propaganda magazine, the Vietnamese, for instance, are collectively identified as the 'territory-swallowing expansionist genocidal *Yuon* aggressor enemy', seemingly justifying a preventive attack against them in order to save the Khmer people.[623] The need to preserve and defend the 'Kampuchean race' was repeatedly expressed in CPK publications.[624] The ostensible threat that the enemy 'others' presents also becomes apparent in a radio broadcast by Pol Pot where he warned that if the Vietnamese '*Yuon* would be able to take Kampuchea, the Kampuchean race would be gone within 30 years'.[625] Not only is race mentioned, othering and the pre-genocidal stages are clearly discernible in that the Khmer Rouge described their revolution's internal enemies in dehumanising language, reminiscent of Nazi terminology, as 'microbes', 'rats,

---

of Cambodian ethnic minorities as victims. Confirmed in: *Prosecutor v Nuon Chea and Khieu Samphân*, Case No 002/19-09-2007/ECCC/TC (16 November 2018), para. 3750. See also Rafter (n 40) 44, 120–127; Greenberg (n 357) 85–86; Hiebert (n 20) 15–17.

619 ECOSOC, UNCHR, Summary Record of the First Part (Public) of the 1510th Meeting, UN Doc. E/CN.4/SR.1510 (1979), para. 22: 'nothing less than autogenocide'. Furthermore: Whitaker (n 7) para. 31; Greenberg (n 357) 85; Drumbl (n 195) 44; Fournet (n 318) 48; Ciorciari (n 156) 413.

620 Schmid (n 254) 226–227; Ratner, Abrams, Bischoff (n 142) 37; Paul (n 103) 287; Vest (n 157) 120.

621 *Prosecutor v Kaing Guek Eav alias Duch*, Case No 001/18-07-2007/ECCC/TC (26 July 2010), para. 388. Furthermore: Akhavan (n 5) 134; Slye, van Schaack (n 160) 228; Wald (n 6) 627.

622 Hiebert (n 41) 174.

623 *Prosecutor v Nuon Chea and Khieu Samphân*, Case No 002/19-09-2007/ECCC/TC (16 November 2018), para. 3833. See also ibid, paras. 3393 and 3403.

624 Ibid paras. 3216 and 3218.

625 Ibid para. 3824. Kiernan (n 138) 549–550.

'abscess', 'germs', or as sources of contamination and poison.[626] The ECCC Trial Chamber even specifically addressed the meaning of the term *Yuon* for the description of the Vietnamese, and concluded that it was used in a 'derogatory fashion in aggressive rhetoric', in order to stir up collective negative sentiments against the Vietnamese, irrespective of their combatant or civilian status.[627] Tantamount to Hutu extremist propaganda, the Khmer Rouge perpetrators used metaphors such as 'pulling out weeds, remove them roots and all'[628] and 'pull up the grass, dig up the roots', and proclaimed that the bodies of their victims would be used as fertiliser.[629] In Cambodia, the hatred and dehumanisation of the perceived enemies was also spread on the radio, using language resemblant of the RTLM radio broadcasts. An announcer stressed that '[o]nly when you have a seething hatred for the enemy . . . , will you stay alert in your efforts to weed out and exterminate the enemy planted within'.[630]

The recent judgment in the case against Nuon Chea and Khieu Samphân was the first to conclusively deal with the crime of genocide. With regard to possible victim groups of genocide, the Closing Order (indictment) focused on the Muslim Cham and Vietnamese, but did not extend to the Khmer. It identified the Cham victim group as an 'ethnic and religious group that distinguishes itself as such, and is identified as such by others' and the Vietnamese group as an 'ethnic and national group, who may also have been considered as a racial group by the CPK'.[631] The adjudication of these genocidal acts was hence the litmus test of a subjective perpetrator-based approach to defining a racial group. The defence lawyers of both defendants submitted that the victim groups had to be determined in adopting an objective approach and that the subjective perception of the perpetrators alone was insufficient to establish group membership.[632] The Trial Chamber largely followed these submissions and considered the subjective element alone insufficient to establish membership of the protected victim group. An analysis that focused on the objective criterion was, according to the ECCC, consistent with the purpose of the Genocide Convention that protects 'relatively stable and permanent groups'.[633] Chapter 3.6.3 has shown

626 Ibid paras. 1176, 3392 and 3407. See also Kiernan (n 138) 549; Hiebert (n 20) 15, 20–22. See Chapter 3.3 for a detailed discussion on the different stages of genocide.

627 *Prosecutor v Nuon Chea and Khieu Samphân*, Case No 002/19-09-2007/ECCC/TC (16 November 2018), paras. 3853, 3379 and 3381.

628 Sixth Investigative Request of Co-Lawyers for Civil Parties Concerning the Charge of Genocide Against the Khmer Nationals, Case No 002/19-09-2007-ECCC/OCIJ (4 February 2010), para. 24. See Chapters 3.6.2 and 3.6.5 on Rwanda.

629 Kiernan (n 138) 547.

630 *Prosecutor v Nuon Chea and Khieu Samphân*, Case No 002/19-09-2007/ECCC/TC (16 November 2018), paras. 3398 and 3821.

631 As quoted in *Prosecutor v Nuon Chea and Khieu Samphân*, Case No 002/19-09-2007/ECCC/TC (16 November 2018), para. 790.

632 Ibid para. 794.

633 Ibid para. 795. See discussion on stability and permanence in Chapter 3.6.3.

that the jurisprudence on the criteria of stability and permanence has been criticised for violating the principle of legality, especially in the manner, by which the *Akayesu* trial judgment broadened the protection of the law of genocide. The ECCC Trial Chamber moreover followed the *ad hoc* tribunals' jurisprudence in determining that the protected group had to have a distinct positive identity and could not be defined by negative criteria.[634]

Nuon Chea and Khieu Samphân were indicted for genocide of the Cham Muslim and the Vietnamese, despite a strong *prima facie* case of genocide against other minority groups like the Chinese, Thai, and possibly the Buddhist monkhood as well.[635] According to witnesses, one Khmer Rouge document explained that 'the Cham race is not to be spared because it has a history of resisting the socialist revolution. . . . So we undertake a policy of discarding them now'.[636] Another directive issued by the leadership read: 'There was no Cham race or Cham country . . ., there were [to be] no Chams, no Chinese, no nothing'.[637] This evidence points to a perception of the Cham as a distinct racial rather than a religious group. The 2010 indictment by the ECCC prosecutors in the *Nuon Chea* et al. case, however, disregarded the racial component in considering the Cham victim group 'an ethnic and religious group that distinguishes itself as such, and is identified as such by others'.[638] Remarkably, while the indictment proposes a double-subjective approach for the determination of the Cham victim group, it clearly suggests a perpetrator-based approach for the identification of the Vietnamese victims. It held that they were systematically killed for being 'an ethnic and national group, who may also have been considered as a racial group by the CPK', thereby acknowledging the perpetrators' definitional power of the victim group.[639]

Although the defendants were indicted for the crime of genocide against the Cham as an ethnic and religious group, the issue of race nonetheless emerges numerous times in the Trial Chamber's examination of criminal acts committed against the group. An expert explained that the 'Khmer Rouge confused the idea of race with that of culture, creed, language, and nation, as had the Nazis'. They arbitrarily determined the minorities that constituted a threat to the

634 Ibid paras. 792–793. See discussion in Chapter 3.9.3.

635 Ratner, Abrams, Bischoff (n 142) 320; Kiernan (n 138) 549, 553; Ciorciari (n 156) 425.

636 Ben Kiernan, *The Pol Pot Regime: Race, Power, and Genocide in Cambodia Under the Khmer Rouge, 1975–1979* (Yale UP 1996) 280.

637 Ibid 279.

638 *Prosecutor v Nuon Chea, Ieng Sary, Khieu Samphan, Ieng Thirith*, Case No 002/19–09–2007-ECCC-OCIJ, Closing Order (Indictment) (15 September 2010), para. 1336. The trial judgment against Nuon Chea and Khieu Samphan confirms that all the parties agree on this qualification of the Cham (*Prosecutor v Nuon Chea and Khieu Samphân*, Case No 002/19–09–2007/ECCC/TC (16 November 2018), para. 3203).

639 *Prosecutor v Nuon Chea, Ieng Sary, Khieu Samphan, Ieng Thirith*, Case No 002/19–09–2007-ECCC-OCIJ, Closing Order (Indictment), (15 September 2010), para. 1343.

Kampuchean nation.[640] While the CPK initially aimed at an assimilation of the Cham (and other minorities) in order to establish an atheistic and homogenous society, the policy eventually evolved into ordering brutal purges of all Cham. This shift coincided with the intensification of the conflict with Vietnam, when the CPK deemed the need to preserve the Khmer race a top priority.[641] Gradually, the Vietnamese '*Yuon*' were considered the most dangerous, acute, and hereditary enemy, based on a perception of long-standing antipathy and animosity between the Kampuchean and the Vietnamese people, whose composition was held to be poisonous.[642]

The perpetrators targeted the Vietnamese not as individuals, but on the basis of their group membership. Similar to the Holocaust or the genocide in Rwanda, in their screening of the population, the CPK drew upon statistical or census lists on village level as well as family record books to identify, single out and separate the Vietnamese from non-Vietnamese.[643] The CPK believed that ethnicity was inherited matrilineally. The Khmer Rouge policy of 'digging up the roots' meant that not only the Vietnamese mothers, but also their children had to be eliminated in order to avoided that Vietnamese blood would be passed down.[644] In other words, the targeting of the Vietnamese encompassed the entire group, irrespective of combatant status, and included women, children, and the elderly. The Chamber was satisfied that the *mens rea* of the crime of genocide was evidenced in the internal and public targeting of the Vietnamese in documents and speeches, the creation of lists, and the adherence to a matrilineal policy.[645]

In its identification of the Vietnamese victim group, the ECCC Trial Chamber notes the existence of distinct features, such as language, cuisine, cultural practices, traditional dresses, and historical heritage. Moreover, most Vietnamese in Cambodia were not fluent in Khmer or spoke it with an accent. In addition to such objective characteristics, the judges consider that the Vietnamese were identified and identified themselves as such because of ancestral connections to Vietnam 'and/or because of their physical traits'. The Chamber concluded that the Vietnamese constituted an ethnic, national, and racial group at the relevant time.[646] The judgment thereby seemingly applies a mixed objective-subjective approach to the identification of the Vietnamese as an ethnic or national group. Without further discussion, the Vietnamese are also held to be, cumulatively or alternatively, a racial group because of their physical traits. It is doubtful that, given the evidence available, the Vietnamese considered themselves a distinct

640 *Prosecutor v Nuon Chea and Khieu Samphân*, Case No 002/19-09-2007/ECCC/TC (16 November 2018), para. 3219, footnote 10844.
641 Ibid paras. 3228 and 3345.
642 Ibid paras. 3381, 3382, 3387, 3388, 3518.
643 Ibid paras. 3421, 3516, and 3517.
644 Ibid paras. 3424–3428, 3518.
645 Ibid para. 3518.
646 Ibid paras. 3419, 3420, 3514.

racial group. Rather, it appears as though the Khmer Rouge and its leadership had an understanding of belonging to a superior race that was under threat by the Vietnamese race, hence a subjective understanding of racial group membership. The fact that the Trial Chamber does not further examine the racial group membership could be seen as an opportunity missed. The prosecution presented substantial indications of the genocidal stages that the judges incorporated in their discussion of the CPK policies. It also demonstrated the perception of the racial otherness of the Vietnamese, including the ostensive matrilineal bloodlines. As such, an exclusive finding that the Vietnamese were a protected racial group could have been anticipated. Chapter 5.5 will demonstrate that the ECCC in its analysis of the crime of crime of persecution conclusively determined that the Vietnamese were targeted for their perceived racial otherness. There, the judges did not consider any group membership other than the racial one. They built their conclusion on the exact same arguments as presented in the analysis of the crime of genocide, namely the perceived matrilineal heritance of Vietnamese blood, the degrading treatment of the Vietnamese as a group, and the dissemination of hatred against the Vietnamese by means of propaganda, speeches, and the like. Conversely, in their legal findings for the crime of genocide, the judges offer three distinct group memberships for the Vietnamese victims. In breach of the principle of effectiveness, the judges do not attempt to classify the victims as one of the four victim groups, but consider them a national, ethnic, and/or a racial group. The Chamber's hesitance to categorise conclusively the Vietnamese as one specific victim group might originate in the fact that none of the parties in the case contested the existence of the Vietnamese as constituting a group, as such. The defence of Nuon Chea agreed with their identification as a distinct ethnic, national and racial group, while the defence of Khieu Samphân accepted their ethnic and national characteristics but rejected their racial qualifications. Note that the civil party lead co-lawyer highlighted evidence pertaining to the Vietnameses' physical features and skin colour, among other, thus objective and contested racial features.[647] Since the racial group categorisation was the only (partially) disputed one, the Chamber did probably not attempt to build a conviction for genocide on it alone.

3.13 Overview of all adjudicated cases

3.13.1 Summing up the different approaches

The objective approach is, in the words of Carsten Stahn, 'more typical in relation to investigation and prosecution', since the prosecutors would begin by looking to evidence that genocidal acts have been committed, before attributing them to the perpetrator of the crime.[648] Hence, they would first determine

647 Ibid para. 3418.
648 Stahn (n 93) 38.

whether crimes have occurred, and then assess whether the perpetrator acted with the *dolus specialis*. In turn, the subjective approach is, according to Stahn, 'more unorthodox' because it 'requires primarily a consideration of the subjective intent of the accused'. As a consequence, a single genocidal act may amount to genocide if it is carried out with a genocidal intent.[649]

There exist four different subjective approaches to defining a racial group apart from a purely objective approach and a mixed objective-subjective approach: first, there is the predominant approach, in which the perpetrator perceives a victim as belonging to a specifically defined group. The second is an inverted approach, in which the victim perceives himself as belonging to a distinct group. A double-subjective approach is the third, in which not only the perception of the perpetrator, but also the self-perception of the victims is relevant. Lastly, an objectivised subjective approach, as introduced by the Darfur Commission, describes a transformation of a subjective approach to gradually becoming an objectivised approach.

This study suggests that any approach other than a purely subjective perpetrator-based approach will incoherently and imperfectly reflect the process of othering, which is inextricably linked to any genocide. The identification, stigmatisation, and dehumanisation of the 'others', the members of the out-group, necessarily depend on the perpetrator's perception and are, as such, inherently subjective. The racial group is created in the mind of the perpetrator, and a judge will need to analyse retrospectively how the victim group looked 'in the eyes of the alleged perpetrators', to paraphrase the *Jelisić* trial judgment.[650]

3.13.2 *Graphical illustration of group membership approaches*

Although the Darfur Commission was not an international criminal body, its report was written by international criminal lawyers and served as a basis for the Security Council's resolution, by which the case of Darfur was referred to the ICC Prosecutor.[651] The Commission's Report contains groundbreaking analyses of group membership for the crime of genocide. It is therefore essential to include the Commission's findings in an illustration of adjudicated cases. Unlike the other judgments discussed, the *Nikolić* case did not deal with the crime of genocide and is therefore excluded. The graphical illustration in Figure 3.1 shows the judicial approaches taken in judgments of the ICTR, ICTY, the ECCC, and the Darfur Commission.

The figure demonstrates that the tribunals have never applied a purely victim-based subjective approach, which for the definition of the protected group of genocide should therefore be disregarded.

Three cases (*Jelisić*, *Krstić*, and *Ndindabahizi*) favoured a subjective approach based on the perpetrator's perception and stigmatisation of the victim group.

649 Ibid.
650 *Prosecutor v Jelisić*, Case No IT-95–10-T (14 December 1999), para. 70.
651 See Chapter 3.11.2.

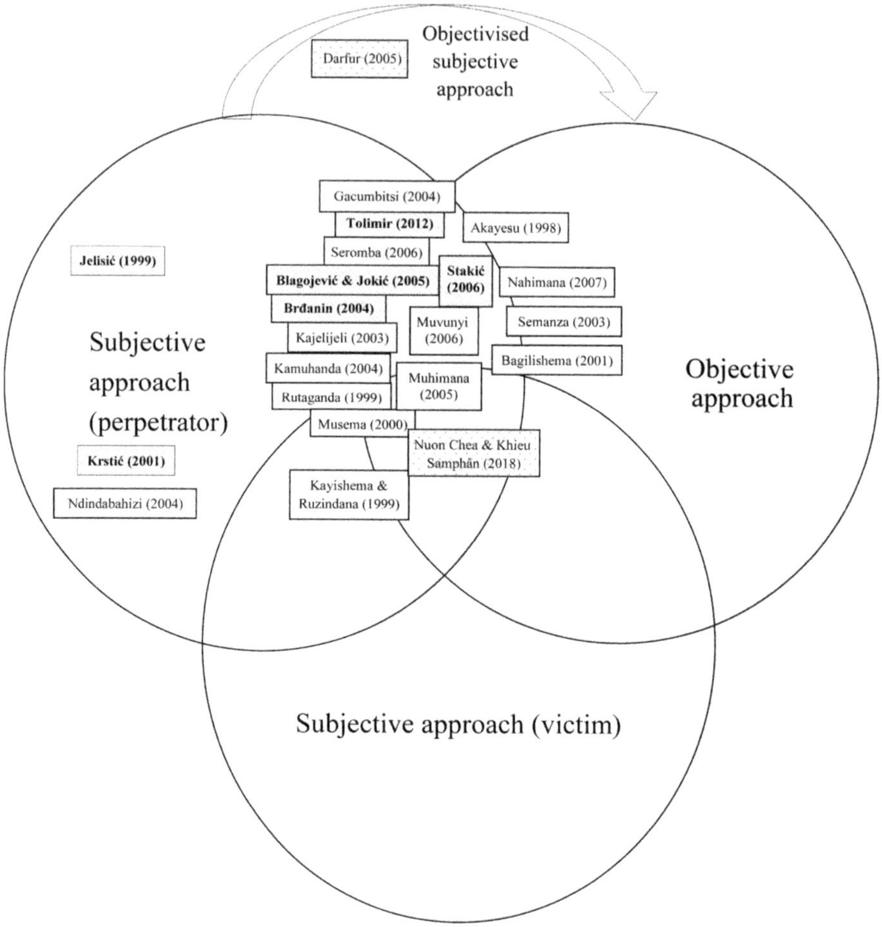

Figure 3.1 Approaches of the ICTR (white), ICTY (diagonal lines), ECCC (dots), and Darfur Commission (dots) to defining group membership (case and year)

The two ICTY judgments were rendered in 1999 and 2001 respectively and represent the early years' of jurisprudence on the matter.

Four cases (*Akayesu*, *Bagilishema*, *Semanza*, and *Nahimana*), all prosecuted by the ICTR, have favoured a predominantly objective approach with a minimal subjective dimension.[652]

One case clearly differs from the others: *Kayishema and Ruzindana* is the only case that seemingly offered all possibilities of group determination in the

652 Amann (n 128) 108, categorises the *Bagilishema* judgment as a primarily perpetrator-based subjective approach.

alternative. It considered either the perception of the victim(s), the perception of the perpetrator(s), or an objective approach decisive in the identification of the protected group.

Three cases (*Muvunyi*, *Muhimana*, and *Stakić*) appear to have relied on a mixed objective-subjective approach, without a clear preference for either. The recent ECCC *Nuon Chea and Khieu Samphân* judgment ought to be included in this category too, since it referred to objective and subjective elements, with a slight preponderance of a subjective approach.

The overwhelming majority of cases essentially adheres to a perpetrator-based subjective approach, yet are based on a case-by-case analysis and always in consultation with objective criteria (*Rutaganda*, *Musema*, *Brđanin*, *Blagojević and Jokić*, *Tolimir*, *Kajelijeli*, *Kamuhanda*, *Seromba*, and *Gacumbitsi*). Of all these nine cases, two stand out for choosing a more objective path in requiring the protected group to be stable and permanent (*Rutaganda* and *Musema*). Both cases considered the victim's perception in some cases admittable.

Finally, the Darfur Commission examined in detail both subjective and objective group membership and concluded in what appears to be a new category of the objectivised subjective approach, thereby placing itself apart from the other cases.

The genocide jurisprudence of the *ad hoc* international criminal tribunals and the Darfur Commission offer an insight into the current developments in the determination of group membership. This analysis has demonstrated the incoherence in the tribunals' jurisprudence, while the next section makes suggestions as to the recommended legal interpretation.

3.14 Interim conclusion

This chapter has shown that there exist two primary methods to define a protected group of genocide. The objective approach relies on provable, 'real' facts to describe a group. In the case of race, this would signify reverting to fallacious methods, such as the classification of people according to their pigmentation, nose shape, or hair texture. Since the natural sciences have long reached the conclusion that there are no distinct human races as bearers of different genes that manifest themselves in phenotypes, it is time for the law to follow suit. Furthermore, also independent of science, the concept of race is inherently subjective in that people assign group membership to individuals they perceive as racially distinct from themselves. Racial group membership usually involves a creation of hierarchies and hence a process of othering. Moreover, an objective approach disrespects the genocidal process in which the *génocidaire* holds the definitional power over his victims' identity.

The subjective approach, on the other hand, is based on either the perpetrator's perception of the victim group as distinct from his own, the victims' perception of their differentness, or a combination of both perceptions. The point of departure is perception, a cognitive element that is difficult to establish and prove. Yet any determination of *mens rea* is challenging, and difficulties alone should not prevent courts from applying a perception-based approach inasmuch as it recognises the identity-based nature of the crime of genocide. The intent to destroy a group for reasons of (perceived) group membership can be inferred from circumstantial evidence such as derogatory speech or violence triggered by genocidal ideology, a fact acknowledged by an increasing number of judgments and scholars. In this sense, 'violence becomes the vehicle . . . in which we can trace back the . . . mental framework of the perpetrators'.[653] The perpetrator's intent and his associated perception of the racial group will manifest themselves in his behaviour, which includes statements, publications, utterances, etc. that communicate his understanding of the racial victim group.

Of the four subjective approaches, jurisprudence has largely relied on the perpetrator-based approach, yet with due consideration of objective elements that generally remain undefined.[654] A perpetrator-based approach is not only consistent with the goal of the Genocide Convention to protect four exclusive groups the perpetrator wishes to destroy qua group. The recognition of the inherent subjectivity of the genocidal process and the concept of race would suggest a full reliance on a perpetrator-based subjective approach, even in the absence of any objective elements.[655] Fournet puts it eloquently and concisely:

> In a sense, the international criminal tribunals cannot be criticised for having turned to subjectivity to define the victim group, insofar as subjectivity is intrinsic to the concept of genocide itself and as the targeted groups might only exist, as groups, in the minds of the genociders: the existence of a 'group' as such might not have any basis in reality and it is the genocider's delirium which will create this group as such. In other words, the crime of genocide aims at the destruction of a group *arbitrarily defined by the genociders*, and the perpetration of the crime of genocide therefore does not necessarily mean that the group actually exists.[656]

The law of genocide puts at the disposal of the courts four categories. The racial category is an analytical tool, which can be used to extrapolate to individual victims the purported characteristic of an imagined archetypal racial group member.[657] In their positivistically framed search for an objective reality, international criminal courts have attempted to provide verifiable definitions of the racial group. The legal classification is treated as an ultimate reality, while it is actually based on a classification originating in the mind of the perpetrator.[658]

653 See Holslag (n 19) 97.
654 Cassese (n 443) 121; Schabas (n 440) 134; Demko (n 35) 230; Lüders (n 156) 55; Jones, Powles (n 3) 154.
655 Similar discussion in Lowenstein (n 211) 43; Ambos (n 189) 8.
656 Fournet (n 188) 108–109, emphasis in original.
657 Eltringham (n 313) 7.
658 Stanton (n 2); Eltringham (n 313) 7–8.

The assignment of victims to a racial group cannot signify that it exists in reality, but rather that the perpetrators, and consequently the judges, assume it does. Thus, rather than looking for an objective legal reality, in our case, an 'ideal' racial group, the perpetrator's perception of the victim group's identity should be the point of departure for a legal classification of the victims.

This chapter has demonstrated wide discrepancy in jurisprudence with regard to the concept of race. Judgments vary from defining race as 'hereditary physical traits' (*Akayesu*), 'externally perceptible quality' (*Jelisić*), to relying on 'the perpetrator of the crime believed that the victim belonged to the group' (*Muhimana*), or 'may be identified by means of the subjective criterion of the stigmatisation of the group, notably by the perpetrators of the crime, on the basis of its perceived racial characteristics' (*Brđanin*). There is therefore no uniform interpretation of race in the crime of genocide. This study suggests an evolutive interpretation of the generic term 'race', building on the perpetrator's perception of the victim group as pertaining to a distinct racial group. Such a subjective approach acknowledges that the racial group is largely created in the mind of the perpetrator. He identifies, singles out, discriminates, dehumanises, and aims at the destruction of a victim group he considers racially distinct from his own. The concept of race has even been held to be the place where the 'psychological, cultural, and ultimately biological dimensions of dehumanisation all converge'.[659]

An application of the subjective approach cannot lead to an expansion of the protection beyond the four exclusively protected victim groups. Instead, in our case, perception has to be limited to cases in which the perpetrator perceives the victim group as racially distinct. For evidentiary reasons, a recognisable pre-genocidal existence of the victim group that does not fully originate in the perpetrator's imagination would be preferable. Such objective recognition of the group is, however, no legal element. Ultimately, the perpetrator's understanding of the group is an issue of proof: the courts need to look for those features the perpetrator took into account when he targeted a certain group, and identify the group based upon these traits.[660] Such a construction will inevitably lead to the protection of groups that exist in the imagination of the perpetrator only.

659 Smith (n 57) 163.
660 Ambrus (n 202) 953; Eltringham (n 313) 30–32.

4 The concept of race in the law of apartheid

> If the belief that there is to be one standard of treatment for the White races and another for the non-White continues to gain strength among the latter, the future for solidarity among the Members of the United Nations and, consequently, for world peace, will indeed be dark.[1]

4.1 Introduction

Of the three crimes examined in this thesis, the crime of apartheid is by far the most controversial and undefined. It is also the only international crime that exclusively protects racial groups, and thus it merits particular attention in this study.[2] This chapter seeks to answer how 'racial group' is defined in the context of the crime against humanity of apartheid, in treaty as well as in customary law. Furthermore, the inclusion of the war crime of apartheid into Art. 85(4) (c) Additional Protocol I to the Geneva Conventions will be examined, albeit with a narrow focus on racial terminology. The meaning of 'racial group' is one of the most important interpretive questions of both the Apartheid Convention and the provision on the crime of apartheid in the Rome Statute.[3] Neither defines the term, nor does the negotiating history shed much light onto this

1 Letter dated 12 July 1948 from the representative of India to the Secretary-General concerning the treatment of Indians in South Africa, UN Doc A/577 (16 July 1948), in UN Blue Book Series, *The United Nations and Apartheid, 1948–1994, Volume 1*, UN Department of Public Information (1994) 222.

2 The author published an article that deals with several issues discussed in this chapter: Carola Lingaas, 'The Crime Against Humanity of Apartheid in a Post-Apartheid World', 2 *Oslo Law Review* (2015).

3 Max Du Plessis, 'International Criminal Law: The Crime of Apartheid Revisited', 24 *South African Journal of Criminal Justice* (2011) 425; Ilias Bantekas, *International Criminal Law* (Hart Publishing 4th ed 2010) 237; Steven Ratner, Jason Abrams, James Bischoff, *Accountability for Human Rights Atrocities in International Law: Beyond the Nuremberg Legacy* (OUP 3rd ed 2009) 126. Similarly: Russell Tribunal on Palestine: Findings of the South African Session, Are Israel's Practices against the Palestinian People in Breach of the Prohibition on Apartheid under International Law (5–7 November 2011), para. 5.20.

issue.[4] Legal scholarship on the crime of apartheid is minimal, as the crime is often considered symbolic rather than legally enforceable. In examining the crime of apartheid through the lens of race, this chapter contributes to a better understanding of the crime and adds to the legal discussion on its applicability, also for future cases of apartheid.

This chapter includes an overview of apartheid's origin in South Africa and its criminalisation, initially as a breach of the prohibition of racial discrimination, later as a crime against humanity *ipso facto* through the Apartheid Convention and the Rome Statute. The codification of the Apartheid Convention was clearly a reaction to the situation in South Africa, but it was drafted sufficiently broadly to be applicable to other regimes of systematic racial discrimination. Despite initial pessimism, the Apartheid Convention remains legally valid and relevant to modern situations of internationalized racial discrimination and has in recent years been ratified by a number of states. The application of the law of apartheid to contemporary situations is, however, dependent on an understanding of race unrelated to the South African context.

Like several other crimes, the crime of apartheid is both a customary crime as well as a treaty crime. The treaty crime, foremost in the Apartheid Convention, remains contentious and appears to be intrinsically linked to the South African apartheid regime. Nonetheless, there exist contemporary situations that involve an institutionalized regime of systematic oppression and domination to which the apartheid terminology is sometimes applied, although often in a colloquial rather than a legal manner.[5] This study focuses exclusively on the legal aspect of the crime and argues that the application in the near future of the law of apartheid should not be ruled out.

4.2 The emergence of apartheid policy in South Africa

South Africa's Prime Minister, Daniel Malan, first used the term 'apartheid', which means 'apartness' or 'separateness' in Afrikaans, in 1944 to denote the country's policies of racial segregation between whites and various non-white racial groups. The term has subsequently been associated with the racial segregation policy of the Afrikaner National Party's government in South Africa (1948–1994).[6] Hendrik

4 Ratner, Abrams, Bischoff (n 3) 126. See Chapters 4.5. (Apartheid Convention) and 4.6.1 (Rome Statute).

5 Julia Gebhard, 'Apartheid', in *Max Planck Encyclopedia of Public International Law* (2016), para. 28, at: <http://opil.ouplaw.com/view/10.1093/law:epil/9780199231690/law-9780199231690-e752?prd=EPIL>. See Chapter 4.5.5 on the examples of North Korea and Palestine.

6 Kai Ambos, *Treatise on International Criminal Law, Volume II: The Crimes and Sentencing* (OUP 2014) 113; Alette Smeulers, Fred Grünfeld, *International Crimes and Other Gross Human Rights Violations: A Multi- and Interdisciplinary Textbook* (Martinus Nijhoff 2011) 109; Johan van der Vyver, 'Apartheid', in Dinah Shelton (ed), *Encyclopedia of Genocide and Crimes Against Humanity* (Thomson Gale 2005) 47; Ellis Cashmore, 'Apartheid', in Ellis Cashmore (ed), *Dictionary of Race and Ethnic Relations* (Routledge 3rd ed 1994) 28.

Verwoerd, who claimed apartheid was a policy of good neighbourliness and an act of God, is considered the principal architect of apartheid. With his appointment as Minister of Native Affairs in 1950, official use of the term apartheid in state programs increased dramatically.[7] The ideological foundation of apartheid lay in an understanding of the separation of nations and groups as divine fate, God being the 'Great Divider'.[8] The social-Darwinist notions of apartheid held that the segregation of blacks from the society of whites was mutually beneficial, protecting whites from an ever-present and increasing black menace (called the *swart gevaar*), but allegedly also benefiting indigenous societies themselves.[9] Differences between humans were explained by race, language, and culture as interdependent variables.[10] Pseudoscientific proof claimed that

> the cerebral capacities of . . . the 'native' are . . . distinctly inferior in comparison with those of the white children' and 'his intellectual development . . . comes to a standstill, as if it were not capable of further development.[11]

In the interest of racial hygiene, it was believed that intermarriage would produce inferior human material prone to poor health, weak constitution, and mental and moral disharmony. Marriages between blacks and whites were therefore undesirable.[12] The white South Africans considered themselves the superior *Herrenvolk* (master race), while all other groups were seen as inferior and hence given fewer rights.[13] For the Afrikaners, black South Africans were

7 Smeulers, Grünfeld (n 6) 109–110; Christine Byron, *War Crimes and Crimes against Humanity in the Rome Statute of the International Criminal Court* (Manchester UP 2009) 239; van der Vyver (n 6) 50; Cashmore (n 6) 28; Paul Rich, 'South Africa', in Jay Sigler (ed), *International Handbook on Race and Race Relations* (Greenwood Press 1987) 250.

8 Paul Maylam, *South Africa's Racial Past: The History and Historiography of Racism, Segregation, and Apartheid* (Ashgate 2001) 186–187; Myres McDougal, Harold Lasswell, Lung-chu Chen, *Human Rights and World Public Order: The Basic Policies of an International Law of Human Dignity* (Yale UP 1980) 531, 578.

9 John Reynolds, 'Third World Approaches to International Law and the Ghosts of Apartheid', in David Keane, Yvonne McDermott (eds), *The Challenge of Human Rights: Past, Present and Future* (Edward Elgar 2012) 197; Adriaan Barnard, 'Slegs Suid Afrikaners – South Africans Only? A Review and Evaluation of the International Crime of Apartheid', 7 *New Zealand Journal of Public and International Law* (2009) 322; Saul Dubow, 'Afrikaner Nationalism, Apartheid and the Conceptualization of 'Race'', 33 *Journal of African History* (1992) 230; Rich (n 7) 239. See Chapter 2.3 on social Darwinism.

10 Dubow (n 9) 220.

11 G.S. Preller quoted in Dubow (n 9) 225. See Chapters 2.6 for discussions on race and intellect in the UNESCO Statement.

12 G. Eloff and G. Cronjé, quoted in Dubow (n 9) 227, 230. See Chapter 2.3 on racial hygiene.

13 John Dugard, John Reynolds, 'Apartheid, International Law, and the Occupied Palestinian Territories', 24 *EJIL* (2013) 873; Max Coleman (ed), *A Crime against Humanity – Analysing the Repression of the Apartheid State* (Human Rights Committee of South Africa 1998) 148; Rich (n 7) 249. See Chapter 2.4 on the Nazi conception of *Herrenvolk*.

the quintessential 'others', the unchosen, uncivilized, unbelievers, and possibly not even human.[14]

4.3 Apartheid legislation in South Africa

Apartheid was an institutionalized system, created by law, enforced by legal institutions, and built on the three pillars of discrimination, territorial fragmentation, and political repression.[15] The cornerstone of the apartheid legal system in South Africa was the Population Registration Act No 30 of 1950. The Act required registration of the South African population and classified each person according to four overarching racial categories: 'whites', 'coloureds' (subdivided into seven sub-groups), 'Asians', and 'Bantus', without, however, defining race as such.[16] This piece of legislation aimed at a rigid classification of the South African people based on appearance, general acceptance, and repute, while an amending Act of 1962 made mandatory the combined consideration of appearance and acceptance.[17] However, the classification of people into the different groups was more difficult than anticipated by the architects of the apartheid system; many simply did not conform to the typologies constructed under the law,[18] and the authorities could themselves reclassify an individual.[19] In ambiguous cases, the individual had the burden of proof. If a person could not be placed in a clear racial category, that person was assumed to be non-white.[20] What became known as 'petty apartheid' was provided for in the Reservation of Separate Amenities Act of 1953, which mandated separate facilities for the different racial groups, affecting all spheres of life including the use of restaurants, public transport, schools, universities, public parks, beaches, etc.[21]

14 Stephen Cornell, Douglas Hartmann, *Ethnicity and Race: Making Identities in a Changing World* (Pine Forge Press 1998) 140. See Chapter 3.2 on othering.

15 Dugard, Reynolds (n 13) 873; Jennifer Balint, *Genocide, State Crime and the Law: In the Name of the State* (Routledge 2012) 50; Smeulers, Grünfeld (n 6) 110; Winston Nagan, Vivile Rodin, 'Racism, Genocide, and Mass Murder: Towards a Legal Theory about Group Deprivations', 17 *National Black Law Journal* (2004) 147.

16 Zimitri Erasmus, 'Apartheid Race Categories', 79 *Transformation* (2012) 1; Barnard (n 9) 323; van der Vyver (n 6) 49; Maylam (n 8) 184; Geoffrey Bowker, Susan Leigh Star, *Sorting Things Out: Classification and Its Consequences* (1999) 196–197; Unit on Apartheid, Apartheid in Practice, UN Doc. ST/PSCA/SER.A/9 (1969), p. 43.

17 Roger Omond, *The Apartheid Handbook* (Penguin Books 2nd ed 1986) 24–25. Until 1962, acceptability was the main criterion used.

18 Bowker, Star (n 16) 201.

19 Unit on Apartheid, Apartheid in Practice, UN Doc. ST/PSCA/SER.A/9 (1969), p. 43. See also Carolyn Fluehr-Lobban, *Race and Racism: An Introduction* (AltaMira Press 2006) 226; Bowker, Star (n 16) 201, 206–207, 213; Omond (n 17) 26.

20 Bowker, Star (n 16) 203, 212.

21 Gebhard (n 5), para. 7.

4.4 The reaction of the international community to apartheid: UN resolutions dealing with apartheid (1946–1994)

4.4.1 Introduction

From the inception of the United Nations in 1946, the international community closely followed developments in South Africa. Already at its very first session, the UN General Assembly dealt with the segregating practices in South Africa and adopted a resolution formally condemning the discriminatory practices of the government.[22] Between 1952 and the early 1990s, the UN General Assembly discussed apartheid policies at every single session except one.[23] Although often exclusively seen in relation to the South African context, the UN resolutions shaped the understanding of apartheid and continue to be significant with regard to the legal definition of the crime. From a historical perspective, these resolutions illustrate the international community's commitment to eradicate apartheid and its determination to declare illegal the South African regime. From a legal perspective, the resolutions reveal how the UN Member States changed their understanding of apartheid and how apartheid grew to be recognised as a crime against humanity. This development justifies a chronological analysis.[24] The resolutions attest in part to the formation of the customary crime of apartheid, insofar as they can be interpreted as demonstrating the *opinio juris* of the UN Member States. This latter issue will be further examined in Chapter 4.8.2.

4.4.2 Actions and reactions 1946–1969

Even before the formalization of apartheid as an official policy in South Africa, racial discrimination against Indians in the Union of South Africa was on the agenda of the UN General Assembly.[25] In its very first session, the General Assembly in a unanimously adopted resolution declared that 'it is in the higher interest of humanity to put an immediate end to religious and so-called racial persecution and discrimination'.[26] Then, in 1950, for the first time ever, a General Assembly resolution was adopted that expressly referred to apartheid: 'the policy of "racial segregation" (Apartheid) is necessarily based on doctrines of racial discrimination'.[27] The UN Member States began to increase pressure

22 UN GA Res.103 (I), 19 November 1946.
23 Barnard (n 9) 334.
24 See Reynolds (n 9) 204–209 for a similar overview.
25 The 1946 Asiatic Land Tenure and Indian Representation Act were reason for the formal complaint by India against South Africa. See Reynolds (n 9) 201; McDougal, Lasswell, Chen (n 8) 533.
26 UN GA Res. 103 (I) of 19 November 1946. UN GA Res. 395 (V) of 2 December 1950 also refers to this resolution.
27 UN GA Res. 395 (V) of 2 December 1950. This resolution dealt with the discriminatory treatment of the Indian population in South Africa only.

on the Security Council. The Sharpeville massacre of March 1960, in which the South African police fired at a peaceful demonstration, killing 68 and injuring more than 200, is considered a turning point in the international community's view of apartheid.[28] The Security Council urged the government of South Africa to abandon its apartheid policies.[29]

The tone of the UN resolutions became increasingly unforgiving. In 1962, the General Assembly 'strongly deprecate[d] the disregard by the Government of South Africa of its obligations [under the UN Charter]'[30] and requested its Member States to take a number of punitive measures such as breaking off diplomatic relations and boycotting South African goods. The General Assembly requested the Security Council to take appropriate measures, including sanctions and, if necessary, to consider action under Art. 6 of the Charter, ie the expulsion of South Africa from the UN.[31] In 1963, the UN adopted the Declaration on the Elimination of All Forms of Racial Discrimination.[32] This non-binding instrument created the foundation for the legally binding mechanism, the International Convention on the Elimination of Racial Discrimination (ICERD).[33] Both instruments refer directly to apartheid, albeit rather as a policy than as an international crime.[34]

From 1964 until 1972, the Security Council remained silent on the issue of apartheid in South Africa.[35] A voting pattern on resolutions passed by the Security Council is clearly visible: before 1964 resolutions were somewhat diluted by frequent abstentions of two of the permanent members, France and the United Kingdom (UK), and occasionally also the US; after the 1976 uprising in Soweto, most resolutions were adopted unanimously.[36]

In 1965, the government of South Africa annexed the territories of South West Africa (now Namibia). The ICJ later issued an advisory opinion on this case (see Chapter 6.4.3). The General Assembly condemned 'the policies of apartheid and racial discrimination practised by the Government of South Africa in South West Africa, which constitute a crime against

28 Paul Eden, 'The Role of the Rome Statute in the Criminalization of Apartheid', 12 *JICJ* (2014) 174; Reynolds (n 9) 205, 207; UN Blue Books Series, The United Nations and Apartheid, 1948–1994 (1994) 13.

29 UN SC Res. 134 (1 April 1960). The Resolution was adopted by nine votes to none, with two abstentions by France and the UK.

30 UN GA Res. 1761 (XVII) of 6 November 1962.

31 Ibid.

32 UN GA Res. 1904 (XVIII) 20 November 1963.

33 UN GA Res. 2106 (XX) 21 December 1965.

34 See discussion on ICERD in Chapter 4.5.4.

35 Reynolds (n 9) 208. It remains unclear why the Council remained silent, but the Cold War might have been the reason.

36 See Chapter 4.4.3 for the reaction in 1976. Furthermore: Dugard, Reynolds (n 13) 879; Reynolds (n 9) 205, 208; Newell Stultz, 'Evolution of the United Nations Anti-Apartheid Regime', 13 *Human Rights Quarterly* (1991) 12.

humanity'.[37] A connection between the practices of apartheid and the crime against humanity was established.

The UN considered not only South Africa. For instance, in a resolution of 1968, the General Assembly condemned 'the Governments of South Africa and Portugal for their persistent defiant stand towards the United Nations and world opinion in respect of their policies of apartheid and colonialism, respectively' and further 'condemns the policy of racial discrimination of the illegal minority regime in Southern Rhodesia'.[38] The reference to 'world opinion' is indicative of the international community's view on apartheid and, as such, of the formation of customary law.[39] Note that the resolution discusses South Africa and Portugal and 'their policies of apartheid and colonialism, respectively'. This wording could indicate that apartheid was exclusively related to South Africa, whereas colonialism referred to Portugal's policy. Although the resolution mentions Portugal's colonial regime, it remains unclear whether Portugal was understood to be an apartheid state, a question of potential relevance to the determination of whether apartheid was a phenomenon limited to South Africa. The connection between the regimes was explicitly mentioned during a later General Assembly meeting when the representative of the Byelorussian Soviet Socialist Republic asked: 'Where can we find those judges who would not condemn crimes committed . . . by the forces of colonialism, apartheid and racism, unless it be in the Republic of South Africa itself, in Southern Rhodesia or in Portugal?'[40]

In 1968, the Convention on the Non-Applicability of Statutory Limitations to War Crimes and Crimes against Humanity (Convention on Non-Applicability of Statutory Limitations) was adopted, whose Art. I(b) included apartheid into the list of crimes against humanity. While expressly mentioning the crime against humanity of apartheid, the Convention does not criminalize apartheid:

> Crimes against humanity whether committed in time of war or time of peace (. . . .) and inhuman acts resulting from the policy of apartheid, and the crime of genocide . . ., even if such acts do not constitute a violation of the domestic law of the country in which they were committed.[41]

This provision was criticised for breaching the principle of legality in making crimes punishable irrespective of the date of their commission.[42] Furthermore,

37 UN GA Res. 2074 (XX) 17 December 1965. The General Assembly, on a yearly basis, restated its condemnation of apartheid as a crime against humanity: UN GA Res. 2202 (XXI) 16 December 1966; UN GA Res. 2307 (XXII) 13 December 1967; UN GA Res. 2391 (XXIII) 26 November 1968.

38 UN GA Res. 2446 (XXIII) 19 December 1968.

39 See Chapter 4.8.2 on *opinio juris*.

40 UN Doc. A/PV.2185 (30 November 1973), p. 12, para. 139.

41 UN GA Res. 2391 (XXIII) 26 November 1968.

42 Eden (n 28) 175: more opposing votes were cast against the adoption of this Convention than any prior international human rights instrument. The corresponding European

the definition of crimes against humanity and, in particular, the inclusion of apartheid, were considered problematic due to their political rather than legal nature; to date only fifty-five states have ratified the Convention.[43]

4.4.3 *Actions and reactions 1970–1979*

In 1971, the Secretary-General submitted a Draft Convention on the Suppression and Punishment of the Crime of Apartheid that declared apartheid a crime against humanity and recognised that a UN convention would be an important contribution to the struggle against apartheid, racism, economic exploitation, colonial domination, and foreign occupation.[44] In the same year, the ICJ rendered the *South West Africa* Advisory Opinion. There, it condemned the establishment and enforcement of distinctions, exclusions, restrictions, and limitations based on grounds of race, colour, descent, or national or ethnic origin as 'flagrant violation of the purposes and principles of the UN Charter'.[45] It considered 'undisputed . . . that the official governmental policy pursued by South Africa in Namibia is to achieve a complete physical separation of races and ethnic groups in separate areas within the Territory'.[46] Albeit not defining either, the Advisory Opinion distinguishes between racial and ethnical groups.

Finally, in 1973, the UN General Assembly adopted the Apartheid Convention and its Art. 1 reads: 'The States Parties to the present Convention declare that apartheid is a crime against humanity'.[47] Another Assembly resolution that year reaffirmed the view of apartheid as a practice constituting a crime against humanity and requested the Security Council to consider measures under Chapter VII of the UN Charter. It furthermore condemned the 'unholy alliance between Portuguese colonialism, South African racism, Zionism and Israeli imperialism'.[48] As in 1968, the resolution distinguishes between Portuguese colonialism and South African racism.

Convention on the Non-Applicability of Statutory Limitations to Crimes against Humanity and War Crimes does not contain the crime of apartheid (Council of Europe, ETS No 82, 25 January 1974).

43 Richard Miller, 'The Convention on the Non-Applicability of Statutory Limitations to War Crimes and Crimes against Humanity', 65 *AJIL* (1971) 491–492. See <https://treaties.un.org/> for ratification status.

44 General Assembly, 26th Session, Third Committee, Draft to the Apartheid Convention presented by Guinea and the Soviet Union in 1971, UN Doc. A/C.3/L.1871 (28 October 1971).

45 *Legal Consequences for States of the Continued Presence of South Africa in Namibia (South West Africa) Notwithstanding Security Council Resolution 276*, ICJ Advisory Opinion (1971), para. 131. Discussed in Goler Teal Butcher, 'Legal Consequences for States of the Illegality of Apartheid', 8 *Human Rights Quarterly* (1986) 407–408, 419.

46 *South West Africa* case, ICJ Advisory Opinion (1971), para. 130.

47 UN GA Res. 3068 (XXVIII), 30 November 1973. See analysis of the Apartheid Convention in Chapter 4.5.

48 UN GA Res 3151 (XXVIII), 14 December 1973.

A Background Paper of 1974, issued by the UN Office of Public Information, declared that a consensus within the UN had developed that the practice of apartheid was a 'crime against humanity' and incompatible with South Africa's obligations under the UN Charter.[49] It is remarkable that the paper refers to a consensus within the UN, given that at this point in time only a few General Assembly resolutions had concluded that apartheid is a crime against humanity. Another ten years would pass until the Security Council would reach such conclusion.[50] Considering that still today scholars contemplate on whether there exists a crime against humanity of apartheid, the Background Paper's conclusion appears premature. While not legally binding, the paper gives expression to a commonly perceived opinion and could be taken as an indication of the customary status of the crime of apartheid.

In consequence of its violations of the UN Charter and the UDHR, by 1975, the South African government was effectively excluded from all UN organs.[51] In 1976, as a direct response to the killing of schoolchildren in Soweto, the Security Council issued a resolution stating that apartheid was a crime against the conscience and dignity of mankind and seriously disturbed international peace and security.[52] Albeit not calling it a crime against humanity, the Security Council nonetheless declared it an international crime. Then in 1977, for 'the first time in the 32-year history of the Organisation', the UN Secretary-General, Kurt Waldheim, stressed 'that action has been taken under Chapter VII of the Charter against a Member State', namely a mandatory, universally applied arms embargo against South Africa.[53]

4.4.4 Actions and reactions 1980–1994

A number of special conferences echoed the universal consensus against apartheid. The 1983 Latin American Regional Conference for Action Against Apartheid declared apartheid not only an inhuman system of racist domination and exploitation, but moreover a crime against humanity.[54] Similarly, the 1984 Lagos Declaration dealt with the crime against humanity of apartheid in a special section and urged the UN Member States to ratify the Apartheid Convention.

49 UN Background Papers, Apartheid and Racial Discrimination (1974), p. 3.

50 See Chapter 4.4.4 on the 1984 Security Council resolution.

51 UN Blue Books Series, The United Nations and Apartheid, 1948–1994 (1994) 30.

52 UN SC Res. 392 (19 June 1976); Ronald Slye, 'Apartheid as a Crime Against Humanity: A Submission to the South African Truth and Reconciliation Commission', 20 *Melbourne Journal of International Law* (1999) 295.

53 UN Doc. S/PV.2046 (4 November 1977) with reference to UN SC Res. 418 (4 November 1977). This mandatory embargo was reaffirmed by UN SC Res. 558 (13 December 1984). Furthermore: Dugard, Reynolds (n 13) 878–879; Butcher (n 45) 432–433.

54 Caracas Declaration for Action Against Apartheid, UN Doc. A/38/451 and S/16009 (1983), para. 1. Mentioned in Butcher (n 45) 413.

Importantly, the states, assembled in Lagos, agreed 'that if non-discrimination is a case of *jus cogens*, apartheid, perhaps the most monstrous form of racial discrimination, also constitutes a specific and particular case of a violation of *jus cogens*'.[55] In other words: racial discrimination is a violation of *jus cogens*. Because of the institutionalized regime of systematic oppression and domination it entails, apartheid is an extreme form of racial discrimination, which must therefore all the more be a violation of a *jus cogens* norm. Chapter 4.8.2 will further discuss this issue, especially whether this conclusion is equally valid for the crime against humanity of apartheid.

In 1984, the UN Security Council for the first time characterised apartheid as a crime against humanity, although not unanimously because the US abstained. The Security Council used the rather cautious wording of "designs further to entrench apartheid, a system characterised as a crime against humanity".[56] By declaring apartheid a crime against humanity, the international community sent a clear signal that apartheid not only threatened its victims, but humanity as a whole.[57] Yet, the Apartheid Convention still was not receiving the anticipated support; all Western states had abstained from ratification. In several resolutions in the early 1990s, the General Assembly tried to persuade its Member States to ratify the Convention, but without success.[58] In a resolution of February 1993, the UN High Commissioner for Human Rights drew attention to the need to strengthen the various mechanisms for combating apartheid by, among other things, establishing an international criminal tribunal as foreseen in Art. 5 Apartheid Convention.[59] The Commissioner's recommendation was certainly influenced by the rapidly deteriorating situation in the Balkans and establishment

55 Declaration of the Seminar on the Legal Status of the Apartheid Régime and Other Legal Aspects of the Struggle Against Apartheid (Lagos Declaration), UN Doc. A/39/423 and S/16709 (1984), pp. 9–10.

56 UN SC Res. 556 (23 October 1984). In 1984, also the General Assembly passed a resolution declaring apartheid a crime against humanity: UN Doc. A/RES/39/72 (13 December 1984). Furthermore Ariel Bultz, 'Redefining Apartheid in International Criminal Law', 24 *Criminal Law Forum* (2013) 213; John Dugard, 'L'Apartheid', in Hervé Ascensio, Emmanuel Decaux, Alain Pellet (eds), *Droit International Pénal* (Editions Pedone 2nd ed 2012) 198; Slye (n 52) 295.

Several General Assembly resolutions confirmed that apartheid was an international crime: UN Doc. A/RES/41/103 (4 December 1986); UN Docs. A/RES/42/56 (30 November 1987); A/RES/43/97 (8 December 1988); UN Doc. A/RES/44/79 (8 December 1989).

57 Coleman (n 13) 203; 243.

58 UN Doc. A/RES/45/90 (14 December 1990); UN Doc. A/RES/46/84 (16 December 1991); UN Doc. A/RES/47/81 (16 December 1992); UN Doc. A/RES/48/89 (20 December 1993).

59 UN Office of the High Commissioner for Human Rights, Implementation of the International Convention on the Suppression and Punishment of the Crime of Apartheid, Commission on Human Rights Resolution 1993/10, UN Doc. E/CN.4/RES/1993/10 (26 February 1993).

of the ICTY only months later. The same year, the General Assembly began lifting sanctions against South Africa, because the transition to democracy had now been enshrined in its laws.[60] In sum, at least fourteen General Assembly resolutions, adopted over a period of forty-eight years (1946–1994), declared apartheid a crime against humanity. Furthermore, the Security Council on one occasion recognised apartheid as a crime against humanity and on another occasion as a 'crime against the conscience and dignity of mankind', by which it avoided a precise legal classification of the crime.

In April 1994, the first non-racial and free democratic elections of a new government in South Africa took place, leading to the formal abolishment of apartheid.[61] Post-apartheid South Africa decided to focus on a process of truth and reconciliation, which made criminal prosecution, domestically or externally in any State Party to the Apartheid Convention, improbable.[62] Despite the availability of the Apartheid Convention as an international legal tool, South Africa opted against criminalisation and victimisation. In favouring transitional justice mechanisms over criminal prosecution, it sought to achieve ***ubuntu***, translated as 'community' or 'humaneness', in the sense of restoring right relationships between people.[63] This conscious choice of the South African society also explains why the ratification of the Apartheid Convention and criminal prosecutions were not prioritised.[64] Ariel Bultz asserted that such use of a reconciliatory mechanism instead of criminal justice impeded the acquisition of customary status for the crime of apartheid.[65] The use of domestic transitional justice, however, cannot be read as affecting the customary international law status of apartheid.[66]

These first sections have drawn a historical background for the rise of apartheid and how South African domestic laws comprehensively legislated and legitimated apartheid policies. They also showed the international community's reaction to the developments in South Africa by imposing sanctions on its regime and eventually by declaring apartheid a crime against humanity. The following three sections will analyse the treaty crime of apartheid in the Apartheid Convention and the Rome Statute and discuss apartheid as a war crime.

60 UN Doc. A/RES/48/1 (8 October 1993); reconfirmed by A/RES/48/159 (20 December 1993).

61 Barnard (n 9) 329; Coleman (n 13) 223.

62 Dugard (n 56) 198–199; Barnard (n 9) 330; Volker Nerlich, *Apartheidskriminalität vor Gericht* (Berlin Verlag 2002) 29; John Dugard, 'International Law and the South African Constitution', 8 *EJIL* (1997) 89. For more information, see Truth and Reconciliation Commission of South Africa, Final Report (29 October 1998), <www.sahistory.org.za/sites/default/files/volume5_0.pdf>.

63 Balint (n 15) 125–126; 164; Dugard (n 56) 198.

64 Reynolds (n 9) 210.

65 Bultz (n 56) 219.

66 See more on apartheid in customary international law in Chapter 4.8.

4.5 The crime of apartheid in the apartheid convention

4.5.1 Introduction

The Apartheid Convention was adopted by a UN General Assembly resolution of 30 November 1973 with ninety-one votes in favour, four votes against (Portugal, South Africa, UK, and US) and twenty-six abstentions.[67] It entered into force in July 1976 with its twentieth ratification. Art. 2 reads:

> For the purpose of the present Convention, the term 'the crime of apartheid', which shall include similar policies and practices of racial segregation and discrimination as practiced in southern Africa, shall apply to the following inhuman acts committed for the purpose of establishing and maintaining domination by one racial group of persons over any other racial group of persons and systematically oppressing them.

The Convention then lists six detailed inhuman acts, including subcategories of prohibited acts.[68] It was adopted for the purpose, among others, of holding criminally liable perpetrators of apartheid by making available an international prosecution mechanism and by providing for universal jurisdiction.[69] Yet significant doubts about the necessity and practicability of declaring apartheid a crime against humanity subject to universal jurisdiction impeded the Convention's ratification.[70] The 109 ratifications it has thus far received are almost entirely from developing countries.[71] States of the industrialized West, including the UK, France, Germany, and the Scandinavian countries have never signed or ratified the Convention, possibly out of fear of exposing their own citizens to prosecution for aiding and abetting apartheid.[72] Especially Art. 3 is constructed so broadly that virtually 'no white South African could escape its reach', and even persons who maintained commercial relations with South Africa during the apartheid regime were at risk of being charged with the crime of apartheid.[73]

67 UN GA Res. 3068 (XXVIII) of 30 November 1973; Dugard (n 56) 198; Hercules Booysen, 'Convention on the Crime of Apartheid', 2 *South African Year Book of International Law* (1976) 57.

68 Art. 2(a)–(f) Apartheid Convention.

69 See Art. 5 Apartheid Convention. Furthermore: Barnard (n 9) 337.

70 Bultz (n 56) 216–217; Du Plessis (n 3) 421; Alexander Zahar, 'Apartheid as an International Crime', in Antonio Cassese (ed), *The Oxford Companion to International Criminal Justice* (OUP 2009) 245; Christian Tomuschat, 'Universal Criminal Jurisdiction With Respect to the Crime of Genocide, Crimes Against Humanity and War Crimes', 71 *Yearbook of the Institute of International Law* (2005) 246; Natan Lerner, *Group Rights and Discrimination in International Law* (Martinus Nijhoff 2nd ed 2003) 125; Slye (n 52) 293; McDougal, Lasswell, Chen (n 8) 545.

71 See <https://treaties.un.org> for ratification status.

72 Slye (n 52) 293.

73 Geoffrey Robertson, *Crimes Against Humanity: The Struggle for Global Justice* (Penguin books 3rd ed 2006) 272; Tomuschat (n 70) 245.

The UK, for example, was concerned that apartheid officials with dual citizenship (South Africa/UK) would be prosecuted and made clear that the universal jurisdiction clause was one of the reasons for voting against the Convention.[74] Moreover, some states did not adopt the Apartheid Convention for prohibiting acts that were not criminalised under their domestic legislation. The obligation to prosecute individuals regardless of nationality was not well received either.[75] The Apartheid Convention was thus criticised because it extended (in the words of the US representative) 'international criminal jurisdiction in a broad and ill-defined manner and seeks to rely upon present powers of domestic jurisdiction for its enforcement'.[76] The fact that neither the ILC nor the General Assembly's Sixth Committee was involved in the drafting is generally considered a weakness of the process.[77] Nonetheless, the adoption of the Convention was important to amalgamate the struggle of the UN Member States against apartheid,[78] but also to establish individual criminal responsibility for the crime of apartheid, as reflected in Art. 3: 'International criminal responsibility shall apply, irrespective of the motive involved, to individuals, members of organisations and institutions and representatives of the State'. The fact that the Apartheid Convention singles out apartheid as one (extreme) form of racial discrimination and provides universal jurisdiction shows the gravity of the crime and its importance to the majority of the international community, at least at the time of its creation.[79]

The term 'apartheid' was applied exclusively by the South African government in denominating its policy. The adoption of that term by the Apartheid Convention is a clear indication that it takes its inspiration from the South African apartheid system. There is some scholarly debate on whether the Apartheid Convention exclusively targeted South Africa or has broader geographical applicability. A literal interpretation of the words 'include' and 'southern Africa' (rather than South Africa) suggests the drafters wanted to leave open application to countries other than South Africa. As indicated previously, the term 'apartheid' was also used for situations in other territories, particularly South West Africa (Namibia) and Rhodesia (Zimbabwe).[80] Yet undoubtedly, the Convention

74 Luc Reydams, *Universal Jurisdiction: International and Municipal Legal Perspectives* (OUP 2003/05) 60; Roger Clark, 'Apartheid', in M. Cherif Bassiouni (ed), *International Criminal Law, Volume I: Sources, Subjects, and Contents* (Martinus Nijhoff 3rd ed 2008) 615.

75 Slye (n 52) 294; Lerner (n 70) 125.

76 Official statement by Mr. Ferguson, UN Doc. A/PV.2185 (30 November 1973), p. 3, para. 23.

77 Lerner (n 70) 126.

78 ECOSOC, Draft Convention and Draft Protocol on the Suppression and Punishment of the Crime of Apartheid, UN Doc. E/RES/1696(LII) (2 June 1973), para. 1.

79 Dugard, Reynolds (n 13) 877–878; Du Plessis (n 3) 420.

80 Natan Lerner, *The UN Convention on the Elimination of all Forms of Racial Discrimination* (Brill Nijhoff 1980/2015) 42, 45–46, 123–127; Dugard (n 56) 199; Clark (n 74) 603; Reydams (n 74) 59; UN Background Papers, Apartheid and Racial Discrimination (1974) 1; Abdulrahim Abby Farah, Statement before the Special Political Committee of the General Assembly, Unit on Apartheid: Notes and Documents, No 20/72 (9 October 1972) 2.

was tailor-made for the South African regime and was intended to be applied, at least initially, only to South Africa.[81] The open formulation of Art. 2, however, allows its application to other situations too, examples of which will be provided in Chapter 4.5.5. The South African system of apartheid is not standard, against which all other possible instances of apartheid must be assessed – and its replication cannot be demanded for a legal determination of the crime of apartheid. Such a comparison is no more useful, from a legal point of view, to demanding that all genocidal situations be compared with the Holocaust. As in other international legal instruments, every violation has to be measured against the provisions of the respective instrument, not against other cases of violation. Earlier cases may illustrate the possible contours that a violation might have, but they cannot provide authoritative guidance for future cases. Rather, every case has to be judged on its own merits.[82]

4.5.2 The racial group in the actus reus

The *actus reus* of the apartheid crime is both complex and in part unclear and does furthermore not define 'racial group'.[83] In his dissenting opinion in the *South West Africa* case before the ICJ, Judge Tanaka noted the difficulties of legally defining race or racial differentiation:

> The reasons therefor [sic] are that the scientific and clear-cut definition of race is not established; that what man considers as a matter of common-sense as criteria to distinguish one race from the other, are the appearance, particularly physical characteristics such as colour, hair, etc., which do not constitute in themselves relevant factors as the basis for different political or legal treatment; and that, if there exists the necessity to treat one race differently from another, this necessity is not derived from the physical

81 The Apartheid Convention is 'a special purpose Convention and it was intended exclusively to combat apartheid as practised until quite recently in South Africa' (Draft Code of Crimes against the Peace and Security of Mankind. Titles and texts of articles adopted by the Drafting Committee; UN Doc. A/CN.4/L.459 (1991), para. 49). Furthermore: Christopher Hall, Larissa van den Herik, 'The Crime of Apartheid', in Otto Triffterer, Kai Ambos (eds), *The Rome Statute of the International Criminal Court: A Commentary* (Verlag CH Beck 3rd ed 2016) 234, 282; Gebhard (n 5), paras. 14, 27; Reynolds (n 9) 210; M. Cherif Bassiouni, 'International Crimes: The *Ratione Materiae* of International Criminal Law', in M. Cherif Bassiouni (ed), *International Criminal Law, Volume I: Sources, Subjects, and Contents* (Martinus Nijhoff 3rd ed 2008) 146; Clark (n 74) 599; Lerner (n 70) 56.

82 Du Plessis (n 3) 423, 427; Victor Kattan, *The Russell Tribunal on Palestine and the Question of Apartheid* (al-Shabaka Policy Brief 2011) 3. Accord: Richard Falk, Virginia Tilley, *Israeli Practices Towards the Palestinian People and the Question of Apartheid: Palestine and the Israeli Occupation,* Economic and Social Commission for Western Asia, UN Doc. E/ESCWA/ECRI/2017/1 (2017) 14.

83 Clark (n 74) 603–616, discloses unclear definitions and 'sloppy drafting'.

> characteristics or other racial qualifications but other factors, namely religious, linguistic, educational, social, etc., which in themselves are not related to race or colour.[84]

The complete lack of jurisprudence on the crime of apartheid does not help clarify the legal uncertainties of the meaning of race. Scholars concur in that race is 'built upon vague, shifting, and erratic references to such factors as skin color, body build, eye cast or colour, hair texture, nose shape, blood type, genetic affiliation, and historical or cultural association'.[85] What is taken as a meaningful 'racial' differentiation depends entirely upon the classifier, the circumstances, and the purposes of the classification.[86]

The Apartheid Convention was modelled after the Genocide Convention.[87] Common to both is that the definition of race was not an issue of debate during their drafting process.[88] Indeed, the draft of the Apartheid Convention makes several references to racial group(s) without however defining them.[89] The demand for precision in the Convention, from some states fearing the weakening of ICERD due to the creation of the Apartheid Convention, did apparently not extend to a demand for a precise definition of race.[90] During the drafting process, the representative of Haiti, Mr. Verret, mentions the 'concept of apartheid on the basis of race and colour',[91] hence suggesting a distinction between the two notions. As mentioned earlier, however, statements by individual state representatives during treaty negotiations are not decisive for the interpretation of a treaty's wording.[92] In a historical-biblical review,

84 *South West Africa Cases* (*Ethiopia* v *South Africa*; *Liberia* v *South Africa*), Second Phase, Dissenting Opinion of Judge Tanaka, ICJ Judgment (1966), p. 308.

85 McDougal, Lasswell, Chen (n 8) 567. Accord: David Livingstone Smith, *Less Than Human: Why We Demean, Enslave, and Exterminate Others* (St. Martin's Press 2011) 165–168.

86 Frederick Osborn, 'Races and the Future of Man', in Richard Osborne (ed), *The Biological and Social Meaning of Race* (WH Freeman & Co. 1971) 161, 164. Similarly: Smith (n 85) 177.

87 Bultz (n 56) 214; Reydams (n 74) 59; Roger Clark, 'Crimes Against Humanity and the Rome Statute of the International Criminal Court', in Mauro Politi, Giuseppe Nesi (eds), *The Rome Statute of the International Criminal Court* (Ashgate 2001) 88; McDougal, Lasswell, Chen (n 8) 542.

88 Ratner, Abrams, Bischoff (n 3) 126. See Chapter 3.4.4 for the Genocide Convention's drafting history.

89 General Assembly, 26th Session, Third Committee, Draft to the Apartheid Convention presented by Guinea and the Soviet Union, UN Doc. A/C.3/L.1871 (28 October 1971). Furthermore. Booysen (n 67) 56.

90 Luvsandanzangiin Ider, Elimination of All Forms of Racial Discrimination, Report of the General Assembly Third Committee, UN Doc. A/8880 (13 November 1972), pp. 8–9; Igor Pavlovich Blishchenko, Study of the International Convention on the Suppression and Punishment of the Crime of Apartheid, UN Unit on Apartheid, Note No 3/74 (March 1974), p. 1.

91 UN Doc. A/PV.2185 (1973) 30 November 1973, p. 4, para. 34.

92 Also recognized by William Schabas, *Genocide in International Law: The Crime of Crimes* (CUP 2nd ed 2009) 637.

going all the way back to the creation of the world, Verret remembers historical clashes that 'have extinguished some races' and in the same breath talks about the 'Jewish people' and the 'black race'.[93] His perception of race more clearly shines through in the statements: 'We consider that all races are equal' and 'we know that beauty is subjective and that black is as beautiful as white'. Moreover, races were moulded from a combination of a nation or place of origin, but also skin colour.[94] In the understanding of Verret, there existed different races, who distinguished themselves on the basis of their skin colour ('black' and 'white').

In going beyond the Apartheid Convention's drafting history, other UN documents also reveal a distinction between race and colour. For example, when in 1947 the UDHR was drafted, the Indian delegate suggested that 'colour' be included along with 'race'. This suggestion was met with consternation. Some delegates expressed their fear that the insertion of 'colour' would lead to the conclusion *a contrario* that 'race' did not cover the term 'colour'. Furthermore, since the idea of race generally covered differences in colour, the addition of colour was superfluous, though not objectionable.[95] Race was not a precise or scientifically defined term and, if there was the slightest doubt, it was better to add the word 'colour' than risk leaving out certain groups.[96] These statements are significant: they demonstrate that as early as 1947, the concept of race was held to lack a scientific foundation and definition. Simultaneously, the notion of race was understood to include but also be broader than (skin) colour. Unlike international criminal law instruments that are narrowly construed, the UDHR as a human rights instrument needed to be drafted as broadly as possible in order to protect against any kind of discrimination.

Returning to apartheid, several sources distinguish between the notions of race and colour. For instance, both the Security Council resolution 417 (1977) and a General Assembly resolution of 1971 referred to 'race, creed or colour'; latter furthermore to 'the white inhabitants'.[97] In the *South West Africa* case, the ICJ notes that distinctions occur 'based on grounds of race, colour, descent or national or ethnic origin'.[98] All these sources differentiate between race and colour, in the belief that there exist distinct racial groups. Even at the time of

93 UN Doc. A/PV.2185 (1973) 30 November 1973, p. 4, para. 35.

94 Ibid, p. 5, para. 41.

95 See discussions in the ECOSOC, UNCHR, Sub-Commission on the Prevention of Discrimination and the Protection of Minorities, Summary Record of the Fourth Meeting, UN Doc. E/CN.4/Sub.2/SR.4 (26 November 1947), pp. 2–5. Furthermore: EW Vierdag, *The Concept of Discrimination in International Law: With Special Reference to Human Rights* (Martinus Nijhoff 1973) 97.

96 Sub-Commission on the Prevention of Discrimination and the Protection of Minorities (n 95), pp. 2–5.

97 UN SC Res. 417 of 31 October 1977; UN GA Res. 2775 (XXVI) 29 November 1971. Similar: Unit on Apartheid, Apartheid in Practice, UN Doc. ST/PSCA/SER.A/9 (1969).

98 *South West Africa* case, ICJ Advisory Opinion (1971), para. 131.

the creation of the Apartheid Convention, the concept of race was far from clear-cut. It appears rather to have consisted of a blend of skin colour with nationality or geographical origin. This understanding is also reflected in South African apartheid literature. In 1939, a hard-line defender of apartheid wrote that colour differences were 'not just an external, skin-deep' matter. Moreover, race was the 'manifestation of a deep, radical physical and psychological difference', a natural 'race-instinct'.[99] In other words, race was more than skin colour. Another apartheid scholar clarified that the

> Bantu and White man in South Africa belong to two different racial groups with distinctive and immutable racial characteristics. Physical differences of skin pigmentation, hair and facial expressions are relatively unimportant . . . racial differences are always accompanied by differences in culture, civilization, the general mode of living, and religion.[100]

The international community's attention focused on the apartheid policies of the South African state, and the regime's black/white dichotomy permeates many UN resolutions, reports, statements, as well as the literature of the time. Frequently, these documents contained references to notions of colour, which hold a meaning beyond that of skin colour, as the following examples show. A Security Council resolution of 1977 talks about 'the Black people . . . , as well as all other opponents of apartheid'.[101] The (capitalized) Black-people terminology was frequently used in UN resolutions to denote all the oppressed people of South Africa: Africans, Coloured people, and Indians, an official UN publication explains.[102] A UN report of 1953 illustrates the complexity of the racial issue in mentioning all the following expressions: 'non-Europeans', 'White ethnic group', 'Bantu', 'Indian', as well as '"Europeans", or of persons regarded as such'.[103] Particularly the ethnic terminology reveals its close interconnectedness with the concept of race. Finally, a letter addressed to the UN Secretary-General by the representatives of thirteen states notes that apartheid 'implies a permanent White superiority over the non-Whites',[104] thereby seemingly recognising that the concept of race entails ideas of a hierarchy between different groups.[105]

99 JD Vorster, quoted in Dubow (n 9) 221.
100 AB du Preez, quoted in Dubow (n 9) 214.
101 UN Doc. S/RES/417 (31 October 1977).
102 UN Blue Books Series, The United Nations and Apartheid (1994) 40.
103 Report of the UN Commission on the Racial Situation in the Union of South Africa, UN Doc. A/2505 and Add. 1, para. 897 (v) (1953). The reference to the perception of a person's racial affiliation is explained by the apartheid jurisdiction of South Africa itself, see further ahead.
104 Letter addressed to the Secretary-General by the permanent representatives of Afghanistan, Burma, Egypt, India, Indonesia, Iran, Iraq, Lebanon, Pakistan, the Philippines, Saudi Arabia, Syria, and Yemen, UN Doc. A72183 (12 September 1952).
105 See Chapters 3.2 and 3.3 on related discussions for the crime of genocide.

The domestic South African apartheid laws did not define race either. Rather, they applied various criteria for classifying a person into a racial group. Individuals were categorised on the basis of their appearance, social acceptance, and descent (or blood, as it commonly was called), the purpose being to define their individual social, economic, and political status.[106] The 1950 Population Registration Act and its later Amendment Acts together laid the legal foundations for the categorisation of the population, but failed to prescribe comprehensive rules for race classifications. Therefore, in contentious cases, tests of 'appearance' and 'general acceptance' were applied. The business of determining a person's racial category included the examination of habits, education and speech, and deportment and demeanour were also taken into account.[107] In borderline cases eyelid and hair tests were applied, and even sporting preferences were considered.[108] According to the Act, a 'white person' meant 'a person who in appearance obviously is, or who is generally accepted as a white person, but does not include a person who, although in appearance obviously a white person, is generally accepted as a coloured person',[109] thus combining physical appearance and social acceptability, including linguistic skills.[110] The Act's definition of a 'coloured person' was 'a person who is not a white person or a native', while "native" was understood as 'a person who in fact is or is generally accepted as a member of any aboriginal race or tribe of Africa'.[111] The absurdity of this legal system of racial classification can be exemplified by way of a 1981 ruling of a Johannesburg magistrate. The magistrate convicted a woman previously considered white for living in a white area. The magistrate held that she was coloured because she had 'a flat nose, wavy hair, a pale skin, and high cheekbones'. On appeal, the Supreme Court set the conviction aside. It ruled that while the woman was obviously not white, she was 'generally accepted' as such.[112]

Despite the fact that the Apartheid Convention was created at a time of white/black binaries, John Dugard and John Reynolds posit that a broader understanding of race is granted. They recognise that the UN Charter, UDHR, ICERD, and the Apartheid Convention all fail to define the content of race itself. However, the Apartheid Convention refers to the ICERD in its preamble and the authors therefore suggest using the latter in the interpretation of race.[113]

106 Dugard, Reynolds (n 13) 873; Bowker, Star (n 16) 208; Omond (n 17) 25.
107 Omond (n 17) 25; Maylam (n 8) 184.
108 Ibid 185, refers to a statement made by the Race Classification Board: 'A soccer player is a Native, a rugby player is a Coloured'. See also Bowker, Star (n 16) 210.
109 §1(1) Population Registration Act 30 (1950), Art. 1.
110 Johan van der Vyver, 'Prosecution and Punishment of the Crime of Genocide', 23 *Fordham International Law Journal* (2000) 303.
111 §1(1) Population Registration Act 30 (1950), Art. 1; Unit on Apartheid, Apartheid in Practice, UN Doc. ST/PSCA/SER.A/9 (1969), p. 41.
112 Omond (n 17) 25.
113 Dugard, Reynolds (n 13) 886. Accord: Falk, Tilley (n 82) 3. Accord: Evelyne Schmid, *Taking Economic, Social and Cultural Rights Seriously in International Criminal Law* (CUP 2015) 142, without further discussing the definition of race.

This suggestion justifies an analysis of how ICERD defines racial discrimination and apartheid. Moreover, the proposal raises the question whether human rights law can be used for the interpretation of international criminal law in general and for race-related crimes in particular.

4.5.3 Reverting to human rights law for the interpretation of international criminal law

The Apartheid Convention was intended to complement the general prohibition of apartheid in Art. 3 ICERD that reads: 'State Parties particularly condemn racial segregation and apartheid and undertake to prevent, prohibit and eradicate all practices of this nature in territories under their jurisdiction'. Apartheid was singled out because, at the time, it was the only instance of racial discrimination in the form of an official government policy.[114] In providing a detailed definition of apartheid, the provision had the aim of taking more effective measures at the international and national levels with a view to the suppression and punishment of the crime.[115] The Apartheid Convention and ICERD are set in two distinct areas of law, namely international criminal law and human rights law, respectively. This study asserts that human rights law cannot be directly invoked as basis for an interpretation of substantive international criminal law, exemplified by the following discussion. On a formal level, international criminal courts are not, and cannot become, party to human rights treaties.[116] Nonetheless, there are compelling arguments for assuming that they should adhere to internationally recognised human rights standards. The ICC contains an explicit reference to human rights in Art. 21(3) Rome Statute. The *ad hoc* tribunals, for their part, were set up as subsidiary organs of the UN Security Council.[117] As such, they are to be expected to follow the principles that underlie various UN instruments, most notably the UN Charter. On a procedural level, the ICTY Appeals Chamber has emphasized that the international tribunals are not bound by the findings of regional or other international courts, such as the jurisprudence of the European Court of Human Rights (ECtHR).[118] But while not binding, both *ad hoc* tribunals consider the jurisprudence a useful and persuasive source of guidance and assistance in the interpretation of the ICTY and ICTR Statutes.[119] Also human rights courts,

114 Lerner (n 70) 51.
115 Last paragraph of the Apartheid Convention's preamble. Furthermore: Lerner (n 80) 210; Dugard, Reynolds (n 13) 877; Du Plessis (n 3) 420.
116 Yvonne McDermott, 'The Influence of International Human Rights Law on International Criminal Procedure', in Philipp Kastner (ed), *International Criminal Law in Context* (Routledge 2018) 283.
117 See Chapters 3.6.2 and 3.9.2.
118 *The Case Against Hartmann*, Case No IT-02–54-R77.5-A (19 July 2011), para. 159.
119 *Prosecutor v Kajelijeli*, Case No ICTR-98–44A-A (23 May 2005), paras. 209, 221, 230; *Prosecutor v Semanza*, Case No ICTR-97–20-A (31 May 2000), para. 78; *Prosecutor v*

like the Inter-American Court for Human Rights (IACHR), have emphasized that human rights law and criminal law have different aims and warned against confusing the international protection of human rights with criminal justice. The objective of international human rights law is not to punish individuals guilty of violations, but rather to protect the victims and provide reparation of damages resulting from state acts.[120] The jurisprudence of the international criminal courts is specked with references to the jurisprudence of international human rights bodies, to the extent of an 'asymmetry of influence',[121] with human rights law having a deeper influence on international criminal law than vice versa.[122] As an example, the ICTY Trial Chamber in *Furundžija* dealt with the question of the direct applicability of the customary law prohibition of torture that originated in interstate treaties[123] for the interpretation of the crime of torture under the ICTY Statute. The judges concluded that a direct application to international criminal law of a rule that imposed state responsibility rather than individual criminal responsibility was not possible.[124] The normative content of a rule has therefore to be taken into consideration before transposing it to another body of law.[125] The *Kunarac* trial judgment also dealt with torture and considered the direct applicability of human rights law in the interpretation of the substantive law of the ICTY Statute. The Trial Chamber held that the definition of torture under human rights law did not comprise the same elements as torture under international humanitarian law and could therefore only serve as an interpretative aid.[126] The same conclusion must be reached for the interpretation of race in international criminal law. Human rights law on race can, at best, assist in the interpretation of its criminal law pendant. The next section analyses whether this conclusion equally applies to the definition of racial discrimination and apartheid.

Kambanda, Case No ICTR-97-23-A (19 October 2000), para. 33; *Prosecutor v Tadić*, Case No IT-94-1-A (15 July 1999), para. 321. Furthermore: Bartłomiej Krzan, 'Human Rights and International Criminal Law', in Bartłomiej Krzan (ed), *Prosecuting International Crimes: A Multidisciplinary Approach* (Brill Nijhoff 2016) 160–161; Vladimir Tochilovsky, *The Law and Jurisprudence of the International Criminal Tribunals and Courts* (Intersentia 2nd ed 2014) 1367.

120 *Velásquez-Rodríguez v Honduras*, IACtHR Judgment (29 July 1988), para. 134.

121 Sergey Vasiliev, 'International Criminal Tribunals in the Shadow of Strasbourg and Politics of Cross-Fertilization', 84 *Nordic Journal of International Law* (2015) 374.

122 McDermott (n 116) 287.

123 Such as the Convention Respecting the Laws and Customs of War on Land (Hague Convention IV), 36 Stat. 2277; Treaty Series 539 (18 October 1907); Lieber Code, based on Francis Lieber, Instructions for the Government of Armies of the United States (1863).

124 *Prosecutor v Furundžija*, Case No IT-95-17/1-T (10 December 1998), paras. 137, 159.

125 Similarly: McDermott (n 116) 284–285; Mohamed Shahabuddeen, *International Criminal Justice at the Yugoslav Tribunal: A Judge's Recollection* (OUP 2012) 231.

126 *Prosecutor v Kunarac* et al., Case Nos. IT-96-23-T and IT-96-23/1-T (22 February 2001), paras. 482, 496.

4.5.4 *Interpreting racial discrimination and apartheid by means of the International Convention on the Elimination of Racial Discrimination*

Of all the international instruments that contain the notion of race, only Art. 1(1) ICERD provides a widely accepted, broad definition of racial discrimination:

> any distinction, exclusion, restriction or preference based on race, colour, descent, or national or ethnic origin which has the purpose or effect of nullifying or impairing the recognition, enjoyment or exercise, on an equal footing, of human rights and fundamental freedoms in the political, economic, social, cultural or any other field of public life.

ICERD contains a stipulative definition rather than one flowing from the usual meaning of race, Patrick Thornberry emphasizes, and is therefore perhaps best considered as a definition solely for the purpose of ICERD itself.[127] The definition of Art. 1(1) ICERD may thus be valid in the context of human rights violations or as a more general principle of non-discrimination; its direct applicability to international criminal law, however, is questionable. Hence, while different branches of law might revert to the same terminology like 'race', their meanings nonetheless differ, owing to the particular assumptions and aims of each legal branch. 'It is far from obvious', Robert Kolb aptly remarks, 'to seek for the natural meaning of a word in another area of the law, without having first established by specific arguments that both areas share the same parameters and aims'.[128] Is the definition of racial discrimination therefore applicable to the interpretation of the law of apartheid? Could ICERD's definition be used in the interpretation of the law of genocide and persecution that contain the word 'racial' too? Racial discrimination is, according to ICERD, such discrimination as is based on, among other things, race. ICERD does not actually define race. Rather, race is listed alongside the ancillary concepts of colour, descent, and national and ethnic origin. Unfortunately, ICERD's drafting history does not clarify the understanding of race, and legal commentators have assumed that the drafters intended to embrace all traditional biological and cultural meanings of race.[129] The academic literature

127 Patrick Thornberry, *International Law and the Rights of Minorities* (Clarendon Press 1991/1992) 160.

128 Robert Kolb, 'The Jurisprudence of the Yugoslav and Rwandan Criminal Tribunals on Their Jurisdiction and on International Crimes (2004–2013)', 84 *BYIL* (2014) 146.

129 Francesco Capotorti, Report of the Sixteenth Session of the Sub-Commission on Prevention of Discrimination and Protection of Minorities to the UNCHR, UN Doc. E/CN.4/873, E/CN.4/Sub.2/241, (11 February 1964), pp. 13–57; McDougal, Lasswell, Chen (n 8) 588; Egon Schwelb, 'The International Convention on the Elimination of All Forms of Racial Discrimination', 15 *International and Comparative Law Quarterly* (1966) 1002.

has notably refrained from discussing the different discriminatory grounds and usually limits itself to juxtaposing them.[130] The efforts of Walter Kälin and Jörg Künzli represent a remarkable exception: they recognise that race terminologically speaking was the 'outcome of a collective ascription' and generally taken to refer to a group of people 'who are perceived as being different and possibly inferior by other groups on account of particular physical and/or cultural attributes'.[131] They acknowledge the association between race and 'social relations involving oppression, subjugation, hatred of the "other", and defence of what is perceived to be one's own'.[132] Albeit suggesting such a timely definition of race, the term's interpretation remains a vexing issue for the determination of racial discrimination.[133]

Steven Ratner and co-authors recognise that the interpretation of a racial group would be an entirely different one if one were to rely on ICERD's definition, which was much wider.[134] Instead, they suggest using the South African classification system of race as a point of reference for the definition of race, since the Apartheid Convention principally addressed South Africa. A racial group would therefore exclude any group defined by itself or by others on terms other than race/skin colour, such as ethnicity or national origin.[135] Relying on ICERD for a definition of race for the crime of apartheid, Corsin Bisaz agrees, would be 'a very broad understanding indeed and will include most if not all groups referred to as "minorities" and "indigenous peoples" as well'.[136] The law of apartheid, however, exclusively protects racial groups. It would therefore be incorrect to expand the scope of that protection to include virtually any discriminated group. Moreover, such an expansion of the protection to embrace minorities as an independent group category has categorically been rejected for the law of genocide although the law more broadly protects the national, ethnic, and religious group in addition to the racial group.[137] It is therefore by no means evident why Art. 1(1) ICERD should be admissible for an expansive interpretation of race for the crime of apartheid.

The Committee on the Elimination of Racial Discrimination (CERD) incorporated groups like non-citizens, migrant workers, and ethno-cultural

130 See criticism in Gro Nystuen, *Achieving Peace or Protecting Human Rights? Conflicts Between Norms Regarding Ethnic Discrimination in the Dayton Peace Agreement* (Martinus Nijhoff 2005) 118.
131 Walter Kälin, Jörg Künzli, *The Law of International Human Rights Protection* (OUP 2009) 369.
132 Ibid.
133 Ibid.
134 Ratner, Abrams, Bischoff (n 3) 126.
135 Ibid.
136 Corsin Bisaz, *The Concept of Group Rights in International Law: Groups as Contested Right-Holders, Subjects and Legal Persons* (Martinus Nijhoff 2012) 103.
137 See Chapter 3.5.2.2 with a discussion of the *Krstić* trial judgment.

groups as nomadic tribes or descent-based caste groups into the definition of racial discrimination.[138] Due to the rule of strict construction that requires the language of a law to be construed such as to fall within the reasonable meaning of its terms and the spirit and scope of the treaty it is contained in, it is doubtful whether such a wide-ranging interpretation of the racial group would stand up to the scrutiny of an international criminal court. The crime against humanity of apartheid cannot be broadened to include migrant workers or nomadic tribes, unless the perpetrator perceives them as belonging to a distinct racial group. Not only would such an interpretation go far beyond the original meaning of race under the South African apartheid regime, it would also exceed any contemporary legal understanding of race for international criminal law. In spite of a subjective approach and a primary reliance on perception for the definition of race, the interpretation cannot be expanded to include any group subjected to discrimination. In sum, it appears unlikely that a criminal tribunal would accept the definition of a racial group as suggested by Dugard and Reynolds. Yet the authors deserve praise for recognising that the question of race is a sociological rather than a biological one.[139] In their further analysis, they claim it was of critical importance whether the respective groups could be identified as having acquired a permanent and irrefutable group membership at birth and were furthermore entwined in a relationship of domination. At first sight, the authors seem to suggest race is an inherent, objective trait, their precise wording being 'identified as groups whose membership is generally understood as fixed and incontestable from acquisition at birth'.[140] However, in coherence with their recognition of race as a sociological concept, it appears more likely that the identification is performed by the perpetrator, based on what he understands to be fixed categories. This interpretation reflects earlier discussions whereby the concept of race for international criminal law is inherently linked to a situation of domination, which Dugard and Reynolds also recognise.[141] More precisely, the question of race is connected to the labelling and stigmatisation of members of a group, singled out by the perpetrator as targets of his criminal acts. The perpetrator dominates a group he considers and treats as inferior. Since the definition of the protected racial group depends on the perpetrator's perception thereof, group membership to it cannot be incontestable from acquisition at birth. It does not matter whether one is born into a group, only whether the perpetrator perceives the victims as being members of the group.[142]

138 CERD, Concluding Observations India, UN Doc. CERD/C/IND/CO/19 (5 May 2007), para. 8. Furthermore: Dugard, Reynolds (n 13) 887.

139 See Dugard, Reynolds (n 13) 889.

140 Ibid.

141 See particularly Chapters 2.7 and 3.2.

142 See discussion in Chapter 3.6.3.

4.5.5 *Contemporary cases of apartheid?*

Despite its contentiousness, there are indications that seem to reveal an understanding of the Apartheid Convention as valid law rather than a dead letter. First, the *Tadić* appeals judgment's explicit reference to the Convention evidences a belief in the treaty's continuing validity.[143] Second, a total of ten states either ratified or acceded to the Apartheid Convention after the South African apartheid regime came to an end in 1994. The latest was the ratification by the State of Palestine in 2014.[144] Palestine's accession is of particular interest given that the situation in the Occupied Palestinian Territories (OPT) commonly is named as an alleged case of apartheid.[145] The Apartheid Convention could indeed experience a similar fate as the Genocide Convention that was considered a *nudum pactum*, an empty, unenforceable pact for which there is no consideration, raising 'serious doubts' about its 'continuing juristic vitality'.[146] Finally, inquiries into the situations in the Democratic People's Republic of Korea (DPRK) and OPT might reawaken interest in the Apartheid Convention, particularly because UN officials describe them as apartheid-like. The subsequent sections will briefly discuss these two situations.

In March 2017, the Economic and Social Commission for Western Asia (ESCWA) published a quasi-legal report on the *Israeli Practices Towards the Palestinian People and the Question of Apartheid: Palestine and the Israeli Occupation* and based its legal analysis on the Apartheid Convention. The report holds that in the 'geopolitical context of Palestine, Jews and Palestinians can be considered racial groups',[147] thereby triggering the question whether (unwritten) contextual elements should be reverted to in the interpretation of the law of apartheid and the 'racial group' element of the crime. The report furthermore concludes that there exists a comprehensive regime created to dominate the non-Jewish population, hence negatively defining the victim group of apartheid.[148] Already in January 2014, the UN Special Rapporteur Richard Falk, who

143 *Prosecutor v Tadić*, Case No IT-94–1-AR72, Decision on the Defence Motion for Interlocutory Appeal on Jurisdiction (2 October 1995), para. 140.

144 The most recent state parties are Uruguay (2012), Montenegro (2006), Georgia (2005), Republic of Moldova (2005); Guatemala (2005), Honduras (2005), Paraguay (2005), Serbia (2001) and Azerbaijan (1996). Clark (n 74) 599, confirms that recent accessions reveal a continuous interest in the Convention.

145 See Carsten Stahn, *A Critical Introduction to International Criminal Law* (CUP 2018) 69; Hall, van den Herik (n 81) 235; Lingaas (n 2) 86–115; Dugard, Reynolds (n 13) 867 et seq; Paul Eden, 'The Practices of Apartheid as a War Crime: A Critical Analysis', in Terry Gill (ed), 16 *Yearbook of International Humanitarian Law* (2013) 101–104.

146 Barry Schiller, 'Life in a Symbolic Universe: Comments on the Genocide Convention and International Law', 9 *Southwestern University Law Review* (1977) 51. For the definition of *nudum pactum*, see <www.publiccontractinginstitute.com/contracts-without-consideration-the-nudum-pactum-mistake-2/>. See also Stahn (n 145) 34.

147 Falk, Tilley (n 82) 3. See also ibid. 20–24.

148 Ibid 6.

co-authored the ESCWA report, presented another report that analysed apartheid as a war crime under Additional Protocol I to the Geneva Conventions; a crime against humanity under Art. 2 Apartheid Convention and Art. 7(2)(h) Rome Statute, and a violation of human rights law under Art. 3 ICERD. In addition to measures on the interstate level, the report suggests a criminal investigation of key individuals before the ICC.[149] Regarding the definition of the Israeli Jews and the Palestinians as two distinct racial groups, the report concludes that 'race is in fact not the sole factor' according to Art. 1 ICERD and that ICERD relates to different races, national or ethnic groups, or indigenous peoples.[150] In other words, Falk submits the application of ICERD's broad definition of race in the interpretation of criminal provisions, a suggestion that this study rejects. In 2011, the Russell Tribunal on Palestine concluded that the perceptions of Israel Jewish and Palestinian identities illustrated that they were two distinct, identifiable groups in the sense of the legal definition of apartheid.[151] Albeit not legally binding, this legal analysis is noteworthy for applying a double-subjective approach to race, based on the groups' mutual perceptions. This study, however, repudiates the application of a double-subjective approach to international criminal law, arguing that it does not reflect the perpetrator's definitional power over the (racial) victim group. In 16 January 2015, on its own initiative, the ICC Prosecutor announced the opening of a preliminary examination into the situation in Palestine. In addition, in May 2018, the State of Palestine referred the situation in Palestine to the ICC for investigation, explicitly requesting an investigation into the crime of apartheid.[152] The situation has now been assigned to the ICC's Pre-Trial Chamber I.[153]

As to North Korea, the Chair of the Commission of Inquiry on Human Rights in the DPRK, Michael Kirby, in a public statement of March 2014 termed the *songbun* social caste system an apartheid system.[154] Conversely, the Commission's official report does not mention apartheid with a word, but does nonetheless urge a referral of the situation to the ICC Prosecutor.[155] In December

149 Richard Falk, Report of the Special Rapporteur on the Situation of Human Rights in the Palestinian Territories Occupied since 1967, UN Doc. A/HRC/25/67 (13 January 2014), paras. 78–80.

150 Ibid para. 54. In 2012, the CERD also referred to apartheid in discussing the racial segregation by Israel (Consideration of Reports Submitted by States Parties under Article 9 of the Convention, Concluding Observations of the CERD, UN Doc. CERD/C/ISR/CO/14–16, 9 March 2012, para. 24).

151 Russell Tribunal on Palestine (n 3) para. 5.20.

152 Referral by the State of Palestine Pursuant to Articles 13(a) and 14 of the Rome Statute (15 May 2018): <www.icc-cpi.int/itemsDocuments/2018-05-22_ref-palestine.pdf>, p. 7.

153 *Situation in the State of Palestine*, Decision assigning the situation in the State of Palestine to Pre-Trial Chamber I, Case No ICC-01/18 (24 May 2018).

154 <www.ohchr.org/EN/NewsEvents/Pages/DisplayNews.aspx?NewsID=14385&LangID=E>.

155 Report of the Detailed Findings of the Commission of Inquiry on Human Rights in the Democratic People's Republic of Korea, UN Doc. A/HRC/25/CRP.1 (7 February 2014),

2014, the UN General Assembly approved a (non-binding) resolution requesting the Security Council to refer the DPRK to the ICC.[156] Thus far, initiatives of referral have been unsuccessful. Unlike the situation in Palestine, the case of DPRK does not appear to be prioritised by either the Security Council, the States Parties to the Rome Statute or the ICC Prosecutor. If the case of North Korea were to be referred to the ICC, a legal analysis of the *songbun* system as a crime against humanity of apartheid should be anticipated. If the *songbun* is structured upon social classes rather than understandings of race, an application of the law of apartheid becomes unlikely.

The crime against humanity of apartheid in Art. 7(1)(j) in conjunction with Art. 7(2)(h) Rome Statute derives from the definition of the crime in the Apartheid Convention. The next section will look at the inclusion of the crime of apartheid onto the ICC's list of crimes against humanity, which by no means could have been foreseen, considering the contentious nature of the crime of apartheid.

4.6 The crime against humanity of apartheid in the Rome Statute

4.6.1 The disputed inclusion of apartheid into the Rome Statute

The ICTY and ICTR had begun working in 1993 and 1994, respectively, and certainly influenced developments leading to the creation of the ICC. The *ad hoc* tribunals did not contain the crime of apartheid in their respective statutes, either as a crime against humanity or as a war crime, notwithstanding the International Committee of the Red Cross's (ICRC) appeal to include it in the ICTY statute.[157] Interestingly, the ICC was drafted upon, inter alia, a formulation of the 1981 Study on Ways and Means of Insuring the Implementation of International Instruments such as the International Convention on the Suppression and Punishment of the Crime of Apartheid, thereby linking the crime of apartheid at an early stage with the prospective international criminal court.[158]

---

paras. 1218 and 1225. The 2017 report does not discuss apartheid or (racial) discrimination (Tomás Ojea Quintana, Report of the Special Rapporteur on the Situation of Human Rights in the DPRK, UN Doc. A/HRC/34/66, 22 February 2017).

156 UN Doc. A/RES/69/188 (21 January 2015), p. 6. On 10 December 2015, the Security Council had the human rights situation in the DPRK on its agenda (UN Doc. S/PV.7575).

157 Hall, van den Herik (n 81) 233; Bultz (n 56) 218. It remains unclear why the crime of apartheid was omitted from the ICTY Statute.

158 UN Doc. E/CN.4/1426 (19 January 1981). See Hall, van den Herik (n 81) 282; M. Cherif Bassiouni, *Introduction to International Criminal Law* (Martinus Nijhoff 2nd ed 2013) 584–585; M. Cherif Bassiouni, *The Legislative History of the International Criminal Court, Volume 1: Introduction, Analysis, and Integrated Text of the Statute, Elements of Crimes and Rules of Procedure and Evidence* (Transnational Publishers 2005) 33, 61–62.

The 1981 study was drafted because Art. 5 Apartheid Convention explicitly demands the creation of an international penal tribunal with jurisdiction over the crimes listed in the Convention. An ILC report of 1991 emphasised that apartheid was an institutionalized form of racial discrimination that aimed at perpetuating domination of a racial group and oppressing it. According to the report, the practice was so deeply condemned by the world's conscience that it was inconceivable for the ILC to exclude it from a future international criminal code. It confirmed that the definition of the crime of apartheid in the Draft Code of Crimes (1989) was based, both in letter and in spirit, on Art. 2 Apartheid Convention.[159] As a result, the ILC Draft Code of Crimes (1991) included a draft statute for an international criminal court,[160] into which the crime of apartheid was incorporated despite 'doubts about its customary nature',[161] and, remarkably, without any reference to the situation in South Africa. Art. 20(2) reads:

> Apartheid consists of any of the following acts based on policies and practices of racial segregation and discrimination committed for the purpose of establishing or maintaining domination by one racial group over any other racial group and systematically oppressing it.[162]

The drafting committee considered the definition of apartheid already incorporated in the Convention as generally acceptable.[163] The only significant modification was to omit reference to the Southern African situation. The chairman of the committee stated that the Apartheid Convention had been drafted to fit the particular situation in southern Africa, but that the definition of apartheid was now reworded so as to look to the future as well,[164] thereby confirming the impression that the Convention was custom-made for the South African situation, yet that the crime could be committed elsewhere in the world.[165]

During the discussions on the report of the Working Group on the Draft Statute for an ICC, there was no agreement among the ILC members on the crime of apartheid. The discussions in the ILC reveal that the position of apartheid as a treaty crime or a crime in customary international law was unclear and unresolved, in part due to the lack of state practice as an indication that

159 UN Doc. A/46/10 (1991), pp. 102–103.

160 Draft Code of Crimes Against the Peace and Security of Mankind (Part II), including a draft statute for an international criminal court, UN Doc. A/CN.4/365 (1983) and UN Doc. A/CN.4/L.459 (1991).

161 Robert Cryer, *Prosecuting International Crimes – Selectivity and the International Criminal Law Regime* (CUP 2005) 259; Dugard (n 56) 200; Gebhard (n 5), para. 25.

162 UN Doc. A/CN.4/L.459 (1991), p. 216, para. 39.

163 Ibid para. 40.

164 Ibid.

165 See discussion in Chapter 4.5.

opinio juris had not crystallized.[166] Chapter 4.8 will discuss these issues further. As a result, the 1994 Draft Statute for an ICC did not include apartheid as an own crime against humanity. It was, however, listed as a treaty crime in the annex and within the context of the Additional Protocol I to the Geneva Conventions that includes apartheid as a war crime.[167]

The 1996 ILC Draft Code of Crimes contained no explicit provision on apartheid either. All the same, apartheid was not completely eliminated from the Draft Code. Art. 18(f) comprised a somewhat generic version of apartheid, prohibiting 'institutionalized discrimination on racial, ethnic or religious grounds involving the violation of fundamental human rights and freedoms and resulting in seriously disadvantaging a part of the population'.[168] The ILC Commentary to the Draft Code held that this institutionalised discrimination was 'in fact the crime of apartheid under a more general denomination', thus expanding the protection beyond the racial group to embrace ethnical and religious groups, too.[169] This expansion is, in the view of this study, the most significant addition of the 1996 Draft Code of Crimes, compared to the Apartheid Convention's definition of the crime. With the inclusion of the crime of apartheid into the Rome Statute, this expansion was, however, reverted and the protection limited to racial groups only.

The Rome Statute was drafted at the UN Diplomatic Conference of Plenipotentiaries on the Establishment of an ICC during the months of June and July of 1998. On the first day, the representative from the South African delegation said that the ICC should make clear that perpetrators of the crimes committed under the apartheid system would no longer go unpunished, acknowledging the failure of the international community to adequately condemn and punish these crimes in the past.[170] Neither the crime against humanity of apartheid nor any institutionalised discrimination was included in any of the draft statutes.[171] On 22 June 1998, a larger group of states formally submitted a proposal to include 'institutionalized racial discrimination, including the practices of apartheid' into the list of crimes against humanity.[172] The very same day, the group

166 ILC, Report of the Working Group on a Draft Statute for an International Criminal Court, A/CN.4/SR.2359 (1994), paras. 33–47; ILC, Report of the Working Group on a Draft Statute for an International Criminal Court, A/CN.4/SR.2360 (29 June 1994), paras. 2 and 15.

167 <http://legal.un.org/ilc/texts/instruments/english/commentaries/7_4_1994.pdf>. See Chapter 4.7 on war crimes.

168 Draft Code of Crimes Against the Peace and Security of Mankind: Titles and Texts of Articles on the Draft Code of Crimes Against the Peace and Security of Mankind, UN Doc. A/51/10 (1996), p. 49.

169 Ibid note 12. See Hall, van den Herik (n 81) 233; Dugard (n 56) 200.

170 UN Doc. A/CONF.183/SR.2, paras. 14–15. See Ronald Slye, Beth van Schaack, *International Criminal Law: The Essentials* (Wolters Kluwer 2009) 234; Clark (n 87) 87.

171 Bultz (n 56) 221.

172 UN Doc. A/CONF.183/C.1/L.12. The group consisted of Bangladesh, India, Lesotho, Malawi, Mexico, Namibia, South Africa, Swaziland, Trinidad and Tobago, and Tanzania.

rephrased its proposal and requested the insertion of a subparagraph with the wording 'as well as the practices of apartheid and other inhumane and degrading practices involving outrage upon personal dignity based on racial discrimination'.[173] On 17 July 1998, the Rome Statute with the crime of apartheid included in the list of crimes against humanity was formally adopted. The inclusion of apartheid in the Rome Statute was a novelty, which some state delegations greeted initially with reluctance.[174] Arguments raised against listing apartheid as a crime against humanity *proprio motu* was that acts of apartheid could be subsumed under the 'other inhumane acts' of Art. 7(1)(k) Rome Statute or under the provisions of persecution on racial grounds (Art. 7(1)(h) Rome Statute).[175] In the end, however, the majority of states agreed that apartheid was of a character and gravity similar to other inhumane acts and had moreover been identified as crime against humanity in earlier instruments, although none of the major precedents to the ICC (Nuremberg Tribunal, Tokyo Tribunal, CCL No 10, ICTY or ICTR) contained this crime.[176] The South African delegation managed to convince the other delegations 'with the unassailable moral authority of its own painful national experience'[177] that the crime of apartheid be included in the list of crimes against humanity. The other delegations surrendered to the coalition's demand, fearing they would otherwise be perceived as contributing to prolonging the South African suffering.[178] In retrospect, it has been argued, the inclusion of apartheid on the list of crimes against humanity increased the harmonisation of international criminal law, since earlier instruments already had determined its status as a crime against humanity, something the Rome Statute now confirmed.[179] The fact that apartheid did not end up in the collective provision of 'other inhumane acts' is a strong reaffirmation of its universal condemnation.[180] Unlike the crime of genocide, the definition of the

173 UN Doc. A/CONF.183/C.1/L.13.

174 Geert-Jan Alexander Knoops, Mens Rea *at the International Criminal Court* (Brill Nijhoff, 2017) 141–142.

175 Timothy McCormack, 'Crimes Against Humanity', in Dominic McGoldrick, Peter Rowe, Eric Donnelly (eds), *The Permanent International Criminal Court: Legal and Policy Issues* (Hart 2004) 198; Herman von Hebel, Darryl Robinson, 'Crimes Within the Jurisdiction of the Court', in Roy Lee (ed), *The International Criminal Court – The Making of the Rome Statute; Issues, Negotiations, Results* (Kluwer Law International 1999) 102. See Chapter 5.4 on the crime against humanity of persecution under the Rome Statute.

176 Note that UN Transitional Administration in East Timor, UNTAET/REG/2000/15 (6 June 2000), Section 6(1)(j) lists the crime of apartheid as a crime against humanity. Furthermore: Gideon Boas, James Bischoff, Natalie Reid, *Elements of Crimes Under International Law: International Criminal Law Practitioners Library Series* (CUP 2008) 109; von Hebel, Robinson (n 175) 102.

177 McCormack (n 175) 198–199.

178 Ibid 199; Clark (n 87) 87.

179 Carline Fournet, *International Crimes: Theories, Practice and Evolution* (Cameron May 2006) 36.

180 Ilias Bantekas, Susan Nash, *International Criminal Law* (Routledge-Cavendish 3rd ed 2007) 136.

crime of apartheid was not 'copy-pasted' from its treaty counterpart, although its reference to racial groups 'still reveals its historic roots'.[181] The definition of the crime of apartheid as adopted in the Rome Statute requires an institutionalised regime actively promoting such an attack against a civilian population, thereby excluding random acts of racial discrimination by individuals.[182]

Considering the often-criticised crime of apartheid in the Apartheid Convention as well as the end of the South African apartheid regime in 1994, it is indeed remarkable that the crime was included into the ICC Statute.[183] Overall, scholars are split: either they approve or they condemn the inclusion of apartheid, the significance of which certainly triggered legal academic analysis. For example, Roger Clark holds that the addition of the crime of apartheid was more symbolic than anything else.[184] John Reynolds even asserts:

> Apartheid has been a largely forgotten and neglected concept in international law since the collapse of the regime in South Africa. . . . Despite the comprehensive treatment of apartheid by the international legal system, there remains a sense among many international lawyers that it was a *sui generis* regime, specific to South Africa, and has now been confined to the annals of legal history.[185]

Christian Tomuschat, former ILC member, criticises the inclusion of apartheid as a 'backward-oriented blunt term' and characterised the crime as 'the most controversial offence',[186] while Margaret deGuzman perceives the inclusion of the crime of apartheid an important clarification of the law.[187] Markus Wagner considers the inclusion of apartheid, as a distinct crime from persecution, in the Rome Statute appropriate: apartheid differs from persecution in that it

181 Hall, van den Herik (n 81) 282. See Chapter 3.4.4 on the drafting history of the crime of genocide.

182 Bultz (n 56) 222; McCormack (n 175) 199–200.

183 Hall, van den Herik (n 81) 233; Tomuschat (n 70) 245; Machteld Boot, *Genocide, Crimes Against Humanity, War Crimes:* Nullum Crimen Sine Lege *and the Subject Matter Jurisdiction of the International Criminal Court* (Intersentia 2002) 472. Disaccord: Karen Parker, Lyn Beth Neylon, '*Jus Cogens*: Compelling the Law of Human Rights', 12 *Hastings International and Comparative Law Review* (1988–1989) 439.

184 Clark (n 87) 88. See also Gerhard Werle, Florian Jessberger *Principles of International Criminal Law* (OUP 3rd ed 2014) 383; Bultz (n 56) 233; Dugard (n 56) 206; Zahar (n 70) 245; Clark (n 74) 619.

185 Reynolds (n 9) 209. Similarly Dugard (n 56) 201.

186 Tomuschat (n 70) 238.

187 Margaret McAuliffe DeGuzman, 'The Road From Rome: The Developing Law of Crimes Against Humanity', 22 *Human Rights Quarterly* (2000) 353. See also Roy Lee, 'The Rome Conference and Its Contribution to International Law', in Roy Lee (ed), *The International Criminal Court – The Making of the Rome Statute; Issues, Negotiations, Results* (Kluwer Law International 1999) 31; Kelly Askin, 'Crimes Within the Jurisdiction of the International Criminal Court', 10 *Criminal Law Forum* (1999) 49.

sought the domination on various levels of one racial group over another racial group. In addition, the crime against humanity of apartheid confirms the stigma attached to it, as already evidenced by the Apartheid Convention.[188] While it is correct that the South African apartheid regime was formally abolished more than twenty years ago, it would nevertheless be bold to assume that there never could be a comparable regime elsewhere. Certain scholars possibly overlook the fact that the crime of apartheid as systematic oppression of one racial group by another, despite its terminological affiliation with South Africa, may occur again.[189] The crime of apartheid is, as such, not bound to the South African experience. Indeed, the international community agreed that apartheid is a crime against humanity, which due to its severity merited its inclusion in the Rome Statute. 'Apartheid constitutes a very specific crime against humanity', Ilias Bantekas observes, 'based solely on racial discrimination. It is relevant even after the collapse of the South African apartheid State'.[190]

Apartheid has been designated a threat to humanity, confirming that it is of international concern because its threshold exceeds a certain degree of gravity or otherwise violates fundamental values of humanity. The crime of apartheid might not necessarily transcend international borders and might therefore lack an internationalisation moment in not directly threatening the sovereignty or stability of another state.[191] While all international crimes shock the conscience of humanity, they do not always threaten global peace and security.[192] Apartheid is a crime of concern to humanity due to its magnitude and horrendousness. Numerous UN resolutions noted its threat against peace and security,[193] although it may not have emerged at the international level. The crime is morally repugnant in that a group of people is systematically discriminated against for reasons the group itself cannot control. The perpetrator classifies the racial group as less worthy. If a state apparatus or any other organisational system is used to enforce such discriminatory measures, the level of gravity is further enhanced. Even though the crime might not have transboundary effects – in the words of *Tadić* – a greater degree of moral turpitude might be attached to it.[194]

188 Markus Wagner, 'The ICC and its Jurisdiction: Myths, Misperceptions and Realities', in Armin von Bogdandy, Rüdiger Wolfrum (eds), 7 *Max Planck Yearbook of United Nations Law* (Martinus Nijhoff, 2003) 450–451. See also Clark (n 74) 600.

189 Accord: McDougal, Lasswell, Chen (n 8) 530.

190 Bantekas (n 3) 237.

191 Bassiouni (n 158) 147, referring to the crime of torture that does not have an international or a transnational element either.

192 Ibid 242, with the examples of slavery, human trafficking or piracy.

193 Eg UN SC Res. 392 (19 June 1976); UN SC Res. 134 (1 April 1960); UN GA Res. 1663 (XVI) (28 November 1961), UN Doc. A/RES/39/72 (13 December 1984). See also Chapter 4.4.3.

194 *Prosecutor v Tadić*, Case No IT-94–1A (15 July 1999), para. 271.

4.6.2 *The legal elements of the crime*

The Rome Statute defines the crime against humanity of apartheid in Art. 7(1)(j) in conjunction with Art. 7(2)(h):

> 1. For the purpose of this Statute, "crime against humanity" means any of the following acts when committed as part of a widespread or systematic attack directed against any civilian population, with knowledge of the attack:
> (j) The crime of apartheid;
> . . .
> 2. For the purpose of paragraph 1:
> (h) "The crime of apartheid" means inhumane acts of a character similar to those referred to in paragraph 1, committed in the context of an institutionalized regime of systematic oppression and domination by one racial group over any other racial group or groups and committed with the intention of maintaining that regime.

The crime of apartheid in Art. 7(1)(j) Rome Statute, according to some legal scholars, is merely a case of a *lex specialis* of, or even absorbed by, the crime of persecution in Art. 7(1)(g) Rome Statute.[195] This section discusses two legal elements of the crime of apartheid, namely 'racial group' and the *mens rea*, showing in the process that the crimes of apartheid and persecution are distinct, as Chapter 5.3.2.2 will also seek to confirm. The definition of the crime of apartheid in the Rome Statute was adjusted to avoid reference to the situation in South(ern) Africa. Instead, the provision is applicable to any similar situation elsewhere. The Rome Statute and the Apartheid Convention both emphasise the systematic, institutionalised, and oppressive character of the racial discrimination.[196] While the crime of apartheid in the Apartheid Convention was contentious and possibly so vaguely defined that it breached the principle of legality,[197] this cannot be said of Art. 7(1)(j) Rome Statute.

4.6.2.1 *The meaning of 'Racial Group'*

The definition of 'racial group' is the perhaps most significant interpretive question of the Apartheid Convention – and the Rome Statute. The ICC will doubtlessly face challenges in interpreting the term if ever an accused stands trial for the crime of apartheid.[198] While the overarching requirements of crimes against humanity have largely been identified, the more specific definition of

195 Eden (n 145) 96; Barnard (n 9) 336; Cryer (n 161) 259; Slye (n 52) 268, 279–282.
196 Du Plessis (n 3) 420; Robert Cryer et al., *An Introduction to International Criminal Law and Procedure* (CUP 2nd ed 2010) 264; Bantekas, Nash (n 180) 136.
197 Booysen (n 67) 82–83 and 90.
198 Du Plessis (n 3) 425; Ratner, Abrams, Bischoff (n 3) 126, 128.

the crime of apartheid, in particular its element of a race or racial group, remains unclear and undefined. Due to the complete lack of case law on the crime of apartheid, both nationally and internationally, legal scholarship as a subsidiary source of law will be consulted in the search of the definition of a racial group. There is only sparse literature on the crime of apartheid in the Rome Statute and there is virtually no academic discourse in relation to racial group. In fact, most scholars refer directly to the corresponding scholarship or jurisprudence on the crime of genocide, which Chapter 3 has dealt with extensively. There is no reason to repeat those findings here.

According to Christine Byron, the definition of 'racial' in the crime of apartheid should be the same as for the crime of persecution, Art. 7(1)(h) in conjunction with Art. 7(2)(g) Rome Statute.[199] In her analysis of the crime of persecution, she refers to ICTR jurisprudence on genocide, quoting the (in)famous definition of race by the *Akayesu* judgment.[200] Byron seems to suggest defining 'racial group' under the crime of apartheid in the same way as 'racial grounds' in the crime of persecution, as well as 'racial group' in the crime of genocide. The validity of her suggestion can be left open at this point. But 'it may be preferable', she concludes, 'to take the two concepts of racial and ethnic group together to cover relevant cases'.[201] It is, however, doubtful whether such interpretation that suggests merging the notions of race and ethnicity would be coherent under the principle of legality and the rights to a fair trial. The merging of two distinct group categories runs counter also to the principle of effectiveness, whereas a reason and meaning has to be attributed to every word, as Chapters 3.5.2.2 and 3.7.2 discussed.

Gerhard Werle and Florian Jessberger suggest defining the term 'racial group' broadly, in accordance with Art. 1 ICERD.[202] Earlier discussions have exposed the broad protection of Art. 1(1) ICERD in international human rights law, the application of which is inconsistent in light of the principle of strict construction and foreseeability under international criminal law.[203] Christopher Hall and co-author Larissa van den Herik, however, recognise that the widely accepted, broad definition of ICERD for human rights law was stretched even further in its application by CERD: '[H]uman rights concepts and interpretations should not be directly transposed to an international criminal law setting without any

199 Byron (n 7) 242.

200 Ibid 231 with reference to *Prosecutor v Akayesu*, ICTR-96-4-T (2 September 1998), para. 514. Similarly, van der Vyver (n 6) 48. See Chapter 3.6.4 on the definition of the racial group in *Akayesu*.

201 Byron (n 7) 231 with reference to William Schabas, *Genocide in International Law: The Crime of Crimes* (CUP 1st ed 2000) 122–123.

202 Werle, Jessberger (n 184) 385. For a similar argument, see Christopher Hall, 'The Crime of Apartheid', in Otto Triffterer (ed), *Commentary on the Rome Statute of the International Criminal Court* (CH Beck 2nd ed 2008) 265.

203 See Chapter 4.5.4.

adjustment'.[204] The ICERD definition and interpretation are not sufficient alone 'to reinterpret the meaning of the word "race" beyond its original meaning in an ICC setting. However, techniques of systematic interpretation may push for reference to the broader discriminatory grounds of persecution'.[205] The authors seem to acknowledge the need for a reinterpretation of race beyond its original meaning as understood in the context of the South African apartheid regime. Whether they are suggesting that a systematic interpretation would lead to a broader interpretation based on human rights law approaches to race (as part of the legal system of public international law that includes human rights as well as international criminal law) – or whether systematic interpretation with its aim of discovering the meaning of race within the international criminal law system could lead to such broadening, remains an open question. This study rejects direct and sole reliance on human rights definitions for the purpose of interpreting substantive criminal law provisions, but does advocate an approach that unifies both the perpetrator's understanding of race as a group perceived as being different from his own group, as well as a contemporary social scientific understanding of race as a social construct, based upon ideas of innate superiority and hierarchies.[206] Such an approach would inevitably lead to an expansion of the definition of race beyond its original understanding when the Apartheid Convention was drafted and the result as such might be identical to that of Hall and van den Herik, albeit grounded on different premises. In sum, this study argues that the concept of race has undergone an evolutive development, because the meaning of race has changed. Race is today understood to be the perception of a person's racial 'otherness'. For international criminal law, the notion of race is inevitably connected to a notion of prejudice and inferiorisation, by which the perpetrator justifies discriminatory treatment of the racially distinct group.[207]

4.6.2.2 The mens rea *of the crime of apartheid*

The *mens rea* of the crime of apartheid embraces not only the intent to maintain an institutionalised regime of systematic oppression and domination, Art. 30 Rome Statute furthermore requires that the perpetrator commits the material elements with intent and knowledge. Thus, the *mens rea* of the crime of apartheid demands awareness by the perpetrator of the factual circumstances, such as the nature and gravity of his acts, and an intention of maintaining the institutionalised regime of systematic oppression and domination over a racial group. Importantly, the systematic oppression and domination not only need to have

204 Hall, van den Herik (n 81) 285.
205 Hall, van den Herik (n 81) 284.
206 See Chapter 4.5.3 for the discussion of the applicability of human rights definitions for international criminal law.
207 See particularly Chapters 2.7, 3.2 and 3.7.

the effect, the perpetrator must also have the purpose of maintaining a regime under which one racial group dominates over another racial group. The crime of apartheid therefore requires a special intent to sustain an institutionalised system of racial discrimination, in addition to the general intent of committing the crime.[208]

This section has shown that the inclusion of the crime against humanity of apartheid into Rome Statute could not have been anticipated. Nonetheless, Art. 7(1)(j) and Art. 7(2)(h) Rome Statute are an indication of the crime's significance, not only as a treaty crime, but also as a crime in customary international law. While the Apartheid Convention served as a legal foundation, the wording of Art. 7(2)(h) deviates from the Convention in removing any reference to the South African context. Apartheid is a crime committed in the context of an institutionalized regime of systematic racial oppression and domination, and a number of present-day regimes could potentially match this description. Corresponding to the discussions in Chapter 3, this study suggests drawing on 'othering' for the interpretation of race in the crime of apartheid. The perpetrator perceives his victims as a racially distinct group and discriminates against them for reasons of their racial group membership. The racial group is therefore constructed subjectively, based on the perpetrator's perception. An evolutive interpretation of race will also lead to this result.[209]

The next section will examine apartheid as a war crime before rounding off the legal analysis of apartheid as a treaty crime. The following section (Chapter 4.8) will then scrutinize apartheid as a customary crime.

4.7 The war crime of apartheid

Not only do the practices of apartheid constitute crimes against humanity, they have also been outlawed as war crimes by international humanitarian law. Additional Protocol I (1977) to the Geneva Conventions of 1949 defines the crime of apartheid in Art. 85(4)(c):

> 4. In addition to the grave breaches defined in the preceding paragraphs and in the Conventions, the following shall be regarded as grave breaches of this Protocol, when committed wilfully and in violation of the Conventions or the Protocol:
>
> . . .
>
> (c) practices of 'apartheid' and other inhuman and degrading practices involving outrages upon personal dignity, based on racial discrimination;

208 Stahn (n 145) 69; Du Plessis (n 3) 427; Bantekas (n 3) 48. This 'special intent' should, however, not be confused with the special intent of the crime of genocide. See Chapter 3.5.3 on the *dolus specialis* of genocide.

209 See Chapter 3.5.2 on the *mens rea* of genocide, Chapter 3.7.2 on evolutive interpretation, and Chapter 3.8.3 with deliberations on the subjective definition of race.

Additional Protocol I was drafted in a time when diplomatic pressure on South Africa was increasing. At the Diplomatic Conference on the Reaffirmation and Development of International Humanitarian Law Applicable in Armed Conflicts, which resulted in the creation of the Additional Protocols I and II, no fewer than eleven national liberation movements participated as observers, among them all the major movements engaged in southern Africa.[210] The inclusion of apartheid is therefore not that surprising. As was the case in respect of the Apartheid Convention, Art. 85(4)(c) Additional Protocol I was criticised for being too vaguely drafted and for not defining apartheid.[211] However, the inclusion of apartheid in the Protocol was deemed justified because of its earlier criminalisation by the Apartheid Convention, which seems to suggest that the ambit of the material element is no wider than the crime of apartheid in the Convention itself.[212] Apartheid practices are already grave breaches of the Geneva Conventions and their inclusion in Protocol I was 'simply a special mention of reprehensible conduct for which the motive is particularly shocking'. The general prohibition of adverse distinction based on race is, as such, contained in several articles of the Geneva Conventions. The explicit inclusion of apartheid policies in Protocol I was therefore not a creation of new law, but rather a recognition of existing law.[213]

The Rome Statute of the ICC does not explicitly list apartheid as a war crime, despite its inclusion in early drafts. In a working paper submitted to the Preparatory Committee, the ICRC also urged the inclusion of the war crime of apartheid in the Rome Statute.[214] It appears that the reference to the war crime of apartheid was removed once apartheid was entered onto the list of crimes against humanity. A number of states would have preferred to have apartheid on the list of war crimes, but their protests were to no avail.[215] Paul Eden suggests two different reasons for this failure by means of anecdotal evidence, namely the hostility of certain states to further strengthening the customary nature of Additional Protocol I and second, the inclusion of the crime against humanity of apartheid in the Statute satisfied the supporters of the criminalisation of apartheid practices.[216]

While there is no explicit mention of apartheid, Art. 8(2)(a) Rome Statute refers to grave breaches of the Geneva Conventions, but only in the strict sense of the term, namely the four Geneva Conventions, not, however, their Additional Protocols. Art. 8(2)(b) Rome Statute mentions outrages upon personal dignity,

210 Eden (n 28) 179. See also Eden (n 145) 92–93 and 98–99 for a brief drafting history of Additional Protocol I and of Rome Statute, respectively.

211 Eden (n 28) 180; Eden (n 145) 93–94.

212 Eden (n 28) 180.

213 Jean Pictet et al., *Commentary on the Additional Protocols of 8 June 1977 to the Geneva Conventions of 12 August 1949* (Martinus Nijhoff 1987) 1002, para. 3515.

214 Jean-Marie Henckaerts, Louise Doswald-Beck, *Customary International Humanitarian Law, Volume II: Practice* (CUP 2005) 2060–2061.

215 Eden (n 145) 98; Barnard (n 9) 349.

216 Eden (n 145) 98.

in particular humiliating and degrading treatment, in international armed conflicts (Art. 8(2)(b)(xxi) Rome Statute). The practice of apartheid as an outrage on personal dignity, as well as humiliating and degrading treatment would certainly be considered a conduct amounting to a war crime.[217] The reference in Art. 8(2)(b) to international armed conflicts notably excludes its application to non-international armed conflicts.

As an extreme form of racial discrimination, apartheid could be subsumed under the provisions of serious violations of Art. 3 common to the Geneva Conventions for non-international armed conflicts, constituting an 'outrage upon personal dignity, in particular humiliating and degrading treatment' (Art. 8(2)(c)(ii) Rome Statute). Customary international law furthermore guarantees respect for all persons *hors de combat* without adverse distinction.[218] In adversely distinguishing between different groups of people, apartheid violates this rule of customary law. In sum, in the situation of a non-international armed conflict, apartheid would constitute a serious violation of Art. 3 common to the Geneva Conventions. The *Tadić* judgment discussed the 'serious' criteria as a breach of a rule protecting important values, affording all the judicial guarantees recognised as indispensable to civilized peoples, and which must involve grave consequences for the victim.[219] None of the provisions on the war crime of apartheid define apartheid or its inherent element of a racial group. The following section will analyse whether the customary crime of apartheid can elucidate the issue of race.

4.8 Apartheid: a crime in customary international law?

4.8.1 Introduction

While the customary crime of genocide corresponds to its treaty counterpart, this might not be the case for the crime of apartheid. Indeed, the customary crime of apartheid might be less intrinsically connected to South Africa than the treaty crime, released from its original association to a specific regime. Customary law is in its origin the oldest source of international law and embodies recognised rules short of any written instrument.[220] The contentiousness of

217 Wording taken from Art. 85(4)(c) Additional Protocol I to the Geneva Conventions. See furthermore: Jean-Marie Henckaerts, Louise Doswald-Beck, *Customary International Humanitarian Law, Volume I: Rules* (CUP 2005) 589.

218 Ibid.

219 *Prosecutor v Tadić*, Case No IT-94–1-T (7 May 1997), para. 612.

220 *North Sea Continental Shelf Cases (Germany v Netherlands, Germany v Denmark)*, ICJ Judgment (1969), para. 74; *Case Concerning Military and Paramilitary Activities in and Against Nicaragua (Nicaragua v United States of America)*, ICJ Judgment (1986), para. 186. Jean d'Aspremont, *Formalism and the Sources of International Law* (OUP 2011) 162; Larissa van den Herik, 'Using Custom to Reconceptualize Crimes Against Humanity', in Shane Darcy, Joseph Powderly (eds), *Judicial Creativity at the International Criminal Tribunal* (OUP 2010) 99; Ian Brownlie, *Principles of Public International Law* (OUP 6th ed 2003) 7–8.

the Apartheid Convention and the as yet not universally ratified Rome Statute as treaty sources reveal the importance of the customary status of the crime of apartheid.[221] In his dissenting opinion in the 1966 ICJ *South West Africa* case, Judge Tanaka held that 'the norm of non-discrimination or non-separation on the basis of race ha[d] become a rule of customary international law'.[222] Not only norms proscribing racial discrimination, but also governmental practices of systematic racial discrimination are prohibited under customary human rights law.[223] Apartheid, in combining racial discrimination with systematic oppression and domination, is an aggravated case of racial discrimination that runs contrary to the most fundamental international human rights law, such as Art. 1(3) UN Charter or Art. 2 UDHR. The prohibition of systematic apartheid-style racial discrimination is customary law beyond doubt,[224] the customary status of the crime against humanity of apartheid remains, however, an issue of debate.

While the existence of customary law is generally acknowledged, its definition in Art. 38 ICJ Statute as 'evidence of a general practice accepted as law' has been 'challenged, questioned, ridiculed, supported, and generally argued over', as Hugh Thirlway puts it.[225] The prevailing positivist approach to customary law demands evidence of subjective recognition by states of what they consider to be a binding rule of international law (*opinio juris*) as well as an objective constant and uniform state practice.[226] In other words, there needs to be a pattern of empirically observable individual instances of state practice and *opinio juris*.[227] These two elements are often intrinsically connected, requiring their examination together or alongside one other.[228] Whether or not the crime against humanity of apartheid has reached customary law status, remains, in the opinion of many scholars, an issue of dispute.[229] This study argues that the crime of

221 Also recognized by Hall, van den Herik (n 81) 235.

222 *South West Africa case* (*Ethiopia v South Africa; Liberia v South Africa*), Second Phase, ICJ Judgment (1966), Dissenting Opinion of Judge Tanaka, p. 293. See Chapter 4.5.2 on Judge Tanaka's definition of race.

223 American Law Institute, Restatement of the Foreign Relations Law of the United States (1986), para. 165; Evan Criddle, Evan Fox-Decent, 'A Fiduciary Theory of *Jus Cogens*', 34 *Yale Journal of International Law* (2009) 331; Thomas Buergenthal, Dinah Shelton, David Stewart, *International Human Rights – In a Nutshell* (West Group 3rd ed 2002) 42.

224 See Kälin, Künzli (n 131) 70; Robertson (n 73) 271.

225 Hugh Thirlway, *The Sources of International Law* (OUP 2014) 7.

226 *Continental Shelf Case (Libyan Arab Jamahiriya v Malta)*, ICJ Judgment (1985), para. 27; *North Sea Continental Shelf Cases (Federal Republic of Germany v Netherlands and Federal Republic of Germany v Denmark)*, ICJ Judgment (1969), paras. 74–77; Noora Arajärvi, *The Changing Nature of Customary International Law* (Routledge 2014) 20; Criddle, Fox-Decent (n 223) 339.

227 Stefan Talmon, 'Determining Customary International Law', 26 *EJIL* (2016) 420.

228 Arajärvi (n 226) 20; Thirlway (n 225) 62; Kälin, Künzli (n 131) 67–68.

229 Gebhard (n 5), para. 25; Roger O'Keefe, *International Criminal Law* (OUP 2015) 140; Ambos (n 6) 113; Eden (n 145) 91; Antonio Cassese et al., *Cassese's International Criminal Law* (OUP 3rd ed 2013) 107; Boas, Bischoff, Reid (n 176) 109; Antonio Cassese, 'Crimes Against Humanity', in Antonio Cassese, Paola Gaeta, John Jones (eds), *The Rome Statute of the International Criminal Court: A Commentary* (OUP 2002) 376.

apartheid has reached customary law status, as to be reasoned in the following sections.

4.8.2 Opinio juris

Evidence of *opinio juris* will often be drawn from debates in the General Assembly or from negotiation of international treaties, where states' opinions on their legal obligations become visible.[230] General Assembly resolutions do not *ipso facto* create new rules of customary law, but they may in some instances constitute evidence of the existence of customary international law, help to crystallise emerging customary law, or contribute to the formation of new law.[231] Numerous UN resolutions have condemned apartheid, indicating the gravity with which apartheid is viewed. In the period from 1946 to 1994, at least fourteen General Assembly resolutions confirmed that apartheid is a crime against humanity, in addition to countless other resolutions and declarations dealing with the South African apartheid regime. Furthermore, the Security Council affirmed on one occasion that apartheid was a crime against humanity, as well as stating once that apartheid was a 'crime against the conscience and dignity of mankind'.[232] Though purely related to the Southern African context, these UN resolutions shaped the understanding of the crime of apartheid and continue to be relevant for its legal definition, since the law of apartheid remains valid for situations others than South Africa, as discussed in Chapters 4.5.1 and 4.6.1. From a historical perspective, these resolutions are of great importance because they illustrate the international community's commitment to eradicate and criminalize apartheid. From a legal point of view, the resolutions show how apartheid grew to be recognised as a crime against humanity and demonstrate the *opinio juris* of the international community.[233]

In the *Nicaragua* case, the ICJ confirmed that '*opinio juris* may . . . be deduced from . . . the attitude of States towards certain General Assembly resolutions'.[234] In its *Advisory Opinion on Nuclear Weapons*, the ICJ repeated that General Assembly resolutions, even though they were not legally binding, could in certain circumstances provide evidence of an *opinio juris.*[235] In the view of

230 Talmon (n 227) 429; Thomas Weatherall, Jus Cogens*: International Law and Social Contract* (CUP 2015) 143–144; William Schabas, 'The Contribution of the Eichmann Trial to International Law', 26 *LJIL* (2013) 691; Kälin, Künzli (n 131) 67.

231 International Law Association, Committee on Formation of Customary (General) International Law, Final Report (2000), Part V, Rule 28, p. 55.

232 UN SC Res. 556 (23 October 1984) and 392 (19 June 1976).

233 Confirmed by Neil Boister, Richard Burchill, 'The Implications of the Pinochet Decision for the Extradition or Prosecution of Former South African Heads of State for Crimes Committed Under Apartheid', 11 *African Journal of International and Comparative Law* (1999) 633–634.

234 *Case Concerning Military and Paramilitary Activities in and Against Nicaragua (Nicaragua v United States of America)*, ICJ Judgment (1986), para. 188.

235 *Legality of the Threat and Use of Nuclear Weapons*, ICJ Advisory Opinion (1996), para 70.

the ICJ, statements made by State representatives in the General Assembly could therefore serve as proof of their *opinio juris*.[236] The fact that the Apartheid Convention reproduced the provisions of the General Assembly resolutions demonstrates their normative character and 'their significance as at least an indirect source of international law'.[237] The UN General Assembly resolutions condemning apartheid had an average of 83.7 percent of Member States voting in favour, with a staggering 91.9 percent support in 1970,[238] and point to a crystallisation of the international community's understanding of apartheid as an unlawful practice.[239] Furthermore, virtually every organ of the UN has dealt with apartheid, from the very beginning of the organisation's inception in 1946.[240] In the midst of the Cold War, apartheid unified the international community in its struggle to bring an end to the South African regime. Schabas stresses the paradigm of the South African apartheid system and notes that no 'other single issue . . . did as much to galvanize the human rights machinery of the United Nations'.[241] The international community stood united in its condemnation of the racially based apartheid system, thus exhibiting an *opinio juris*. In Adriaan Barnard's view, although the treaties containing the crime of apartheid were broadly accepted, they had not reached a universal level of participation that would indicate customary status. Indeed, none of the *ad hoc* criminal tribunals' statutes incorporated the crime of apartheid, which was particularly notable in the case of the Special Court for Sierra Leone and the Iraq Special Tribunal that, apart from the crime of apartheid, effectively replicated the Rome Statute's list of crimes against humanity.[242] The ILC, however, seems to rebut Barnard's argumentation and instead confirms the crystallisation of customary law. In its 2013 Report on the Formation and Evidence of Customary Law, it considered the prohibition against racial discrimination and apartheid as peremptory norms, formed as a result of a process of widespread acceptance and recognition by the international community as a whole.[243] Scholars agree: the status of apartheid 'as an international crime has long been undisputed'.[244] In addition, the proposed International Convention on the Prevention and Punishment of Crimes Against Humanity, which in 2010 was

236 Talmon (n 227) 432; Thirlway (n 225) 79–80. Confirmed on a general level in the Report of the ILC, UN Doc. A/71/10 (2016), Chapter V, Conclusion 10.
237 Blishchenko (n 90) 4.
238 Stultz (n 36) 14.
239 McDougal, Lasswell, Chen (n 8) 536.
240 Clark (n 74) 600.
241 William Schabas, *Unimaginable Atrocities – Justice, Politics, and Rights at the War Crimes Tribunals* (OUP 2012) 192.
242 Barnard (n 9) 352–353.
243 ILC, Formation and Evidence of Customary International Law, UN Doc. A/CN.4/659 (14 March 2013), pp. 29–30.
244 See Timothy McCormack, Gerry Simpson, 'The International Law Commission's Draft Code of Crimes Against the Peace and Security of Mankind: An Appraisal of the Substantive Provisions', 5 *Criminal Law Forum* (1994) 42. Similar: O'Keefe (n 229) 235.

drafted by several eminent international lawyers and in 2017 provisionally adopted by the ILC Drafting Committee on first reading, includes the crime of apartheid in its Art. 3(1)(j).[245] The condemnation of apartheid as a crime against humanity and, as such, an affront to human dignity by 'the majority of Member states' was noted as early as in 1972, which could suggest the existence of an *opinio juris* already prior to the ratification of the Convention in 1973.[246] Similarly, a 1974 UN-sponsored study of the Apartheid Convention viewed apartheid as an international crime seen from the perspective of generally accepted principles of international law.[247] On a more general level, the States Parties to the Rome Statute intended Art. 7 to reflect but not expand existing customary law.[248] Hence, Art. 7, by including the crime of apartheid, 'reflects a simultaneous statement of *opinio juris* by 120 States'.[249] There are therefore strong indications that an *opinio juris* as to the prohibition of apartheid as a crime against humanity exists and has existed for more than four decades. If this *opinio juris* can be shown to have been associated with corresponding state practices, the crime of apartheid might well by now have acquired the status of customary law.

4.8.3 State practice

In order for a rule to be considered a customary norm, there has to be state practice in addition to an *opinio juris.* This is because custom grows from the action – or inaction – of states and the active or passive reaction of the other subjects of law concerned.[250] State practice has to be widespread, consistent, and uniform but it need not embrace the practice of every single member of the UN.[251] In order for state practice to manifest, a certain passage of time is

245 <http://sites.law.wustl.edu/docs/harris/cah/EnglishTreatyFinal.pdf>; ILC, Crimes against Humanity: Texts and titles of the draft preamble, the draft articles and the draft annex provisionally adopted by the Drafting Committee on first reading, UN Doc. A/CN.4/L.892 (26 May 2017).

246 Farah (n 80) 7. See furthermore General Assembly, 28th Session, Third Committee, 2003rd meeting, UN Doc. A/C.3/SR.2003 (22 October 1973), paras. 29 and 38.

247 Blishchenko (n 90) 1.

248 Christopher Hall, Kai Ambos, 'Crimes Against Humanity', in Otto Triffterer, Kai Ambos (eds), *The Rome Statute of the International Criminal Court: A Commentary* (CH Beck 3rd ed 2016) 158; Werle, Jessberger (n 184) 57, 61; Leila Nadya Sadat, 'Crimes Against Humanity in the Modern Age', 107 *AJIL* (2013) 351; Cryer (n 196) 264; Patricia Wald, 'Genocide and Crimes against Humanity', 6 *Washington University Global Studies Law Review* (2007) 621–622; McCormack (n 175) 181, 200; deGuzman (n 187) 353; von Hebel, Robinson (n 175) 91, 122; Askin (n 187) 41.

249 Cryer (n 196) 245.

250 Arajärvi (n 226) 21; Thirlway (n 225) 63.

251 International Law Association, Committee on Formation of Customary (General) International Law, Final Report (2000), p. 24, Rule 14(i); Thirlway (n 225) 64, 67; Brownlie (n 220) 7.

necessary, although there is no general rule as to how much time has to elapse before state practice becomes apparent.[252]

There exists no state practice of criminal prosecution of the crime of apartheid: it has never been prosecuted by any court; no person has ever been tried for this crime.[253] While state practice might not manifest itself in the prosecution of the crime, it could, however, be reflected in domestic criminal law.[254] The crime of apartheid has been included into the national legislation of at least thirty-five countries (in addition to a multitude of national military manuals that prohibit apartheid), suggesting a high level of acceptance of the crime and state practice.[255] Remarkably, these are national laws from European, Asian, North and South American and only a number of African and Middle East countries.[256] Thus, in contrast to the ratification of the Apartheid Convention, the national legislation prohibiting apartheid originates largely in states of the industrialized West, such as Canada, Ireland, the Netherlands, and so forth. In sum, a respectable number of states have criminalised apartheid, either by means of national legislation or as States Parties to the Apartheid Convention.

On the international level, several treaties contain provisions on apartheid, all of which have reached a significant number of ratifications, thereby indicating state acceptance of the unlawfulness of apartheid. As of February 2019, the ICERD, for example, has 179 member states.[257] Art. 3 ICERD singled out apartheid as a specific form of discrimination in order to counter the South African government's claim that apartheid was not a form of racial discrimination, but rather a policy of separate development.[258] While the reference to apartheid in Art. 3 may have targeted South Africa, it nevertheless prohibited all forms of racial segregation in all countries.[259] Additional Protocol I to the Geneva Conventions also achieved a high level of ratification with 174 signatory States Parties.[260] In 1998, the Rome negotiations for the ICC reaffirmed apartheid as a crime against humanity, believed by certain scholars to be confirmation of the crime's customary status.[261] To date, the Rome Statute has been ratified by 123 States. Last, but not least, the Apartheid Convention with 109 ratifications confirms a generally high-level acceptance of apartheid as an international

252 Thirlway (n 225) 64; Brownlie (n 220) 7.
253 Zahar (n 70) 245; Barnard (n 9) 332; Robertson (n 73) 272; Henckaerts, Doswald-Beck (n 214) 2058 and 2060; Reydams (n 74) 60.
254 *Prosecutor v Tadić*, Case No 94–1-A (15 July 1999), para. 290; Weatherall (n 230) 239.
255 Accord: Henckaerts, Doswald-Beck (n 214) 2055–2058. Disaccord: Barnard (n 9) 352.
256 Henckaerts, Doswald-Beck (n 214) 2055–2058.
257 See <https://treaties.un.org/> on ratification status.
258 Dugard, Reynolds (n 13) 877; Bantekas (n 3) 236; Bantekas, Nash (n 180) 166.
259 CERD, General Recommendation No 19 on Art. 3 of the Convention (1995), reprinted in UN Doc. HRI/GEN/1/Rev.6, p. 208. Furthermore Lerner (n 80) 47; Du Plessis (n 3) 423.
260 <https://ihl-databases.icrc.org/applic/ihl/ihl.nsf/INTRO/470>.
261 Bantekas, Nash (n 180) 135; deGuzman (n 187) 353.

crime.[262] Admittedly, the majority of ratifications of the Apartheid Convention occurred during the 1970s and 1980s. However, a not-insignificant number took place in the early 1990s, ie in the final years of the South African apartheid regime.[263] Moreover, there are no indications of hostility to the law of apartheid by states that are not party to the discussed treaties. A clear signal is also the acceptance by previous non-States Parties to the Apartheid Convention (such as South Africa or the UK) of later instruments prohibiting apartheid.[264] The prohibition of racial discrimination itself is an undisputed rule of customary law. The prohibition of apartheid as an example of aggravated racial discrimination that also constitutes an international crime is recognised by an increasing number of states and can therefore be asserted to have reached the level of customary law.[265] A trial for the crime would arguably confirm the *opinio juris* while strengthening state practice.[266] As indicated in Chapter 4.5.5, there are currently two potential cases of apartheid, namely the situations in the OPT and DPRK, which might be brought before the ICC. As such, the crime of apartheid could experience an awakening in future applications.

In the analysis of this study, the Apartheid Convention did not codify the customary definition of apartheid as a crime against humanity. The ratification of the Convention was, however, an expression of the *opinio juris* of the ratifying States Parties. The repeated reference to apartheid as a crime against humanity in UN resolutions, treaties, as well as domestic legislation, are all examples of state practice. Finally, the codification of the crime of apartheid in the Rome Statute is a strong indication of the status of apartheid as an international and customary crime. This conclusion is supported by the ICTY in the *Tadić* trial judgment, which provided an important clarification: 'Additional codifications of international law have also confirmed the customary law status of the prohibition of crimes against humanity, as well as two of its most egregious manifestations: genocide and apartheid'.[267] Apartheid as institutionalized racism is a particularly malicious manifestation of racial discrimination. The prohibition of racial discrimination as a fundamental principle of international law is listed in Art. 55 UN Charter and Art. 2 UDHR. The crime of apartheid undoubtedly constitutes a case of aggravated racial discrimination and as such has, in the view of this study, acquired customary law status.[268]

262 <https://treaties.un.org> for ratification status.

263 From 1990 until 1994, Armenia, Bahrain, Bosnia, Croatia, Czech Republic, Estonia, Latvia, Oman, and Zimbabwe became party to the Apartheid Convention: <https://treaties.un.org/Pages/ViewDetails.aspx?src=TREATY&mtdsg_no=IV-7&chapter=4&lang=en>.

264 Dugard, Reynolds (n 13) 882–883.

265 Accord: Du Plessis (n 3) 421–422; Boister, Burchill (n 233) 634. Disaccord: Schmid (n 113) 141.

266 Report of the ILC, sixty-fourth session, UN Doc. A/67/10 (2012), p. 8.

267 *Prosecutor v Tadić*, Case No 94-1-T (7 May 1997), para. 622.

268 Accord: Dugard, Reynolds (n 13) 882.

4.9 Interim conclusion

This chapter has argued that race was not a controversial matter in any of the drafting processes, either of the Apartheid Convention, ICERD, Additional Protocol I to the Geneva Conventions or the Rome Statute. Race was not a disputed issue because the focus of apartheid was on the situation of South Africa, especially in the drafting of the Apartheid Convention and Additional Protocol I. The Rome Statute built its definition of the crime against humanity of apartheid on the Apartheid Convention and thus largely relied on those discussions in its drafting process. As such, race was seen as a combination of skin colour and group membership. It has to be recalled that numerous references mention 'race and colour', ie two distinct concepts. Yet, at the same time, resolutions often referred to the 'black' and 'white' people, thereby apparently distinguishing between peoples' skin colour. Thus, historically, the meaning of race under the Apartheid Convention mirrored the understanding of race adopted by the apartheid government in South Africa – an amalgam of national origin, blood relationship, as well as skin colour.

Akin to the crime of genocide, certain scholars have suggested defining the racial group according to Art. 1(1) ICERD. This proposal is unconvincing. Owing to the principle of strict legality and its corollaries of specificity and foreseeability, criminal law needs to be narrowly and precisely defined. The term 'racial' was not meant to include a nearly unlimited number of protected groups, ranging from race, colour, or descent, to national or ethnic origin. The law of apartheid exclusively protects the racial group, and this limited protection has to be respected. Since the Apartheid Convention was drafted the understanding of the term 'race' has evolved. The meaning of race has adopted a subjective understanding. It is therefore suggested that 'racial group' ought to be defined as a group perceived by the perpetrator as having racial characteristics.[269] For reasons of proof and in order to attach some objectivity to the group's existence, it is preferable (though not legally required) that the group is identifiable to people other than the perpetrator.

This chapter has found that the law of apartheid is applicable to situations in countries other than South Africa. This goes for the Apartheid Convention as much as for Additional Protocol I to the Geneva Conventions and the Rome Statute. There were notably some doubts as to the Apartheid Convention's spatial applicability. The wording of the Convention – 'similar policies and practices of racial segregation and discrimination as practised in southern Africa' – however, makes it clear that there is no exclusive applicability to South Africa. Recent ratifications of the Convention furthermore confirm the belief in its deterrent effect and its continued validity. The Rome Statute makes no reference to the South African apartheid regime and is therefore applicable to any

269 See also Chapter 3.8 on the related discussion of the definition of 'racial group' for the crime of genocide.

situation in which an institutionalised regime of systematic oppression and domination by one racial group is perpetrated over any other racial group(s).

The analysis here shows that apartheid is a customary crime, codified in the Rome Statute. While the Apartheid Convention is seen as ill-defined and too broadly drafted, this cannot be claimed of the Rome Statute. The provision on the crime against humanity of apartheid in the Rome Statute points to customary law, which is narrower than the crime envisaged by the Apartheid Convention. However, there appears to be no difference in the definition of the racial group for the treaty or the customary crime of apartheid. It can, in fact, be assumed that the protected group under both customary international law and treaty law is identical.

This chapter showed that the crime of apartheid to a certain extent experienced a similar fate as the crime of genocide: their criminalisation was a reaction to atrocities, which the international community in both situations condemned. The Apartheid Convention was the legal response to the apartheid regime in South Africa, just as the Genocide Convention was the legal response to the Holocaust. At the time of drafting, neither crime defined 'racial group', and although the notion was rather vague, it was nonetheless uncontested. Unlike for genocide, the law of apartheid has to date not been applied by any criminal court. This study argues that the definition of the racial group for the crime of apartheid is significant in projecting possible application of the crime. In relying on the perpetrator's perception of the victim group's racial 'otherness', the racial group is subjectively defined, thus avoiding reverting to the practices of apartheid officials who believed you could determine race objectively.

5 The concept of race in the law of persecution

Every person and every nation at one time or other becomes the weak. For that reason, nobody should tolerate persecution, let alone extermination, as a precedent[1]

5.1 Introduction

The crime of persecution is considered instrumental to and a 'key chapter in the development of international criminal law'[2] in that it lifted widespread or systematic discrimination from being a matter of concern to the territorial state to the level of the international community as a whole. The recognition of persecution as an international crime emphasises the accountability for harm upon an individual's membership of, affiliation, or identification with a group.[3] Persecution is one of the most widely indicted crimes against humanity.[4] Nevertheless, it does not play a major role in the analysis of the concept of race in international criminal law, owing mostly to its extensive range of protections. This chapter discusses how the crime of persecution developed and what distinguishes persecution from genocide and from apartheid. The identification of the victim group, which is based on racially grounded discriminatory acts, is central to the discussion. In concluding, this chapter holds that unlike genocide or apartheid, a perpetrator-based subjective approach to the racial group is broadly accepted in the jurisprudence for the crime of persecution. In allowing the perpetrator to define the contours of his victim groups, the judges clearly accept the identity-based nature of the crime without requiring objectivity of

1 Franz Werfel, *Die vierzig Tage des Musa Dagh*, Paul Zsolnay Verlag (1933) 177. The original wording is: 'Jede Person und jede Nation kommt einmal in die Lage, die schwächere zu sein. Deshalb darf man einen Präzedenzfall der Ausrottung, ja ach nur der Schädigung nicht dulden'.

2 Helen Brady, Ryan Liss, 'The Evolution of Persecution as a Crime Against Humanity', in Morten Bergsmo, Wui Ling Cheah, Tianying Song, Ping Yi (eds), *Historical Origins of International Criminal Law: Vol 3* (Torkel Opsahl Academic EPublisher 2015) 429.

3 Ibid 429–430.

4 Patricia Wald, 'Genocide and Crimes Against Humanity', 6 *Washington University Global Studies Law Review* (2007) 630.

the protected groups. The Rome Statute of the ICC defines the crime of persecution in Art. 7(1)(h) in conjunction with Art. 7(2)(g):

> 1. For the purpose of this Statute, 'crime against humanity' means any of the following acts when committed as part of a widespread or systematic attack directed against any civilian population, with knowledge of the attack:
> (h) Persecution against any identifiable group or collectivity on political, racial, national, ethnic, cultural, religious, gender as defined in paragraph 3, or other grounds that are universally recognised as impermissible under international law, in connection with any act referred to in this paragraph or any crime within the jurisdiction of the Court;
>
> 2. For the purpose of paragraph 1:
> (g) 'Persecution' means the intentional and severe deprivation of fundamental rights contrary to international law by reason of the identity of the group or collectivity;

According to Art. 7(1)(h) Rome Statute, persecution can be committed on political, racial, national, ethnic, cultural, religious, gender or other grounds universally recognised as impermissible under international law. In doing so, the law on persecution offers more discriminatory grounds than apartheid or genocide and hence embraces more victim groups.[5] The Elements of Crimes to the Rome Statute do not define the term 'racial' for the crime of persecution. Instead, paragraphs 2 and 3 to Art. 7(1)(h) declare the targeting of persons by reason of race a ground universally recognised as impermissible under international law.

Persecution in international criminal law has never been comprehensively defined. Neither international treaty law nor case law provides an all-inclusive list of prohibited acts encompassed by the charge of persecution, and persecution is not known in the world's major criminal justice systems.[6] Persecution is, in particular, not a self-standing crime, but rather an umbrella crime that can only be committed by way of underlying acts or omissions amounting to serious human rights violations.[7] From a procedural point of view, it would be insufficient to indict someone for 'persecution' alone. Rather, in order to observe

5 Ibid.

6 *Prosecutor v Tadić*, Case No IT-94–1-T (7 May 1997), para. 694; *Prosecutor v Kordić and Čerkez*, Case No IT-95–14/2-T (26 February 2001), para. 192. See also Gerhard Werle, Florian Jessberger *Principles of International Criminal Law* (OUP 3rd ed 2014) 373; M. Cherif Bassiouni, *Crimes Against Humanity: Historical Evolution and Contemporary Application* (CUP 2011) 396; Mohamed Elewa Badar, 'From the Nuremberg Charter to the Rome Statute: Defining the Elements of Crimes Against Humanity', 73 *San Diego International Law Journal* (2004) 122.

7 *Prosecutor v Stanišić and Zupljanin*, Case No IT-08–91-T (27 March 2013), para. 67; *Prosecutor v Banović*, Case No IT-02–65/1-S (28 October 2003), para. 38; *Prosecutor v Kupreškić* et al., Case No IT-95–16-A (23 October 2001), para. 98; *Prosecutor v Todorovic*,

the principle of legality, the prosecution must indict the person for particular acts.[8]

5.2 A brief history of the crime of persecution

Frequently, defendants have challenged the crime of persecution due to its vagueness as a breach of the principle of *nullum crimen sine lege*. However, the *ad hoc* tribunals repeatedly confirmed that the principle did not prevent a court from interpreting and clarifying the elements of a crime.[9] This is also the position taken here: the crime of persecution – and its element of race – must be interpreted in order to clarify the crime's contours. Recourse to its drafting history according to Art. 32 VCLT is therefore justified. Resort to the *travaux préparatoires* is furthermore warranted for reasons of comprehensiveness. Since the concept of persecution only emerged in positive law after WWII, the following section begins with an examination of how the Nuremberg Tribunal dealt with persecution. Thereafter, the development of the crime until today is discussed.

5.2.1 The crime of persecution in post-WWII trials

Art. 6(c) of the IMT Charter defined crimes against humanity as including 'inhumane acts committed against any civilian population, before or during the war, or persecutions on political, racial or religious grounds in execution of or in connection with any crime within the jurisdiction of the Tribunal'.[10] During

Case No IT-95–9/1-S (31 July 2001), para. 32. Brady, Liss (n 2) 530; Kai Ambos, *Treatise on International Criminal Law, Volume II: The Crimes and Sentencing* (OUP 2014) 104–105; Robert Kolb, 'The Jurisprudence of the Yugoslav and Rwandan Criminal Tribunals on Their Jurisdiction and on International Crimes (2004–2013)', 84 *British Yearbook of International Law* (2014) 169; Alexander Murray, 'Does International Criminal Law Still Require a 'Crime of Crimes'? A Comparative Review of Genocide and Crimes against Humanity', 3 *Goettingen Journal of International Law* (2011) 599; David Nersessian, *Genocide and Political Group* (OUP 2010) 155, 168; Wald (n 4) 630; Badar (n 6) 126.

8 *Prosecutor v Stanišić and Zupljanin*, Case No IT-08–91-T (27 March 2013), para. 67. Furthermore: Vladimir Tochilovsky, *Jurisprudence of the International Criminal Courts and the European Court of Human Rights: Procedure and Evidence* (Martinus Nijhoff 2008) 30.

9 *Prosecutor v Delalić* et al., Case No IT-96–21-A (20 February 2001), para. 173; *Prosecutor v Aleksovski*, Case No IT-95–14/1-A (24 March 2000), paras. 126–127. Furthermore: Steven Ratner, Jason Abrams, James Bischoff, *Accountability for Human Rights Atrocities in International Law: Beyond the Nuremberg Legacy* (OUP 3rd ed 2009) 77.

10 Art. 6(c) Charter of the IMT, appended to the Agreement for the Prosecution and Punishment of the Major War Criminals of the European Axis (8 August 1945), 82 UNTS 279. The original definition of crimes against humanity used a semicolon: 'before or during the war; or persecution on political, racial or religious grounds', thus strictly distinguishing between so-called murder type crimes and persecution type crimes. The Berlin Protocol of 6 October 1945 replaced the semi-colon with a comma, which was later confirmed by the IMT. See Ken Roberts, 'Striving for Definition: The Law of Persecution from Its

the drafting of the Nuremberg Charter, concerns were expressed that the introduction of crimes against humanity as a new category of crimes breached the principle of ***nullum crimen sine lege***. Therefore, crimes against humanity were jurisdictionally connected to other crimes within the jurisdiction of the Tribunal. This way, no defendant was convicted for crimes against humanity only, and the principle of legality was not violated.[11] Despite the fact that persecution was recognised and expressly listed as a crime against humanity, the Charter did not provide sufficient definition and it left the concept largely void of legal content or specificity.[12] Persecution was also included in CCL No 10 and the Tokyo Charter. However, the latter limited itself to political and racial grounds and omitted religious grounds, thereby reflecting the factual pattern of persecution that had occurred in the Far East.[13] Although the judgment of the International Military Tribunal for the Far East (IMTFE or Tokyo Tribunal) repeatedly refers to racial habits, customs, manners, ties, and conflict, which could indicate persecution on racial grounds, it did not consider the crime of persecution.[14] Conversely, the Nuremberg Tribunal devoted a large section of its judgment to the persecution. 'With the seizure of power', the tribunal writes in a frequently quoted section,[15]

> the persecution of the Jews was intensified. A series of discriminatory laws was passed, which limited the offices and professions permitted to Jews; and

---

Origins to the ICTY', in Hirad Abtahi, Gideon Boas (eds), *The Dynamics of International Criminal Justice: Essays in Honour of Sir Richard May* (Brill Nijhoff 2006) 263.

11 Richard Ashby Wilson, 'Propaganda and History in International Criminal Trials', 14 *JICJ* (2016) 522; William Schabas, 'Synergy or Fragmentation? International Criminal Law and the European Convention on Human Rights', 9 *JICJ* (2011) 613–614; Robert Cryer, Håkan Friman, Darryl Robinson, Elizabeth Wilmshurst, *An Introduction to International Criminal Law and Procedure* (CUP 2nd ed 2010) 112–114; Antonio Cassese, *The Human Dimension of International Law: Selected Papers of Antonio Cassese* (OUP 2008) 460–461.

12 Roberts (n 10) 263.

13 Charter of the IMTFE: <www.un.org/en/genocideprevention/documents/atrocity-crimes/Doc.3_1946%20Tokyo%20Charter.pdf>. *Prosecutor v Tadić*, Case No IT-94-1-T (7 May 1997), para. 711; *Prosecutor v Nyiramasuhuko* et al., Case No ICTR-98-42-A (14 December 2015), footnote 4959. Furthermore: James Larry Taulbee, *International Crime and Punishment: A Guide to the Issues* (ABC Clio 2009) 91; Christine Byron, *War Crimes and Crimes Against Humanity in the Rome Statute of the International Criminal Court* (Manchester UP 2009) 225; Kriangsak Kittichaisaree, *International Criminal Law* (OUP 2001) 119. Note that the 25 Japanese leaders tried at Tokyo were sentenced for war crimes only [Brady, Liss (n 2) 459; Ratner, Abrams, Bischoff (n 9) 49; Roberts (n 10) 264].

14 Judgment IMTFE (4 November 1948), reproduced in <http://werle.rewi.hu-berlin.de/tokio.pdf>. Furthermore: David Nersessian, *Genocide and Political Groups* (OUP 2010) 155; Olivia Swaak-Goldman, 'Persecution', in Gabrielle Kirk McDonald, Olivia Swaak-Goldman (eds), *Substantive and Procedural Aspects of International Criminal Law: The Experience of International and National Courts* (Kluwer Law International 2000) 249.

15 Eg Jonas Nilsson, 'The Crime of Persecution in the ICTY Case-law', in Bert Swart, Alexander Zahar, Göran Sluiter (eds), *The Legacy of the International Criminal Tribunal for the Former Yugoslavia* (OUP 2011) 220–221.

> restrictions were placed on their family life and their rights of citizenship. By the autumn of 1938, the Nazi policy . . . was directed towards the complete exclusion of Jews from German life. Pogroms were organised, which included the burning and demolishing of synagogues, the looting of Jewish businesses, and the arrest of prominent Jewish business men. A collective fine of 1 billion marks was imposed on the Jews, the seizure of Jewish assets was authorised, the movement of Jews was restricted . . . . The creation of the ghettos was carried out on an extensive scale, and . . . Jews were compelled to wear a yellow star to be worn on the breast and back.[16]

The Tribunal classified the crimes committed against the Jews as racial persecution, whereas today they more likely would be seen as religious, possibly even ethnic, persecution. According to the IMT and the prosecutions under CCL No 10, persecution did not require a physical element: the application of the Nuremberg racial laws, for example, was considered an act of persecution.[17]

The 1961 decision of the Israeli District Court in the *Attorney General of Israel v Eichmann* is probably the most famous judgment on the crime of persecution prior to the establishment of the ICTY and ICTR.[18] Concerning Eichmann, the Court held that '[a]ll his acts carried out with the intent of exterminating the Jewish People also amount, in fact, to the persecution of Jews on national, racial, religious, and political grounds'.[19] The Court recognised that the perpetrator's motive for committing international crimes was irrelevant,[20] as long as it could be demonstrated that he acted with the required knowledge of an overarching attack, and, in the case of persecution, harboured a discriminatory intent.[21] Eichmann appealed the judgment for breaching the principle of legality because of the *ex post facto* application of the 1950 Nazi and Nazi

16 Trial of the Major War Criminals before the International Military Tribunal (14 November 1945–1 October 1946), Vol. 1, Judgment (1947), pp. 247–249.

17 *United States of America v Josef Altstoetter* et al. (*Justice* Case), Trials of War Criminals Before the Nuremberg Tribunals Under Control Council Law No 10, Vol. 3, p. 54. See Chapter 2.5.1 on the Nuremberg laws.

18 Chapter 3.4.4 discussed the *Eichmann* judgment with regard to the crime of genocide.
Note that several judgments under CCL No 10 dealt with persecution, as did national courts, eg the *Greiser* case (Poland), the *Zühlke* and *Rauter* cases (Netherlands), or the *Barbie* case (France). For an overview: *Prosecutor v Kupreškić* et al., Case No IT-95–16-T (14 January 2000), paras. 598–602, 611–613.

19 *The Attorney General of Israel v Eichmann*, Case No 40/61, Judgment (11 December 1961), para. 201, at: <www.asser.nl/upload/documents/DomCLIC/Docs/NLP/Israel/Eichmann_Judgement_11-12-1961.pdf>.

20 Same is valid today. See *Prosecutor v Vasiljević*, Case No IT-98–32-T (29 November 2002), para. 228; *Prosecutor v Tadić*, Case No IT-94–1-A (15 July 1999), para. 272. Furthermore: Brady, Liss (n 2) 535; Murray (n 7) 602; Ratner, Abrams, Bischoff (n 9) 37; William Fenrick, 'The Crime Against Humanity of Persecution in the Jurisprudence of the ICTY', 32 *Netherlands Yearbook of International Law* (2001) 88.

21 *The Attorney General of Israel v Eichmann* (n 19) paras. 183, 227–241.

Collaborators (Punishment) Law, but his appeal was quashed by the Israeli Supreme Court in 1962.[22]

5.2.2 *The ILC Draft Codes of Crimes*

The 1954 ILC Draft Code of Crimes defined the crime of persecution in its Art. 2(11) as 'persecutions, committed against any civilian population on social, political, racial, religious or cultural grounds by the authorities of a State or by private individuals acting at the instigation or with the toleration of such authorities'.[23] Compared to the earlier formulations in the IMT Charter and CCL No 10, the ILC added social and cultural grounds of discrimination and also explicitly included the requirement of state involvement. In the wake of the Cold War, the development of international criminal law subsided, and it was not until 1991 that the ILC deemed it necessary to update the Draft Code in form and substance in order to accommodate developments in international law in recent decades. Its 1991 Draft Code defined persecution as related to human rights violations

> committed in a systematic manner or on a mass scale by government officials or by groups that exercise de facto power over a particular territory and seek to subject individuals or groups of individuals to a life in which enjoyment of some of their basic rights is repeatedly or constantly denied.[24]

The 1996 ILC Draft Code of Crimes also included persecution in the list of crimes against humanity and defined it as a discriminatory act on political, racial, religious or ethnic grounds. Its commentary did not elaborate on the discriminatory grounds, and the ICTY in *Kupreškić* considered that the ILC Draft provided little guidance in the interpretation of persecution.[25]

The following section will analyse the jurisprudence of the ICTY and ICTR on the crime of persecution. It will also look at the relationship between the crime of persecution, the crime of genocide, and the crime of apartheid. Thereafter, the *mens rea*, including the discriminatory intent, will be discussed, before moving on to the examination of 'racial grounds'.

22 *The Attorney General of Israel v Eichmann*, Case No 40/61, Judgment, Israel Supreme Court (29 May 1962), at: www.asser.nl/upload/documents/DomCLIC/Docs/NLP/Israel/Eichmann_Appeals_Judgement_29-5-1962.pdf. Furthermore: Matthew Lippman, 'Genocide: The Trial of Adolf Eichmann and the Quest for Global Justice', 8 *Buffalo Human Rights Law Review* (2002) 67–105.

23 ILC Draft Code of Offences Against the Peace and Security of Mankind (1954), <http://legal.un.org/ilc/texts/instruments/english/draft_articles/7_3_1954.pdf>.

24 Draft Code of Crimes against the Peace and Security of Mankind with commentaries 1991, UN Doc. A/46/10 (1991), p. 104.

25 *Prosecutor v Kupreškić* et al., Case No IT-95–16-T (14 January 2000), para. 590.

5.3 Jurisprudence of the *ad hoc* international criminal tribunals

5.3.1 *Introduction*

Persecution was rarely charged in criminal trials prior to the creation of the ICTY, when it experienced a kind of renaissance.[26] Through frequent adjudications of persecution, the crime has become known as the tribunal's 'flagship crime'.[27] Counts alleging persecution have captured the serious dimension of the conflict in the former Yugoslavia, the historical backdrop of which is reviewed in the acclaimed *Tadić* trial judgment. The Trial Chamber held that although Serbs, Muslims, and Croats resided in separate villages, there were frequent intermarriages and good interrelations between the groups. All three groups considered themselves Slavs.[28] When in 1991 Slovenia and later Croatia declared independence in response to a perceived Serbian domination of the Federation, Yugoslavia began disintegrating along its republics' borders. Eventually, this development led to brutal conflicts in Croatia and in Bosnia and Herzegovina, converting an apparently friendly atmosphere between Muslims, Croats, and Serbs into one of fear, distrust, and mutual hostility.[29] Such polarisation forced each individual to either leave his group altogether or to fully identify with it.[30] Prior to the eruption of military hostilities, propaganda emphasised the myth that the Muslims had taken the land that belonged to 'us'. As in Nazi Germany and Rwanda, a legend of origin was created that essentialised each group's

26 Brady, Liss (n 2) 500; Nilsson (n 15) 219.

27 Brady, Liss (n 2) 500; Gideon Boas, James Bischoff, Natalie Reid, *Elements of Crimes Under International Law: International Criminal Law Practitioners Library Series*, Volume II (CUP 2008) 116.

28 *Prosecutor v Tadić*, Case No IT-94-1-T (7 May 1997), para. 67. Furthermore: Stephen Cornell, Douglas Hartmann, *Ethnicity and Race: Making Identities in a Changing World* (Pine Forge Press 1998) 144–148; Russell Hardin, *One for All: The Logic of Group Conflict* (Princeton UP 1995) 148, 156, 158–159.

29 *Prosecutor v Tadić*, Case No IT-94-1-T (7 May 1997), para. 83; Tadeusz Mazowiecki, Report by Special Rapporteur of the UNCHR, Pursuant to Paragraph 32 of Commission Resolution 1993/7 of 23 February 1993, on the Situation of Human Rights in the Territory of the Former Yugoslavia, UN Doc. E/CN.4/1994/47 (17 November 1993); Elisabeth Rehn, Report by Special Rapporteur of the UNCHR, Pursuant to Commission Resolution 1995/89, on the Situation of Human Rights in the Territory of the Former Yugoslavia, ECOSOC, UN Doc. E/CN.4/1996/63 (14 March 1996). Furthermore: Taulbee (n 13) 60; Robert Hayden, 'Imagined Communities and Real Victims: Self-Determination and Ethnic Cleansing in Yugoslavia', in Alexander Laban Hinton (ed), *Genocide: An Anthropological Reader* (Blackwell Publishers 2002) 233; Lori Lyman Bruun, 'Beyond the 1948 Convention: Emerging Principles of Genocide in Customary International Law', 17 *Maryland Journal of International Law and Trade* (1993) 199–200.

30 Toon Zwaan, 'Crisis and Genocide in Yugoslavia, 1985–1995', in Maria van Haperen et al. (eds), *The Holocaust and Other Genocides: An Introduction* (NIOD 2012) 126; Hayden (n 29) 236–237; Anton Blok, *Honour and Violence* (Polity Press 2001) 127–128; Hardin (n 28) 143, 148, 159.

identity, reinforcing the differences between 'us' and 'them' that legitimised the removal or extinction of the 'others'.[31] In removing all but one identity marker and thereby creating a unifying identity of the out-group, the process of othering is intensified. As in other cases, the perpetrators were preoccupied with their own group's susceptibility to threats, despite proclaiming to be superior.[32] The *Kupreškić* trial judgment gives a good description of the process of othering that beset the former Yugoslavia:

> In a matter of a few months, persons belonging to different ethnic groups, who used to enjoy good neighbourly relations, and who previously lived side by side in a peaceful manner and who once respected one another's different religious habits, customs and traditions, were transformed into enemies. Nationalist propaganda gradually fuelled a change in the perception and self-identification of members of the various ethnic groups. Gradually the 'others', ie the members of other ethnic groups, originally perceived merely as 'diverse', came instead to be perceived as 'alien' and then as 'enemy'; as potential threats to the identity and prosperity of one's group. What was earlier friendly neighbourly coexistence turned into persecution of those 'others'.[33]

Persecution is the most common conviction under crimes against humanity at the ICTY. By the time of the closure of the ICTY at the end of 2017, 161 individuals had been indicted and fifty-nine convicted of persecution.[34] The ICTY's jurisprudence on the crime is considered one of its most important contributions to international criminal law in that it truly developed the substantive content of the crime.[35] Despite providing substance and clarity to the crime, the Tribunal did not define racial grounds. While the crime against humanity of persecution was less relevant for ICTR cases, which were dominated by prosecutions for genocide,[36] the ICTR *Butare* appeals judgment, however,

31 Mark Rapley, '"How to do X without doing Y": Accomplishing Discrimination without "Being Racist" – "Doing Equity"', in Martha Augoustinos, Katherine Reynolds (eds), *Understanding Prejudice, Racism, and Social Conflict* (Sage Publications 2001) 232; Zwaan (n 30) 126; Ben Kiernan, *Blood and Soil: A World History of Genocide and Extermination from Sparta to Darfur* (Yale UP 2007) 588–590.

32 Kiernan (n 31) 588.

33 *Prosecutor v Kupreškić* et al., Case No IT-95–16-T (14 January 2000), para. 750.

34 <www.icty.org/en/cases/key-figures-cases> and <http://icr.icty.org/>. In comparison, the next highest number of convictions is twenty-one individuals for murder. Figures confirmed by Dr. Barbora Holá, Associate Professor, VU University Amsterdam (in file with author). Accord: Brady, Liss (n 2) 500; Fausto Pocar, 'Persecution as a Crime Under International Criminal Law', 2 *Journal of National Security Law and Policy* (2008) 358.

35 Valerie Oosterveld, 'Crimes Against Humanity', in Ann-Marie de Brouwer, Alette Smeulers (eds), *The Elgar Companion to the International Criminal Tribunal for Rwanda* (Edward Elgar 2016) 135; Brady, Liss (n 2) 500; Nilsson (n 15) 219–220; Bassiouni (n 6) 405; Roberts (n 10) 257 and 299; Fenrick (n 20) 89.

36 Kolb (n 7) 169; Larissa van den Herik, *The Contribution of the Rwanda Tribunal to the Development of International Law* (Martinus Nijhoff Publishers 2005) 194.

made some significant contributions to the distinction between race and ethnicity for the crime of persecution and will be discussed subsequently in Chapter 5.3.4.2.

Discrimination is the main feature that distinguishes persecution from other crimes against humanity, and the 'discriminatory intent must be characterizable in terms of politics, race, and religion'.[37] ICTY case law in this regard has consistently defined persecution as an

> act or omission which discriminates in fact and which: denies or infringes upon a fundamental right laid down in international customary or treaty law (*actus reus*); and was carried out deliberately with the intention to discriminate on one of the listed grounds, specifically race, religion or politics (the *mens rea*).[38]

Race is clearly positioned within the mental elements, which confirms that it is part of the perpetrator's discriminatory impetus and behaviour. In genocide, however, the perpetrator must have an intent to destroy the racial group and commit one of the enumerated acts against the racial group, which, ostensibly places race within the objective and subjective elements of the crime. In sum, race appears to have a distinctly different position in the crime of persecution than in the crime of genocide.

According to *Tadić*, the crime of persecution required some kind of discrimination that was intended to be, and resulted in, an infringement of an individual's fundamental rights, especially the right of equality. In order to constitute persecution under the ICTY Statute, this discrimination had to be on one of the listed grounds, namely political, racial, or religious.[39] There is no definitive list of protected fundamental rights, the Trial Chamber in *Kupreškić* held. Rather, it depends on whether the right in question can be considered so fundamental that its denial amounts to persecution and the denial has a severe enough impact on the victim.[40] The ICTY held that the crime against humanity of persecution 'derives its unique character from the requirement of a specific discriminatory

37 *Prosecutor v Kvočka* et al., Case No IT-98–30/1-T (2 November 2001), para. 194; Simon Chesterman, 'An Altogether Different Order: Defining the Elements of Crimes Against Humanity', 10 *Duke Journal of Comparative and International Law* (2000) 328.

38 *Prosecutor v Krajišnik*, Case No IT-00–39-T (27 September 2006), para. 734; *Prosecutor v Krnojelac*, Case No IT- 97–25-T (15 March 2002), paras. 431–432 and confirmed by Appeals Judgment (17 September 2003), para. 185. Similarly *Prosecutor v Mladić*, Case No IT-09–92-T (22 November 2017), para. 3228; *Prosecutor v Kordić and Čerkez*, Case No IT-95–14/2-A (17 December 2004), para. 101; *Prosecutor v Kordić and Čerkez*, Case No IT-95–14/2-T (26 February 2001), para. 188 and confirmed by *Prosecutor v Nahimana* et al., Case No ICTR-99–52-A (28 November 2007), para. 985.

39 *Prosecutor v Tadić*, Case No IT-94–1-T (7 May 1997), para. 697.

40 *Prosecutor v Kupreškić* et al., Case No IT-95–16-T (14 January 2000), paras. 630–631. Similarly *Prosecutor v Mladić*, Case No IT-09–92-T (22 November 2017), para. 3229.

intent'.[41] The accused must consciously intend to discriminate on one of the listed grounds of persecution. It is, in other words, not sufficient that the accused merely was aware that he was acting in a discriminatory way. Nevertheless, a conscious intent to discriminate does not require the existence of a discriminatory policy or the accused's participation in the formulation of such a policy or practice by an authority.[42] Importantly, and similar to the crimes of genocide and apartheid, the perpetrator must intend to commit the discrimination because of the victim's membership of a community or a group.[43] The victims are discriminated on political, racial or religious grounds; thus, they belong to a group of which the perpetrator is not part.[44] As such, the crime of persecution resembles the crime of genocide, where the perpetrator singles out a group, in whole or in part, for destruction. The two crimes will be further compared in the subsequent section.

5.3.2 *Positioning persecution*

This section will attempt to position the crime of persecution in relation to the crime of genocide and the crime of apartheid. Not only do all three crimes contain the term 'racial', they also all exhibit a discriminatory element against a specific group. Not least, the relationship between persecution and genocide is unclear, with persecution commonly portrayed as a form of lesser genocide.

5.3.2.1 *Persecution and genocide*

The boundaries between persecution and genocide tend to be blurred: both crimes consist of an attack against an individual for belonging to a specific group.[45] The ICTY Trial Chamber in *Jelisić* even concluded that 'genocide is closely related to the crime of persecution'[46] and 'a crime characterised as genocide constitutes, of itself, crimes against humanity within the meaning of persecution'.[47] However, despite the grey zones where the crimes overlap, they nonetheless have different legal elements and vary considerably in their *mens*

41 *Prosecutor v Krnojelac*, Case No IT-97–25-T (15 March 2002), para. 435. Furthermore: William Schabas, *An Introduction to the international Criminal Court* (CUP 4th ed 2011) 119; Boas, Bischoff, Reid (n 27) 89.

42 *Prosecutor v Prlić* et al., Case No IT-04–74-T (29 May 2013), para. 76; *Prosecutor v Blaškić*, Case No IT-95–14-A (29 July 2004), para. 165; *Prosecutor v Vasiljević*, Case No IT-98–32-T (29 November 2002), para 248. Furthermore: Nersessian (n 14) 160; Fenrick (n 20) 93.

43 *Prosecutor v Blaškić*, Case No IT-95–14-T (3 March 2000), para. 235.

44 Ibid para. 236; *Prosecutor v Tadić*, Case No IT-94–1-T (7 May 1997), paras. 714–715.

45 Brady, Liss (n 2) 491.

46 *Prosecutor v Jelisić*, Case No IT-95–10-T (14 December 1999), para. 68.

47 Ibid.

rea and *actus reus*.[48] While a discriminatory element is essential to both crimes, in that the perpetrator selects his victims because of their membership of a certain group, the crime of genocide takes discrimination one step further.[49] In genocide, the perpetrator intends to destroy the group as such, whereas the crime of persecution limits itself to an intentional and severe deprivation of fundamental rights by reason of the identity of the group. As such, the crime of genocide requires the highest level of proof of the *mens rea*.[50] The *génocidaire* targets the group as such and intends its destruction, while the persecutory act stops with the individual.[51] In persecution, the protection of the larger group is purely incidental because the law criminalises the unlawful deprivation of fundamental rights of individual characteristics, such as race.[52] The victim is, however, selected precisely due to his membership of a particular political, racial, or religious group the perpetrator does not intend to destroy. In sum, the crime of persecution does not protect the group as such, but rather its members in their political, racial, or religious differences.[53] In this regard, the ICTY in *Sikirica* clarified that

> the ultimate victim of genocide is the *group* . . .. This is what differentiates genocide from the crime against humanity of persecution. Even though they both have discriminatory elements, . . . in the case of persecution, the perpetrator commits crimes against *individuals*, on political, racial or religious grounds.[54]

Furthermore, the discriminatory intent in terms of political, racial, or religious characteristics is the main feature that distinguishes the crime of persecution

48 *Prosecutor v Rutaganda*, Case No ICTR-96–3-T (6 December 1999), para. 117. Furthermore: Nersessian (n 14) 160, 165; Badar (n 6) 124; William Schabas, 'The Crime of Genocide in the Jurisprudence of the International Criminal Tribunals', in Horst Fischer, Claus Kress, Sascha Rolf Lüder (eds), *International and National Prosecution of Crimes Under International Law* (Berliner Verlag 2001) 461–462.

49 William Schabas, *The International Criminal Court: A Commentary on the Rome Statute* (OUP 2nd ed 2016) 194, 201; Murray (n 7) 596; John RWD Jones, Steven Powles, *International Criminal Practice: The International Criminal Tribunal for the Former Yugoslavia, The International Criminal Tribunal for Rwanda, The International Criminal Court, The Special Court of Sierra Leone, The East Timor Special Panels for Serious Crimes, War Crimes Prosecutions in Kosovo* (OUP 3rd ed 2003) 215.

50 *Prosecutor v Krstić*, Case No IT-98–33-T (2 August 2001), para. 553. Furthermore: Murray (n 7) 596; Schabas (n 48) 462. See Chapter 3.5.3 on genocidal intent.

51 Brady, Liss (n 2) 491; Nersessian (n 14) 174–176.

52 Nersessian (n 14) 260.

53 Ibid 258; Guénaël Mettraux, *International Crimes and the* ad hoc *Tribunals* (OUP 2005) 334; Ken Roberts, 'The Law of Persecution Before the International Criminal Tribunal for the Former Yugoslavia', 15 *LJIL* (2002) 628.

54 *Prosecutor v Sikirica*, Case No IT-95–8, Judgment on Defense Motion to Acquit (3 September 2001), para. 89, emphasis added.

from other crimes against humanity.[55] The *mens rea* requirement of the crime of persecution has been determined to be higher than that required for ordinary crimes against humanity, but lower than is required for genocide.[56] This 'necessary heightened *mens rea*'[57] leads to the conclusion that the ICTY treated the crime of persecution as some kind of 'super crime against humanity' or 'lower genocide', without having appropriate regard to the principle of legality.[58]

Persecution thus comprises criminal acts that are motivated by racial, religious or political animus, *Kupreškić* held, but its discriminatory *mens rea* stops short of the genocidal intent to destroy.[59] Formulated differently, genocidal intent necessarily implies the discriminatory intent required for persecution.[60]The closeness of persecution to genocide is further demonstrated in the analysis of the *mens rea* in the *Kupreškić* trial judgment. The Trial Chamber held that persecutory acts were aimed at 'singling out and attacking certain individuals on discriminatory grounds' with the ultimate aim of 'removal of those persons from the society in which they live alongside the perpetrators, or eventually even from humanity itself'.[61] Singling out and attacking victims discriminatorily is symptomatic of any genocidal process, as Chapters 3.2 and 3.3 demonstrated. Detached from its context, the wording in *Kupreškić* on 'the removal from humanity' reads like a textbook description of the *dolus specialis* of genocide. The crimes of persecution and genocide are deeply intertwined in that – from a sociological perspective – discriminatory measures, such as persecution, commonly are the first step in a genocidal enterprise.[62] While persecution might indeed be considered a mitigated form of genocide, the ICTY Trial Chamber seems to juxtapose the two crimes' intent. However, the intent to destroy in

55 *Prosecutor v Kvočka* et al., Case No IT-98–30/1-T (2 November 2001), para. 194. Furthermore: Nersessian (n 14) 155–160.

56 *Prosecutor v Stakić*, Case No IT-97–24-T (31 July 2003), para. 738; *Prosecutor v Kordić and Čerkez*, Case No 95–14/2-T (26 February 2001), para. 212; *Prosecutor v Kupreškić* et al., Case No IT-95–16-T (14 January 2000), para. 636; *Prosecutor v Tadić*, Case No 94–1-A (15 July 1999), para. 305; *Prosecutor v Tadić*, Case No 94–1-T (7 May 1997), para. 716. Furthermore: Nersessian (n 14) 155, 174; Kai Ambos, 'What Does 'Intent to Destroy' in Genocide Mean?', 91 *International Review of the Red Cross* (2009) 835–836; Byron (n 13) 229 and 234; Badar (n 6) 134; Roberts (n 53) 635.

57 *Prosecutor v Kordić and Čerkez*, Case No 95–14/2-T (26 February 2001), para. 220.

58 Caroline Fournet, Clotilde Pégorier, '"Only One Step Away From Genocide": The Crime of Persecution in International Criminal Law', 10 *International Criminal Law Review* (2010) 718. Similarly: Nilsson (n 15) 221.

59 *Prosecutor v Kupreškić* et al., Case No IT-95-16-T (14 January 2000), para. 606.

60 *Prosecutor v Nahimana* et al., Case No ICTR-99–52-A (28 November 2007), para. 1010.

61 *Prosecutor v Kupreškić* et al., Case No IT-95–16-T (14 January 2000), para. 634. *Prosecutor v Kordić and Čerkez*, Case No IT -95–14/2-T (26 February 2001), para. 214 endorsed this approach.

62 Mettraux (n 53) 336. The persecutor intends to discriminate individuals for reasons of their group membership, whereas the *génocidaire* intends to destroy a group [Nersessian (n 14) 174]. Both crimes consist of discrimination, but genocide can grow out of persecution by taking discrimination one step further to destruction.

the crime of genocide is significantly stronger than the intent to discriminate in the crime of persecution. The main distinguishing element for the two crimes is therefore their distinct *mens rea*,[63] a fact that the ICTY did not respect in blurring their definitional boundaries. Oddly, in the very same judgment, the Trial Chamber emphasized how the *mens rea* of genocide is limited to the intent to destroy and, as such, is an extreme form of persecution.[64]

The position of the crime of persecution, particularly in relation to the crime of genocide, has not yet been fully resolved. At times, persecution is treated as a special kind of crime against humanity, while at others, the ICTY performs a 'quasi-merger between persecution and genocide'.[65] As early as 1944, Lemkin acknowledged the close connection between the two crimes in noting that genocide is a composite of different acts of persecution or destruction.[66] The ICTY in *Kupreškić* explored this interconnectedness further. 'Persecution', it declared,

> is an offence belonging to the same *genus* as genocide. Both . . . are crimes perpetrated against persons that belong to a particular group and who are targeted because of such belonging. . . . [F]rom the viewpoint of *mens rea*, genocide is an extreme and most inhuman form of persecution. To put it differently, when persecution escalates to the extreme form of wilful and deliberate acts designed to destroy a group or part of a group, it can be held that such persecution amounts to genocide.[67]

Unlike the *génocidaire*, whose ulterior motive is the destruction of the group, in the crime of persecution the perpetrator chooses his victims because they belong to a specific community, but without seeking to destroy the community as such.[68] Ethnic cleansing, 'although it is not a term of art',[69] is an example of persecution that falls short of genocide. It includes practices aimed at expelling or inducing the departure of persons who do not belong to the perpetrator's group from a defined area.[70] In practical terms, lower-level perpetrators seem to be charged with persecution rather than genocide, since persecution does

63 Taulbee (n 13) 16.
64 *Prosecutor v Kupreškić* et al., Case No IT-95–16-T (14 January 2000), para. 636. Related discussion: Roberts (n 53) 625.
65 Fournet, Pégorier (n 58) 718.
66 Raphael Lemkin, *Axis Rule in Occupied Europe: Laws of Occupation, Analysis of Government, Proposals for Redress* (Carnegie Endowment for International Peace 1944) 92.
67 *Prosecutor v Kupreškić* et al., Case No IT-95–16-T (14 January 2000), para. 636.
68 *Prosecutor v Jelisić*, Case No IT-95–10-T (14 December 1999), para. 79.
69 *Prosecutor v Kupreškić* et al., Case No IT-95–16-T (14 January 2000), para. 606.
70 William Schabas, 'Judicial Activism and the Crime of Genocide', in Shane Darcy, Joseph Powderly (eds), *Judicial Creativity at the International Criminal Tribunal* (OUP 2010) 74–77; Fenrick (n 20) 82. See *Prosecutor v Mladić*, Case No IT-09–92-T (22 November 2017), para. 3315.

not require the proof of a *dolus specialis.* The crime of persecution therefore becomes the 'gap-filling criminal prohibition' preferred by the prosecution.[71] Higher-level perpetrators would, in return, supposedly be charged with the crime of genocide, to which is attached a higher stigma, if the prosecution can prove a special intent to destroy a group.[72]

5.3.2.2 Persecution and apartheid

Prior to the inclusion of apartheid in the Rome Statute, legal scholars discussed whether or not apartheid constituted the crime of persecution on racial grounds. 'Since apartheid was a state-wide system of racial discrimination', Ronald Slye wrote, 'it is reasonable to conclude that apartheid constitutes a crime against humanity under this category'.[73] The inclusion of persecution on racial grounds (Art. 7(1)(h) Rome Statute) could arguably facilitate the prosecution of any widespread or systematic policy of apartheid. Indeed, the argument against including apartheid on the list of crimes against humanity was made at the Rome Diplomatic Conference on the grounds that the crime of apartheid had become superfluous.[74] The 1996 ILC Draft Code of Crimes notably distinguished between persecution and institutionalised discrimination. According to the Draft Code, persecution would apply to acts that lacked the specific intent required for the crime of genocide. Whereas the categories of prohibited acts of persecution and institutionalised discrimination had to be committed in a systematic manner or on a large scale to constitute a crime against humanity, institutional discrimination further required that the discriminatory plan or policy has been institutionalised, for example, by the adoption of a series of legislative measures denying individuals who are members of a particular racial, ethnic or religious group of their human rights or freedoms. The ILC concluded that this in fact was the crime of apartheid under a more general denomination.[75] Hence, the crime of apartheid does not require a special discriminatory intent, but rather an intent to maintain an institutionalised regime. Nevertheless, the crime consists of the oppression and domination of one racial group over another because of a (perceived or real) membership of a racial group. The perpetrator thus makes a selection and discriminates against his victims because of their racial affiliation.

71 Eyal Mayroz, 'Genocide: To Prevent and Punish "Radical Evil"', in Philipp Kastner (ed) *International Criminal Law in Context* (Routledge 2018) 86; Mettraux (n 53) 336.

72 Taulbee (n 13) 101. See discussion in Chapter 3.5.3.2 on issues of proving the intent.

73 Ronald Slye, 'Apartheid as a Crime Against Humanity: A Submission to the South African Truth and Reconciliation Commission', 20 *Michigan Journal of International Law* (1999) 280.

74 Timothy McCormack, 'Crimes Against Humanity', in Dominic McGoldrick, Peter Rowe, Eric Donnelly (eds), *The Permanent International Criminal Court: Legal and Policy Issues* (Hart Publishing 2004) 198; Ariel Bultz, 'Redefining Apartheid in International Criminal Law', 24 *Criminal Law Forum* (2013) 226. See Chapter 4.6.1 on the drafting of the Rome Statute.

75 ILC Draft Code of Crimes against Peace and Security of Mankind (1996), p. 49.

While persecution demands a discriminatory intent, such a mental element is not needed for the crime of apartheid. Can apartheid be committed without discriminatory intent, despite this not being an explicit legal requirement? Might an intrinsic discriminatory *mens rea* be contained in apartheid? While these questions need not be answered conclusively, an answer of the latter in the affirmative would be expected.

5.3.3 The mens rea *of persecution*

In contrast to other crimes, a persecutory act is neither inherently inhumane nor criminal as long as it is not committed with the required discriminatory intent, the *mens rea*.[76] The act is automatically criminalised if it is based on political, racial, or religious grounds and 'thereby attacks humanity through some of the most basic groups into which it is organised'.[77] Thus, it is the discrimination itself that makes the act inhumane – and the discriminatory intent becomes the hallmark of persecution.[78] In *Kvočka*, the ICTY Trial Chamber discussed discriminatory acts such as denying bank accounts, educational, or employment opportunities that were not considered criminal, but would nevertheless become criminal and persecutorial if committed with discriminatory intent.[79] While the discriminatory intent need not be the primary intent with respect to the underlying acts committed, it nonetheless has to be a significant one.[80] As with the crime of genocide, prosecutors have found it difficult to prove such discriminatory intent, although it is uncontested from a legal standpoint.[81] Furthermore, the perpetrator need not have a persecutory intent, as

76 *Prosecutor v Krnojelac*, Case No IT-97–25-A, Separate Opinion of Judge Shahabuddeen (17 September 2003), paras. 6–7; *Prosecutor v Tadić*, Case No IT-94–1-T (7 May 1997), para. 715; *Prosecutor v Lukić and Lukić*, Case No IT-98–32/1-T (20 July 2009), para. 993; *Prosecutor v Krajišnik*, Case No IT-00–39-T (27 September 2006), para. 735. Furthermore: Geert-Jan Alexander Knoops, Mens Rea *at the International Criminal Court* (Brill Nijhoff 2017) 139; Nersessian (n 14) 156–157; Dermot Groome, 'Persecution', in Antonio Cassese (ed), *The Oxford Companion to International Criminal Justice* (OUP 2009) 453; Boas, Bischoff, Reid (n 27) 89–90.

77 Steven Ratner, Jason Abrams, *Accountability for Human Rights Atrocities in International Law* (OUP 2nd ed 2001) 63 (omitted from the 3rd ed). Furthermore: Knoops (n 76) 137; Fournet, Pégorier (n 58) 729. Similarly, *Prosecutor v Kupreškić*, Case No IT-95–16-T (14 January 2000), para. 622; *Prosecutor v Naletilić and Martinović*, Case No IT-98–34-T (31 March 2003), para. 634; *Prosecutor v Semanza*, Case No ICTR-97–20-T (15 May 2003), para. 469; *Prosecutor v Kordić and Čerkez*, Case No IT-95–14/2-T (26 February 2001), paras. 202–207.

78 See Boas, Bischoff, Reid (n 27) 90; Olivia Swaak-Goldman, 'The Crime of Persecution in International Criminal Law', 11 *LJIL* (1998) 148.

79 *Prosecutor v Kvočka* et al., Case No IT-98–30-T (2 November 2001), para. 186.

80 *Prosecutor v Krnojelac*, Case No IT-97–25-T (15 March 2002), para. 435. Furthermore: Nersessian (n 14) 159.

81 Brady, Liss (n 2) 536; Pocar (n 34) 358; Boas, Bischoff, Reid (n 27) 95; Badar (n 6) 140. See Chapter 3.5.3.2 on the proof of genocidal intent.

opposed to a discriminatory intent.[82] The ICTY Trial Chamber in *Prlić*, *Stakić* and *Lukić and Lukić* even labelled this discriminatory intent for the crime of persecution a *dolus specialis*,[83] whereas the term commonly is associated with the crime of genocide. Most importantly for this study, the perpetrator's intention to discriminate has to be based on specific grounds, namely race, religion, or politics (in the case of the ICTY and ICTR).[84] Thus, discrimination on racial, religious, or political grounds is inherently linked to the perpetrator's intent or, in the words of the ICTY Trial Chamber, 'carried out deliberately with the intention to discriminate on one of the listed grounds'.[85] While jurisprudence has confirmed that the crime of persecution requires an intent to discriminate on racial grounds, among others, the question remains how racial grounds are defined.

5.3.4 *Defining the victim group of persecution*

5.3.4.1 *Introduction*

The definition of the victim group, especially the racial group, is central to this study. As in the crime of genocide, the perpetrator of the crime of persecution commits his crime against 'persons that belong to a particular group and who are targeted because of such belonging. In both categories what matters is the intent to discriminate'.[86] Persecution is, in other words, a label attached to underlying offences characterised by discrimination against particular groups of persons.[87] The following sections will analyse persecution on racial grounds under the ICTY and ICTR Statutes, discuss whether there is a difference between racial groups and racial grounds, and explore discussions on inferiorisation and dehumanisation in the jurisprudence of the *ad hoc* tribunals. The analysis will demonstrate that the perpetrator's perception is central to the identification of the victims of persecution and that, contrary to the case of genocide, a negative group definition is admissible.

5.3.4.2 *Acts of persecution on racial grounds*

Art. 7(1)(h) Rome Statute of the ICC broadly lists the discriminatory grounds for the crime against humanity of persecution to include political, racial, national,

82 Mettraux (n 53) 186.

83 *Prosecutor v Prlić* et al., Case No IT-04–74-T (29 May 2013), para. 76; *Prosecutor v Stakić*, Case No IT-97–24-A (22 March 2006), para. 328; *Prosecutor v Lukić and Lukić*, Case No 98–32/1-T (20 July 1999), para. 994.

84 *Prosecutor v Tadić*, Case No IT-94–1-T (7 May 1997), para. 697; *Prosecutor v Krstić*, Case No IT-98–33-T (2 August 2001), para. 553. Furthermore: Mettraux (n 53) 182.

85 *Prosecutor v Vasiljević*, Case No IT-98–32-T (29 November 2002), para. 244.

86 *Prosecutor v Kupreškić*, Case No IT-95–16-T (14 January 2000), para. 636.

87 Boas, Bischoff, Reid (n 27) 89.

ethnic, cultural, religious, gender, or other grounds that are universally recognised as impermissible under international law.[88] The definition of persecution in Art. 3(h) ICTR and Art. 5(h) ICTY Statute, on the other hand, is significantly narrower, criminalising only 'persecutions on political, racial and religious grounds'. This definition caused problems for the ICTY and ICTR for two reasons: first, for seemingly listing the discriminatory grounds in a cumulative fashion (indicated by the word 'and'), and second, for excluding ethnic grounds. The tribunals had therefore to engage in an interpretational balancing act in order to include ethnic groups in the definition of the crime of persecution. The Trial Chamber in *Bagosora* recognised that the crime of persecution did not include ethnic grounds, despite being contained in the *chapeau* on crimes against humanity. Nonetheless, it considered that discrimination on ethnic grounds could nevertheless constitute persecution if the violated rights were sufficiently serious, as was also confirmed by the *Nahimana* appeals judgment.[89] The Trial Chamber in *Brđanin* considered racial grounds for the crime of persecution to include ethnicity, 'which it finds more appropriate to refer to in the context of the present case'.[90]

Similarly, the Prosecution in the *Butare* case argued that targeting the Tutsi ethnic group meant targeting a group on racial grounds, because 'racial grounds' in Art. 3(h) ICTR Statute included ethnic grounds.[91] The Prosecution further asserted that the ICTR Trial Chamber had taken judicial notice of the Tutsi as an ethnic group, making them a racial group also under customary international law.[92] While race and ethnicity are indeed related, it would nevertheless be wrong to conclude that racial grounds included ethnic grounds *per se* or that an ethnic group was identical to a racial group under customary international law. There are no indications that customary law would treat the two groups identically. On appeal, the accused Ntahobali argued that the Trial Chamber had not relied on evidence that the Tutsi were a different racial group from the Hutu. He reiterated that the ICTR Statute distinguished between race and ethnicity, as did Arts. 4, 5 and 7 ICERD.[93] The conclusion on appeal was that the Trial Chamber had convicted Ntahobali of persecution on ethnic grounds. The crime of persecution, the majority stressed, only protected three distinct

88 See discussion in Chapter 5.4.

89 *Prosecutor v Bagosora* et al., Case No ICTR-98–41-T (18 December 2008), para. 2209 with reference to *Prosecutor v Nahimana* et al., Case No ICTR-99–52-A (28 November 2007), para. 986.

90 *Prosecutor v Brđanin*, Case No IT-99–36-T (1 September 2004), para. 992, footnote 2484.

91 *Prosecutor v Nyiramasuhuko* et al. (*Butare* case), Case No ICTR-98–42-A (14 December 2015), para. 2130.

92 Ibid. Footnote 4945 refers to Art. 1(1) ICERD, possibly implying that it reflects customary law.

93 *Prosecutor v Nyiramasuhuko* et al., Case No ICTR-98–42-A (14 December 2015), para. 2132 and footnote 4952.

groups: political, racial, and religious. A contextual reading of Art. 3 made 'clear that "ethnicity" cannot be encapsulated in "race". Indeed, interpreting the discriminatory ground of "race" . . . as including "ethnicity" would render the distinction in the chapeau of Art. 3 of the Statute redundant, illogical, and superfluous'.[94] The Appeals Chamber also pointed to the established distinction between race and ethnicity in the definition of genocide.[95] However, since the *chapeau* to all crimes against humanity in Art. 3 ICTR Statute offers protection to 'any civilian population on national, political, ethnic, racial or religious grounds', the discriminatory ground of ethnicity is applicable for the crime of persecution too.[96] In accepting discrimination on the basis of ethnicity as one of the protected grounds of persecution, the *ad hoc* tribunals effectively expanded the exhaustive list in their statutes.[97]

In his dissenting opinion, Judge Agius argued that it would contradict customary international law to narrow the protection to these three groups only, particularly because the *chapeau* also included the ethnic group. Rather, he considered, persecution on 'racial grounds' included discrimination on grounds of ethnicity.[98] Judge Agius believed the interpretation of the majority was 'overly restrictive' because it 'mechanically [led] to the conclusion that discrimination on the basis of ethnicity cannot overlap or be encompassed in other discriminatory grounds for persecution, in particular, "racial" grounds'.[99] In his opinion, the majority placed too much emphasis on the *chapeau* of Art. 3, which was an additional jurisdictional requirement rather than a discriminatory intent.[100] His argument in this matter is confirmed by the *Nahimana* Trial Chamber, for which the overarching discriminatory motive was not considered to be part of the definition of crimes against humanity as a matter of customary law, but rather a jurisdictional limitation, not a substantive element of the offense.[101] Judge Agius examined several international sources to strengthen his argument. First, he discussed Art. 1(1) ICERD for the definition of racial discrimination. He recognised that ICERD differentiated between race and ethnicity, but that discrimination based on either ground constituted racial discrimination.[102] Reviewing the Genocide Convention's drafting history, he concluded that

94 Ibid para. 2137.
95 Ibid footnote 4963.
96 Ibid para. 2134.
97 *Prosecutor v Milutinović* et al., Case No IT-05–87-T (26 February 2009), para. 176; Kolb (n 7) 169.
98 *Prosecutor v Nyiramasuhuko* et al., Case No ICTR-98–42-A, Dissenting and Separate Opinions of Judge Agius (14 December 2015), paras. 29–43.
99 Ibid para. 33.
100 Ibid para. 34.
101 *Prosecutor v Nahimana* et al., Case No ICTR-99–52-T (3 December 2003), para. 1071. Furthermore: William Schabas, *The UN International Criminal Tribunals: The Former Yugoslavia, Rwanda and Sierra Leone* (CUP 2006) 219.
102 *Prosecutor v Nyiramasuhuko* et al., Case No ICTR-98–42-A, Dissenting and Separate Opinions of Judge Agius (14 December 2015), para. 36.

'ethnical' and 'racial' appeared not to have autonomous meanings. Rather, ethnicity overlapped or was largely synonymous with race and was added to the Genocide Convention late in the drafting process.[103] Agius is correct in saying that ethnicity was included in an eleventh-hour compromise.[104] When the Genocide Convention was drafted, Jews or Poles, who nowadays would be considered an ethnic (or national or religious) group, were then understood as distinct racial groups.[105] Yet drawing on such an interpretation for the ICTR Statute – created in an era when it was unlikely that anyone referred to Jews or Poles as racial groups – arguably weakens rather than strengthens Agius' argument. To this extent, recourse to the *travaux préparatoires* of the Genocide Convention does not seem intuitively significant for the interpretation of the crime of persecution in the ICTR Statute. Nonetheless, it is acknowledged that the ICTY and ICTR Statutes were based on what was considered customary law in 1993 and 1994, respectively.[106] While this fact is not contested, the interpretation of a racial ground for the crime of persecution by reference to ICERD and the drafting history of the Genocide Convention, however, is. This study has already shown that Art. 1(1) ICERD cannot readily be transposed to a provision entailing individual criminal responsibility.[107] Judge Agius would seem to have realised this too when he blames the majority for their 'overly restrictive' interpretation and for placing 'too much emphasis' on the *chapeau*. The application of international criminal law has direct consequences for the accused, thus demanding a restrictive interpretation.

The practical implications of the discriminatory motive for the crime of persecution are of little significance, Schabas asserts, because while national and ethnic groups were not included in Art. 3(h) ICTR Statute, they would 'fit within the parameters of the somewhat archaic term "racial"'.[108] In Schabas' opinion, and as discussed earlier with regard to genocide, the Tutsi could be adequately described as either an 'ethnic' or a 'racial' group.[109] No prosecution for persecution before the ICTR should fail because the Tutsi were not considered a racial group, he maintains.[110] Yet this was the outcome of the *Semanza* case, which is controversial inasmuch as it convicted the perpetrator for genocide, but acquitted him for persecution with respect to the killing of moderate Hutu and Tutsi sympathizers. The prosecution had failed to demonstrate to the judges that the victims were a political group in the sense of Art. 3(h)

103 Ibid para. 37.
104 See Chapter 3.4.4 on the drafting history of the Genocide Convention.
105 *Prosecutor v Nyiramasuhuko* et al., Case No ICTR-98–42-A, Dissenting and Separate Opinions of Judge Agius (14 December 2015), para. 38.
106 See Chapters 3.6.2 on the creation of the ICTR and 3.9.2 on the creation of the ICTY.
107 See Chapters 4.5.3 and 4.5.4.
108 Schabas (n 101) 219.
109 Ibid. See Chapter 3.6.5.
110 Schabas (n 101) 219.

ICTR Statute.[111] Schabas argues that *Semanza* would have been a prime example of persecution, rather than genocide. The Hutu victims were not members of the targeted ethnic or racial group, while persecution on political grounds would have been the better legal classification of the crimes.[112] Notably, in *Nahimana* another ICTR Trial Chamber concluded that attacks on Hutu were acts of 'persecution on political grounds of an ethnic character'.[113]

The definition of 'racial' is as problematic for the crime of persecution as it is for the crime of genocide or apartheid. As with the crime of genocide, legal scholars have preferred to avoid the contentious issue of defining race for the crime of persecution. Werle and Jessheimer bypass definitional challenges when noting that 'if the perpetrator discriminates against the victim because the victim is of a certain race, the perpetrator is acting on racial grounds'.[114] Discrimination on ethnic grounds, which they do not further examine, 'probably has little independent scope outside racial grounds'.[115] For additional information on conduct on 'national' and 'ethnic grounds', the authors refer to their analysis of the protected groups of genocide where they seem to equate national and ethnic *grounds* with national and ethnic *groups*,[116] a topic to be discussed in the next section. With regard to persecution on the grounds of gender, Werle and Jessheimer conclude that the term 'gender' embraces both biological and sociological differences,[117] in coherence with Art. 7(3) Rome Statute, which defines gender as referring 'to the two sexes, male and female, within the context of society',[118] thus taking into account factual as well as constructed realities. If gender can be constructed sociologically, the same must be all the more valid for race and ethnicity.

5.3.4.3 *Racial group vs racial ground*

While the provisions on the crimes of genocide and apartheid expressly protect members of a certain *group*, the crime of persecution is a bit more diffuse in protecting victims targeted on a number of *grounds*. Nevertheless, it will be shown here that the treatment of the victim's group membership by the ICTR and ICTY is not significantly different for the crime of persecution than for that of genocide. According to the judges, it apparently does not matter

111 *Prosecutor v Semanza*, Case No ICTR-97–20-T (15 May 2003), para. 471.
112 Schabas (n 101) 219.
113 *Prosecutor v Nahimana* et al., Case No ICTR-99–52-T (3 December 2003), para. 1071.
114 Werle, Jessberger (n 6) 378.
115 Ibid.
116 Ibid footnote 303.
117 Ibid 379.
118 In the UN context, gender has been defined as 'observed differences between women and men based on socially assigned roles', see Report by the Secretary-General, Implementation of the Outcome of the Fourth World Conference on Women, UN Doc. A/51/322 (3 September 1996), para. 9.

whether a victim is a member of a racial group or persecuted on racial grounds. This fact could indicate that the concept of race is considered identically for all the crimes examined within the framework of this study. The following examples will demonstrate the manner in which the victim groups are defined in the ICTR and ICTY jurisprudence. While not all cases deal with the racial group, their discussions can nonetheless be extrapolated to this analysis on race.

According to *Blaškić*, 'the victimised persons were specially selected on grounds linked to their belonging to a particular community'[119] and similarly, *Krstić* holds that the perpetrator targeted individuals 'because of their membership in a specific community'.[120] It is remarkable that these two judgments use the term 'community' rather than 'group', despite the fact that the (identical) criminal provisions of both statutes do not mention the word 'community'. Whether this was a deliberate choice of wording is not apparent at first sight. However, *Blaškić* suggests that the ICTY Trial Chamber understood 'community' to signify the same as 'group', when it noted that 'the perpetrator of the acts of persecution does not initially target the individual but rather membership in a specific racial, religious or political group'.[121] Indeed, a full clarification comes from *Blaškić* itself, when, in the discussion of the *mens rea* of the crime of persecution, it emphasises that '[i]t is the specific intent to cause injury to a human being because he belongs to a particular community or group'.[122] Group and community can therefore be interpreted as having synonymous meanings. To this extent it should be noted that Art. 7(2)(g) Rome Statute reconciles earlier ambiguities by referring to the identity of the group or collectivity. Chapter 5.4.3 will discuss these two notions further.

The *Kvočka* trial judgment concluded that '[t]he victims were targeted for attack on discriminatory grounds. . . . [D]iscriminatory grounds form the requisite criteria, not membership in a particular group'.[123] The Trial Chamber apparently distinguishes between 'grounds' and 'groups' – and does not consider the latter an element of the crime. This conclusion was later rejected by the Trial Chamber in *Krnojelac*, emphasizing that 'the argument in the *Kvočka* Trial Judgment . . . would appear to deny the interests protected by the crime. Even the relevant discriminatory intent necessarily assumes that the victim is a member of a political, racial or religious group'.[124] Although the ICTY Statute does not expressly require discrimination to have been perpetrated against a member of

119 *Prosecutor v Blaškić*, Case No IT-95–14-T (3 March 2000), para. 233.

120 *Prosecutor v Krstić*, Case No IT-98–33-T (2 August 2001), para. 553. Similarly: *Prosecutor v Blaškić*, Case No IT-95–14-T (3 March 2000), para. 220.

121 *Prosecutor v Blaškić*, Case No IT-95–14-T (3 March 2000), para. 235. Similarly: *Prosecutor v Kupreškić* et al., Case No IT-95-16-T (14 January 2000), para. 636.

122 *Prosecutor v Blaškić*, Case No IT-95–14-T (3 March 2000), para. 235.

123 *Prosecutor v Kvočka* et al., Case No IT-98–30/1-T (2 November 2001), para. 197.

124 *Prosecutor v Krnojelac*, Case No IT-97–25-T (15 March 2002), footnote 1294.

the targeted group, it is a necessary implication of an act committed on a discriminatory basis.[125] Put differently: the crime of persecution is directed against members of a specific group for reasons of their group membership. The interpretation of 'grounds' and 'group' leads apparently to the same result.

Similarly, the ICTY Trial Chamber in *Blagojević* held that an act was discriminatory when a victim was targeted for membership of a group defined by the perpetrator on a political, racial, or religious basis. The act or omission needed to discriminate in fact and have discriminatory consequences, thus discriminatory intent was not sufficient in itself.[126] This statement is interesting for two reasons: first, in acknowledging that the perpetrator defines the victim group, the Tribunal applied a subjective perpetrator-based approach.[127] The victims' perception of their own group membership was seemingly considered insignificant. Second, the crime was not completed unless the discriminatory act also had discriminatory consequences, ie persecution is not an inchoate crime. Unlike the crime of genocide that is fulfilled also without the destruction of a group, the perpetrator of persecution cannot be convicted for intending to discriminate against a group.

5.3.4.4 The perpetrator's perception of the victim group

In cases of genocide, the jurisprudence generally admitted mixed objective-subjective approaches for the classification of the victim group. In a few isolated cases, a victim-based approach was deemed acceptable.[128] As to the crime of persecution, however, the ICTY Trial Chamber in *Naletilić and Martinović* made it clear that the victim's perception did not define his status as a member of a protected group. Rather, for classification as a targeted group of persecution, only the perpetrator's perception mattered:

> [T]he targeted group does not only comprise persons who *personally* carry the (religious, racial or political) criteria of the group. The targeted group must be interpreted broadly, and may . . . include such persons who are *defined by the perpetrator as belonging to the victim group due to their close affiliations or sympathies for the victim group*. The Chamber finds this interpretation consistent with the underlying *ratio* of the provision prohibiting

125 Ibid para. 432.

126 *Prosecutor v Blagojević* et al., Case No IT-02–60-T (17 January 2005), para. 583. Confirmed in: *Prosecutor v Lukić and Lukić*, Case No 98–32/1-A (4 December 2012), para. 455; *Prosecutor v Stakić*, Case No IT-97–24-T (31 July 2003), para. 733; *Prosecutor v Nahimana* et al., Case No ICTR-99–52-T (3 December 2003), para. 1073; *Prosecutor v Vasiljević*, Case No IT-98–32-T (29 November 2002), paras. 244–245; *Prosecutor v Krnojelac*, Case No IT-97–25-T (15 March 2002), para. 432. See discussion in Schabas (n 49) 201.

127 Also recognised by Kolb (n 7) 170.

128 See discussion in Chapters 3.9.2 and 3.13.

> persecution, as it is the perpetrator who defines the victim group while the targeted victims have no influence on the definition of their status. The Chamber finds that in such cases, a factual discrimination is given as the victims are ***discriminated in fact*** for who or what they are on the basis of the perception of the perpetrator.[129]

In a footnote, the Trial Chamber further explained that this interpretation took into account

> the fact that the power to define the 'targeted group' rest solely in the hands of the perpetrator group. If a certain person is defined by the perpetrator as belonging to the targeted group, this definition thus becomes 'discriminatory in fact' for the victim as it may not be rebutted, even if such classification may be incorrect under objective criteria.[130]

The Tribunal applied a perpetrator-based subjective approach, acknowledging that the targeted group may be defined subjectively by the perpetrator.[131] Also other cases recognised the definitional power of the perpetrator. For instance, the ICTY Trial Chamber in *Blagojević and Jokić* held that the victim was targeted because of his membership 'of a group defined by the perpetrator on a political, racial or religious basis'.[132] Similarly, the *Đorđević* trial judgment opined that an 'act is discriminatory when a victim is targeted because of his or her membership in a group defined by the perpetrator on a political, racial or religious basis'.[133] Interestingly, the Trial Chamber convicted Đorđević for '[p]ersecutions, on racial grounds . . . , for having . . . aided and abetted the persecutions against Kosovo Albanians',[134] thereby determining that the perpetrator had discriminated against the Kosovo Albanian victims on racial grounds. Most other ICTY judgments, however, considered the victims an ethnic group. In this case, the racial grounds were either progressively interpreted as a perception of differentness or – more likely – were included in the ethnic grounds of discrimination.[135] Overall, the victim's group membership is deemed a subjective criterion.

129 *Prosecutor v Naletilić and Martinović*, Case No IT-98–34-T (31 March 2003), para. 636 (emphasis in original). Endorsed by *Prosecutor v Stakić*, Case No IT-97–24-T (31 July 2003), para. 734 and *Prosecutor v Simić*, Case No IT-95–9-T (17 October 2003), para 49.

130 *Prosecutor v Naletilić and Martinović*, Case No IT-98–34-T (31 March 2003), para. 636, footnote 1572.

131 Also recognized by: Boas, Bischoff, Reid (n 27) 93; Roberts (n 10) 277, 280; Badar (n 6) 136.

132 *Prosecutor v Blagojević and Jokić*, Case No IT-02–60-T (17 January 2005), para. 583.

133 *Prosecutor v Đorđević*, Case No IT-05–87/1-T (23 February 2011), para. 1758.

134 Ibid, para. 2230.

135 Criticised in *Prosecutor v Nyiramasuhuko* et al., Case No ICTR-98–42-A, Dissenting and Separate Opinions of Judge Agius (14 December 2015), para. 41. See discussion in Chapter 5.3.4.2.

In holding the definitional power, the perpetrator identifies persecutory victims based on his perception. An objective characterisation of the victims' group membership is therefore not necessary.[136]

The ICTY Trial Chamber in *Milutinović* concluded that the perpetrator's intent to discriminate against members of a specific group for their group membership can be inferred from the circumstances, including the attitude of the 'perpetrator as demonstrated by his behaviour'.[137] Hate speech as a means of behaviour was used to determine the perpetrator's *mens rea* in the trial judgment in the *Ruggiu* case, the first decision by the ICTR on the crime of persecution. It dealt with the hate speech broadcasts by the radio station RTLM, which had 'all aimed at singling out and attacking the Tutsi ethnic group . . . on discriminatory grounds, by depriving them of the fundamental rights to life, liberty and basic humanity'.[138] The ICTR *Bikindi* trial judgment equally confirmed that hate speech could lead to persecutory discrimination; moreover, the Chamber did not exclude the possibility that songs too could constitute persecution.[139] Hate speech reduces the status of the victims, not only in the eyes of the group itself, but in the eyes of others who perceive and treat them as less than humans, and the derogatory position assigned to the victims of persecution can cause an irreversible harm.[140] The ICTY *Kupreškić* case also discussed how the perpetrators discriminated and targeted members of the victim group solely because of their identity. The judgment recognised that the victims were treated as inferior due to their shared ethnic, racial, or religious bonds, which were different to those of the dominant group.[141] The inferiorisation and dehumanisation of the Bosnian Muslims resurfaces elsewhere in the judgment:

> Bosnian Croat persecution of the Bosnian Muslim population was designed to dehumanise the latter so that it would be easier to commit acts of violence against them. Croats started to call Muslims by the derogatory term 'balijas', expel them from their homes, threaten them and otherwise harass them on the sole basis of their ethnicity.[142]

136 *Prosecutor v Prlić* et al., Case No IT-04–74-T (29 May 2013), para. 73; *The Prosecutor v Milutinović* et al., Case No IT-05–87-T (26 February 2009), para. 177. See also Kolb (n 7) 170; Nersessian (n 14) 158. See Chapters 3.2 and 3.8.3 on genocide.

137 *Prosecutor v Kvočka* et al., Case No IT-98–30/1-A (28 February 2005), para. 460.

138 *Prosecutor v Ruggiu*, Case No ICTR-97–23-I, Trial Judgment (1 June 2000), para. 22. Identical wording used in *Prosecutor v Kupreškić* et al., Case No IT-95–16-T (14 January 2000), para. 634. See also Chapter 3.6.5.

139 *Prosecutor v Bikindi*, Case No ICTR-01–72-T (2 December 2008), paras. 394–395.

140 *Prosecutor v Nahimana* et al., Case No ICTR-99–52-T (3 December 2003), para. 1071.

141 *Prosecutor v Kupreškić* et al., Case No IT-95–16-T (14 January 2000), para. 751. See Chapters 3.2 on othering and 3.3 on the stages of genocide, including the inferiorisation of the victim group.

142 *Prosecutor v Kupreškić* et al., Case No IT-95–16-T (14 January 2000), para. 85. See Ellen Elias-Bursać, *Translating Evidence and Interpreting Testimony at a War Crimes Tribunal* (Palgrave 2015) 145–148 on the meaning of 'Balijas' and how it was understood.

The use of such offensive or derogatory language in reference to non-Serbs was a topic in the *Brđanin*, *Krajišnik,* and the recent *Mladić* trial judgments too. The defendants had been calling the victims '*Balijas*' (Muslims), '*Ustaša*' (Croats), '*Šiptar*' (Albanians), 'Islamic tribe', 'Turks', 'vermin', 'scum', 'infidel', and 'second rate people'.[143] Also the *Karadžić* trial judgment recognised the importance of the perpetrators' selection of victims based on their identity. These acts, the Trial Chamber held, were carried out deliberately with the intent to discriminate on the basis of the victim's identity.[144] In doing so, the judges acknowledged the identity-based nature of the crime of persecution. As with other cases of persecution and genocide, the media played an important role in stirring up hatred and violence. In the context of the Yugoslav conflict, Serbian television ran 'a campaign of virulent anti-Bosniac propaganda',[145] increasingly highlighting the division between Bosniacs and Croats,[146] creating two allegedly distinct groups: 'us' and 'them'. Such othering is symptomatic of any genocide, but equally indicative of persecution.

5.3.4.5 *Positive and negative group definition*

The *Krnojelac* appeals judgment did not define all of the separate discriminatory grounds, but did observe that crimes of persecution were committed 'against the non-Serb detainees because of their political or religious affiliation',[147] without answering whether the non-Serb detainees were discriminated against due to their political or religious affiliation. In another case, that of *Kvočka*, the Appeals Chamber concluded that since the attack was directed only against the non-Serbian population, it was indicative of the perpetrator's discriminatory intent.[148] Both judgments negatively categorise the victims, as 'non-Serbs', a categorisation

143 *Prosecutor v Krajišnik*, Case No IT-00–39-T (27 September 2006), paras. 793, 802; *Prosecutor v Brđanin*, Case No IT-99–36-T (1 September 2004), para. 325; *Prosecutor v Mladić*, Case No IT-09–92-T (22 November 2017), paras. 2707, 2776, 3270, 3275, 3281, 3305, 3414, 3552.

144 *Prosecutor v Karadžić*, Case No IT-95–5–18-T (25 March 2016), para. 2568. Note that in *Prosecutor v Mladić*, Case No IT-09–92-T (22 November 2017), the Trial Chamber does not discuss the perpetrator's perception.

145 *Prosecutor v Kupreškić* et al., Case No IT-95–16-T (14 January 2000), para. 48.

146 Ibid; *Prosecutor v Brđanin*, Case No IT-99–36-T (1 September 2004), para. 323.

147 *Prosecutor v Krnojelac*, Case No IT- 97–25-A (17 September 2003), para. 187. Similarly: *Prosecutor v Nahimana*, Case No ICTR-99–52-T (3 December 2003), para. 1071; *Prosecutor v Kvočka* et al., Case No IT-98–30/1-T (2 November 2001), paras. 196–198; *Prosecutor v Blaškić*, Case No IT-95–14-T (3 March 2000), para. 236; *Prosecutor v Tadić*, Case No IT-94–1-T (7 May 1997), paras. 652 and 714.

148 *Prosecutor v Kvočka* et al., Case No IT-98–30/1-A (28 February 2005), paras. 340–347. Also the ECCC Appeals Chamber confirmed that negative approaches to the victim group were admissible for the crime of persecution (*Prosecutor v Kaing Guek Eav alias Duch*, Case No 001/18-07-2007/ECCC/SC, Appeal Judgement (3 February 2012), para. 272).

that was deemed incorrect for the crime of genocide.[149] The ICTR trial judgment in the *Media* case expressly confirmed the admissibility of the negative categorisation of the victim group for the crime of persecution.[150]

So far, three pronounced differences between the crimes of genocide and persecution have become apparent: first, the range of discriminatory grounds is more limited for genocide; second, the victim's perception of group membership for persecution is irrelevant; and finally, unlike for genocide, persecution allows a negative group categorisation.

5.3.4.6 *Mistake of fact*

If the perpetrator is objectively mistaken as to the victim's membership of the targeted group, it raises the question of whether discrimination has in fact taken place. A mistake about a fact that leads to the loss of the subjective requirements of responsibility, results in an exclusion of criminal liability.[151] Art. 32(1) Rome Statute clarifies that a mistake of fact excludes criminal responsibility only if it negates the mental element of the crime. The Statutes of the ICTY and ICTR lack a corresponding provision.

The issue of a mistake of fact was explicated in the case of *Kvočka*. The trial judges held that 'the detainees in Omarska camp were selected on the basis of political, ethnic, or religious criteria; their specific attributes differing from those, and being defined in distinction to those, of their Bosnian Serb captors and abusers'.[152] The judgment suggests that distinct attributes enabled the perpetrators to select their victims. If these attributes are distinct from the perpetrators', they must be objectively detectable. As such, they would not be covered by the *mens rea* only but be part of the crime's *actus reus* too. However, the judgment clarifies that even if the victim did not actually belong to the group, but was targeted for his assumed membership of it, the crime would nevertheless constitute persecution 'even if the suspicion proves inaccurate'.[153] The judges further hold that 'discriminatory grounds form the requisite criteria, not membership in a particular group'.[154] This key sentence establishes that the perpetrator's perception outweighs any objective classification of the victims. Furthermore, in holding that the victim did not actually have to belong to one of the victim groups, despite the perpetrator believing so, the Tribunal did not apparently consider the wrong group determination as an *error in persona*.

A parallel can be drawn to the discussions on the crime of genocide and the assault on Hutu individuals who sympathized with the Tutsi.[155] For genocide,

149 See Chapter 3.9.3. *Prosecutor v Mladić*, Case No IT-09–92-T (22 November 2017), para. 3358 also mentions non-Serbs as a category of victims of persecution.
150 *Prosecutor v Nahimana* et al., Case No ICTR-99–52-T (3 December 2003), para. 1071.
151 Werle, Jessberger (n 6) 245.
152 *Prosecutor v Kvočka* et al., Case No IT-98–30/1-T (2 November 2001), para. 195.
153 Ibid.
154 Ibid para. 197.
155 See Chapter 3.9.4 on mistake of fact for the crime of genocide.

the perpetrator's *mens rea* determined whether a victim was granted protection. If a Hutu was attacked because the perpetrator believed him a Tutsi, the law of genocide would apply. However, if a Hutu was attacked for taking a political side, namely in supporting the Tutsi and thereby disavowing Hutu policy, it would not be considered a genocidal attack because there was no genocidal intent to destroy the Hutu group. Moreover, the Genocide Convention does not cover political groups. For persecution, the same is valid: if a person is attacked because he is believed to be a Muslim, but later turns out to be an atheist, he was nevertheless attacked for being a Muslim, even though he – objectively – was not a member of the religious group. The crime would be persecution on religious grounds, not a mistake of fact. While the persecutory act must have discriminatory consequences, these consequences do not necessarily have to affect a member of the targeted group. It 'is not necessary that the victim of the crime of persecution be a member of the group against whom the perpetrator of the crime intended to discriminate', the Trial Chamber in *Brđanin* concluded.[156] This conclusion reflects settled jurisprudence, whereby even if there exists an *error in persona*, the act is still discriminatory in fact. This is exemplified in *Martic* holding that 'it is not necessary that a victim actually *be* a member of the targeted group. Thus, a Serb mistaken for a Muslim may still be the victim of the crime of persecution'.[157] In a similar case, the Appeals Chamber in *Krnojelac* explained that 'the act committed . . . institutes discrimination in fact, *vis-à-vis* the other Serbs who were not subject to such acts, effected with the will to discriminate against a group on grounds of ethnicity'.[158]

In sum it appears as though the victim does not have to be an actual member of one of the victim groups; he could even be mistaken as such, and still fulfil the criteria of the crime of persecution. However, Guénaël Mettraux argues, if the perpetrator acted with an intent to discriminate on racial grounds, but failed to do so because he mistook the racial identity of the victim, his act would not amount to persecution because there would be no discrimination *in fact*. Mettraux believes this situation to constitute a mistake of fact, insofar as the victim did not actually belong to a specific racial group.[159] However, Mettraux seems to ignore the circumstance that factual discrimination has occurred, albeit not against a concrete racial group. Earlier chapters have shown that human beings cannot be separated into distinct racial groups. There exist only racial beliefs that manifest themselves in discriminatory behaviour against individuals whom the perpetrator identifies as racially distinct. For the victims, the consequences of persecution are very real, regardless of the group's actual existence

156 *Prosecutor v Brđanin*, Case No IT-99–36-T (1 September 2004), para. 993.

157 *Prosecutor v Martic*, Case No IT-95–11-T (12 June 2007), para. 118 (emphasis in original). Confirmed in: *Prosecutor v Prlić* et al., Case No IT-04–74-T (29 May 2013), para. 73.

158 *Prosecutor v Krnojelac*, Case No IT- 97–25-A (17 September 2003), para. 185.

159 Mettraux (n 53) 185.

in racial terms. It would therefore be incorrect to treat factual discrimination against a non-existent racial group – because there is no such thing as a racial group – as a mistake of fact.

David Nersessian suggests a slightly different method of defining the victim's group membership for the crime of persecution. Akin to the crime of genocide, he advocates a subjective approach to the group's defining characteristics. Yet, once established, these subjective criteria became objectively dispositive for an analysis, and thus an objective manifestation of the perpetrator's subjective determination.[160] While recognizing that this was contrary to the ICTY Appeals Chamber in *Knorjelac*, Nersessian nevertheless believes that once such objective criteria were established, any erroneous categorisation of a victim would have to be treated as a mistake of fact.[161] Similar to Nersessian's opinion, this study also advocates a perpetrator-based subjective approach. The perpetrator holds the definitional power, and he alone determines the victims of his discriminatory behaviour. However, the protection cannot be expanded to include any group created by the perpetrator's fantasy. Rather, the discriminatory act has to be aimed at members of groups that are protected under the law of persecution. Due to the lack of objective criteria, the perpetrator's perception of the racial group becomes the sole manifestation of the group's contours. From a point of view of evidence, discriminatory acts against a group that is objectively determinable prior to the persecutory acts is easier to prove. Especially (repeated) acts of stigmatisation, discrimination, and inferiorisation could assist in an objective determination of the victims. If evidentiary proof of the perpetrator's intent can be produced, even groups who lack an objectively determinable existence prior to the persecutory acts would be embraced by the protection of the law. As such, the group's existence is not so much an objective manifestation of a subjective belief, but rather an issue of prosecutorial proof. As a consequence, there can be no mistake of fact as long the perpetrator's mental element is given.

5.4 The crime against humanity of persecution in the Rome Statute

5.4.1 Introduction

Since earlier instruments comprised the crime against humanity of persecution, its inclusion in the Rome Statute of the ICC was, despite the lack of an agreed definition, not contentious.[162] Persecution according to Art. 7(1)(h) in conjunction

160 Nersessian (n 14) 158.

161 Ibid.

162 Christopher Hall, Joseph Powderly, Niamh Hayes, 'Persecution', in Otto Triffterer, Kai Ambos (eds), *The Rome Statute of the International Criminal Court: A Commentary* (CH Beck 3rd ed 2016) 220. Disaccord: Boas, Bischoff, Reid (n 27) 108.

with Art. 7(2)(g) Rome Statute is a crime against humanity in which the perpetrator targets individuals based on their membership of a specific community, respectively an identifiable group.[163] The provision protects any identifiable group or collectivity on political, racial, national, ethnic, cultural, religious, gender, or other grounds that are universally recognised as impermissible under international law. This significant expansion of discriminatory grounds should, according to one commentator, be welcomed 'despite its vagueness and the possible difficulty in application'[164] and has been interpreted to exemplify the progressive development of international law, albeit going beyond the boundaries of customary law.[165]

The illustrative list given in the Rome Statute ('or other grounds') makes clear that the enumerated grounds are not exhaustive, yet not open-ended either, because universal recognition is a high threshold.[166] Rather than requiring a universal recognition, some scholars argue that 'universally recognised' should be understood as 'widely recognised' grounds, like those contained in the International Covenant on Civil and Political Rights (ICCPR) and the UDHR.[167] For the ICC, the direct application of these rights is possible due to Art. 21(3) Rome Statute, which holds that the application and interpretation of the law 'must be consistent with internationally recognised human rights, and be without any adverse distinction founded on grounds such as . . . race'.[168] A debate is still ongoing as to whether Art. 21(3) Rome Statute applies to procedural rights only or is applicable to the interpretation of substantive international criminal law too, in our case of the term 'race' for the crime of persecution. The following section will briefly examine these questions, providing an additional nuance for the Rome Statute's relationship to human rights law.

5.4.2 Art. 21(3) Rome Statute: human rights references for procedural rights only?

Art. 21(3) Rome Statute has been described as forming a 'super-hierarchy', seemingly containing an overriding rule of general consistency in requiring adherence to the most fundamental principles of human rights.[169] Yet, there

163 Elements of Crimes. Furthermore: Byron (n 13) 230.

164 Pocar (n 34) 363.

165 William Schabas, 'Atrocity Crimes (Genocide, Crimes against Humanity, War Crimes)', in William Schabas (ed), *The Cambridge Companion to International Criminal Law* (CUP 2016) 205; Groome (n 76) 454.

166 Schabas (n 49) 198; Cryer et al. (n 11) 260; Kittichaisaree (n 13) 119.

167 Hall, Powderly, Hayes (n 162) 226; Schabas (n 49) 199; Nersessian (n 14) 156; *Prosecutor v Kupreškić* et al., Case No IT-95-16-T (14 January 2000), para. 621.

168 Hall, Powderly, Hayes (n 162) 224. Furthermore: Leena Grover, *Interpreting Crimes in the Rome Statute of the International Criminal Court* (CUP 2014) 277.

169 Sanji Mmasenono Monageng, Alexander Heinze, 'The Rome Statute and Universal Human Rights', in Evelyn Ankumah (ed), *The International Criminal Court and Africa: One*

remains dissent as to whether Art. 21(3) serves as a guide in the interpretation of the Rome Statute, as a basis for filling gaps or whether it, under the most extreme interpretation, might set aside a provision of the Rome Statute that contradicts human rights law.[170] Thus, the normative effect of Art. 21(3) remains a contentious issue, in particular the issue of whether human rights law should be considered *lex specialis* for all substantive and procedural norms of the Statute.[171] The ICC is aided by the jurisprudence of other criminal tribunals and human rights jurisprudence, the latter providing a 'persuasive authority which may be of assistance in applying and interpreting' the law.[172] While human rights law is not determinative or binding, since it arises in a very different context, it is a source of inspiration and guidance for ensuring the rights of the accused.[173] The discussion in Chapter 4.5.3 raised the same considerations. Nonetheless, to date, the ICC has often looked to human rights norms and commonly included references to global instruments such as the UDHR in its jurisprudence.[174] Yet, there remains an insurmountable ambiguity: on the one hand, all ICC jurisprudence should cohere with international human right law; on the other, the ICC is clear in its judgment that it was 'not established to be an international court of human rights'.[175] Hence, Art. 21(3) might function as a

---

Decade On (Intersentia 2016) 66; Krit Zeegers, *International Criminal Tribunals and Human Rights Law: Adherence and Contextualization* (Asser Press 2016) 73–74, 360; Rebecca Young, '"Internationally Recognized Human Rights" Before the International Criminal Court', 60 *International and Comparative Law Quarterly* (2011) 189–193, 207.

170 Marina Aksenova, 'Human Rights at the International Criminal Court: Testing the Limits of Judicial Discretion', 86 *Nordic Journal of International Law* (2017) 74–75; Bartłomiej Krzan, 'Human Rights and International Criminal Law', in Bartłomiej Krzan (ed), *Prosecuting International Crimes: A Multidisciplinary Approach* (Brill Nijhoff 2016) 168, 170; Zeegers (n 169) 78; Annika Jones, 'Insights Into an Emerging Relationship: Use of Human Rights Jurisprudence at the International Criminal Court', 16 *Human Rights Law Review* (2016) 711–712, 721.

171 *Prosecutor v Katanga*, Case No ICC-01/04–01/07, Trial Judgment (7 March 2014), para. 50. Furthermore: Zeegers (n 169) 74, 78.

172 *Barayagwiza v Prosecutor*, Case No ICTR-97–19-AR72 (3 November 1999), para. 40. See discussion in Yvonne McDermott, 'The Influence of International Human Rights Law on International Criminal Procedure' in Philipp Kastner (ed), *International Criminal Law in Context* (Routledge 2018) 285.

173 McDermott (n 172) 285, 295; Herman von Hebel, Darryl Robinson, 'Crimes Within the Jurisdiction of the Court', in Roy Lee (ed), *The International Criminal Court – The Making of the Rome Statute: Issue, Negotiations, Results* (Kluwer Law International 1999) 124.

174 See for instance: *Prosecutor v Katanga and Chui*, Case No ICC-01/04–01/07–3003, Decision on an Amicus Curiae application and on the 'Requête tendant à obtenir presentations des témoins DRC-D02-P-0350, DRC-D02-P-0236, DRC-D02-P-0228 aux autorités néerlandaises aux fins d'asiles (Articles 68 and 93(7) of the Statute) (9 June 2011) para 73. Furthermore: McDermott (n 172) 288; Jones (n 170) 701–729.

175 *Prosecutor v Gaddafi and Al-Senussi*, Case No ICC-01/11–01/11-OA6, on the appeal of Mr Abdullah Al-Senussi against the decision of Pre-Trial Chamber I of 11 October 2013 entitled 'Decision on the admissibility of the case against Abdullah Al-Senussi' (24 July 2014) para. 219.

rule of consistency and interpretation. It also emphasizes the overarching importance of human rights and may contribute to the coherence of international law in matters of shared concern, thereby strengthening the effectiveness of international criminal and human rights law.[176] This book, however, argues that Art. 21(3) cannot be used to interpret the concept of race for purposes concerning the law of persecution by directly applying human rights definitions. Rather, Art. 21(3) primarily secures procedural rights and defines the standard of proof for criminal trials before the ICC.[177] A correct reading of Art. 21(3) leads to an application and interpretation of the Rome Statute consistent with the principle of legality as part of internationally recognised human rights law, especially with the aim of maximizing the rights of the accused to a fair trial and with due regard for the protection of victims and witnesses.[178] Also the UN High Commissioner for Human Rights expressed a belief that the terminology 'internationally recognised human rights' refers above all to the right to a fair trial.[179] The drafting process, as well as the practice of the ICC, confirm this understanding.[180]

5.4.3 *Identifiable group or collectivity*

The Elements of Crimes to Art. 7(1)(h) Rome Statute clarify that, for the crime of persecution to have occurred, the perpetrator must have targeted the victims 'by reason of the identity of a group of collectivity or targeted the group or collectivity as such'. This discriminatory requirement is a key element of persecution.[181] The formulation apparently originated due to the need for a

176 Jones (n 170) 728.

177 Accord: Krzan (n 170) 170–174; Zeegers (n 169) 360; Jones (n 170) 715, 719; Grover (n 168) 115, 119. Disaccord: Aksenova (n 170) 75.

178 Aksenova (n 170) 87; Zeegers (n 169) 76; Grover (n 168) 114–115.

179 UN High Commissioner for Human Rights, Position Paper on the Establishment of a Permanent International Criminal Court, UN Doc. UNICC/NONE/98/1 (15 June 1998), paras. 46–53.

180 *Prosecutor v Lubanga*, Case No ICC-01/04–01/06–772, Judgment on the Appeal of Mr Thomas Lubanga Dyilo against the Decision on the Defence Challenge to the Jurisdiction of the Court Pursuant to Art. 19(2)(a) of the Statute of 3 October 2006 (14 December 2006), para. 37; *Prosecutor v Lubanga*, Case No ICC-01/04–01/06–424, Decision on the Prosecutor's Application for Leave to Reply to 'Conclusions de la defense en réponse au mémoire d'appel du Procureur', Appeals Chamber, Separate opinion of Judge Georghios M. Pikis (12 September 2006), para. 3; *Situation in the Democratic Republic of the Congo*, Case No ICC-01/04–168, Judgment on the Prosecutor's Application for Extraordinary Review of Pre-Trial Chamber I's 31 March Decision Denying Leave to Appeal, Appeals Chamber (13 July 2006), paras. 38–39. See also Aksenova (n 170) 75, Zeegers (n 169) 93–96; Jones (n 170) 715; Young (n 169) 198, 200; Leena Grover, 'A Call to Arms: Fundamental Dilemmas Confronting the Interpretation of Crimes in the Rome Statute of the International Criminal Court', 21 *EJIL* (2010) 559.

181 Evelyne Schmid, *Taking Economic, Social and Cultural Rights Seriously in International Criminal Law* (CUP 2015) 137.

compromise at the Rome Diplomatic Conference, where some delegations wished to extend protection to those who sympathised with the group or collectivity, such as members of NGOs or humanitarian aid workers. The suggestion was criticised by others for overly expanding the scope of protection. Finally, the UK's suggestion to include the phrase 'by reason of identity of the group' was accepted.[182]

Art. 7(1)(h) Rome Statute refers to 'any identifiable group or collectivity,' while Art. 7(2)(g) holds that the persecutory conduct must occur 'by reason of the identity of the group or collectivity'. Scholars point to an inconsistency, in that targeting a group by reason of its identity required a higher threshold than just targeting the group as such.[183] However, element 2 of the Elements of Crimes to Art. 7(1)(h) offers both possibilities in the alternative: 'The perpetrator targeted such person or persons by reason of the identity of a group or collectivity or targeted the group or collectivity as such'. The special discriminatory intent requires the group to have been targeted on particular grounds, namely political, racial, national, ethnic, cultural, religious, gender, or other grounds impermissible under international law. The rationale is that the perpetrator chooses a particular victim on particular grounds. If the perpetrator selects a victim independent of these particular characteristics, he lacks the discriminatory intent. The victim is chosen for reasons of the special characteristics the perpetrator ascribes to him.[184] The discriminatory intent appears to have the same result as a subjective approach to defining the victim group, namely that the perpetrator defines the victim group according to his own perception. As Hall and his co-authors clarify, 'identifiable' is either based on objective criteria or on the mind of the accused.[185] The group or collectivity is identifiable by the accused by virtue of objective criteria or, alternatively, as a group or collectivity distinct from the group or collectivity to which the accused belongs himself.[186] As to the racial grounds, this study has shown that race cannot be defined objectively. Since there are no different human races, there exist no objective criteria to define them either. The perpetrator's perception of the victim's racial group membership therefore remains the only option.

Not unlike the crime of genocide, in the crime of persecution, the perpetrator targets individuals for their membership of the group or collectivity, and the discriminatory acts are directed against members of that group.[187] The ICTY clarified that 'the perpetrator of the acts of persecution does not initially target the individual but rather membership in a specific racial, religious or political

182 Kittichaisaree (n 13) 122.
183 Schabas (n 49) 197; Ambos (n 7) 107.
184 Brady, Liss (n 2) 553; Ambos (n 7) 107. Similarly: *Prosecutor v Kupreškić* et al., Case No IT-95-16-T (14 January 2000), para. 636.
185 Hall, Powderly, Hayes (n 162) 221.
186 Ibid. Disaccord: Roberts (n 10) 279.
187 Schabas (n 49) 197; Hall, Powderly, Hayes (n 162) 220.

group'.[188] Nevertheless, the crime of persecution covers conduct against both individuals and groups, whereas groups consist of individual members. The acts committed against the group are necessarily effectuated against its individual members.[189] Furthermore, the Trial Chamber in *Tadić* clarified that 'the persecutory act must be intended to cause, and result in, an infringement of an *individual's* enjoyment of a basic or fundamental right'.[190]

It is not obvious what the difference between a group and a collectivity is or why both terms are used.[191] One dictionary defines a group as 'a number of people or things that are together or in the same place; a number of people who are connected by some shared activity, interest, or quality; a number of things that are related in some way'.[192] It defines a collectivity as 'the quality or state of being collective or a collective whole; especially: the people as a body'.[193] Both terms refer to how individuals are brought together. The only relevant difference appears to be the strength of the connection: 'group' seems to be a looser association, whereas 'collectivity' implies a strong bond of interconnectedness. Helen Brady and Ryan Liss suggest another interpretation: while the terms are interchangeable, when a number of groups are attacked, the sum of these groups can be referred to as a collectivity.[194] Yet, the *chapeau* of all crimes against humanity assigns protection to 'any civilian population' only. The word 'population' intends to exclude attacks against a limited and randomly selected number of individuals.[195] This threshold is also valid for the crime of persecution, in addition to its requirement of a discrimination of an identifiable group or collectivity.

The requirement that a group or collectivity has to be discernible (ICTY and ECCC) or identifiable (ICC) at first sight appears to entail its objective determination. Nevertheless, the fact that a group is identifiable does not automatically imply its objective existence. Rather, the group may be identifiable to the perpetrator or to the general public because of the discriminatory treatment imposed on it by the perpetrator. A historical example of such identifiability would be the persecutory treatment of the Jews prior to and during the Holocaust. Initially, the Jews in Germany were not distinguishable from the rest of the population due to their high cultural and social assimilation.[196] Yet the

188 *Prosecutor v Blaškić*, Case No IT-95–14-T (3 March 2000), para. 235.
189 Hall, Powderly, Hayes (n 162) 220.
190 *Prosecutor v Tadić*, Case No IT-94–1-T (7 May 1997), para. 715 (emphasis added).
191 Accord: Hall, Powderly, Hayes (n 162) 220.
192 <www.merriam-webster.com/dictionary/group>.
193 <www.merriam-webster.com/dictionary/collectivity>.
194 Brady, Liss (n 2) 550.
195 *Prosecutor v Kunarac* et al., Case Nos. IT-96–23 & IT-96–23/1-A, Appeals Judgment (12 June 2002), para. 90.
196 Maureen Hiebert, *Constructing Genocide and Mass Violence: Society, Crisis, Identity* (Routledge 2017) 150; Bradley Campbell, *The Geometry of Genocide* (University of Virginia Press 2015) 20.

Nuremberg Laws determined who was considered Jewish, and the obligation to wear a yellow Star of David made these individuals externally identifiable, irrespective of their factual membership of the Jewish community.[197]

5.4.4 *Racial grounds*

Neither the earlier instruments nor the Rome Statute define racial grounds. Hall and co-authors suggest that persecution on racial grounds 'should be given at least as broad a reading as the widely accepted definition of racial discrimination'[198] in Art. 1 ICERD, namely 'any distinction, exclusion, restriction or preference based on race, colour, descent, or national or ethnic origin'. The authors note that, so far, the ICC Prosecutor has never charged on racial, but only on ethnic grounds, probably because the concept of race has become increasingly outmoded since the adoption of the Genocide Convention.[199] While it is correct that race in a biological sense is outmoded, the authors' reference to the Genocide Convention remains unclear because the Convention does not deal with the crime of persecution. Rather, the notion of race was included under the Rome Statute's crime against humanity of persecution as late as 1998. Moreover, the scholars seem to ignore that crimes are being committed for reasons of race even today, although there are no such things as different human races. This conclusion is, partially, confirmed by Schabas who considers the term 'grounds' to suggest a specific intent or motive for the act of persecution.[200] Unlike their suggestion for the interpretation of racial grounds, Hall and his co-authors choose not to revert to ICERD's definition of 'national grounds', despite the fact that ICERD includes the related notion of 'national origin'. Instead, they suggest defining 'national' as broader than citizenship and to include 'attributes of a group which considers that it is a nation even though the members . . . are located in more than one State'.[201] Although this study agrees with the suggested definition of national ground, the selective reference to ICERD definitions could nurture some doubt over the applicability of a human rights provision *per analogiam* for the interpretation of race for the Rome Statute. Furthermore, while the scholars recommend a broad approach to race, they simultaneously hold that since 'most definitions of race are now discredited and . . . there is no universally accepted definition, this term should be given a broad reading'.[202] In other words, albeit suggesting that the concept of race is discredited and lacks a universal definition, Art. 1 ICERD should nevertheless be applied, which offers precisely such a definition of race within the framework of human rights law. A discrepancy becomes apparent: either there is a way to define race, or race is discredited and should therefore

197 See Chapter 2.5.1 on the Nuremberg Laws.
198 Hall, Powderly, Hayes (n 162) 223.
199 Ibid 224.
200 Schabas (n 49) 197.
201 Hall, Powderly, Hayes (n 162) 224.
202 Ibid.

be avoided. In the spirit of the principle of effectiveness, this study proposes not to ignore or discredit race, but rather to define it contemporaneously for international criminal law as the perpetrator's perception of the victim's racial differentness.[203] As discussed earlier, this study rejects the applicability of Art. 1 ICERD when defining international crimes, the reason being that an interpretation based on the definition of racial discrimination in Art. 1 ICERD expands the notion of race too extensively for the purposes of international criminal law.[204]

5.4.5 *Jurisprudence of the ICC*

Unlike its rather limited jurisprudence on genocide, the ICC has rendered several decisions on the crime of persecution to date. Cases originating from the situations in Darfur, Democratic Republic of Congo (DRC), Libya, Kenya, Uganda, Ivory Coast, and Georgia, will be discussed in a consecutive order, with a narrow angle on the definition of the victim groups of persecution.

As already deliberated in Chapter 3.11.2, the UN Security Council referred the situation in Darfur to the ICC due to its continued threat to international peace and security, taking note of the Darfur Commission's report.[205] In its confirmation of the arrest warrants in the case against Ahmed Muhammad Harun and Ali Muhammad Ali Abd-Al-Rahman, the ICC Pre-Trial Chamber held that there were 'reasonable grounds to believe that these acts [of persecution] were committed as part of a policy designed to attack the civilian population who were perceived as being associated with the rebels'.[206] In doing so, the judges of the Pre-Trial Chamber refer to the perpetrators' perception of their victims, whom allegedly belonged primarily to the Fur population.[207] The warrant of March 2012 for the arrest of Abdel Raheem Muhammad Hussein also construes the attacks perpetrated by the Sudanese armed forces and/or the Janjaweed as having been committed in the context of a systematic and widespread attack on 'the civilian population, belonging largely to the Fur, Masalit and Zaghawa groups, perceived as being associated with the rebels'.[208] According to the warrant, a common plan was formulated at the highest level of the government of Sudan to carry out counter-insurgency campaigns against parts of 'the civilian population perceived by the Government of the Republic of the

203 See Chapter 3.7.2 on the principle of effectiveness.
204 See Chapter 4.5.4.
205 UN Doc. S/RES/1593 (2005), 31 March 2005.
206 *Prosecutor v Harun and Abd-Al-Rahman*, Case No ICC-02/05–01/07, Pre-Trial Chamber I, Decision on the Prosecution Application under Article 58(7) of the Statute (27 April 2007), para. 74.
207 Ibid. It could, however, be argued that the Pre-Trial Chamber refers to 'perception' rather than factual group membership because of the lower standard of proof of 'sufficient evidence to establish substantial grounds to believe that the person committed each of the crimes charged' (Art. 61(7) Rome Statute).
208 *Prosecutor v Hussein*, Case No ICC-02/05–01/12, Warrant of Arrest for Abdel Raheem Muhammad Hussein (1 March 2012), p. 5.

Sudan as being close to the rebel groups'.[209] Pre-Trial Chamber I confirmed that there were reasonable grounds to believe such attacks on civilians perceived as associated with the rebels had occurred.[210] Yet again, the emphasis is on the perceived membership of the victims rather than their factual one.

In the *Mbarushimana* case in the situation in the DRC, the ICC Pre-Trial Chamber in 2011 repeatedly mentions in its discussion, that, while not confirming the charges, the targeted civilians were perceived as affiliated with the government forces based on their political affiliation.[211] Hence, the perpetrator's perception outweighed the actual group membership of the victims. In another case from the DRC, the Pre-Trial Chamber unanimously confirmed charges against Bosco Ntaganda. There was a widespread and systematic attack against the civilian population, the Chamber found, pursuant to an organisational policy to attack civilians perceived to be non-Hema, such as those belonging to Lendu, Bira, and Nande ethnic groups.[212] The Chamber confirmed the charges, including the commission of persecution of the non-Hema civilian population.[213] The perpetrator's perception of the victims of persecutorial conduct is noted as is the negative definition of the victims as non-Hema. In July 2019, the Trial Chamber convicted Ntaganda, among other, of persecution. In its presentation of the background of the case, the judgment notes that tensions between the different groups were based on a perception that the opposing ethnicity was the enemy.[214] It confirmed settled practice that the victim groups can be defined in a positive or a negative manner, as Chapter 5.3.4.5 showed. The groups' definition included 'the objective factors relevant to the discriminatory ground alleged, [and] the subjective perception of belonging of both the perpetrator and the victim'.[215] In doing so, the judgment applies objective factors and the victims' own perception, in addition to the perpetrator's perception, thereby seemingly overturning earlier practice. Indeed, the Chamber presents as a fact that the Lendu were an ethnic group and that certain villages were predominantly Lendu, but does not further discuss the perpetrator's perception.[216] The blurred boundaries between the crime of

209 Ibid.

210 *Prosecutor v Hussein*, Case No ICC-02/05–01/12, Public redacted version of 'Decision on the Prosecutor's application under article 58 relating to Abdel Raheem Muhammad Hussein' (1 March 2012), paras. 18 and 21.

211 *Prosecutor v Mbarushimana*, Case No ICC-01/04–01/10, Decision on the Confirmation of Charges (16 December 2011), paras. 175, 196, 225, 265.

212 *Prosecutor v Ntaganda*, Case No ICC-01/04–02/06–309, Decision Pursuant to Article 61(7)(a) and (b) of the Rome Statute on the Charges of the Prosecutor Against Bosco Ntaganda (9 June 2014).

213 *Prosecutor v Ntaganda*, Case No ICC-01/04–02/06, Document Containing the Charges (10 January 2014), para. 155.

214 *Prosecutor v Ntaganda*, Case No ICC-01/04-02/06, Trial Judgment (8 July 2019), para. 22.

215 ibid paras. 1009–1010.

216 ibid paras. 1012–1014.

genocide and persecution become apparent in the singling out of the victims: the judgment provides numerous examples where the Lendu were killed, while members of other ethnic groups were spared.[217] Furthermore, several instances of dehumanisation are mentioned: the Lendu were perceived not as human beings, but as 'wild animals' and beasts that would be 'exterminated' within three days.[218] Given this evidence, it could be argued that a conviction of genocide would have been more appropriate.

In 2011, acting upon a Security Council referral based on Chapter VII of the UN Charter, the ICC Prosecutor issued arrest warrants for three accused in the situation in the Libyan Arab Jamahiriya.[219] The Pre-Trial Chamber held that there were reasonable grounds to believe that the accused attacked the civilian population 'taking part in demonstrations against Muammar Gaddafi's regime or perceived to be dissidents'[220] and that therefore acts of persecution based on political grounds were committed. In the opinion of the Chamber, the civilians were targeted 'on the basis of their political opposition (whether actual or perceived) to Muammar Gaddafi and his regime'.[221] Again, rather than requiring actual group membership, emphasis was placed on whether the victims were targeted for real or perceived political opposition.

In the case of Kenya, the Pre-Trial Chamber in January 2012 confirmed the charges against William Samoei Ruto and Joshua Arap Sang of, among others, crimes against humanity of persecution committed in the context of post-election violence in Kenya in 2007/2008.[222] Equally, on 23 January 2012, the ICC Pre-Trial Chamber confirmed the charges against Francis Muthaura and Uhuru Kenyatta, the sitting president of Kenya. The Chamber found substantial grounds to believe that victims were targeted based on their identity as perceived supporters of the competing Orange Democratic Movement.[223]

217 ibid paras. 1016–1022.

218 ibid para. 1021.

219 *Prosecutor v Gaddafi, Gaddafi and Al-Senussi*, Case No ICC-01/11, Decision on the Prosecutor's Application Pursuant to Article 58 as to Muammar Mohammed Abu Minyar Gaddafi, Saif Al-Islam Gaddafi and Abdullah Al-Senussi, Pre-Trial Chamber I (27 June 2011), paras. 1 and 4. See also *Prosecutor v Al-Tuhamy Mohamed Khaled*, Case No ICC-01/11–01/13, Warrant of Arrest (18 April 2013), para. 5. The ICC Pre-Trial Chamber I unsealed this warrant of arrest on 27 April 2017.

220 *Prosecutor v Gaddafi, Gaddafi and Al-Senussi*, Case No ICC-01/11, Decision on the Prosecutor's Application Pursuant to Article 58 as to Muammar Mohammed Abu Minyar Gaddafi, Saif Al-Islam Gaddafi and Abdullah Al-Senussi, Pre-Trial Chamber I (27 June 2011), para. 32. See also ibid paras. 23, 24, 32, 35, 65, 77, 79, 81, and 88, all using the same terminology ('perceived to be [political] dissidents').

221 Ibid para. 65.

222 *Prosecutor v Ruto and Sang*, Case No ICC-01/09–01, Decision on the Confirmation of Charges Pursuant to Article 61(7)(a) and (b) of the Rome Statute, ICC-01/09–01/11–373 (23 January 2012), paras. 349, 367.

223 *Prosecutor v Muthaura, Kenyatta, Ali*, Case No ICC-01/09–02/11, Decision on the Confirmation of Charges Pursuant to Article 61(7)(a) and (b) of the Rome Statute (23 January 2012), paras. 428–430.

Despite terminating the procedures because of weak evidence,[224] the Pre-Trial Chamber acknowledged the importance of the perceived membership of the victims.

In the situation of Uganda, the ICC Pre-Trial Chamber confirmed the charges against Dominic Ongwen, considering the objective elements of the crime of persecution as sufficiently established by evidence. Ongwen is accused of persecution on political grounds of civilians perceived as being affiliated with or supportive of the Ugandan government.[225] The confirmation of charges repeatedly refers to how the perpetrator(s) perceived the victims.[226] The trial against Ongwen commenced on 6 December 2016. In early 2019, Ongwen's defence alleged that the Confirmation of Decision suffered from various defects and requested the Trial Chamber to dismiss, among others, the charge of persecution due to deficient pleadings that failed to define the contextual elements and the required *mens rea*. The trial judges did not grant the relief sought in the Defects Series.[227]

The Ivory Coast investigation was the first to be opened by the ICC *proprio motu* in which a country accepted the Court's jurisdiction (Art. 12(3) Rome Statute), without being a State Party to the Rome Statute. The Decision on the Confirmation of Charges against the former president of the Ivory Coast, Laurent Gbagbo, held that there were substantial grounds to believe that at least 316 victims were targeted for reason of their identity as perceived political supporters of the oppositional Ouattara party.[228] The Trial Hearing in January 2016 confirmed that former minister Charles Blé Goudé prompted 'the killing, burning and persecution of perceived Ouattara supporters'.[229] Yet again, the decision emphasises the perpetrator's perception of the discriminated victims, confirming that actual group membership is not required for the provision on persecution to apply. In January 2019, Gbagbo and Blé Goudé were acquitted from all charges.[230]

224 *Prosecutor v Ruto and Sang*, Case No ICC-01/09–01, Public redacted version of Decision on Defence Applications for Judgments of Acquittal, ICC-01/09–01/11–2027-Red-Corr (16 June 2016).

225 *Prosecutor v Ongwen*, Case No ICC-02/04–01/15, Pre-Trial Chamber II, Decision on the Confirmation of Charges Against Dominic Ongwen (23 March 2016), pp. 75, 77, 80–81, 84–85, 88–89.

226 Ibid, para. 66, 73. Confirmation of Charges: para. 25, 39, 52, 65 with corresponding Counts No 10, 23, 36, 49.

227 *Prosecutor v Ongwen*, Case No ICC-02/04–01/15, Decision on Defence Motions Alleging Defects in the Confirmation Decision (7 March 2019).

228 *Prosecutor v Gbagbo and Blé Goudé*, Case No ICC-02/11–01/15, Decision on the Confirmation of Charges Against Laurent Gbagbo (12 June 2014), para. 204.

229 *Prosecutor v Gbagbo and Blé Goudé*, Case No ICC-02/11–01/15, Trial Hearing, ICC-02/11–01/15-T-10-ENG ET WT 29–01–2016 1/61 SZ T (29 January 2016), p. 30, paras. 17–18.

230 *Prosecutor v Gbagbo and Blé Goudé*, Case No ICC-02/11–01/15-T-232-ENG ET WT 15–01–2019 1–7 SZ T, Oral Judgment (15 January 2019).

Lastly, in January 2016, the ICC Pre-Trial Chamber granted the prosecutor's request to open an investigation into the situation of Georgia, in relation to crimes committed in and around South Ossetia in 2008, including crimes against humanity of persecution. In its decision, the Pre-Trial Chamber held that 'the civilian population, in particular ethnic Georgian civilians, was attacked by South Ossetian forces' and 'acts were reportedly committed with a view to forcibly expelling ethnic Georgians from the territory of South Ossetia in furtherance of the overall objective to change the ethnic composition of the territory'.[231] The decision mentions the ethnicity of the victims, without reference to the perpetrator's perception. It thereby resembles the recent *Ntaganda* judgment that in addition to objective factors also discusses the victims' ethnicity. While *Ntaganda* refers to the perpetrators's perception, it does not further rely on it in the identification of the victims. The investigation is currently ongoing.

Until the *Ntaganda* judgment of July 2019, the ICC did seemingly not require an objective determination of the victims for the crime of persecution. Rather, it fully relied on the perpetrator's perception. Being the first ICC judgment to comprehensively deal with the crime of persecution, *Ntaganda* appears to have moved away from relying on perception to setting a more objective course. It remains to be seen if later ICC judgments will follow suit. This study urges the ICC to adhere to the earlier practice of defining the victims of persecution based on the perpetrator's perception. The following section analyses the ECCC's jurisprudence on the crime of persecution.

5.5 Jurisprudence of the ECCC

Art. 5 of the Law on the Establishment of the ECCC defines persecution as a crime against humanity committed on political, racial, and religious grounds.[232] The ECCC has dealt with the crime of persecution in numerous cases. This study chooses the following cases for their discussion of the victim groups: Case 001 (*Duch*) and Case 002/02 (*Nuon Chea and Khieu Samphân*). In the appeal judgment against Duch, the ECCC Supreme Court Chamber confirmed the trial judgment's findings that 'a victim is targeted because of the victim's membership in a group *defined by the perpetrator* on specific grounds, namely on political, racial or religious basis'.[233] More specifically, it held that 'the perpetrator may define the targeted victims based on a subjective assessment as to what group or

231 *Situation in Georgia*, Pre-Trial Chamber I, Decision on the Prosecutor's request for authorization of an investigation, ICC-01/15 (27 January 2016), paras. 20–21.

232 Law on the Establishment of the Extraordinary Chambers, with inclusion of amendments as promulgated on 27 October 2004 (NS/RKM/1004/006), <www.eccc.gov.kh/sites/default/files/legal-documents/KR_Law_as_amended_27_Oct_2004_Eng.pdf>.

233 *Prosecutor v Kaing Guek Eav alias Duch*, Case No 001/18-07-2007/ECCC/SC, Appeal Judgment (3 February 2012), para. 272 (emphasis in original) with reference to *Prosecutor v Kaing Guek Eav alias Duch*, Case No 001/18-07-2007/ECCC/TC, Trial Judgement (26 July 2010), para. 377.

groups pose a political threat or danger'.[234] As with the crime of genocide, the persecuted victim group apparently can be constructed on a notion of threat the perpetrator perceives it to constitute to his own group. At first sight, the Supreme Court Chamber seems to have taken a perpetrator-based approach in fully relying on the perpetrator's subjective assessment. It held that the Trial Chamber did not err in its conclusion that the discrimination in fact embraced 'all real or perceived political opponents'.[235] For its part, the Trial Chamber noted:

> It was the Party Centre which defined the nature and composition of the targeted groups, encapsulating all real or perceived political opponents. . . . While many of these offences were perpetrated against individuals merely perceived to be enemies of the CPK, the Chamber finds that all victims suffered the same grave discriminatory consequences of acts perpetrated in furtherance of this specific discriminatory intent.[236]

Both chambers refer to the perpetrator's group categorisation. Nonetheless, the Supreme Court Chamber also stated that 'discrimination in fact is connected to the requirement that the victim *actually belong* [sic] to a sufficiently *discernible* political, racial or religious group'.[237] The judgment seems to juxtapose discrimination in fact with actual membership of a discernible group. However, unless a victim becomes a member of a discernible group because of factual discrimination, the two requirements should be analytically separated. Indeed, it might be conceivable for a victim to experience discrimination in fact without actually belonging to a discernible group. In November 2018, the Trial Chamber clarified that discrimination in fact occurred where a victim was targeted because of his membership in a group defined by the perpetrator. More specifically, the group had to be sufficiently discernible; however, it was the perpetrator who defined the group.[238] In doing so, the Trial Chamber placed the full emphasis on the perpetrator's definition of the group and thereby removed any analytical confusion between actual membership to a discernible victim group and discrimination in fact. The judges also seemingly quashed the conclusion of the Supreme Court Chamber in *Duch* of 2012 that held that there could be no discrimination in fact where there was a mistake of fact by the perpetrator as

234 *Prosecutor v Kaing Guek Eav alias Duch*, Case No 001/18-07-2007/ECCC/SC, Appeal Judgment (3 February 2012), para. 272.

235 Ibid para. 273.

236 *Prosecutor v Kaing Guek Eav alias Duch*, Case No 001/18-07-2007/ECCC/TC (26 July 2010), para. 390.

237 *Prosecutor v Kaing Guek Eav alias Duch*, Case No 001/18-07-2007/ECCC/SC (3 February 2012), para. 274 (emphasis in original). Confirmed by: *Prosecutor v Nuon Chea and Khieu Samphân*, Case No 002/19-09-2007/ECCC/TC (16 November 2018), para. 714.

238 *Prosecutor v Nuon Chea and Khieu Samphân*, Case No 002/19-09-2007/ECCC/TC (16 November 2018), paras. 714 and 1174.

to whether a victim actually belonged to the defined target group.[239] In confirming that the victim group determination can be based on the perpetrator's perception alone, independent of an actual, objective group membership, the Trial Chamber's interpretation corresponds to the progressive jurisprudence for the crime of persecution.

In the appeals judgment in Case 002 against Nuon Chea and Khieu Samphân, the ECCC Supreme Court Chamber discussed an alleged legal error related to the definition of political persecution. The Trial Chamber found that the crime can be committed against not only political groups, but also against discernible groups who are discriminated against for political motivations or the political agenda of their persecutors.[240] The Supreme Court Chamber relied heavily on the deliberations in the *Duch* appeals judgment, one element of which should be highlighted. In the *Nuon Chea and Khieu Samphân* appeals judgment, the Supreme Court Chamber refers to a passage in the *Duch* appeal judgment in which the judges held that 'while the group that is the object of persecution must be discernible, it is the perpetrator who defines the group',[241] thereby apparently allowing for a perpetrator-based approach for the crime of persecution. However, albeit discussing the perpetrator's intent, in its conclusion, the *Duch* appeals judgment does not allow a definition of the group based on intent alone. Rather, *Duch* reads: 'This Chamber rejects . . . the Trial Chamber's holding to the extent that it allows for persecutory intent alone to suffice for establishing the crime of persecution regardless of whether the victim is actually a member of a discernible targeted group'.[242] This apparent discrepancy was resolved in the November 2018 trial judgment against Nuon Chea and Khieu Samphân. In discussing the *mens rea* of the crime of persecution, the Chamber holds that persecution on political grounds may target groups, which include various categories of persons other than members of a political group or those holding political views, including perceived political opponents.[243] In admitting perception of group membership, the judges clearly allow

239 *Prosecutor v Kaing Guek Eav alias Duch*, Case No 001/18–07–2007/ECCC/SC, Appeal Judgment (3 February 2012), para. 277. See Chapter 5.3.4.6 on mistake of fact.

240 *Prosecutor v Nuon Chea and Khieu Samphân*, Case No 002/19–09–2007-ECCC/SC, Appeal Judgment (23 November 2016), para. 663 with reference to Nuon Chea's Appeal Against the Judgment in Case 002/01, Case No 002/19–09–2007-ECCC-SC (29 December 2014), paras. 355–364 and *Prosecutor v Nuon Chea and Khieu Samphân*, Case No 002/19–09–2007-ECCC/TC (7 August 2014), para. 430.

241 *Prosecutor v Nuon Chea and Khieu Samphân*, Case No 002/19–09–2007-ECCC/SC (23 November 2016), para. 669 with reference to *Prosecutor v Kaing Guek Eav alias Duch*, Case No 001/18–07–2007/ECCC/SC, Appeal Judgment (3 February 2012), paras. 272–273.

242 *Prosecutor v Kaing Guek Eav alias Duch*, Case No 001/18–07–2007/ECCC/SC (3 February 2012), para. 275.

243 *Prosecutor v Nuon Chea and Khieu Samphân*, Case No 002/19–09–2007/ECCC/TC (16 November 2018), para. 718. See also ibid para. 314 that refers to the negative characterisation of the targeted group and its affiliates or sympathisers.

a subjective approach to defining the victim group. The judges open the group category to victims other than members of political parties and include those who were perceived as political enemies.

Importantly, in the earlier Closing Order of September 2010 for Case 002, the ECCC Office of the Co-Investigating Judges discussed racial persecution and held:

> Vietnamese people were persecuted on the basis that the CPK considered the Vietnamese to be racially distinct from Cambodian people, based on biological and particularly matrilineal descent. . . . Vietnamese people were deliberately and systematically identified and targeted due to their perceived race. . . . Vietnamese people were often identified through the use of pre-prepared statistical lists or registration of those people as Vietnamese, and the perpetrators often took steps to ensure that they were Vietnamese before they were killed.[244]

This statement is intriguing for several reasons: first, the prosecutors clearly refer to race as a matter of perception in that the CPK considered the Vietnamese as racially distinct and targeted them on the basis of this perception.[245] They implicitly confirm that racial group membership should not be evaluated using 'objective and scientifically irreproachable criteria', reverting to the apt formulation of the *Jelisić* trial judgment.[246] Second, the CPK used certain biological criteria, foremost the perceived matrilineal inheritance of Vietnamese blood, to create a racial distinction between the Cambodian and the Vietnamese. Third, the process of singling out, the othering, becomes apparent in that the Vietnamese were identified by means of lists. The fact that the perpetrators explicitly ensured that their victims were Vietnamese before they killed them appears to be a strong indication of a genocidal intent rather than merely racial persecution.[247]

In its judgment of November 2018, the Trial Chamber confirmed its satisfaction that the victims were targeted on the discriminatory basis that they were Vietnamese. It moreover held that the Vietnamese living in Cambodia were considered sufficiently discernible as a racial group. In its discussion of the *mens rea*, the Chamber concludes that the Vietnamese individuals were systematically targeted due to their perceived race, hence taking a purely subjective approach to defining their racial group membership. The evidence it refers to are instructions, orders, reports, and contemporaneous publications in the *Revolutionary Flag*. The racial discriminatory animus that the perpetrators held against the Vietnamese is evidenced in their reference as 'half-breed' or 'pure *Yuon*',

244 *Prosecutor v Nuon Chea, Ieng Sary, Khieu Samphan, Ieng Thirith*, Case No 002/19–09–2007-ECCC-OCIJ, Closing Order (Indictment) (15 September 2010).

245 See Chapter 3.12 on the same issue with regard to the crime of genocide.

246 *Prosecutor v Jelisić*, Case No IT-95–10-T (14 December 1999), para. 70.

247 See Chapter 3 on the crime of genocide and Chapter 3.12 on the ECCC jurisprudence on genocide.

meaning Vietnamese.[248] The Vietnamese were, according to the Chamber, identified as and targeted for their hereditary racial otherness. They were referred to in a derogatory and degrading manner, thus seen as of a lesser value.[249]

The ECCC convicted the defendants of the crime of persecution on racial grounds based on their perception of the Vietnamese as a distinct race, as exemplified in an understanding of matrilineal bloodlines. In relying fully on the perpetrators' perception, the trial judges avoided any discussion of objective racial criteria. Evidence before the court demonstrated that the victims were discriminated against, targeted, and persecuted due to their perceived racial differentness. Their otherness was disseminated in official documents and speeches as well as CPK propaganda materials. In its judgment, the ECCC thereby fully endorsed a subjective approach to race for the crime of persecution.

5.6 Interim conclusion

Unlike the crime of genocide, it is 'clear from the start', regarding the crime of persecution, 'that only the perpetrator's identification of the group is decisive'.[250] This chapter has demonstrated that most international judgments adhered to such a perpetrator-based subjective approach. Although the recent *Ntaganda* judgment casts some doubt, objective group-constitutive characteristics that connect victim group members are not necessary.[251] The question of why international criminal courts allow the perpetrator to identify his racial victim group for the crime of persecution, while they only reluctantly – and generally only in connection with certain objective elements – admit such subjective approach for the crime of genocide, remains unanswered. This study suggests that this inconsistency originates in the distinct placement of race in the legal elements of the respective crime. The racial group is part of the *mens rea* and the *actus reus* of the crime of genocide, while it is only linked to the *mens rea* of the crime of persecution. This comparative question has yet to be answered by an international criminal court.

Other than for cases of genocide, the international judiciary has been cautious in defining race for the crime of persecution. Reasons for its reluctance are not

248 *Prosecutor v Nuon Chea and Khieu Samphân*, Case No 002/19-09-2007/ECCC/TC (16 November 2018), paras. 1188–1192, 2607 (discussing national hatred of the Vietnamese in establishing racial distinctiveness), and 3513.

249 Ibid., paras. 2608 and 2996. See also paras. 3428 and 3510 (discussing ethnicity in establishing racial discrimination).

250 See Werle, Jessberger (n 6) 373. Confirmed in: *Prosecutor v Blagojević and Jokić*, Case No IT-02-60-T (17 January 2005), para. 583; *Prosecutor v Naletilić and Martinović*, Case No IT-98-34-T (31 March 2003), para. 636; *Prosecutor v Stakić*, Case No IT-97-24-T (31 July 2003), para. 734; *Prosecutor v Krnojelac*, Case No 97-25-A (17 September 2003), para. 185.

251 See Werle, Jessberger (n 6) 378.

immediately apparent but may be due to the general discomfort when discussing race or the extended possibilities to prosecute persecution on other grounds. The recent judgment of the ECCC with convictions for the crime of persecution on racial grounds could indicate a change. The judgment's endorsement of the perpetrators' subjective understanding of racial otherness made an important contribution to the interpretation of the concept of race for the crime of persecution. The judges carefully avoided any discussion of the accuracy of the racial inheritance or the objective otherness of the Vietnamese victim group. Instead, they fully relied on the perpetrators' perception of race, especially the notion of full- or half-bloodedness and the degrading treatment of victims ostensibly affected by matrilineal heritance.

Generally, it can be concluded that the international tribunals have not hesitated to define victims of persecution subjectively, occasionally relying entirely on the perpetrator's perception. Notably, the analysis of judgments also reveals that mistakes of fact are not accepted if the victims experienced factual discrimination, irrespective of their objective belonging to the targeted group.

There appear to be no substantial differences between racial grounds and racial groups for the crime of persecution. As a starting point, the provision on persecution in the Rome Statute could certainly have been formulated more clearly by referring to racial groups rather than racial grounds. The drafters could therefore have avoided any ambiguity originating from the 'racial grounds' formulation. The clarification by case law has, however, resolved any uncertainty. The jurisprudence treats discrimination on racial grounds as equal to discrimination of a racial group. The tribunals define persecution as discrimination of a group for reasons of its group membership, thereby including racial group membership.

6 Conclusion

The painter Pablo Picasso allegedly once said: 'Everything you can imagine is real'.[1] Is this valid for the concept of race too? Does race become real when we imagine its existence? The laws of genocide, apartheid, and persecution all contain the term 'racial', but being legally categorised as a member of a 'racial group' does not signify that different human races in fact exist. When these laws were drafted, there was little controversy that race was objectively determinable, and that every human being could be classified as a member of a specific racial group. Since then, the social and natural sciences have convincingly refuted this assumption. Humanity cannot be divided into distinct groups that share common racial characteristics, let alone DNA.

Given that research has proved beyond doubt that race has no basis in science, how should international criminal courts and tribunals deal with the term 'race' when it presents itself within a treaty provision? Should they simply ignore it? If not, how should they interpret it? These are the questions that have been at the heart of this book.

In answer to the first question, this study has argued that courts cannot turn a blind eye to race. As a consequence of the principle of effectiveness, according to which each term in a legal provision has significance, the term 'race' may not be disregarded or treated as superfluous. A reason and meaning must be attributed to every component of a legal provision. The concept of race, despite its historical burden, is part and parcel of the legal protection afforded to members of certain victim groups.

However, as the term 'race' must not be disregarded, how should it be interpreted in light of the fact that the concept has no scientific basis? The study has shown that the concept of race in international criminal law has undergone an evolutive interpretation. Accordingly, it is no longer aligned with dubious race science as it was prior to and following WWII but is rather concerned with a purely subjective understanding of racial differences in groups, irrespective of their actual existence. The result of this evolutive interpretation leads to race

1 Although this quote is commonly attributed to the painter Pablo Picasso, no written source exists to confirm this.

being defined as the product of social construction rather than heredity. Recent and prevailing social science scholarship, which this book has repeatedly made use of, maintains that racial identities are the result of continuous interpretation and re-interpretation of how the 'others' differ from 'us'. Once these racial binaries are established, the perpetrator considers that discriminatory treatment of the 'others' is justified.

An evolutive, and thus subjective, interpretation of race will inevitably broaden the protection of the law. This book has argued that such an expansion remains within the ambits of the principle of legality if the perpetrator perceives the victims to be members of a different group, to which he assigns racial characteristics. The principle of legality functions here as an interpretative boundary, 'constitut[ing] a clear and explicit restriction on all interpretative activity',[2] in that the crime cannot be expanded beyond the groups that are already protected by the law. As such, the principle limits the interpretative freedom of judges who are dealing with the concept of race.

Following the introductory chapter that outlined the basis for this study, Chapter 2 of the book showed that the history of race went hand in hand with the history of colonialism, slavery, and eugenics. Based on discoveries in the eighteenth century, scientists developed a theory of racial scientism. They classified the different racial groups according to their phenotypical features and characteristics that were allegedly transmitted by blood. What is not commonly known is that intellectual and public opinion fully embraced these theories, which was significant for their later misuse by the Nazi regime. Much of the race thinking today is influenced by these racial sciences of the past. The research in this book shows that the assumption that international criminal tribunals were to a certain degree also influenced by historical ideas of racial categories appears to be justified given that they reverted to objective, biological definitions of race.

Chapter 3 demonstrated that in adjudicating the crime of genocide, the international criminal tribunals gradually moved away from a purely objective approach to race. However, in contrast to the majority of legal scholarship that appears to concur with the mixed objective-subjective approach that the courts have taken since, this study advocates a purely subjective perpetrator-based approach to the definition of the concept of race. This approach finds support in established social science research that has convincingly demonstrated how the perpetrator identifies, singles out, stigmatises, discriminates, and dehumanises his victims. This book therefore recommends that the international judiciary should more actively consider the legal relevance of othering for the definition of membership within a racial group, without reverting to dangerous objective determinations of distinct racial groups. Above all, this study recommends the discontinuation of the legal practice of the courts determining a targeted group

2 *Prosecutor v Katanga*, Case No ICC-01/04–01/07, Trial Judgment (7 March 2014), para. 51.

by means of – generally unspecified and undefined – objective criteria.[3] The same is valid for the requirement that the group ought to 'be an objective feature of the society in question'.[4] As explored in Chapter 3, and expanded further in Chapters 4 and 5, the perpetrator stigmatises the victim group that he believes to exhibit innate and therefore unchangeable phenotypical traits. These traits signify, in the eyes of the perpetrator, the belonging of the victim to a group distinct from the perpetrator's own group. Whether these groups, in fact, exist and are 'an objective feature of the society in question', is irrelevant, as long as the perpetrator perceives and treats the 'other' group and its members as distinct, inferior, and a threat to his own group.

The book then considered two types of crimes against humanity where the interpretation of race is important: apartheid and persecution. To the surprise of many legal commentators, the crime of apartheid was included in the Rome Statute.[5] The research in Chapter 4 showed that this development was heavily criticised to the point of ridiculing the inclusion of what was considered an archaic legal construct. Undoubtedly, the insertion of apartheid into the list of crimes against humanity was controversial. Yet, unlike a number of legal scholars, this book predicts that the provisions on the crime of apartheid could experience a fate similar to the crime of genocide. It argues that, by evolutively interpreting race, the international criminal tribunals are provided with a tool to hold perpetrators of systematic oppression and domination of ostensible racial groups accountable. Contrary to common (legal and colloquial) understanding, this study has shown that the crime of apartheid remains legally enforceable and is not intrinsically linked to the apartheid regime of South Africa. Recent ratifications of the Apartheid Convention confirm this view. In particular, a judicial examination of the situation in Palestine appears to be within reach, bringing closer the possibility of the first ever judgment on the crime of apartheid.

Finally, Chapter 5 on the crime of persecution revealed that, although the courts consistently relied on the perpetrator's identification of the victim group and uniformly recognised the perpetrator's role in its stigmatisation and discrimination, they circumvented the issue of race. Arguably, the multitude of discriminatory grounds listed in the law of persecution encourages courts to rely on other, safer grounds than race. The study was unable to conclusively answer the question of why courts allow a perpetrator-based approach for the

3 For instance in *Prosecutor v Gacumbitsi*, Case No ICTR-2001–64-T (17 June 2004), para. 254; *Prosecutor v Kajelijeli*, Case No ICTR-98–44A-T (1. December 2003), para. 811; *Prosecutor v Muvunyi*, Case No ICTR-00–55A-T (12 September 2006), para 484.

4 Prosecutor v Bagilishema, Case No ICTR-95–1A-T (7 June 2001), para. 65.

5 The most recent draft of the ILC Convention on the Prevention and Punishment of Crimes against Humanity of May 2019 adopted verbatim the wording of the Rome Statute, there including the crime of apartheid. See ILC, Crimes against humanity: Texts and titles of the draft preamble, the draft articles and the draft annex provisionally adopted by the Drafting Committee on second reading, UN Doc. A/CN.4/l.935 (15 May 2019).

crime of persecution, when they (reluctantly) admit it for the closely related crime of genocide.[6] The chapter concluded that the distinct placement of race in the *mens rea* of the crime of persecution leads to the courts taking a distinct approach.

When examining the jurisprudence of the international criminal tribunals on crimes concerning race, several important themes have arisen throughout the book. One recurring topic has been the inconclusive protection that the international criminal tribunals offer to victims of crimes of identity, such as genocide or persecution. In their judgments, the courts commonly avoid discussing race, although it is a legal element of several treaty provisions.[7] One of the key recommendations of the study is to urge judges to step out of the shadow of racial science and fully embrace a contemporary approach to race that builds on the perception of racial otherness.

Moreover, the review of the jurisprudence demonstrated that the international criminal tribunals at times do not distinguish between the notions of race and ethnicity, but treat them as one.[8] The most recent conviction by the ECCC, for example, consistently refers to the Vietnamese *ethnicity*, even where it discusses matrilineal heredity of Vietnamese group membership and then establishes that genocide and persecution against the Vietnamese *racial* group had been committed.[9] While an approach which blends ethnicity and race might be justifiable for areas other than international criminal law, this book recommends that a clear and verifiable judicial examination of each victim group, including the racial group, be undertaken in order to comply fully with the principle of legality. Critical voices might claim that this is legal hair splitting, as long as the victims of these atrocities, notwithstanding their exact classification, are awarded protection. This study, however, argues that for reasons of legal certainty, the group categorisation has to be unambiguous.[10] The courts should in particular be mindful that by avoiding discussions of race, they limit legal protection to fewer victim groups. Consequently, international criminal tribunals should make greater use of the notion of race,

6 Chapter 5.3.2.1 explores the relationship between the two crimes.

7 The concept of race is an element of Arts. 6 on genocide, 7(1)(h) on persecution, 7(1)(j) in conjunction with 7(2)(h) on apartheid of the Rome Statute, Art. 2 Genocide Convention, Art. 2 Apartheid Convention as well as of the corresponding provision in the statutes of the *ad hoc* and internationalized criminal tribunals.

8 For example in Prosecutor v Brđanin, Case No IT-99–36-T (1 September 2004), para. 992, footnote 2484 or *Prosecutor v Đorđević*, Case No IT-05–87/1-T (23 February 2011), para. 2230.

9 Prosecutor v Nuon Chea and Khieu Samphân, Case No 002/19–09–2007/ECCC/TC (16 November 2018) paras. 3418–3428 and 3510. See discussion in Chapter 3.12.

10 The study is therefore also critical to the ICTY's ensemble approach in *Krstić* that built on the scholarship of William Schabas. According to this approach, the four protected groups of genocide are seen as a single phenomenon and are in a dynamic relationship, where each group contributes to the construction of the other. See discussion in Chapter 3.5.2.2.

thereby giving more protection to more victims of genocide, persecution, and apartheid.

The review of legal scholarship in the book showed that, with a few exceptions, international criminal lawyers are either silent or contentious on the matter of race. By way of example, Daniel Ntanda Nsereko writes that a racial group is a grouping into which the entire human species is divided, the members of which are easily identifiable and constitute distinct, clearly determinable communities.[11] Matthew Lippman, for his part, states that '[t]he concept of racial groups is self-evident'.[12] This book has shown that race is neither self-evident nor that members of so-called racial groups are easily identifiable or clearly determinable. In providing a detailed analysis of the adjective 'racial' for the crimes of genocide, persecution, and apartheid, this study makes a contribution to legal scholarship that does not blatantly dismiss race as a historical and outdated concept.

The key recommendation of this book is that courts apply a purely subjective approach when interpreting race. In practical terms, how can the racial group membership be proven, given it might exist in the imagination of the perpetrator only? For the purposes of a criminal trial, the approach advocated within this book requires proof not of objective variations among the involved groups' phenotypes, but rather as to the perpetrator's understanding of such. The judiciary's task to find such evidence is challenging and complex, but not impossible. In the recent ECCC case against Nuon Chea and Khieu Samphân, such evidence was, for example, readily available.[13] Notwithstanding the fact that no conclusive finding was made that a genocide against a racial group had occurred, the judgment repeatedly discusses the perpetrators' belief of the heredity Vietnamese group membership, passed down through the mothers' blood. Although neither biologically nor genetically correct, these ideas involved an understanding of innate and unfalsifiable markers and would, as such, have been sufficient for a subjective construction of the racial group. This book has shown that speeches, publications, orders, and the like can reflect a racialized understanding, evidence that the ECCC – and other tribunals in similar cases – should have taken into account to a higher degree.

Comparable indications were equally available for other cases where ostensible racial groups were targeted, including the Holocaust, the Rwandan genocide, and the conflict in the former Yugoslavia, all of which have been recurring topics in this book. It has been shown how perpetrators' communications in the form

11 Daniel Ntanda Nsereko, 'Genocide: A Crime against Mankind', in Gabrielle Kirk McDonald, Olivia Swaak-Goldman (eds), *Substantive and Procedural Aspects of International Criminal Law: The Experience of International and National Courts* (Kluwer Law International 2000) 130.

12 Matthew Lippman, 'Genocide', in M. Cherif Bassiouni (ed), International Criminal Law, Volume I: Sources, Subjects, and Contents (Martinus Nijhoff 3rd ed 2008) 412.

13 See Chapters 3.12. and 5.5 for a discussion of the case and the evidence of racial group membership.

of written or spoken statements, publications, radio broadcasts, or diary entries can be used as evidence of a racialized perception of the victims. For example, a year before the genocide in Rwanda a local magazine cited a discovery made by 'specialists in human genetics' that Tutsi could only reproduce with each other and therefore remained a small minority. Or, before the war erupted in Bosnia, a Serbian nationalist leader claimed that intermarriages between Serbs and Muslims led to the genetic 'degeneration of Serb nationality'.[14] In addition to these historical cases of animosities, more contemporary cases like the Rohingya in Myanmar or the Yazidi in Northern Iraq indicate racialized patterns of attacks. This study argues that these recent atrocities might be, legally speaking, crimes against racial groups.

Since the concept of race in international criminal law is an evidentiary matter, it is up to the prosecutor to reconstruct the dynamics and patterns of the atrocities, also beyond the *actus reus*. No crime of identity against a racial group is committed without a manifestation of othering, as this study consistently has argued. The othering can acquire evidentiary value and assist in proving the perpetrator's intent to target the victims for ostensible racial differences. In sum, the racial otherness will vary from case to case, and potentially also from perpetrator to perpetrator because it is constructed upon an individual or collective understanding of biologically innate variations in groups. Criteria range from blood ties to skin tone and nose width, to name a few, none of which bear any scientific, legal, or moral legitimacy. Nonetheless, in the mind of the perpetrator, these criteria create racial differences and this is what has to be proven by the prosecutor in order for there to be a successful conviction for the crime of genocide, persecution, or apartheid against a racial group.

Recent years have seen a disquieting rise in race thinking and race science.[15] According to a newly published survey, one in four of us believe that 'some human races are more intelligent than others'.[16] We live in a time where race science and the interconnected discourse of the threatening, inferior 'others' has powerfully re-emerged into public discourse. Politicians unabashedly use

14 Ana Swanson, 'The disturbing thing that happens when you tell people they have different DNA', www.washingtonpost.com/news/wonk/wp/2016/05/13/the-disturbing-thing-that-happens-when-you-tell-people-they-have-different-dna/?utm_term=.a53dafe008fb (13 May 2016). See discussions in Chapters 2.4 (Holocaust), 3.6.5 (Rwanda) and 5.3.1 and 5.3.4.4 (former Yugoslavia).

15 Angela Saini, 'Why Race Science is on the Rise Again', www.theguardian.com/books/2019/may/18/race-science-on-the-rise-angela-saini (18 May 2019); Gavin Evans, 'The Unwelcome Revival of "Race Science"', www.theguardian.com/news/2018/mar/02/the-unwelcome-revival-of-race-science (2 March 2018). Christian Sundquist, 'Science Fiction and Racial Fables: Navigating the Final Frontier of Genetic Interpretation', 25 *Harvard Blackletter Law Journal* (2009) 57–93 already pointed to these developments.

16 This is based on a survey of the Norwegian population. Guri Tyldum, *Holdninger til Diskriminering, Likestilling og Hatprat i Norge*, Fafo report (2019) 75. Interrelated: Jon Røyne Kyllingstad, 'The Absence of Race in Norway?', 95 *Journal of Anthropological Sciences* (2017) 1–9.

race thinking as a tool to defend and justify nationalist identity politics. Populist thoughts are disseminated with arguments originating in race sciences.[17] Race still heavily influences the perceptions of individuals although science has long discredited it. Even though race is, scientifically speaking, a fiction, it is an everyday reality, and the need to take a stand against crimes which have a racial element is more important than ever. International courts can play a unique role in this respect. For this reason, this book encourages international prosecutors and the international judiciary to make increased use of the racial group category in its adjudication of crimes of genocide, persecution, and apartheid and hold accountable perpetrators who commit crimes against ostensible racial groups. Because, for the perpetrator, race is real and the consequences of his racial thinking are equally real for the victims.

17 Francis Fukuyama, 'The Heart of Populism Is Identity, Not Race', https://spectator.us/populism-identity/ (17 October 2018); Francis Fukuyama, Robert Muggah, 'Populism Is Poisoning the Global Liberal Order', www.theglobeandmail.com/opinion/populism-is-poisoning-the-global-liberal-order/article37777370/ (29 January 2018).

Table of legislation

International legislation and other legal instruments

Charter of the International Military Tribunal, 8 August 1945.

Charter of the International Military Tribunal for the Far East, Special Proclamation by the Supreme Commander for the Allied Powers at Tokyo, 19 January 1946.

Charter of the United Nations, 1 UNTS XVI, 26 June 1945.

Control Council Law No 10, Punishment of Persons Guilty of War Crimes, Crimes Against Peace and Against Humanity, 20 December 1945, 3 Official Gazette Control Council for Germany, 50–55 (1946).

Convention on the Non-Applicability of Statutory Limitations to War Crimes and Crimes against Humanity, UN Doc. Res. 2391 (XXIII), 78 UNTS 277, 26 November 1968.

Convention on the Prevention and Punishment of the Crime of Genocide, UN Doc. A/RES/3/260 (9 December 1948), 78 UNTS 277.

Elements of Crimes of the Rome Statute, reproduced from the Official Records of the Assembly of States Parties to the Rome Statute of the International Criminal Court, First session, 3–10 September 2002.

Geneva Conventions I-IV of 12 August 1949, consisting of:

- Convention (I) for the Amelioration of the Condition of the Wounded and Sick in Armed Forces in the Field.
- Convention (II) for the Amelioration of the Condition of Wounded, Sick and Shipwrecked Members of Armed Forces at Sea.
- Convention (III) relative to the Treatment of Prisoners of War.
- Convention (IV) relative to the Protection of Civilian Persons in Time of War.

Hague Convention (IV), Convention Respecting the Laws and Customs of War on Land, 36 Stat. 2277; UNTS 539, 18 October 1907.

International Covenant on Civil and Political Rights, UN Doc. Res. 2200 (XXI), 16 December 1966, ***999 UNTS 171*** .

International Convention on the Elimination of All Forms of Racial Discrimination, UN GA Res. 2106 (XX), 21 December 1965, 660 UNTS 9464.

International Convention on the Suppression and Punishment of the Crime of Apartheid, UN Doc. A/9030, UN GA Res. 3068 (XXVIII), 30 November 1973, 1015 UNTS 243.

Lieber Code, based on Francis Lieber, Instructions for the Government of Armies of the United States (1863).

London Agreement by the Governments of the UK, USA, the Provisional Government of the French Republic and the USSR for the Prosecution and Punishment of the Major War Criminals of the European Axis, and Charter of the International Military Tribunal, 8 August 1945.

Protocol Additional I to the Geneva Conventions of 12 August 1949, and relating to the Protection of Victims of International Armed Conflicts (Protocol I), 8 June 1977.

Rome Statute of the International Criminal Court, UN Doc. A/CONF.183/9, 17 July 1998, 2187 UNTS 90.

Statute of the International Court of Justice, 33 UNTS 993, 26 June 1945.

Universal Declaration of Human Rights, UN GA Res. 217 A (III), 10 December 1948.

UN Transitional Administration in East Timor (UNTAET), Regulation No 2000/15 on the Establishment of Panels with Exclusive Jurisdiction over Serious Criminal Offences, UN Doc. UNTAET/REG/2000/15, 6 June 2000.

Vienna Convention on the Law of Treaties (VCLT), 1155 UNTS, 23 May 1969, UN Doc. A/CONF.39/11/Add.2 and A/CONF.39/27.

Regional legislation and other legal instruments

European Convention on the Non-Applicability of Statutory Limitations to Crimes against Humanity and War Crimes, Council of Europe, ETS No 82, 25 January 1974.

Law on the Establishment of the Extraordinary Chambers, with inclusion of amendments as promulgated on 27 October 2004 (NS/RKM/1004/006).

Table of cases

International Military Tribunal (IMT)

Internationaler Militärgerichtshof Nürnberg, *Der Prozess gegen die Hauptkriegsverbrecher vor dem Internationalen Militärgerichtshof, Nürnberg 14. November 1945–1. Oktober 1946*, veröffentlicht in Nürnberg 1947 gemäss den Weisungen des Internationalen Militärgerichtshofes vom Sekretariat des Gerichtshofes unter der Autorität des Obersten Kontrollrats für Deutschland, Band I: Amtlicher Wortlaut in Deutscher Sprache. International Military Tribunal in Nuremberg, *Trial Against the Main War Criminals Before the International Military Tribunal*, Nuremberg 14 November 1945–1 October 1946, published in Nuremberg 1947 according to the Instructions of the International Military Tribunal by the Secretariat of the Tribunal, under the Authority of the Control Council for Germany, Volume I: Official text in German.

Hermann Göring et al., Trial of the Major War Criminals Before the International Military Tribunal, Vol. XIX, Proceedings (14 November 1945–1 October 1946).

Trial of the Major War Criminals before the International Military Tribunal, Nuremberg 14 November 1945–1 October 1946, Volume I, Nuremberg (1947).

International Criminal Tribunal for the Former Yugoslavia (ICTY)

The Case Against Hartmann, Case No IT-02–54-R77.5-A, Appeals Judgment (19 July 2011).

The Prosecutor v Aleksovski, Case No IT-95–14/1-A, Appeals Judgment (24 March 2000).

The Prosecutor v Banović, Case No IT-02–65/1-S, Sentencing Judgment (28 October 2003).

The Prosecutor v Blagojević and Jokić, Case No IT-02–60-T, Trial Judgment (17 January 2005).

The Prosecutor v Blaškić, Case No IT-95–14-A, Appeals Judgment (29 July 2004).

The Prosecutor v Blaškić, Case No IT-95–14-AR108bis, Judgment on the Request of the Republic of Croatia for Review of the Decision on Trial Chamber II of 18 July 1997 (29 October 1997).

The Prosecutor v Blaškić, Case No IT-95–14-T, Trial Judgment (3 March 2000).

The Prosecutor v Brđanin, Case No IT-99–36-T, Trial Judgment (1 September 2004).

The Prosecutor v Delalić et al., Case No IT-96–21-A, Appeals Judgment (20 February 2001).

The Prosecutor v Đorđević, Case No IT-05–87/1-T, Trial Judgment (23 February 2011).

The Prosecutor v Erdemović, Case No IT-96–22-T, Trial and Sentencing Judgment (29 November 1996).

The Prosecutor v Furundžija, Case No IT-95–17/1-T, Trial Judgment (10 December 1998).

The Prosecutor v Galić, Case No IT-98–29-T, Trial Judgment (5 December 2003).

The Prosecutor v Hadžihasanović et al., Case No IT-01–47-PT, Decision on Joint Challenge to Jurisdiction (12 November 2002).

The Prosecutor v Jelisić, Case No IT-95–10-A, Appeals Judgment (5 July 2001).

The Prosecutor v Jelisić, Case No IT-95–10-A, Appeals Judgment, Separate Opinion of Judge Nieto-Navia (5 July 2001).

The Prosecutor v Jelisić, Case No IT-95–10-T, Trial Judgment (14 December 1999).

The Prosecutor v Jelisić and Češić, Prosecutor's Pre-Trial Brief, Case No IT-95–10-PT (19 November 1998).

The Prosecutor v Karadžić, Case No IT-95–5/18-AR98bis.l, Appeals Judgment (11 July 2013).

The Prosecutor v Karadžić, Case No 95–5/18-T, Rule 98bis Judgment (28 June 2012).

The Prosecutor v Karadžić, Case No IT-95–5–18-T, Trial Judgment (25 March 2016).

The Prosecutor v Karadžić and Mladić, Case No IT-95–5-R61 and IT-95–18-R61, Review of the Indictments Pursuant to Rule 61 of the Rules of Procedure and Evidence (11 July 1996).

The Prosecutor v Kordić and Čerkez, Case No IT-95–14/2-A, Appeals Judgment (17 December 2004).

The Prosecutor v Kordić and Čerkez, Case No IT-95–14/2-T, Trial Judgment (26 February 2001).

The Prosecutor v Krajišnik, Case No IT-00–39-T, Trial Judgment (27 September 2006).

The Prosecutor v Krnojelac, Case No IT-97–25-A, Appeals Judgment (17 September 2003).

The Prosecutor v Krnojelac, Case No IT-97–25-A, Appeals Judgment (17 September 2003), Separate Opinion of Judge Shahabuddeen.

The Prosecutor v Krnojelac, Case No IT-97–25-T, Trial Judgment (15 March 2002).

The Prosecutor v Krstić, Case No IT-98–33-A, Appeals Judgment (19 April 2004).

The Prosecutor v Krstić, Case No IT-98–33-T, Trial Judgment (2 August 2001).

The Prosecutor v Kunarac et al., Case Nos. IT-96–23 and IT-96–23/1-A, Appeals Judgment (12 June 2002).

The Prosecutor v Kunarac et al., Case Nos. IT-96–23-T and IT-96–23/1-T, Trial Judgment (22 February 2001).

The Prosecutor v Kupreškić et al., Case No IT-95–16-A, Appeals Judgment (23 October 2001).

The Prosecutor v Kupreškić et al., Case No IT-95–16-T, Trial Judgment (14 January 2000).

The Prosecutor v Kvočka et al., Case No IT-98–30/1-A, Appeals Judgment (28 February 2005).

The Prosecutor v Kvočka et al., Case No IT-98–30/1-T, Trial Judgment (2 November 2001).

The Prosecutor v Lukić and Lukić, Case No IT-98–32/1-A, Appeals Judgment (4 December 2012).

The Prosecutor v Lukić and Lukić, Case No 98–32/1-T, Trial Judgment (20 July 2009).

The Prosecutor v Martic, Case No IT-95–11-T, Trial Judgment (12 June 2007).

The Prosecutor v Milosević, Case No IT-02–54-T, Decision on Motion for Judgment of Acquittal (16 June 2004).

The Prosecutor v Milutinović et al., Case No IT-05–87-T, Trial Judgment (26 February 2009).

The Prosecutor v Mladić, Case No IT-09–92-T, Trial Judgment (22 November 2017).

The Prosecutor v Mrkšić and Šljivančanin, Case No IT-95–13/1-A, Appeals Judgment (5 May 2009).

The Prosecutor v Naletilić and Martinović, Case No IT-98–34, Trial Judgment (31 March 2003).

The Prosecutor v Nikolić, Case No IT-94–2-R61, Review of Indictment Pursuant to Rule 61 of the Rules of Procedure and Evidence (20 October 1995).

The Prosecutor v Popović et al., Case No IT-05–88-T, Trial Judgment (10 June 2010).

The Prosecutor v Prlić et al., Case No IT-04–74-T, Trial Judgment (29 May 2013).

The Prosecutor v Sikirica, Case No IT-95–8-T, Judgment on Defence Motions to Acquit (3 September 2001).

The Prosecutor v Simić, Case No IT-95–9-T, Trial Judgment (17 October 2003).

The Prosecutor v Stakić, Case No IT-97–24-A, Appeals Judgment (22 March 2006).

The Prosecutor v Stakić, Case No IT-97–24-A, Appeals Judgment, Partly Dissenting Opinion of Judge Shahabuddeen (22 March 2006),

The Prosecutor v Stakić, Case No IT-97–24-T, Trial Judgment (31 July 2003).

The Prosecutor v Stanišić and Zupljanin, Case No IT-08–91-T, Trial Judgment (27 March 2013).

The Prosecutor v Tadić, Case No IT-94–1-A, Appeals Judgment (15 July 1999).

The Prosecutor v Tadić, Case No IT-94–1-AR72, Decision on the Defence Motion for Interlocutory Appeal on Jurisdiction (2 October 1995).

The Prosecutor v Tadić, Case No IT-94–1-T, Trial Judgment (7 May 1997).

The Prosecutor v Todorovic, Case No IT-95–9/1-S, Sentencing Judgment (31 July 2001).

The Prosecutor v Tolimir, Case No IT-05–88/2-A, Appeals Judgment (8 April 2015).

The Prosecutor v Tolimir, Case No IT-05–88/2-T, Trial Judgment (12 December 2012).

The Prosecutor v Trbić, Case No IT-05–88/1-PT, Decision on Referral of Case Under Rule 11bis with Confidential Annex (27 April 2007).

The Prosecutor v Vasiljević, Case No IT-98–32-T, Trial Judgment (29 November 2002).

International Criminal Tribunal for Rwanda (ICTR)

Barayagwiza v The Prosecutor, Case No ICTR-97–19-AR72, Decision, 3 November 1999.

The Prosecutor v Akayesu, Case No ICTR-96–4-A, Appeals Judgment (1 June 2001)

The Prosecutor v Akayesu, Case No ICTR-96–4-T, Trial Judgment (2 September 1998).

The Prosecutor v Akayesu, Case No ICTR-96–4-T, Trial Judgment, Statement by President Kama (2 September 1998).

The Prosecutor v Bagilishema, Case No ICTR-95–1A-T, Trial Judgment (7 June 2001).

The Prosecutor v Bagosora et al., Case No ICTR-98–41, Amended Indictment (12 August 1999).

The Prosecutor v Bagosora et al., Case No ICTR-98–41-T, Trial Judgment (18 December 2008).

The Prosecutor v Barayagwiza, Case No ICTR-97–19-AR72, Decision, Separate Opinion of Judge Shahabuddeen (3 November 1999).

The Prosecutor v Bikindi, Case No ICTR-01–72-A, Appeals Judgment (18 March 2010).

The Prosecutor v Bikindi, Case No ICTR-01–72-T, Trial Judgment (2 December 2008).

The Prosecutor v Gacumbitsi, Case No ICTR-2001–64-T, Trial Judgment (17 June 2004).

The Prosecutor v Kajelijeli, Case No ICTR-98–44A-A, Appeals Judgment (23 May 2005).

The Prosecutor v Kajelijeli, Case No ICTR-98–44A-T, Trial Judgment (1 December 2003).

The Prosecutor v Kambanda, Case No ICTR-97–23-A, Appeals Judgment (19 October 2000).

The Prosecutor v Kambanda, Case No ICTR-97–23-S, Trial Judgment and Sentence (4 September 1998).

The Prosecutor v Kamuhanda, Case No ICTR-95–54A-T, Trial Judgment (22 January 2004).

The Prosecutor v Karemera et al., Case No ICTR-98–44-AR73(C), Decision on Prosecutor's Interlocutory Appeal of Decision on Judicial Notice (16 June 2006).

The Prosecutor v Kayishema, Case No ICTR-95–1-A, Appeals Judgment (1 June 2001).

The Prosecutor v Kayishema and Ruzindana, Case No ICTR-95–1-T, Sentence (21 May 1999).

The Prosecutor v Kayishema and Ruzindana, Case No ICTR-95–1-T, Trial Judgment (21 May 1999).

The Prosecutor v Mpambara, Case No ICTR-01–65-T, Trial Judgment (11 September 2006).

The Prosecutor v Muhimana, Case No ICTR-95–1B-T, Trial Judgment (28 April 2005).

The Prosecutor v Musema, Case No ICTR-96–13-A, Trial Judgment (27 January 2000).

The Prosecutor v Muvunyi, Case No ICTR-00–55A-T, Trial Judgment (12 September 2006), annulled.

The Prosecutor v Muvunyi, Case No ICTR-00–55A-T, Trial Judgment (11 February 2010).

The Prosecutor v Nahimana et al., Case No ICTR-99–52-A, Appeals Judgment (28 November 2007).

The Prosecutor v Nahimana et al., Case No ICTR-99–52-T, Trial Judgment (3 December 2003).

The Prosecutor v Nchamihigo, Case No ICTR-01–63-T, Trial Judgment (12 November 2008).

The Prosecutor v Ndindabahizi, Case No ICTR-2001–71-I, Trial Judgment (15 July 2004).

The Prosecutor v Niyitegeka, Case No ICTR-96–14-A, Appeals Judgment (9 July 2004).

The Prosecutor v Niyitegeka, Case No ICTR-96–14-T, Trial Judgment (16 May 2003).

The Prosecutor v Ntagerura, Bagambiki, Imanishimwe, Case No ICTR-99–46-T, Trial Judgment (25 February 2004).

The Prosecutor v Ntakirutimana and Ntakirutimana, Case Nos. ICTR-96–10-A and ICTR-96–17-A, Appeals Judgment (13 December 2004).

The Prosecutor v Ntakirutimana and Ntakirutimana, Case Nos. ICTR-96–10-T and ICTR-96–17-T, Trial Judgment (21 February 2003).

The Prosecutor v Ntawukulilyayo, Case No ICTR-05–82-T, Trial Judgment (3 August 2010).

The Prosecutor v Nyiramasuhuko et al., Case No ICTR-98–42-A, Appeals Judgment (14 December 2015).

The Prosecutor v Nyiramasuhuko et al., Case No ICTR-98–42-A, Appeals Judgment, Dissenting and Separate Opinions of Judge Agius (14 December 2015).

The Prosecutor v Rukundo, Case No ICTR-2001–70-T, Trial Judgment (27 February 2009).

The Prosecutor v Ruggiu, Case No ICTR-97–32, Amended Indictment (18 December 1998).

The Prosecutor v Ruggiu, Case No ICTR-97–32-I, Trial Judgment and Sentence (1 June 2000).

The Prosecutor v Rutaganda, Case No ICTR-96–3-T, Trial Judgment (6 December 1999).

The Prosecutor v Semanza, Case No ICTR-97–20-A, Appeals Chamber Decision (31 May 2000).

The Prosecutor v Semanza, Case No ICTR-97–20-T, Trial Judgment (15 May 2003).

The Prosecutor v Seromba, Case No ICTR-2001–66-T, Trial Judgment (13 December 2006).

The Prosecutor v Serushago, Case No ICTR-98–03-S, Sentence (5 February 1999).

International The Residual Mechanism for Criminal Tribunals

The Prosecutor v Karadžić, Case No MICT-13–55-A, Appeals Judgment (20 March 2019).

International Criminal Court (ICC)

Referral by the State of Palestine Pursuant to Articles 13(a) and 14 of the Rome Statute (15 May 2018).

Situation in Georgia, Pre-Trial Chamber I, Decision on the Prosecutor's request for authorization of an investigation, ICC-01/15 (27 January 2016).

Situation in the Democratic Republic of the Congo, Case No ICC-01/04–168, Judgment on the Prosecutor's Application for Extraordinary Review of Pre-Trial Chamber I's 31 March 2006 Decision Denying Leave to Appeal (13 July 2006).

Situation in the State of Palestine, Case No ICC-01/18, Decision Assigning theSituation in the State of Palestine to Pre-Trial Chamber I (24 May 2018).

The Prosecutor v Al Bashir, Case No ICC-02/05–01/09, Decision on the Prosecution's Application for a Warrant of Arrest against Omar Hassan Ahmad Al Bashir (4 March 2009).

The Prosecutor v Al Bashir, Case No ICC-02/05–01/09, Decision on the Prosecution's Application for a Warrant of Arrest against Omar Hassan Ahmad Al Bashir, Separate and Partly Dissenting Opinion of Judge Anita Ušacka (4 March 2009).

The Prosecutor v Al Bashir, Case No ICC-02/05–01/09-OA, Judgment on the Appeal of the Prosecutor against the 'Decision on the Prosecution's Application for a Warrant of Arrest against Omar Hassan Ahmad Al Bashir' (3 February 2010).

The Prosecutor v Al Bashir, Case No ICC-02/05–01/09–94, Second Decision on the Prosecution's Application for a Warrant of Arrest against Omar Hassan Ahmad Al Bashir (12 July 2010).

The Prosecutor v Al-Tuhamy Mohamed Khaled, Case No ICC-01/11–01/13, Warrant of Arrest (18 April 2013).

The Prosecutor v Gaddafi and Al-Senussi, Case No ICC-01/11–01/11-OA6, on the appeal of Mr Abdullah Al-Senussi against the decision of Pre-Trial Chamber

I of 11 October 2013 entitled 'Decision on the Admissibility of the Case Against Abdullah Al-Senussi', Appeals Judgment (24 July 2014).

The Prosecutor v Gaddafi, Gaddafi and Al-Senussi, Case No ICC-01/11, Decision on the Prosecutor's Application Pursuant to Article 58 as to Muammar Mohammed Abu Minyar Gaddafi, Saif Al-Islam Gaddafi and Abdullah Al-Senussi, Pre-Trial Chamber I (27 June 2011).

The Prosecutor v Gbagbo and Blé Goudé, Case No ICC-02/11–01/15, Decision on the Confirmation of Charges against Laurent Gbagbo (12 June 2014).

The Prosecutor v Gbagbo and Blé Goudé, Case No ICC-02/11–01/15-T-232-ENG ET WT 15–01–2019 1–7 SZ T, Oral Judgment (15 January 2019).

The Prosecutor v Gbagbo and Blé Goudé, Case No ICC-02/11–01/15, Trial Hearing, ICC-02/11–01/15-T-10-ENG ET WT 29–01–2016 1/61 SZ T (29 January 2016).

The Prosecutor v Hussein, Case No ICC-02/05–01/12, Public redacted version of 'Decision on the Prosecutor's Application Under Article 58 Relating to Abdel Raheem Muhammad Hussein' (1 March 2012).

The Prosecutor v Hussein, Case No ICC-02/05–01/12, Warrant of Arrest for Abdel Raheem Muhammad Hussein (1 March 2012).

The Prosecutor v Harun and Abd-Al-Rahman, Case No ICC-02/05–01/07, Pre-Trial Chamber I, Decision on the Prosecution Application under Article 58(7) of the Statute (27 April 2007).

The Prosecutor v Katanga, Case No ICC-01/04–01/07, Trial Judgment Pursuant to Article 74 of the Statute (7 March 2014).

The Prosecutor v Katanga and Chui, Case No ICC-01/04–01/07–3003, Decision on an Amicus Curiae Application and on the 'Requête tendant à obtenir presentations des témoins DRC-D02-P-0350, DRC-D02-P-0236, DRC-D02-P-0228 aux autorités néerlandaises aux fins d'asiles (Articles 68 and 93(7) of the Statute) (9 June 2011).

The Prosecutor v Lubanga, Case No ICC-01/04–01/06–424, Decision on the Prosecutor's Application for Leave to Reply to "Conclusions de la defense en réponse au mémoire d'appel du Procureur", Appeals Chamber, Separate opinion of Judge Georghios M. Pikis (12 September 2006).

The Prosecutor v Lubanga, Case No ICC-01/04–01/06–772, Judgment on the Appeal of Mr. Thomas Lubanga Dyilo against the Decision on the Defence Challenge to the Jurisdiction of the Court Pursuant to Art. 19(2)(a) of the Statute of 3 October 2006 (14 December 2006).

The Prosecutor v Mbarushimana, Case No ICC-01/04–01/10, Decision on the Confirmation of Charges (16 December 2011).

The Prosecutor v Muthaura, Kenyatta, Ali, Case No ICC-01/09–02/11, Decision on the Confirmation of Charges Pursuant to Article 61(7)(a) and (b) of the Rome Statute (23 January 2012).

The Prosecutor v Ntaganda, Case No ICC-01/04–02/06, Decision Pursuant to Article 61(7)(a) and (b) of the Rome Statute on the Charges of the Prosecutor Against Bosco Ntaganda (9 June 2014).

The Prosecutor v Ntaganda, Case No ICC-01/04–02/06, Document Containing the Charges (10 January 2014).

The Prosecutor v Ntaganda, Case No ICC-01/04–02/06, Trial Judgment (8 July 2019).

The Prosecutor v Ongwen, Case No ICC-02/04–01/15, Decision on Defence Motions Alleging Defects in the Confirmation Decision (7 March 2019).

The Prosecutor v Ongwen, Case No ICC-02/04–01/15, Decision on the Confirmation of Charges against Dominic Ongwen (23 March 2016).

The Prosecutor v Ruto and Sang, Case No ICC-01/09–01, Decision on the Confirmation of Charges Pursuant to Article 61(7)(a) and (b) of the Rome Statute, ICC-01/09–01/11–373 (23 January 2012).

The Prosecutor v Ruto and Sang, Case No ICC-01/09–01, Public Redacted Version of Decision on Defence Applications for Judgments of Acquittal, ICC-01/09–01/11–2027-Red-Corr (16 June 2016).

Extraordinary Chambers in the Courts of Cambodia (ECCC)

Nuon Chea's Appeal against the Judgment in Case 002/01, Case No 002/19–09–2007-ECCC-SC (29 December 2014).

Sixth Investigative Request of Co-Lawyers for Civil Parties Concerning the Charge of Genocide Against the Khmer Nationals, Case No 002/19–09–2007-ECCC/OCIJ (4 February 2010).

The Prosecutor v Kaing Guek Eav alias Duch, Case No 001/18–07–2007/ECCC/SC, Appeal Judgment (3 February 2012).

The Prosecutor v Kaing Guek Eav alias Duch, Case No 001/18–07–2007/ECCC/TC, Trial Judgment (26 July 2010).

The Prosecutor v Nuon Chea, Ieng Sary, Khieu Samphân, Ieng Thirith, Case No 002/19–09–2007-ECCC-OCIJ, Closing Order (Indictment), (15 September 2010).

The Prosecutor v Nuon Chea et al., Case No 002/19–09–2007-ECCC-OCIJ, Ieng Sary's Supplemental Alternative Submission to His Motion Against the Applicability of Genocide at the ECCC (21 December 2009).

Prosecutor v Nuon Chea and Khieu Samphân, Case No 002/19–09–2007/ECCC/TC, Trial Judgment (16 November 2018).

The Prosecutor v Nuon Chea and Khieu Samphân, Case No 002/19–09–2007-ECCC/SC, Appeal Judgment (23 November 2016).

The Prosecutor v Nuon Chea and Khieu Samphân, Case No 002/19–09–2007-ECCC/TC, Trial Judgment (7 August 2014).

International Court of Justice (ICJ)

Aegean Sea Continental Shelf (*Greece v Turkey*), Judgment, ICJ Reports 1978.

Anglo-Iranian Oil Co. Case (*United Kingdom v Iran*), Preliminary Objection, Judgment, ICJ Reports 1952.

Application of the Convention on the Prevention and Punishment of the Crime of Genocide (Bosnia and Herzegovina v Serbia and Montenegro), ICJ Judgment (26 February 2007).

Application of the Convention on the Prevention and Punishment of the Crime of Genocide (Bosnia and Herzegovina v Serbia and Montenegro), Public sitting, Document Nr. CR/2006/43 (8 May 2006).

Application of the Convention on the Prevention and Punishment of the Crime of Genocide (*Bosnia and Herzegovina v Serbia and Montenegro*), Supplement to the Application and to the Second Request for the Indication of Provisional Measures of Protection Submitted by the Government of the Republic of Bosnia and Herzegovina, ICJ Reports 1993.

Application of the Convention on the Prevention and Punishment of the Crime of Genocide (Bosnia and Herzegovina v Yugoslavia), Preliminary Objections, Joint Declaration of Judge Shi and Judge Vereshchetin, Judgment, ICJ Reports 1996.

Application of the Convention on the Prevention and Punishment of the Crime of Genocide (Bosnia and Herzegovina v Yugoslavia), Preliminary Objections, Judgment, ICJ Reports 1996.

Application of the Convention on the Prevention and Punishment of the Crime of Genocide (Croatia v Serbia), ICJ Summary Judgment (15 February 2015).

Application of the Convention on the Prevention and Punishment of the Crime of Genocide (Croatia v Serbia), Judgment, ICJ Reports 2015.

Arbitral Award of 31 July 1989 (*Guinea Bissau v Senegal*), Judgment, ICJ Reports 1991.

Case Concerning Armed Activity on the Territory of the Congo (Democratic Republic of the Congo v Rwanda), Judgment on Jurisdiction of the Court and Admissibility of the Application, ICJ Reports 2006.

Case concerning Kasikili/ Sedudu Island (*Botswana* v *Namibia*), Declaration of Judge Higgins, Judgment, ICJ Reports 1999.

Case Concerning Military and Paramilitary Activities in and Against Nicaragua (Nicaragua v United States of America), Judgment, ICJ Reports 1986.

Case Concerning the Barcelona Traction, Light and Power Company Limited (*Barcelona Traction Case*) (New Application: 1962) (*Belgium v Spain*), Second Phase, Judgment, ICJ Reports 1970.

Case concerning the Gabčikovo-Nagymaros Project (Hungary vs Slovakia), Danube Dams case, Judgment, ICJ Reports 1997.

Case Concerning the Territorial Dispute (*Libyan Arab Jamahiriya v Chad*), Judgment, ICJ Reports 1994.

Competence of the General Assembly for the Admission of a State to the United Nations, Advisory Opinion, ICJ Reports 1950.

Competence of the General Assembly for the Admission of a State to the United Nations, Advisory Opinion, Dissenting Opinion of Judge Alvarez, ICJ Reports 1950.

Continental Shelf Case (Libyan Arab Jamahiriya v Malta), Judgment, ICJ Reports 1985.

Dispute Regarding Navigational and Related Rights (*Costa Rica v Nicaragua*), Judgment, ICJ Reports 2009.

Legal Consequences for States of the Continued Presence of South Africa in Namibia (South West Africa) Notwithstanding Security Council Resolution 276 (1970), Advisory Opinion, ICJ Reports 1971.

Legality of the Threat and Use of Nuclear Weapons, Advisory Opinion, ICJ Reports 1996.

North Sea Continental Shelf Cases (*Federal Republic of Germany v Netherlands, Federal Republic of Germany v Denmark*), Judgment, ICJ Reports 1969.

Reservations to the Convention on the Prevention and Punishment of the Crime of Genocide, Advisory Opinion, ICJ Reports 1951.

Reservations to the Convention on the Prevention and Punishment of the Crime of Genocide, Advisory Opinion, Dissenting Opinion of Judge Alvarez, ICJ Reports 1951.

Reservations to the Convention on the Prevention and Punishment of the Crime of Genocide, Advisory Opinion, Dissenting Opinion of Judges Guerrero, McNari, Read and Hsu Mo, ICJ Reports 1951.

South West Africa Cases (Ethiopia v South Africa; Liberia v South Africa), Preliminary Objections, Joint Dissenting Opinion of Judges Spender and Fitzmaurice, Judgment (21 December 1962), ICJ Reports (1962).

South West Africa Cases (*Ethiopia v South Africa; Liberia v South Africa*), Second Phase, Judgment, Dissenting Opinion of Judge Tanaka, ICJ Reports 1966.

Permanent Court of Arbitration (PCA)

Award in the Arbitration Regarding the Iron Rhine ("Ijzeren Rijn") Railway between the Kingdom of Belgium and the Kingdom of the Netherlands (Iron Rhine case), UNRIAA Vol. XXVII (24 May 2005).

International Centre for Settlement of Investment Disputes (ICSID)

Wintershall Aktiengesellschaft v Argentine Republic, International Centre for Settlement of Investment Disputes, ICSID Case No ARB/04/14, Award, 8 December 2008.

World Trade Organisation (WTO) appellate body

US – Import Prohibition of Certain Shrimp and Shrimp Products, WTO Appellate Body Report, Case No WT/DS58/AB/R, 12 October 1998.

The European Court of Human Rights

C.R. v The United Kingdom, Application No 20190/92, Judgment, 22 November 1995.

S.W. v The United Kingdom, Application No 20166/92, Judgment, 22 November 1995.

Timishev v Russia, Applications Nos 55762/00 and 55974/00, Judgment, 13 December 2005.

Vasiliauskas v Lithuania, Application No 35343/05, Grand Chamber Judgment, 20 October 2015.

Vasiliauskas v Lithuania, Application No 35343/05, Grand Chamber Judgment, Dissenting Opinion of Judges Villiger, Power-Forde, Pinto de Albuquerque and Kūris, 20 October 2015.

The Inter-American Court of Human Rights

The Right to Information on Consular Assistance in the Framework of the Guarantees of the Due Process of Law, Case No OC-16/99, Advisory Opinion, 1 October 1999.

Velásquez-Rodríguez v Honduras, Series C., No 4, Judgment, 29 July 1988.

Domestic and other courts

Israel

The Attorney-General of the Government of Israel v Eichmann, Criminal Case No 40/61, Judgment, District Court of Jerusalem (11 December 1961).

The Attorney-General of the Government of Israel v Eichmann, Criminal Case No 40/61, Judgment, Israel Supreme Court (29 May 1962).

United States of America

Loving v Virginia, Indictment for Felony (6 January 1959), at: <https://lva.omeka.net/items/show/54>.

Nuremberg Military Tribunals

United States of America v Josef Altstoetter et al. (*Justice* Case), Trials of War Criminals Before the Nuremberg Tribunals Under Control Council Law No 10, Vol. 3 (October 1946--April 1949), Washington: US Government Printing Office, 1950.

United States of America v Otto Ohlendorf et al. (*Einsatzgruppen* Case), Trials of War Criminals Before the Nuremberg Military Tribunals Under Control Council Law No 10, Vol. 4, Opening Statement of the Prosecution, (October 1946–April 1949), Washington: US Government Printing Office, 1950.

United States of America v Otto Ohlendorf et al. (*Einsatzgruppen* Case), Trials of War Criminals Before the Nuremberg Military Tribunals Under Control Council Law No 10, Vol. 4, Opinion and Judgment (October 1946–April 1949), Washington: US Government Printing Office, 1950.

United States of America v Ulrich Greifelt et al. (*RuSHA Case*), Trials of War Criminals Before the Nuremberg Military Tribunals Under Control Council Law No 10, Vol. 4, Indictment (October 1946--April 1949), Washington: US Government Printing Office, 1950.

United States of America v Ulrich Greifelt et al. (*RuSHA* Case), Trials of War Criminals Before the Nuremberg Military Tribunals Under Control Council Law No 10, Vol. 4, Opening Statement of the Prosecution (October 1946–April 1949), Washington: US Government Printing Office, 1950.

United States of America v Ulrich Greifelt et al. (*RuSHA* Case), Trials of War Criminals Before the Nuremberg Military Tribunals Under Control Council Law No 10, Vol. 5, General Defenses and Special Issues (October 1946–April 1949), Washington: US Government Printing Office, 1950.

United States of America v Ulrich Greifelt et al. (*RuSHA* Case), Trials of War Criminals Before the Nuremberg Military Tribunals Under Control Council Law No 10, Vol. 5, Judgment (October 1946–April 1949), Washington: US Government Printing Office, 1950.

Table of UN documents and other official publications

General Assembly resolutions

UN GA Res. 96 (I) of 11 December 1946.
UN GA Res. 103 (I) of 19 November 1946.
UN GA Res. 217 A (III) of 10 December 1948.
UN GA Res. 260 (III) of 9 December 1948.
UN GA Res. 395 (V) of 2 December 1950.
UN GA Res. 1663 (XVI) of 28 November 1961.
UN GA Res. 1761 (XVII) of 6 November 1962.
UN GA Res. 1904 (XVIII) of 20 November 1963.
UN GA Res. 2074 (XX) of 17 December 1965.
UN GA Res. 2106 (XX) of 21 December 1965.
UN GA Res. 2202 (XXI) of 16 December 1966.
UN GA Res. 2307 (XXII) of 13 December 1967.
UN GA Res. 2391 (XXIII), 26 November 1968.
UN GA Res. 2446 (XXIII) of 19 December 1968.
UN GA Res. 2775 (XXVI) of 29 November 1971.
UN GA Res. 3068 (XXVIII) of 30 November 1973.
UN GA Res. 3151 (XXVIII) of 14 December 1973.
UN Doc. A/RES/39/72 of 13 December 1984.
UN Doc. A/RES/41/103 of 4 December 1986.
UN Doc. A/RES/42/56 of 30 November 1987.
UN Doc. A/RES/43/97 of 8 December 1988.
UN Doc. A/RES/44/79 of 8 December 1989.
UN Doc. A/RES/45/90 of 14 December 1990.
UN Doc. A/RES/46/84 of 16 December 1991.
UN Doc. A/RES/47/81 of 16 December 1992.
UN Doc. A/RES/48/1 of 8 October 1993.
UN Doc. A/RES/48/89 of 20 December 1993.
UN Doc. A/RES/48/159 of 20 December 1993.
UN Doc. A/RES/69/188 of 21 January 2015.

Security Council resolutions

UN SC Res. 134 of 1 April 1960.
UN SC Res. 392 of 19 June 1976.
UN SC Res. 417 of 31 October 1977.
UN SC Res. 418 of 4 November 1977.
UN SC Res. 556 of 23 October 1984.
UN SC Res. 558 of 13 December 1984.
UN Doc. S/RES/827 of 25 May 1993.
UN Doc. S/RES/935 of 1 July 1994.
UN Doc. S/RES/955 of 8 November 1994.
UN Doc. S/RES/1564 of 18 September 2004.
UN Doc. S/RES/1593 of 31 March 2005.

UN reports by commissions of experts, Secretary-General, and special rapporteurs

Azkoul, Karim, Rapporteur of the Ad Hoc Committee on Genocide, *Report of the Committee and Draft Convention Drawn Up by the Committee*, UN Doc. E/794 (24 May 1948).

Blishchenko, Igor Pavlovich, *Study of the International Convention on the Suppression and Punishment of the Crime of Apartheid*, UN Unit on Apartheid, Department of Political and Security Council Affairs, Note No 3/74, March 1974.

Capotorti, Francesco, *Report of the Sixteenth Session of the Sub-Commission on Prevention of Discrimination and Protection of Minorities to the Commission on Human Rights*, ECOSOC, Commission on Human Rights, Sub-Commission on Prevention of Discrimination and Protection of Minorities, UN Doc. E/CN.4/873, E/CN.4/Sub.2/241, 11 February 1964.

Degni-Ségui, René, Special Rapporteur of the Commission on Human Rights, *Report on the Situation of Human Rights in Rwanda Under Paragraph 20 of Resolution S-3/1 of 25 May 1994*, ECOSOC, Commission on Human Rights, Question of the Violation of Human Rights and Fundamental Freedoms in Any Part of the World, With Particular Reference to Colonial and Other Dependent Countries and Territories, UN Doc. E/CN.4/1995/71, 17 January 1995.

Falk, Richard, *Report of the Special Rapporteur on the Situation of Human Rights in the Palestinian Territories Occupied since 1967*, UN Doc. A/HRC/25/67, 13 January 2014.

Falk, Richard, Tilley, Virginia, *Israeli Practices Towards the Palestinian People and the Question of Apartheid: Palestine and the Israeli Occupation, Issue No 1*, Economic and Social Commission for Western Asia, UN Doc. E/ESCWA/ECRI/2017/1 (2017).

Identical Letters Dated 15 March 1999 from the Secretary-General to the President of the General Assembly and the President of the Security Council, UN Doc. S/1999/231 and UN Doc. A/53/850, Annex: *Report of the Group of Experts for Cambodia Established Pursuant to General Assembly Resolution 52/135*, 15 March 1999.

Ider, Luvsandanzangiin, Elimination of All Forms of Racial Discrimination, Report of the General Assembly Third Committee, UN Doc. A/8880, 13 November 1972.

Interim Report of the Commission of Experts Established Pursuant to Security Council Resolution 780 (1992), UN Doc. S/25274, 9 February 1993.

Letter Dated 5 October 1993 from the Secretary-General to the President of the Security Council, UN Doc. S/26545, Annex: *Second Interim Report of the Commission of Experts Established Pursuant to Security Council Resolution 780 (1992)*.

Letter Dated 24 May 1994 from the Secretary-General to the President of the Security Council, UN Doc. S/1994/674, Annex: *Final Report of the Commission of Experts Established Pursuant to Security Council Resolution 780 (1992)*.

Letter Dated 9 December 1994 from the Secretary-General to the President of the Security Council, UN Doc. S/1994/1405, Annex: *Final Report of the Commission of Experts Established Pursuant to Security Council Resolution 935 (1994)*.

Letter Dated 1 October 1994 from the Secretary-General to the President of the Security Council, UN Doc. S/1994/1125, Annex: *Preliminary Report of the Independent Commission of Experts Established in Accordance With Security Council Resolution 935* (1994).

Mazowiecki, Tadeusz, *Report by Special Rapporteur of the Commission on Human Rights, Pursuant to Paragraph 32 of Commission Resolution 1993/7 of 23 February 1993 on the Situation of Human Rights in the Territory of the Former Yugoslavia*, ECOSCO, UN Doc. E/CN.4/1994/47, 17 November 1993.

Office of the Special Advisor on the Prevention of Genocide (OSAPG), *Framework of Analysis for Atrocity Crimes: a Tool for Prevention* (2014), at: www.un.org/en/preventgenocide/adviser/pdf/framework%20of%20analysis%20for%20atrocity%20crimes_en.pdf.

Quintana, Tomás Ojea, *Report of the Special Rapporteur on the Situation of Human Rights in the Democratic People's Republic of Korea*, UN Doc. A/HRC/34/66, advance edited version, 22 February 2017.

Rehn, Elisabeth, *Report by Special Rapporteur of the Commission on Human Rights, Pursuant to Commission Resolution 1995/89, on the Situation of Human Rights in the Territory of the Former Yugoslavia*, ECOSOC, UN Doc. E/CN.4/1996/63, 14 March 1996.

Report of the Secretary-General, *Implementation of the Outcome of the Fourth World Conference on Women*, UN Doc. A/51/322, 3 September 1996.

Report of the Secretary-General on the Implementation of the Five Point Action Plan and the Activities of the Special Adviser on the Prevention of Genocide, UN Doc. E/CN.4/2006/84, 9 March 2006.

Report by the Secretary-General, *Review of Studies of Problems of Race Relations and of the Creation and Maintenance of Racial Attitude*, Commission on Human Rights, Twenty-Ninth Session, UN Doc. E/CN.4/1105, 14 November 1972.

Report of the Secretary-General pursuant to para. 2 of Security Council Resolution 808 (1993), UN Doc. S/25704, 3 May 1993.

Ruhashyankiko, Nicodème, *Study of the Question of the Prevention and Punishment of the Crime of Genocide*, UN Doc. E/CN.4/Sub. 2/416, 4 July 1978.

Whitaker, Benjamin, *Revised and Updated Report on the Question of the Prevention and Punishment of the Crime of Genocide*, UN Doc. E/CN.4/Sub. 2/1985/6, 2 July 1985.

Commissions of inquiry (UN and others)

Report of the Detailed Findings of the Commission of Inquiry on Human Rights in the Democratic People's Republic of Korea, UN Doc. A/HRC/25/CRP.1 (7 February 2014).

Report of the International Commission of Inquiry on Darfur to the United Nations Secretary-General, Pursuant to Security Council Resolution 1564 of 18 September 2004, UN Doc. S/2005/60 (25 January 2005).

Russell Tribunal on Palestine: Findings of the South African Session, Are Israel's Practices Against the Palestinian People in Breach of the Prohibition on Apartheid Under International Law, 5–7 November 2011.

International Law Commission

Crimes Against Humanity: Texts and titles of the draft preamble, the draft articles and the draft annex provisionally adopted by the Drafting Committee on first reading, UN Doc. A/CN.4/L.892, 26 May 2017.

Draft Articles on Responsibility of States for Internationally Wrongful Acts, with commentaries, adopted by the International Law Commission at its fifty-third session, Report of the ILC on the work of its fifty-third session, 23 April – 1 June and 2 July – 10 August 2001, UN Doc. A/56/10.

Draft Code of Offences against the Peace and Security of Mankind (1954), at: http://legal.un.org/ilc/texts/instruments/english/draft_articles/7_3_1954.pdf

Draft Code of Crimes against the Peace and Security of Mankind with commentaries, UN Doc. A/46/10 (1991).

Draft Code of Crimes Against the Peace and Security of Mankind (Part II), including a Draft Statute for an International Criminal Court, UN Doc. A/CN.4/365 (1983) and UN Doc. A/CN.4/L.459 (1991).

Draft Code of Crimes Against the Peace and Security of Mankind, Report of the Working Group on a Draft Statute for an International Criminal Court, Summary Record of the 2359th meeting, UN Doc. A/CN.4/SR.2359, 29 June 1994.

Draft Code of Crimes Against the Peace and Security of Mankind. Titles and texts of articles adopted by the Commission at its forty-eighth session, UN Doc. A/CN.4/L.532, 1996.

Draft Code of Crimes Against the Peace and Security of Mankind: Titles and texts of articles on the Draft Code of Crimes Against the Peace and Security of Mankind, UN Doc. A/51/10, 1996.

International Law Commission, Sixty-fifth session (5 May-7 June and 8 July-9 August 2013), Formation and Evidence of Customary International Law, Memorandum by the Secretariat, UN Doc. A/CN.4/659, 14 March 2013.

Report of the International Law Commission on the work of its forty-eighth session, 6 May – 26 July 1996, Official Records of the General Assembly, Fifty-first session, Supplement No 10, including a Draft Code of Crimes with commentaries, UN Doc. A/51/10, 1996.

Report of the International Law Commission, sixty-fourth session (7 May–1 June and 2 July–3 August 2012), General Assembly Official Records, Sixty-seventh session, Supplement No 10, UN Doc. A/67/10, 2012.

Report of the International Law Commission, sixty-eighth session (2 May–10 June and 4 July – 12 August 2016), General Assembly Official Records, Seventy-first session, Supplement No 10, UN Doc. A/71/10, 2016.

Report of the Study Group of the International Law Commission, Fragmentation of International Law: Difficulties Arising from the Diversification and Expansion of International Law, UN Doc. A/CN.4/L.682, 13 April 2006.

Report of the Working Group on a Draft Statute for an International Criminal Court, UN Doc. A/CN.4/SR.2360, 29 June 1994.

Report of the UN Commission on the Racial Situation in the Union of South Africa, UN Doc. A/2505 and Add. 1, 1953.

Thiam, Doudou, Fourth Report on the Draft Code of Offences Against the Peace and Security of Mankind, UN Doc. A/CN.4/398, 11 March 1986.

Waldock, Humphrey, ILC Special Rapporteur, Third Report on the Law of Treaties, Yearbook of the International Law Commission, UN Doc. A/CN.4/SER.A/1964/Add.1, 1964.

Committee on the Elimination of Racial Discrimination (CERD)

Concluding Observations India, UN Doc. CERD/C/IND/CO/19, 5 May 2007.

Consideration of Reports Submitted by States Parties under Article 9 of the Convention, Concluding Observations of the Committee on the Elimination of Racial Discrimination, Israel, UN Doc. CERD/C/ISR/CO/14–16, 9 March 2012.

General Recommendation No 19 on Article 3 of the Convention, Forty-seventh Session (1995), reprinted in UN Doc. HRI/GEN/1/Rev.6, p. 208.

Hagan v Australia, No 26/2002, Communication (20 March 2003), UN Doc. CERD/C/62/D/26/2002.

UN Economic and Social Council (ECOSOC)

UN Economic and Social Council, Ad Hoc Committee on Genocide, Summary Record of the Third Meeting, UN Doc. E/AC.25/SR.3, 6 April 1948.

UN Economic and Social Council, Ad Hoc Committee on Genocide, Summary Record of the Thirteenth Meeting, UN Doc. E/AC.25/SR.13, 20 April 1948.

UN Economic and Social Council, Commission on Human Rights, Sub-Commission on the Prevention of Discrimination and the Protection of Minorities, Summary Record of the Fourth Meeting, UN Doc. E/CN.4/Sub.2/SR.4, 26 November 1947.

UN Economic and Social Council, Commission on Human Rights, Summary Record of the First Part (Public) of the 1510th Meeting, UN Doc. E/CN.4/SR.1510, 9 March 1979.

UN Economic and Social Council, Draft Convention and Draft Protocol on the Suppression and Punishment of the Crime of Apartheid, UN Doc. E/RES/1696 (LII), 2 June 1973.

General Assembly, Third Committee (drafting of the Apartheid Convention)

General Assembly, 26th Session, Third Committee, Draft to the Apartheid Convention presented by Guinea and the Soviet Union in 1971, UN Doc. A/C.3/L.1871, 28 October 1971.

General Assembly, 28th Session, Third Committee, 2003rd meeting, UN Doc. A/C.3/SR.2003, 22 October 1973.

UN General Assembly, Sixth Committee (drafting of the Genocide Convention)

UN Doc. A/C.6/SR.63, 30 September 1948.

UN Doc. A/C.6/SR.64, 1 October 1948.

UN Doc. A/C.6/SR.69, 7 October 1948.

UN Doc. A/C.6/SR.74, 14 October 1948.

UN Doc. A/C.6/SR.75, 15 October 1948.

UN Doc. A/C.6/SR.132, 1 December 1948.

UN Doc. A/C.6/211, 1 October 1948.

UN Doc. A/PV.55, 11 December 1946.

UN Doc. A/PV.178, 9 December 1948.

UN Doc. A/PV.179, 9 December 1948.

UN Doc. A/PV.2185, 30 November 1973.

UN diplomatic conference of plenipotentiaries on the establishment of an international criminal court (1998)

UN Doc. A/CONF.183/C.1/L.53.

UN Doc. A/CONF.183/C.1/L.58.

UN Doc. A/CONF.183/C.1/L.91.

UN Doc. A/CONF.183/C.1/SR.3.

UN Doc. A/CONF.183/C.1/L.12.

UN Doc. A/CONF.183/C.1/L.13.
UN Doc. A/CONF.183/SR.2.

UN Secretary-General

UN Secretary-General, Draft Convention on the Crime of Genocide and Comments, UN Doc. E/447, 26 June 1947.

Letter addressed to the Secretary-General by the permanent representatives of Afghanistan, Burma, Egypt, India, Indonesia, Iran, Iraq, Lebanon, Pakistan, the Philippines, Saudi Arabia, Syria and Yemen, UN Doc. A72183, 12 September 1952.

UNESCO

'Proposals on the Biological Aspects of Race' (1964), in UNESCO, *Four Statements on the Race Question*, 1969.

'Statement on Race' (1950), in UNESCO, *Four Statements on the Race Question*, 1969.

'Statement on Race and Racial Prejudice of 1967', in UNESCO, *Four Statements on the Race Question*, 1969.

'Statement on the Nature of Race and Race Differences' (1951), in UNESCO, *Four Statements on the Race Question*, 1969.

The Race Question, Vol. 3, 1950, File No 341.16:001.

The Race Concept: Results of an Inquiry, Paris: UNESCO, 1952.

UN High Commissioner for Human Rights

UN Commission on Human Rights, Implementation of the International Convention on the Suppression and Punishment of the Crime of Apartheid: Study on Ways and Means of Insuring the Implementation of International Instruments Such as the Convention on the Suppression and Punishment of the Crime of Apartheid, Including the Establishment of International Jurisdiction Envisaged by the Convention, UN Doc. E/CN.4/1426, 19 January 1981.

UN Office of the High Commissioner for Human Rights, Implementation of the International Convention on the Suppression and Punishment of the Crime of Apartheid, Commission on Human Rights Resolution 1993/10, UN Doc. E/CN.4/RES/1993/10, 26 February 1993.

UN Office of the High Commissioner for Human Rights, The High Commissioner's Position Paper on the Establishment of a Permanent International Criminal Court, UN Doc. UNICC/NONE/98/1, 15 June 1998.

Other UN documents

Caracas Declaration for Action Against Apartheid, UN Doc. A/38/451 and S/16009 (1983).

Declaration of the Seminar on the Legal Status of the Apartheid Régime and Other Legal Aspects of the Struggle Against Apartheid (Lagos Declaration) UN Doc. A/39/423 and S/16709 (1984).

Letter dated 12 July 1948 from the representative of India to the Secretary-General concerning the treatment of Indians in South Africa, UN Doc A/577, 16 July 1948.

Report of the Ad Hoc Committee on the Establishment of an International Criminal Court, GAOR, Fiftieth Session, Supplement No 22, UN Doc. A/50/22, 1995.

Security Council, 2046th Meeting, UN Doc. S/PV.2046, 4 November 1977.

Security Council, 7575th Meeting, UN Doc. S/PV.7575, 10 December 2015.

Other UN publications

Farah, Abdulrahim Abby, Statement before the Special Political Committee of the General Assembly, in Unit on Apartheid: Notes and Documents, No 20/72, 9 October 1972.

UN Background Papers, *Apartheid and Racial Discrimination*, New York: UN Office of Public Information, 1974.

UN Blue Book Series, *The United Nations and Apartheid, 1948–1994, Volume 1*, New York: UN Department of Public Information, 1994.

Unit on Apartheid, *Apartheid in Practice*, UN Doc. ST/PSCA/SER.A/9, 1969.

International Law Association

Committee on Formation of Customary (General) International Law, Final Report, 2000.

American Law Institute

Restatement of the Foreign Relations Law of the United States (1986).

Table of online sources

(all last accessed 30 April 2019)

Reichsbürgergesetz (1935), published by the Austrian National Library: http://alex.onb.ac.at/cgi-content/alex?apm=0&aid=dra&datum=19350004&seite=00001146&zoom=2

Erste Verordnung zur Ausführung des Gesetzes zum Schutze des Deutschen Blutes und der Deutschen Ehre (1935). published by the Austrian National Library: http://alex.onb.ac.at/cgi-content/alex?aid=dra&datum=1935&page=1480&size=45

Hans Günther: Eine Kleine Rassenkunde des Deutschen Volkes: https://archive.org/details/Guenther-Hans-Kleine-Rassenkunde-des-deutschen-Volkes-Text

Attorney-General of Israel v Eichmann, Case No 40/61, Judgment (11 December 1961): www.asser.nl/upload/documents/DomCLIC/Docs/NLP/Israel/Eichmann_Judgement_11-12-1961.pdf

Attorney-General of Israel v Eichmann, Case No 40/61, Appeals Judgment (29 May 1962): www.asser.nl/upload/documents/DomCLIC/Docs/NLP/Israel/Eichmann_Appeals_Judgement_29-5-1962.pdf

London Agreement by the Governments of the UK, USA, the Provisional Government of the French Republic and the USSR for the Prosecution and Punishment of the Major War Criminals of the European Axis, (8 August 1945): http://avalon.law.yale.edu/imt/imtchart.asp

Charter of the International Military Tribunal: http://avalon.law.yale.edu/imt/imtconst.asp

Introduction to the ECCC: www.eccc.gov.kh/en/about-eccc/introduction

Thomas Theorem: www.encyclopedia.com/doc/1O88-ThomasTheorem.html

Treaties, States Parties and Commentaries, Protocol Additional to the Geneva Conventions of 12 August 1949, and relating to the Protection of Victims of International Armed Conflicts (Protocol I), 8 June 1977: https://ihl-databases.icrc.org/applic/ihl/ihl.nsf/INTRO/470

ICTY Court Records: http://icr.icty.org/

ICTY Key Figures of the Cases: www.icty.org/en/cases/key-figures-cases.

UN Audiovisual Library of International Law: Procedural History of the Convention on the Prevention and Punishment of the Crime of Genocide: http://legal.un.org/avl/ha/cppcg/cppcg.html

ILC Draft Statute for an International Criminal Court (1994): http://legal.un.org/ilc/texts/instruments/english/commentaries/7_4_1994.pdf
ILC Draft Code of Offences against the Peace and Security of Mankind (1954): http://legal.un.org/ilc/texts/instruments/english/draft_articles/7_3_1954.pdf
Merriam Webster dictionary: www.merriam-webster.com
Collectivity: www.merriam-webster.com/dictionary/collectivity
Group: www.merriam-webster.com/dictionary/group
Hereditary: www.merriam-webster.com/dictionary/hereditary
Objective: www.merriam-webster.com/dictionary/objective
UNESCO Declaration on Race and Racial Prejudice (1978): www.ohchr.org/Documents/ProfessionalInterest/race.pdf
Statement by Mr Michael Kirby Chair of the Commission of Inquiry on Human Rights in the Democratic People's Republic of Korea to the 25th session of the Human Rights Council, Geneva, 17 March 2014: www.ohchr.org/EN/NewsEvents/Pages/DisplayNews.aspx?NewsID=14385&LangID=E
American Association of Physical Anthropologists, Statement on Race and Racism (March 2019): <www.physanth.org/about/position-statements/aapa-statement-race-and-racism-2019/>
Les actes constituant un danger general (interétatique) consideres comme delites des droit des gens par Raphaël Lemkin: www.preventgenocide.org/fr/lemkin/madrid1933.htm
Contracts without Consideration: The 'Nudum Pactum' Mistake: www.public-contractinginstitute.com/contracts-without-consideration-the-nudum-pactum-mistake-2/
Nuremberg Racial Laws: www.rassengesetze.nuernberg.de/
Truth and Reconciliation Commission of South Africa, Final Report (1998): www.sahistory.org.za/sites/default/files/volume5_0.pdf
Proposed International Convention on the Prevention and Punishment of Crimes Against Humanity:http://sites.law.wustl.edu/docs/harris/cah/EnglishTreaty-Final.pdf
United Nations Treaty Collection: https://treaties.un.org States Parties to the Apartheid Convention: https://treaties.un.org/Pages/ViewDetails.aspx?src=TREATY&mtdsg_no=IV-7&chapter=4&lang=en
Charter of the International Military Tribunal for the Far East, Special Proclamation by the Supreme Commander for the Allied Powers at Tokyo:www.un.org/en/genocideprevention/documents/atrocity-crimes/Doc.3_1946%20Tokyo%20Charter.pdf
History of the United Nations War Crimes Commission and the Development of the Laws of War (1948): www.unwcc.org/documents/
The Nuremberg Race Laws: www.ushmm.org/outreach/en/article.php?ModuleId=10007695
Judgment IMTFE: http://werle.rewi.hu-berlin.de/tokio.pdf

Bibliography

Abtahi, Hirad, Webb, Philippa, *The Genocide Convention: The Travaux Préparatoires*, Volume 1, Leiden: Martinus Nijhoff, 2008.

Ackermann, Josef, *Heinrich Himmler als Ideologe* [Heinrich Himmler, the Ideologue], Göttingen: Musterschmidt, 1970.

Akande, Dapo, 'Sources of International Criminal Law', in Cassese, Antonio (ed), *The Oxford Companion to International Criminal Justice*, Oxford: Oxford University Press, 2009.

Akhavan, Payam, 'Balkanizing Jurisdiction: Reflections on Article IX of the Genocide Convention in *Croatia v Serbia*', *Leiden Journal of International Law*, Volume 28, 2015, pp. 893–897.

———, 'The Crime of Genocide in the ICTR Jurisprudence', *Journal of International Criminal Justice*, Volume 3, No 4, 2005, pp. 989–1006.

———, 'Enforcement of the Genocide Convention: A Challenge to Civilization', *Harvard Human Rights Journal*, Volume 8, 1995, pp. 229–258.

———, 'Genocide', in de Brouwer, Ann-Marie, Smeulers, Alette (eds), *The Elgar Companion to the International Criminal Tribunal for Rwanda*, Cheltenham: Edward Elgar, 2016.

———, *Reducing Genocide to Law: Definition, Meaning, and the Ultimate Crime*, Cambridge: Cambridge University Press, 2012.

Aksenova, Marina, 'Human Rights at the International Criminal Court: Testing the Limits of Judicial Discretion', *Nordic Journal of International Law*, Volume 86, 2017, pp. 68–90.

Allard K. Lowenstein International Human Rights Clinic, Yale Law School, *Persecution of the Rohingya Muslims: Is Genocide Occurring in Myanmar's Rakhine State? A Legal Analysis*, 2015.

Allport, Gordon W., *The Nature of Prejudice*, New York: Doubleday Anchor Books, 2nd edn, 1958.

Alonzo-Maizlish, David, 'In Whole or in Part: Group Rights, The Intent Element of Genocide, and the "Qualitative Criterion",' *New York University Law Review*, Volume 77, 2002, pp. 1369–1403.

Amann, Diane Marie, 'Group Mentality, Expressivism, and Genocide', *International Criminal Law Review*, Volume 2, 2002, pp. 93–143.

———, 'Prosecutor v Akayesu, Case ICTR-96-4-T', *American Journal of International Law*, Volume 93, No 1, 1999, pp. 195–199.

Amatrudo, Anthony, Blake, Leslie William, *Human Rights and the Criminal Justice System*, Abingdon: Routledge, 2015.

Ambos, Kai, 'Some Preliminary Reflections on the *Mens Rea* Requirements of the Crimes of the ICC Statute and of the Elements of Crimes', in Vohrah, Lal Chand *et al.* (eds), *Man's Inhumanity to Man: Essays on International Law in Honour of Antonio Cassese*, The Hague: Kluwer Law International, 2003.

———, 'The Crime of Genocide and the Principle of Legality under Article 7 of the European Convention on Human Rights', *Human Rights Law Review*, Volume 17, 2017, pp. 175–186.

———, *Treatise on International Criminal Law, Volume II: The Crimes and Sentencing*, Oxford: Oxford University Press, 2014.

———, 'What Does 'Intent to Destroy' in Genocide Mean?', *International Review of the Red Cross*, Volume 91, No 876, 2009, pp. 833–858.

Ambrus, Monika, 'Genocide and Discrimination: Lessons to Be Learnt from Discrimination Law', *Leiden Journal of International Law*, Volume 25, 2012, pp. 935–954.

Anderson, Benedict, *Imagined Communities: Reflections on the Origin and Spread of Nationalism*, London: Verso, 3rd revised edn, 2006.

Anonymous, 'Genocide: A Commentary on the Convention', *Yale Law Journal*, Volume 58, 1948–1949, pp. 1142–1160.

Aptel, Cécile, 'The Intent to Commit Genocide in the Case Law of the International Criminal Tribunal for Rwanda', *Criminal Law Forum*, Volume 13, 2002, pp. 273–291.

Arajärvi, Noora, *The Changing Nature of Customary International Law*, London: Routledge, 2014.

Arato, Julian, 'Subsequent Practice and Evolutive Interpretation: Techniques of Treaty Interpretation over Time and Their Diverse Consequences', *The Law and Practice of International Courts and Tribunals*, Volume 9, 2010, pp. 443–494.

Arendt, Hannah, *Eichmann in Jerusalem: A Report on the Banality of Evil*, Middlesex: Penguin Books, 1963/1987.

———, *The Origins of Totalitarianism*, New York: Harcourt, Brace & Co., 1951.

Arnold, Roberta, 'The *Mens Rea* of Genocide under the Statute of the International Criminal Court', *Criminal Law Forum*, Volume 14, 2003, pp. 127–151.

Arsanjani, Mahnoush, 'The Rome Statute of the International Criminal Court', *American Journal for International Law*, Volume 93, No 1, 1999, pp. 22–43.

Askin, Kelly, 'Crimes within the Jurisdiction of the International Criminal Court', *Criminal Law Forum*, Volume 10, 1999, pp. 33–59.

Aspegren, Lennart, Williamson, Jamie, 'The Rwanda Tribunal and Genocide', in Decaux, Emmanuel, Dieng, Adama, Sow, Malick (eds), *From Human Rights to International Criminal Law: Studies in Honour of an African Jurist, the Late Judge Laïty Kama*, Leiden: Martinus Nijhoff, 2007.

Augoustinos, Martha, Reynolds, Katherine, 'Prejudice, Racism, and Social Psychology', in Augoustinos, Martha, Reynolds, Katherine (eds), *Understanding Prejudice, Racism, and Social Conflict*, London: Sage Publications, 2001.

Aydin, Devrim, 'The Interpretation of Genocidal Intent under the Genocide Convention and the Jurisprudence of International Courts', *Journal of Criminal Law*, Volume 78, 2014, pp. 423–441.

Badar, Mohamed Elewa, 'From the Nuremberg Charter to the Rome Statute: Defining the Elements of Crimes Against Humanity', *San Diego International Law Journal*, Volume 73, 2004, pp. 73–144.

———, *The Concept of* Mens Rea *in International Criminal Law: The Case for a Unified Approach*, Oxford: Hart Publishing, 2013.

Balint, Jennifer, *Genocide, State Crime and the Law: In the Name of the State*, Abingdon: Routledge, 2012.

Bamshad, Michael, *et al.*, 'Human Population Genetic Structure and Inference of Group Membership', *American Journal of Human Genetics*, Volume 72, 2003, pp. 578–589.

Bantekas, Ilias, *International Criminal Law*, Oxford: Hart Publishing, 4th edn, 2010.

———, 'The Anthropological Dimension of International Crimes and International Criminal Justice', in Bantekas, Ilias, Mylonaki, Emmanouela (eds), *Criminological Approaches to International Criminal Law*, Cambridge: Cambridge University Press, 2014.

Bantekas, Ilias, Nash, Susan, *International Criminal Law*, London: Routledge-Cavendish, 3rd edn, 2007.

Banton, Michael, *International Action against Racial Discrimination*, Oxford: Clarendon Press, 1996.

———, 'Race: As Classification', in Cashmore, Ellis (ed), *Encyclopedia of Race and Ethnic Studies*, London: Routledge, 2004.

———, *Racial Theories*, Cambridge: Cambridge University Press, 2nd edn, 1998.

———, 'Social Aspects of the Race Question', in UNESCO, *Four Statements on the Race Question*, 1969.

———, *What We Now Know About Race and Ethnicity*, New York: Berghahn, 2015.

Barkan, Elazar, 'Mobilizing Scientists against Nazi Racism, 1933–1939', in Stocking, George (ed), *Bones, Bodies, Behavior: Essays on Biological Anthropology*, Madison: University of Wisconsin Press, 1988.

Barnard, Adriaan, 'Slegs Suid Afrikaners – South Africans Only? A Review and Evaluation of the International Crime of Apartheid', *New Zealand Journal of Public and International Law*, Volume 7, 2009, pp. 317–365.

Barth, Fredrik, 'Introduction', in Barth, Fredrik (ed), *Ethnic Groups and Boundaries: The Social Organization of Culture Difference*, Long Grove: Waveland Press, 1969/1998.

Bassiouni, Cherif M., *Crimes Against Humanity: Historical Evolution and Contemporary Application*, Cambridge: Cambridge University Press, 2011.

———, 'International Crimes: The *Ratione Materiae* of International Criminal Law', in Bassiouni, M. Cherif (ed), *International Criminal Law, Volume I: Sources, Subjects, and Contents*, Leiden: Martinus Nijhoff, 3rd edn, 2008.

———, *Introduction to International Criminal Law*, Ardsley: Transnational Publishers, 2003.

———, *Introduction to International Criminal Law: Second Revised Edition*, Leiden: Martinus Nijhoff, 2013.

———, *The Legislative History of the International Criminal Court, Volume 1: Introduction, Analysis, and Integrated Text of the Statute, Elements of Crimes and Rules of Procedure and Evidence*, Ardsley: Transnational Publishers, 2005.

———, 'The Protection of "Collective Victims" in International Law', in Bassiouni, M. Cherif (ed), *International Protection of Victims*, Paris: Association International de Droit Pénal, Editions Érès, 1988.

Bauer, Yehuda, 'The Evolution of Nazi Jewish Policy, 1933–1938', in Chalk, Frank, Jonassohn, Kurt (eds), *The History and Sociology of Genocide*, New Haven: Yale University Press, 1990.

Baumann, Gerd, *The Multicultural Riddle: Rethinking National, Ethnic, and Religious Identities*, New York: Routledge, 1999.

Bazyler, Michael, *Holocaust, Genocide, and the Law: A Quest for Justice in a Post-Holocaust World*, New York: Oxford University Press, 2016.

Beckman, Lars, *Ras och Rasfördomar* [Race and Racial Prejudice], Falköping: Prisma, 1966.

Behrens, Paul, 'A Moment of Kindness? Consistency and Genocidal Intent', in Henham, Ralph, Behrens, Paul (eds), *The Criminal Law of Genocide: International, Comparative and Contextual Aspects*, Aldershot: Ashgate, 2007.

———, 'Art. 6: Genocide', in Klamberg, Mark (ed), *Commentary on the Law of the International Criminal Court*, Brussels: Torkel Opsahl Academic EPublisher, 2017.

———, 'Between Abstract Event and Individualized Crime: Genocidal Intent in the Case of Croatia', *Leiden Journal of International Law*, Volume 28, 2015, pp. 923–935.

———, 'Genocide and the Question of Motives', *Journal of International Criminal Justice*, Volume 10, 2012, pp. 501–523.

———, 'The Crime of Genocide and the Problem of Subjective Substantiality', *German Yearbook of International Law*, Volume 59, Berlin: Duncker & Humblot, 2016.

Bernath, Julie, 'The Politics of Difference in Transitional Justice: Genocide and the Construction of Victimhood at the Khmer Rouge Tribunal', *Journal of Intervention and Statebuilding*, Volume 12, 2018, pp. 367–384.

Berreby, David, *Us and Them: The Science of Identity*, Chicago: The University of Chicago Press, 2008.

Bertallo, Alain, 'Von der Ethnisierung zum Genozid: Mechanismen der Mobilisierung Unbeteiligter zu Akteuren kollektiver Gewaltexzesse' [From Ethnization to Genocide: Mechanisms to Mobilizing Uninvolved Persons to Becoming Actors of Collective Violence], in Schaller, Dominik, Boyadjian, Rupen, Berg, Vivianne, Scholtz, Hanno (eds), *Enteignet – Vertrieben – Ermordet: Beiträge zur Genozidforschung* [Dispossessed – Displaced – Murdered: Contributions to Genocide Research], Zürich: Chronos Verlag, 2004.

Bettwy, David Shea, 'The Genocide Convention and Unprotected Groups: Is the Scope of Protection Expanding under Customary International Law?', *Notre Dame Journal of International and Comparative Law*, Volume 2, No 1, 2011, pp. 167–196.

Bialas, Wolfgang, 'The Eternal Violence of the Blood: Racial Science and Nazi Ethics', in Weiss-Wendt, Anton, Yeomans, Rory (eds), *Racial Science in Hitler's New Europe, 1938–1945*, Lincoln: University of Nebraska Press, 2013.

Bisaz, Corsin, *The Concept of Group Rights in International Law: Groups as Contested Right-Holders, Subjects and Legal Persons*, Leiden: Martinus Nijhoff, 2012.

Bjørge, Eirik, *The Evolutionary Interpretation of Treaties*, Oxford: Oxford University Press, 2014.

Blok, Anton, *Honour and Violence*, Cambridge: Polity Press, 2001.

Bloxham, Donald, 'The Holocaust on Trial: Crimes Against Humanity, Justice, and the Writing of the Historical Record', in Schaller, Dominik, Boyadjian, Rupen, Berg, Vivianne, Scholtz, Hanno (eds), *Enteignet – Vertrieben – Ermordet: Beiträge zur Genozidforschung* [Dispossessed – Displaced – Murdered: Contributions to Genocide Research], Zürich: Chronos Verlag, 2004.

Blumer, Herbert, 'Race Prejudice as a Sense of Group Position', *The Pacific Sociological Review*, Volume 1, No 1, 1958, pp. 3–7.

Boas, Gideon, Bischoff, James, Reid, Natalie, *Elements of Crimes Under International Law: International Criminal Law Practitioners Library Series*, Volume II, Cambridge: Cambridge University Press, 2008.

Bobo, Lawrence, 'Foreword', in Koenig, Barbara, Lee, Sandra Soo-Jin, Richardson, Sarah (eds), *Revisiting Race in a Genomic Age*, New Brunswick: Rutgers University Press, 2008.

Boghossian, Paul, 'The Concept of Genocide', *Journal of Genocide Research*, Volume 12, No 1, 2010, pp. 69–80.

Boister, Neil, Burchill, Richard, 'The Implications of the Pinochet Decision for the Extradition or Prosecution of Former South African Heads of State for Crimes Committed Under Apartheid', African Journal of International and Comparative Law, Volume 11, 1999, pp. 619–637.

Boot, Machteld, *Genocide, Crimes Against Humanity, War Crimes:* Nullum Crimen Sine Lege *and the Subject Matter Jurisdiction of the International Criminal Court*, Antwerpen: Intersentia, 2002.

Booysen, Hercules, 'Convention on the Crime of Apartheid', South African Year Book of International Law, Volume 2, 1976, pp. 56–96.

Bowen, John, 'The Myth of Global Ethnic Conflict', in Hinton, Alexander Laban (ed), *Genocide: An Anthropological Reader*, Malden: Blackwell Publishers, 2002.

Bowker, Geoffrey, Star, Susan Leigh, *Sorting Things Out: Classification and Its Consequences*, Cambridge: The MIT Press, 1999.

Brady, Helen, Liss, Ryan, 'The Evolution of Persecution as a Crime against Humanity', in Bergsmo, Morten, Cheah, Wui Ling, Song,Tianying, Yi, Ping (eds), *Historical Origins of International Criminal Law: Volume 3*, Brussels: Torkel Opsahl Academic EPublisher, 2015.

Brattain, Michelle, 'Race, Racism, and Antiracism: UNESCO and the Politics of Presenting Science to the Postwar Public', *American Historical Review*, December 2007, pp. 1386–1413.

Brown, Chester, *A Common Law of International Adjudication*, Oxford: Oxford University Press, 2007.

Brownlie, Ian, *Principles of Public International Law*, Oxford: Oxford University Press, 6th edn, 2003.

Brubaker Rogers, *Ethnicity Without Groups*, Cambridge: Harvard University Press, 2004.

Bruun, Lori Lyman, 'Beyond the 1948 Convention: Emerging Principles of Genocide in Customary International Law', *Maryland Journal of International Law and Trade*, Volume 17, 1993, pp. 193–226.

Buergenthal, Thomas, Shelton, Dinah, Stewart, David, *International Human Rights – In a Nutshell*, St. Paul: West Group, 3rd edn, 2002.

Bultz, Ariel, 'Redefining Apartheid in International Criminal Law', *Criminal Law Forum* Volume 24, 2013, pp. 205–233.

Butcher, Goler Teal, 'Legal Consequences for States of the Illegality of Apartheid', *Human Rights Quarterly*, Volume 8, 1986, pp. 404–442.

Byamukama, Shivon, Kapranos Huntley, John, 'Criminal Justice in the Aftermath of the 1994 Rwanda Genocide', in Henham, Ralph, Behrens, Paul (eds), *The Criminal Law of Genocide: International, Comparative and Contextual Aspects*, Aldershot: Ashgate, 2007.

Byron, Christine, *War Crimes and Crimes against Humanity in the Rome Statute of the International Criminal Court*, Manchester: Manchester University Press, 2009.

Calvo-Goller, Karin, *The Trial Proceedings of the International Criminal Court: ICTY and ICTR Precedents*, Leiden: Martinus Nijhoff, 2006.

Campbell, Bradley, *The Geometry of Genocide: A Study in Pure Sociology*, Charlottesville: University of Virginia Press, 2015.

Carlton, Eric, *War and Ideology*, London: Routledge, 1990.

Carney, Amy, 'Preserving the "Master Race": SS Reproductive and Family Policies during the Second World War', in Weiss-Wendt, Anton, Yeomans, Rory (eds), *Racial Science in Hitler's New Europe, 1938–1945*, Lincoln: University of Nebraska Press, 2013.

Cashmore, Ellis, 'Apartheid', in Cashmore, Ellis (ed), *Dictionary of Race and Ethnic Relations*, London: Routledge, 3rd edn, 1994.

———, 'Ethnicity', in Cashmore, Ellis (ed), *Dictionary of Race and Ethnic Relations*, London: Routledge, 3rd edn, 1994.

———, 'Race', in Cashmore, Ellis (ed), *Dictionary of Race and Ethnic Relations*, London: Routledge, 3rd edn, 1994.

Cassese, Antonio, 'Crimes against Humanity', in Cassese, Antonio, Gaeta, Paola, Jones, John (eds), *The Rome Statute of the International Criminal Court: A Commentary*, Oxford: Oxford University Press, 2002.

———, *International Criminal Law*, Oxford: Oxford University Press, 2nd edn, 2008.

Cassese, Antonio, Gaeta, Paola, et al., *Cassese's International Criminal Law*, Oxford: Oxford University Press, 3rd edn, 2013.

Chalk, Frank, Jonassohn, Kurt, *The History and Sociology of Genocide: Analyses and Case Studies*, New Haven: Yale University Press, 1990.

Chaumont, Jean-Michel, *Die Konkurrenz der Opfer: Genozid, Identität und Anerkennung* [The Concurrence of the Victims: Genocide, Identity, and Recognition], Lüneburg: zu Klampen Verlag, 2001.

Chesterman, Simon, 'An Altogether Different Order: Defining the Elements of Crimes against Humanity', *Duke Journal of Comparative and International Law*, Volume 10, No 2, 2000, pp. 307–345.

Christensen, Claus Bundgård, Poulsen, Niels Bo, Smith, Peter Scharff, Waffen-SS: *Europas Nazistiske Soldater* [Waffen-SS: Europe's Nazi Soldiers], København: Gyldendal, 2015.

Churchill, Winston, *The World Crisis: The Aftermath*, London: Thornton Butterworth, 1929.

Ciorciari, John, '"Auto-Genocide" and the Cambodian Reign of Terror', in Schaller, Dominik, Boyadjian, Rupen, Berg, Vivianne, Scholtz, Hanno (eds), *Enteignet – Vertrieben – Ermordet: Beiträge zur Genozidforschung* [Dispossessed – Displaced – Murdered: Contributions to Genocide Research], Zürich: Chronos Verlag, 2004.

Clark, Janine Natalya, 'Elucidating the *Dolus Specialis*: An Analysis of ICTY Jurisprudence on Genocidal Intent', *Criminal Law Forum*, Volume 26, 2015, pp. 497–531.

Clark, Roger S., 'Apartheid', in Bassiouni, M. Cherif (ed), *International Criminal Law, Volume I: Sources, Subjects, and Contents*, Leiden: Martinus Nijhoff, 3rd edn, 2008.

———, 'Crimes against Humanity and the Rome Statute of the International Criminal Court', in Politi, Mauro, Nesi, Giuseppe (eds), *The Rome Statute of the International Criminal Court – A Challenge to Impunity*, Aldershot: Ashgate, 2001.

Coleman, Max (ed), *A Crime against Humanity – Analysing the Repression of the Apartheid State*, Johannesburg: Human Rights Committee of South Africa, 1998.

Confino, Alon, *A World Without Jews: The Nazi Imagination from Persecution to Genocide*, New Haven: Yale University Press, 2014.

Cornell, Stephen, Hartmann, Douglas, 'Conceptual Confusions and Divides: Race, Ethnicity, and the Study of Immigration', in Foner, Nancy, Fredrickson, George (eds), *Not Just Black and White: Historical and Contemporary Perspectives on Immigration, Race, and Ethnicity in the United States*, New York: Russell Sage, 2004.

———, *Ethnicity and Race: Making Identities in a Changing World*, Thousand Oaks: Pine Forge Press, 1998.

Cosmides, Leda, Tooby, John, Kurzban, Robert, 'Perceptions of Race', *Trends in Cognitive Sciences*, Volume 7, No 4, 2003, pp. 173–179.

Criddle, Evan, Fox-Decent, Evan, 'A Fiduciary Theory of *Jus Cogens*', *Yale Journal of International Law*, Volume 34, 2009, pp. 331–387.

Crowe, David, *War Crimes, Genocide, and Justice*, New York: Palgrave Macmillan, 2014.

Cryer, Robert, *Prosecuting International Crimes – Selectivity and the International Criminal Law Regime*, Cambridge: Cambridge University Press, 2005.

Cryer, Robert, Friman, Håkan, Robinson, Darryl, Wilmshurst, Elizabeth, *An Introduction to International Criminal Law and Procedure*, Cambridge: Cambridge University Press, 2nd edn, 2010 (Cryer, 2010).

Cupido, Marjolein, 'The Contextual Embedding of Genocide: A Casuistic Analysis of the Interplay Between Law and Facts', *Melbourne Journal of International Law*, Volume 15, 2014, pp. 378–413.

Dahlberg, Gunnar, *Race, Reason and Rubbish: An Examination of the Biological Credentials of the Nazi Creed*, London: Unwin Brothers Ltd., 1942.

d'Aspremont, Jean, *Formalism and the Sources of International Law*, Oxford: Oxford University Press, 2011.

Davis, David Brion, 'Constructing Race: A Reflection', *The William and Mary Quarterly: A Magazine of Early American History and Culture*, Volume 54, No 1, 1997, pp. 7–18.

Dawidowicz, Lucy, *The War Against the Jews: 1933-1945*, New York: Bantam Books, 1975.

deGuzman, Margaret McAuliffe, 'The Road from Rome: The Developing Law of Crimes against Humanity', *Human Rights Quarterly*, Volume 22, 2000, pp. 335–403.

Demko, Daniela, 'Die von der Genozidkonvention geschützten "Gruppen" als Regelungsgegenstand des "Specific Intent"' [The Protected "Groups" of the Genocide Convention as Subject Matter of the "Specific Intent"], *Schweizerische Zeitschrift für Internationales und Europäisches Recht*, Volume 2, 2009, pp. 223–246.

Deng, Francis, 'The Challenge of Managing Identity Conflicts', in Zartman, I. William, Anstey, Mark, Meerts Paul (eds), *The Slippery Slope to Genocide*, Oxford: Oxford University Press, 2012.

Derenzo, Judith, Garcia, Michael, 'Genocide: Legal Precedent Surrounding the Definition of the Crime', *Congressional Research Service Report for Congress*, Code RL32605, 14 September 2004.

Deutsch, David, Yanay, Niza, 'The Politics of Intimacy: Nazi and Hutu Propaganda as Case Studies', *Journal of Genocide Research*, Volume 1, No 1, 2016, pp. 21–39.

de Waal, Alex, 'Genocide in Rwanda', *Anthropology Today*, Volume 10, No 3, June 1994, pp. 1–2.

———, 'Group Identity, Rationality, and the State', *Critical Review*, Volume 11, No 2, Spring 1997, pp. 279–289.

———, 'Reflections on the Difficulties of Defining Darfur's Crisis as Genocide', *Harvard Human Rights Journal*, Volume 20, 2007, pp. 25–33.

Djeffal, Christian, *Static and Evolutive Treaty Interpretation: A Functional Reconstruction*, Cambridge: Cambridge University Press, 2016.

Drost, Pieter, *The Crime of State: Penal Protection for Fundamental Freedoms of Persons and Peoples, Book II: Genocide: United Nations Legislation on International Criminal Law*, Leyden: A.W. Sythoff, 1959.

Drumbl, Mark, *Atrocity, Punishment, and International Law*, Cambridge: Cambridge University Press, 2007.

———, 'The Crime of Genocide', in Brown, Bartram (ed), *Research Handbook on International Criminal Law*, Cheltenham: Edward Elgar, 2011.

Dubow, Saul, 'Afrikaner Nationalism, Apartheid and the Conceptualization of 'Race'', *Journal of African History*, Volume 33, 1992, pp. 209–237.

Duedahl, Poul, UNESCO Man: Changing the Concept of Race, 1945–65, http://vbn.aau.dk/files/61248765/UNESCO_Man_Paper_Poul_Duedahl.pdf.

Dugard, John, 'International Law and the South African Constitution', *European Journal of International Law*, Volume 8, No 1, 1997, pp. 77–92.

———, 'L'Apartheid' [Apartheid], in Ascensio, Hervé, Decaux, Emmanuel, Pellet, Alain (eds), *Droit International Pénal* [International Penal Law], Paris: Editions Pedone, 2nd edn, 2012.

———, Reynolds, John, 'Apartheid, International Law, and the Occupied Palestinian Territories', *European Journal of International Law*, Volume 24, No 3, 2013, pp. 867–913.

Du Plessis, Max, 'International Criminal Law: The Crime of Apartheid Revisited', *South African Journal of Criminal Justice*, Volume 24, No 3, 2011, pp. 417–428.

Earl, Hilary, 'Legacies of the Nuremberg SS-Einsatzgruppen Trial After 70 Years', *Loyola of Los Angeles International And Comparative Law Review*, Volume 39, 2017, pp. 95–115.

———, *The Nuremberg SS-Einsatzgruppen Trial, 1945–1958: Atrocity, Law, and History*, New York: Cambridge University Press, 2009.

Eden, Paul, 'The Practices of Apartheid as a War Crime: A Critical Analysis', in Gill, Terry (ed), *Yearbook of International Humanitarian Law*, Volume 16, 2013, pp. 89–117.

———, 'The Role of the Rome Statute in the Criminalization of Apartheid', *Journal of International Criminal Justice*, Volume 12, 2014, pp. 171–191.

Elias-Bursać, Ellen, *Translating Evidence and Interpreting Testimony at a War Crimes Tribunal: Working in a Tug-of-War*, Basingstoke: Palgrave, 2015.

Eltringham, Nigel, *Accounting for Horror: Post-Genocide Debates in Rwanda*, London: Pluto Press, 2004.

———, '"Illuminating the Broader Context": Anthropological and Historical Knowledge at the International Criminal Tribunal for Rwanda', *Journal of the Royal Anthropological Institute*, Volume 19, 2013, pp. 338–355.

———, '"Invaders Who Have Stolen the Country": The Hamitic Hypothesis, Race and the Rwandan Genocide', *Social Identities: Journal for the Study of Race, Nation and Culture*, Volume 12, No 4, 2006, pp. 425–446.

Emberland, Terje, 'Pure-Blooded Vikings and Peasants – Norwegians in the Racial Ideology of the SS', in Weiss-Wendt, Anton, Yeomans, Rory (eds), *Racial Science in Hitler's New Europe, 1938–1945*, Lincoln: University of Nebraska Press, 2013.

Erasmus, Zimitri, 'Apartheid Race Categories', *Transformation*, Volume 79, 2012, pp. 1–11.

Eriksen, Thomas Hylland, *Ethnicity and Nationalism*, London: Pluto Press, 3rd edn, 2010.

Feierstein, Daniel, *Genocide as Social Practice: Reorganizing Society under the Nazis and Argentina's Military Juntas*, New Brunswick: Rutgers University Press, 2014.

Fein, Helen, 'States of Genocide and other States', in Carol Rittner, John Roth, James Smith (eds), *Will Genocide Ever End?*, St. Paul: Paragon, 2002.

Fenrick, William, 'The Crime Against Humanity of Persecution in the Jurisprudence of the ICTY', *Netherlands Yearbook of International Law*, Volume 32, 2001, pp. 81–96.

Fletscher, George, Ohlin, Jens David, 'Reclaiming Fundamental Principles of Criminal Law in the Darfur Case', *Journal of International Criminal Justice*, Volume 3, 2005, pp. 539–561.

Fluehr-Lobban, Carolyn, *Race and Racism: An Introduction*, Lanham: AltaMira Press, 2006.

Fournet, Caroline, *Genocide and Crimes against Humanity: Misconceptions and Confusion in French Law and Practice*, Oxford: Hart Publishing, 2013.

———, *International Crimes: Theories, Practice and Evolution*, London: Cameron May, 2006.

———, *The Crime of Destruction and the Law of Genocide: Their Impact on Collective Memory*, Aldershot: Ashgate, 2007.

Fournet, Caroline, Pégorier, Clotilde, 'Only One Step Away From Genocide': The Crime of Persecution in International Criminal Law', *International Criminal Law Review*, Volume 10, 2010, pp. 713–738.

Friedlander, Henry, 'Nazi Crimes and the German Law', in Stoltzfus, Nathan, Friedlander, Henry (eds), *Nazi Crimes and the Law*, Washington: Cambridge University Press, 2008.

Friedländer, Saul, *The Years of Extermination: Nazi Germany and the Jews, 1939–1945*, London: Weinfeld & Nicolson, 2007.

Fronza, Emanuela, 'Genocide in the Rome Statute', in Lattanzi, Flavia, Schabas, William (eds), *Essays on the Rome Statute of the International Criminal Court*, Ripa Fagnano Alto: il Sirente, 1999.

Fujimura, Joan, et al., 'Clines Without Classes: How to Make Sense of Human Variation', *Sociological Theory*, Volume 32, No 3, 2014, pp. 208–227.

Gallant, Kenneth, *The Principle of Legality in International and Comparative Criminal Law*, Cambridge: Cambridge University Press, 2009.

Galton, Francis, 'Hereditary Talent and Character', Second Paper, *Macmillan's Magazine*, Volume 12, 1865, pp. 318–327.

Gardiner, Richard, *Treaty Interpretation*, Oxford: Oxford University Press, 2008.

Gazzini, Tarcisio, *Interpretation of International Investment Treaties*, Oxford: Hart Publishing, 2016.

Gebhard, Julia, 'Apartheid', in Max Planck Encyclopedia of Public International Law, 2016, http://opil.ouplaw.com/view/10.1093/law:epil/9780199231690/law-9780199231690-e752?prd=EPIL.

Gellately, Robert, 'The Third Reich, the Holocaust, and Visions of Serial Genocide', in Gellately, Robert, Kiernan, Ben (eds), *The Specter of Genocide: Mass Murder in Historical Perspective*, Cambridge: Cambridge University Press, 2003.

Gilroy, Paul, *Against Race: Imagining Political Culture Beyond the Color Line*, Cambridge: Harvard University Press, 2000.

Glaser, Kurt, Possony, Stefan, *Victims of Politics: The State of Human Rights*, New York: Columbia University Press, 1979.

Gould, Stephan Jay, *The Mismeasure of Man*, London: Penguin Books, 3rd edn, 1997.

Gourevitch, Philip, *We Wish to Inform You that Tomorrow We Will Be Killed with Our Families: Stories from Rwanda*, New York: Picador, 1998.

Grady, Katy, 'The Genocide Convention's Protected Groups: A Place for Gender?', in Eboe-Osuji, Chile (ed), *Protecting Humanity: Essays in International Law and Policy in Honour of Navanethem Pillay* (2010), Leiden: Martinus Nijhoff.

Greenawalt, Alexander, 'Rethinking Genocidal Intent: The Case for a Knowledge-Based Interpretation', *Columbia Law Review*, Volume 99, 1999, pp. 2259–2294.

Greenberg, Douglas, 'Citizenship, National Identity, and Genocide', in Provost, René, Akhavan, Payam (eds), *Confronting Genocide*, Dordrecht: Springer, 2011.

Grosswald Curran, Vivian, 'Fear of Formalism: Indications from the Fascist Period in France and Germany of Judicial Methodology's Impact on Substantive Law', *Cornell International Law Journal*, Volume 35, 2001–2002, pp. 101–187.

———, 'Racism's Past and Law's Future', *Vermont Law Review*, Volume 28, 2004, pp. 683–712.

Grover, Leena, 'A Call to Arms: Fundamental Dilemmas Confronting the Interpretation of Crimes in the Rome Statute of the International Criminal Court', *European Journal of International Law*, Volume 21, No 3, 2010, pp. 543–583.

———, *Interpreting Crimes in the Rome Statute of the International Criminal Court*, Cambridge: Cambridge University Press, 2014.

Gunn, Jeremy, 'The Complexity of Religion and the Definition of "Religion" in International Law', *Harvard Human Rights Journal*, Volume 16, 2003, pp. 189–215.

Haas, François, 'German Science and Black Racism: Roots of the Nazi Holocaust', *The FASEB Journal*, Volume 22, 2008, pp. 332–337.

Hagan, John, Rymond-Richmond, Wenona, *Darfur and the Crime of Genocide*, Cambridge: Cambridge University Press, 2009.

Hall, Christopher, 'The Crime of Apartheid', in Triffterer, Otto (ed), *Commentary on the Rome Statute of the International Criminal Court: Observer's Notes, Article by Article*, München: Verlag C.H. Beck, 2nd edn, 2008.

Hall, Christopher, Ambos, Kai, 'Crimes against Humanity', in Triffterer, Otto, Ambos, Kai (eds), *The Rome Statute of the International Criminal Court: A Commentary*, München: Verlag C.H. Beck, 3rd edn, 2016.

Hall, Christopher, Powderly, Joseph, Hayes, Niamh, 'Persecution', in Triffterer, Otto, Ambos, Kai (eds), *The Rome Statute of the International Criminal Court: A Commentary*, München: Verlag C.H. Beck, 3rd edn, 2016.

Hall, Christopher, van den Herik, Larissa, 'The Crime of Apartheid', in Triffterer, Otto, Ambos, Kai (eds), *The Rome Statute of the International Criminal Court: A Commentary*, München: Verlag C.H. Beck, 3rd edn, 2016.

Hamilton, Jennifer, 'Revitalizing Difference in the HapMap: Race and Contemporary Human Genetic Variation Research', *Journal of Law, Medicine and Ethics*, 2008, pp. 471–477.

Haque, Adil Ahmad, 'Group Violence and Group Vengeance: Toward a Retributive Theory of International Criminal Law', *Buffalo Criminal Law Review*, Volume 9, 2005, pp. 273–328.

Hardin, Russell, *One for All: The Logic of Group Conflict*, Princeton: Princeton University Press, 1995.

Haslam, Nick, Bastian, Brock, Laham, Simon, Loughnan, Stephen, 'Humanness, Dehumanization, and Moral Psychology', in Mario Mikulincer and Phillip Shaver (eds), *The Social Psychology of Morality: Exploring the Causes of Good and Evil*, American Psychological Association, 2012.

Hayden, Robert, 'Imagined Communities and Real Victims: Self-Determination and Ethnic Cleansing in Yugoslavia', in Hinton, Alexander Laban (ed), *Genocide: An Anthropological Reader*, Malden: Blackwell Publishers, 2002.

Heideman, Richard, 'Legalizing Hate: The Significance of the Nuremberg Laws and the Post-War Nuremberg Trials', *Loyola of Los Angeles International and Comparative Law Review*, Volume 39, 2017, pp. 5–24.

Heinemann, Isabel, 'Defining "(Un)Wanted Population Addition": Anthropology, Racial Ideology, and Mass Murder in the Occupied East', in Weiss-Wendt, Anton, Yeomans, Rory (eds), *Racial Science in Hitler's New Europe, 1938–1945*, Lincoln: University of Nebraska Press, 2013.

Helmersen, Sondre Torp, 'Evolutive Treaty Interpretation: Legality, Semantics and Distinctions', *European Journal of Legal Studies*, Volume 6, 2013, pp. 127–148.

Henckaerts, Jean-Marie, Doswald-Beck, Louise, *Customary International Humanitarian Law, Volume I: Rules*, Cambridge: Cambridge University Press, 2005.

———, *Customary International Humanitarian Law, Volume II: Practice*, Cambridge: Cambridge University Press, 2005.

Hiebert, Maureen, *Constructing Genocide and Mass Violence: Society, Crisis, Identity*, Abingdon: Routledge, 2017.

———, 'The Three "Switches" of Identity Construction in Genocide: The Nazi Final Solution and the Cambodian Killing Fields', *Genocide Studies and Prevention: An International Journal*, Volume 3, No 1, 2008, pp. 5–29.

Hintjens, Helen, 'When Identity Becomes a Knife: Reflecting on the Genocide in Rwanda', *Ethnicities*, Volume 1, No 1, 2001, pp. 25–55.

Hinton, Alexander Laban, 'Genocide and Anthropology: Introduction', in Laban Hinton, Alexander (ed), *Genocide: An Anthropological Reader*, Malden: Blackwell Publishers, 2002.

———, 'The Dark Side of Modernity: Toward an Anthropology of Genocide', in Hinton, Alexander Laban (ed), *Annihilating Difference: The Anthropology of Genocide*, Berkeley: University of California Press, 2002.

Hirschfeld, Lawrence, *Race in the Making: Cognition, Culture, and the Child's Construction of Human Kinds*, Cambridge: Massachusetts Institute of Technology, 1996.

Hitler, Adolf, *Mein Kampf* [My Struggle], München: Verlag Franz Eher Nachfolger, 13th edn, 1932.

Hoffman, Sharona, 'Is There a Place for "Race" as a Legal Concept?', *Arizona State Law Journal*, Volume 36, 2004, pp. 1093–1159.

Holá, Barbora, Smeulers, Alette, 'Rwanda and the ICTR: Facts and Figures', in de Brouwer, Ann-Marie, Smeulers, Alette (eds), *The Elgar Companion to the International Criminal Tribunal for Rwanda*, Cheltenham: Edward Elgar, 2016.

Holslag, Anthonie, 'The Process of Othering from the "Social Imaginaire" to Physical Acts: An Anthropological Approach', *Genocide Studies and Prevention: An International Journal*, Volume 9, No 1, 2015, pp. 96–113.

Howard, Erica, 'Race and Racism – Why does European Law have Difficulties with Definitions?', *International Journal of Comparative Labour Law and Industrial Relations*, Volume 24, No 1, 2008, pp. 5–29.

Huttenbach, Henry, 'Locating the Holocaust on the Genocide Spectrum: Towards a Methodology of Definition and Categorization', *Holocaust and Genocide Studies*, Volume 3, No 3, 1988, pp. 289–303.

Jackson, Jesse, 'Deportation of Armenians', Letter to Henry Morgenthau, American Ambassador in Constantinople, Document No Aleppo 333 (3 August 1915), US State Dept. Index No 867.4016/126, in Sarafian, Ara (compiler), *United States Official Documents on the Armenian Genocide, Volume I: The Lower Euphrates*, Watertown: Armenian Review, 1993.

Jacobs, Dov, 'Positivism and International Criminal Law: The Principle of Legality as a Rule of Conflict of Theories', in d'Aspremont, Jean, Kammerhofer, Jörg (eds), *International Legal Positivism in a Post-Modern World*, Cambridge: Cambridge University Press, 2014.

Jallow, Hassan Bubacar, The ICTR's Elaboration of the Core International Crimes of Genocide, Crimes against Humanity and War Crimes and Modes of Liability, in de Brouwer, Ann-Marie, Smeulers, Alette (eds), *The Elgar Companion to the International Criminal Tribunal for Rwanda*, Cheltenham: Edward Elgar, 2016.

Jarvis, Helen, 'Trials and Tribulations: The Long Quest for Justice for the Cambodian Genocide', in Meisenberg, Simon, Stegmiller, Ignaz (eds), *The Extraordinary Chambers in the Courts of Cambodia: Assessing Their Contribution to International Criminal Law*, The Hague: TMC Asser Press, 2016.

Jarvis, Michelle, Tieger, Alan, 'Applying the Genocide Convention at the ICTY: The Influence of Paradigms Past', *Journal of International Criminal Justice*, Volume 14, 2016, pp. 857–877.

Jaynes, Gerald, 'Immigration and the Social Construction of Otherness: "Underclass" Stigma and Intergroup Relations', in Foner, Nancy, Fredrickson, George (eds), *Not Just Black and White: Historical and Contemporary Perspectives on Immigration, Race, and Ethnicity in the United States*, New York: Russell Sage, 2004.

Jenkins, Richard, *Rethinking Ethnicity*, London: Sage Publications, 2nd edn, 2008.

Jones, Adam, *Genocide: A Comprehensive Introduction*, Abingdon: Routledge, 2nd edn, 2011.

———, *The Scourge of Genocide*, Abingdon: Routledge, 2013.

Jones, Annika, 'Insights Into an Emerging Relationship: Use of Human Rights Jurisprudence at the International Criminal Court', *Human Rights Law Review*, Volume 16, 2016, pp. 701–729.

Jones, John RWD, '"Whose Intent is it Anyway?" Genocide and the Intent to Destroy a Group', in Vohrah, Lal Chand *et al.* (eds), *Man's Inhumanity to Man: Essays on International Law in Honour of Antonio Cassese*, The Hague: Kluwer Law International, 2003.

Jones, John RWD, Powles, Steven, *International Criminal Practice: The International Criminal Tribunal for the Former Yugoslavia, The International Criminal Tribunal for Rwanda, The International Criminal Court, The Special Court of Sierra Leone, The East Timor Special Panels for Serious Crimes, War Crimes Prosecutions in Kosovo*, Oxford: Oxford University Press, 3rd edn, 2003.

Jørgensen, Nina, 'The Definition of Genocide: Joining the Dots in the Light of Recent Practice', *International Criminal Law Review*, Volume 1, Nos 3–4, 2001, pp. 285–313.

Kahn, Jonathan, 'The Troubling Persistence of Race in Pharmagenomics', *Journal of Law, Medicine and Ethics*, Volume 40, 2012, pp. 873–885.

Kälin, Walter, Künzli, Jörg, *The Law of International Human Rights Protection*, Oxford: Oxford University Press, 2009.

Kattan, Victor, *The Russell Tribunal on Palestine and the Question of Apartheid*, al-Shabaka Policy Brief, November 2011.

Kielsgard, Mark, *Responding to Modern Genocide: At the Confluence of Law and Politics*, Abingdon: Routledge, 2016.

Kiernan, Ben, *Blood and Soil: A World History of Genocide and Extermination from Sparta to Darfur*, New Haven: Yale University Press, 2007.

———, *The Pol Pot Regime: Race, Power, and Genocide in Cambodia under the Khmer Rouge, 1975–79*, New Haven: Yale University Press, 1996.

———, 'Twentieth-Century Genocides: Underlying Ideological Themes from Armenia to East Timor', in Gellately, Robert, Kiernan, Ben (eds), *The Specter of Genocide: Mass Murder in Historical Perspective*, Cambridge: Cambridge University Press, 2003.

King, Henry Jr., 'Genocide and Nuremberg', in Henham, Ralph, Behrens, Paul (eds), *The Criminal Law of Genocide: International, Comparative and Contextual Aspects*, Aldershot: Ashgate, 2007.

Kirsch, Stefan, 'The Social and the Legal Concept of Genocide', in Behrens, Paul, Henham, Ralph (eds), *Elements of Genocide*, Abingdon: Routledge, 2013.

———, 'The Two Notions of Genocide: Distinguishing Macro Phenomena and Individual Misconduct', *Creighton Law Review*, Volume 42, 2008–2009, pp. 347–360.

Kittichaisaree, Kriangsak, *International Criminal Law*, Oxford: Oxford University Press, 2001.

Klann, Helen, McKenzie, Phillipa, *Judge Laïty Kama: Five Cases to Develop International Criminal Law*, in Decaux, Emmanuel, Dieng, Adama, Sow, Malick (eds), *From Human Rights to International Criminal Law: Studies in Honour of an African Jurist, the Late Judge Laïty Kama*, Leiden: Martinus Nijhoff, 2007.

Knoops, Geert-Jan Alexander, Mens Rea *at the International Criminal Court*, Leiden: Brill Nijhoff, 2017.

Koenig, Barbara, Lee, Sandra Soo-Jin, Richardson, Sarah, 'Introduction', in Koenig, Barbara, Lee, Sandra Soo-Jin, Richardson, Sarah (eds), *Revisiting Race in a Genomic Age*, New Brunswick: Rutgers, 2008.

Kolb, Robert, 'The Jurisprudence of the Yugoslav and Rwandan Criminal Tribunals on Their Jurisdiction and on International Crimes (2004–2013)', *British Yearbook of International Law*, Volume 84, No 1, 2014, pp. 131–186.

Koskenniemi, Martti, 'Race, Hierarchy and International Law: Lorimer's Legal Science', *European Journal of International Law*, Volume 27, No 2, 2016, pp. 415–429 (Koskenniemi, 2016).

Koursami, Nasour, *The 'Contextual Elements' of the Crime of Genocide*, Berlin: Springer, 2018.

Kress, Claus, 'The Crime of Genocide Under International Law', *International Criminal Law Review*, No 6, 2006, pp. 461–502.

———, 'The Darfur Report and Genocidal Intent', *Journal of International Criminal Justice*, Volume 3, 2005, pp. 562–578.

———, 'The ICC's First Encounter with the Crime of Genocide: The Case against Al Bashir', in Stahn, Carsten (ed), *The Law and Practice of the International Criminal Court*, Oxford: Oxford University Press, 2015.

Krzan, Bartłomiej, 'Human Rights and International Criminal Law', in Krzan, Bartłomiej (ed), *Prosecuting International Crimes: A Multidisciplinary Approach*, Leiden: Brill Nijhoff, 2016.

Kyllingstad, Jon Røyne, *Kortskaller og Langskaller: Fysisk Antropologi i Norge og Striden om det Nordiske Herremennesket* [Short-sculls and Long-sculls: Physical Anthropology in Scandinavia and the Debate about the Nordic Master Race], Oslo: Scandinavian Academic Press, 2004.

Lauterpacht, Hersch, 'Restrictive Interpretation and the Principle of Effectiveness in the Interpretation of Treaties', *British Yearbook of International Law*, 1949, pp. 48–85.

LeBlanc, Lawrence, 'The United Nations Genocide Convention and Political Groups: Should the United States Propose an Amendment?', *Yale Journal of International Law*, Volume 13, 1988, pp. 268–295.

Lee, Roy, 'The Rome Conference and its Contribution to International Law', in Lee, Roy S. (ed), *The International Criminal Court – The Making of the Rome Statute; Issues, Negotiations, Results*, The Hague: Kluwer Law International, 1999.

Lemkin, Raphael, *Axis Rule in Occupied Europe: Laws of Occupation, Analysis of Government, Proposals for Redress*, Washington: Carnegie Endowment for International Peace, Division of International Law, 1944.

———, 'Genocide as a Crime under International Law', *American Journal of International Law*, Volume 41, 1947, pp. 145–151.

Lerner, Natan, *Group Rights and Discrimination in International Law*, The Hague: Martinus Nijhoff, 2nd edn, 2003.

———, 'New Concepts in the UNESCO Declaration on Race and Racial Prejudice', *Human Rights Quarterly*, Volume 3, No 1, 1981, pp. 48–61.

———, *The UN Convention on the Elimination of all Forms of Racial Discrimination*, Leiden: Brill Nijhoff, 1980/2015 (revised reprint).

Levene, Mark, 'A Twentieth-Century Phenomenon?', in Rittner, Carol, Roth, John, Smith, James (eds), *Will Genocide Ever End?*, St. Paul: Paragon, 2002.

Levy, Guillermo, 'Considerations on the Connections between Race, Politics, Economics, and Genocide', *Journal of Genocide Research*, Volume 8, No 2, 2006, pp. 137–148.

Lingaas, Carola, *The Concept of Race*, unpublished PhD thesis, University of Oslo, 2017.

———, 'The Crime against Humanity of Apartheid in a Post-Apartheid World', *Oslo Law Review*, Volume 2, No 2, 2015, pp. 86–115.

———, 'Defining the Protected Groups of Genocide through the Case Law of International Courts', *International Crimes Database Brief*, 2015 (Lingaas, 2015a), www.internationalcrimesdatabase.org/upload/documents/20151217T122733-Lingaas%20Final%20ICD%20Format.pdf.

———, 'Enhancing the Effectiveness of the Law of Genocide', in Nicholson, Joanna (ed), *Strengthening the Validity of International Criminal Tribunals*, Leiden: Brill Nijhoff, 2018.

———, 'Imagined Identities: Defining the Racial Group in the Crime of Genocide', *Genocide Studies and Prevention: An International Journal*, Volume 10, No 1, Article 9, 2016, pp. 79–106.

Lippman, Matthew, 'A Road Map to the 1948 Convention on the Prevention and Punishment of the Crime of Genocide', *Journal of Genocide Research*, Volume 4, No 2, 2002, pp. 177–195.

———, 'Genocide', in Bassiouni, M. Cherif (ed), *International Criminal Law, Volume I: Sources, Subjects, and Contents*, Leiden: Martinus Nijhoff, 3rd edn, 2008.

———, 'Genocide: The Crime of the Century. The Jurisprudence of Death at the Dawn of the New Millennium', *Houston Journal of International Law*, Volume 23, 2000–2001, pp. 467–535.

Lisson, David, 'Defining 'National Group' in the Genocide Convention: A Case Study of Timor-Leste', *Stanford Law Review*, Volume 60, March 2008, pp. 1459–1496.

Livingston, Michael, *The Fascists and the Jews of Italy: Mussolini's Race Laws, 1938–1943*, Cambridge: Cambridge University Press, 2013.

López, Ian Haney, *White by Law: The Legal Construction of Race*, New York: New York University Press, 2006.

Lopez, Julia Costa, 'Beyond Eurocentrism and Orientalism: Revisiting the Othering of Jews and Muslims Through Medieval Canon Law', *Review of International Studies*, Volume 42, No 3, 2016.

Luban, David, 'Calling Genocide by Its Rightful Name: Lemkin's Word, Darfur, and the UN Report', *Chicago Journal of International Law*, Volume 7, No 1, 2006–2007, pp. 303–320.

Lüders, Barbara, *Die Strafbarkeit von Völkermord nach dem Römischen Statut für den Internationalen Strafgerichtshof* [The Criminal Liability for Genocide in the Rome Statute of the International Criminal Court], Berlin: Berliner Wissenschafts-Verlag, 2004.

Luke, Carmen, Carrington, Vicki, 'Race Matters', *Journal of Intercultural Studies*, Volume 21, No 1, 2000, pp. 5–24.

Magnarella, Paul, 'Recent Developments in the International Law of Genocide: An Anthropological Perspective on the International Criminal Tribunal for Rwanda', in Hinton, Alexander Laban (ed), *Annihilating Difference: The Anthropology of Genocide*, Berkeley: University of California Press, 2002.

Marks, Jonathan, 'Race: Past, Present, and Future', in Koenig, Barbara, Soo-Jin Lee, Sandra, Richardson, Sarah (eds), *Revisiting Race in a Genomic Age*, New Brunswick: Rutgers University Press, 2008, pp. 21–38.

———, 'Solving the Riddle of Race', *Studies in History and Philosophy of Biological and Biomedical Sciences*, Volume 59, 2016, pp. 161–164.

Marrus, Michael, 'Hitler's Antisemitism', in Chalk, Frank, Jonassohn, Kurt (eds), *The History and Sociology of Genocide*, New Haven, Yale University Press, 1990.

Martin, Fanny, 'The Notion of 'Protected Group' in the Genocide Convention and Its Application', in Gaeta, Paola (ed), *The UN Genocide Convention: A Commentary*, Oxford: Oxford University Press, 2009.

May, Larry, *Genocide: A Normative Account*, Cambridge: Cambridge University Press, 2010.

———, 'Identifying Groups in Genocide Cases', in May, Larry, Hoskins, Zachary (eds), *International Criminal Law and Philosophy*, Cambridge: Cambridge University Press, 2010.

May, Richard, Wierda, Marieke, 'Is There a Hierarchy of Crimes in International Law?', in Vohrah, Lal Chand *et al.* (eds), *Man's Inhumanity to Man: Essays on International Law in Honour of Antonio Cassese*, The Hague: Kluwer Law International, 2003.

May, Werner, *Deutscher Nationalkatechismus: Dem jungen Deutschen in Schule und Beruf* [German National Catechism: For the Young German in School and Profession], Breslau: Heinrich Handels Verlag, 2nd edn, 1934.

Maylam, Paul, *South Africa's Racial Past: The History and Historiography of Racism, Segregation, and Apartheid*, Aldershot: Ashgate, 2001.

Mayroz, Eyal, 'Genocide: To Prevent and Punish "Radical Evil"', in Kastner, Philipp (ed) *International Criminal Law in Context*, Abingdon: Routledge, 2018.

McCormack, Timothy, 'Crimes Against Humanity', in McGoldrick, Dominic, Rowe, Peter, Donnelly, Eric (eds), *The Permanent International Criminal Court: Legal and Policy Issues*, Oxford: Hart Publishing, 2004.

McCormack, Timothy, Simpson, Gerry, 'The International Law Commission's Draft Code of Crimes against the Peace and Security of Mankind: An Appraisal of the Substantive Provisions', *Criminal Law Forum*, Volume 5, No 1, 1994, pp. 1–55.

McDermott, Yvonne, 'The Influence of International Human Rights Law on International Criminal Procedure', in Philipp Kastner (ed), *International Criminal Law in Context*, Abingdon: Routledge, 2018.

McDougal, Myres, Lasswell, Harold, Chen, Lung-chu, *Human Rights and World Public Order: The Basic Policies of an International Law of Human Dignity*, New Haven: Yale University Press, 1980.

McDougal, Myres, Lasswell, Harold, Miller, James, *The Interpretation of Agreements and World Public Order: Principles of Content and Procedure*, New Haven: Yale University Press, 1967.

Merkouris, Panos, *Article 31(3)(c) VCLT and the Principle of Systemic Integration: Normative Shadows in Plato's Cave*, Leiden: Brill Nijhoff, 2015.

Merrills, J.G., 'Two Approaches to Treaty Interpretation', *Australian Yearbook of International Law*, 1968–1969, pp. 55–82.

Mettraux, Guénaël, *International Crimes and the* ad hoc *Tribunals*, Oxford: Oxford University Press, 2005.

Miller, Richard, 'The Convention on the Non-Applicability of Statutory Limitations to War Crimes and Crimes against Humanity', *American Journal of International Law*, Volume 65, 1971, pp. 476–501.

Monageng, Sanji Mmasenono, Heinze, Alexander, 'The Rome Statute and Universal Human Rights', in Ankumah, Evelyn (ed), *The International Criminal Court and Africa: One Decade On*, Cambridge: Intersentia, 2016.

Moshman, David, 'Us and Them: Identity and Genocide', *Identity: An International Journal of Theory and Research*, Volume 7, No 2, 2007, pp. 115–135.

Mugwanya, George William, *The Crime of Genocide in International Law: Appraising the Contribution of the UN Tribunal for Rwanda*, London: Cameron May, 2007.

Müller-Wille, Staffan, 'Race and History: Comments from an Epistemological Point of View', *Science, Technology and Human Values*, Volume 39, No 4, 2014, pp. 597–606.

Murray, Alexander, 'Does International Criminal Law Still Require a 'Crime of Crimes'? A Comparative Review of Genocide and Crimes against Humanity', *Goettingen Journal of International Law*, Volume 3, No 2, 2011, pp. 589–615.

Nagan, Winston, Rodin, Vivile, 'Racism, Genocide, and Mass Murder: Towards a Legal Theory about Group Deprivations', *National Black Law Journal*, Volume 17, 2004, pp. 133–221.

Nerlich, Volker, *Apartheidskriminalität vor Gericht* [Apartheid Criminality in Court], Berlin: Berlin Verlag, 2002.

Nersessian, David, 'Comparative Approaches to Punishing Hate: The Intersection of Genocide and Crimes Against Humanity', *Stanford Journal of International Law*, Volume 43, 2007, pp. 221–264.

———, 'The Contours of Genocidal Intent: Troubling Jurisprudence from the International Criminal Tribunals', *Texas International Law Journal*, Volume 37, 2002, pp. 231–276.

———, *Genocide and Political Groups*, Oxford: Oxford University Press, 2010.

———, 'The Razor's Edge: Defining and Protecting Human Groups Under the Genocide Convention', *Cornell International Law Journal*, Volume 36, 2003, pp. 293–327.

Nilsson, Jonas, 'The Crime of Persecution in the ICTY Case-law', in Swart, Bert, Zahar, Alexander, Sluiter, Göran (eds), *The Legacy of the International Criminal Tribunal for the Former Yugoslavia*, Oxford: Oxford University Press, 2011.

Ntanda Nsereko, Daniel, 'Genocide: A Crime against Mankind', in Kirk McDonald, Gabrielle, Swaak-Goldman, Olivia (eds), *Substantive and Procedural Aspects of International Criminal Law: The Experience of International and National Courts, Volume I*, The Hague: Kluwer Law International, 2000.

Nystuen, Gro, *Achieving Peace or Protecting Human Rights? Conflicts Between Norms Regarding Ethnic Discrimination in the Dayton Peace Agreement*, Leiden: Martinus Nijhoff, 2005.

O'Keefe, Roger, *International Criminal Law*, Oxford: Oxford University Press, 2015.

Omond, Roger, *The Apartheid Handbook*, Harmondsworth: Penguin Books, 2nd ed 1986.

Oosterveld, Valerie, 'Crimes against Humanity', in de Brouwer, Ann-Marie, Smeulers, Alette (eds), *The Elgar Companion to the International Criminal Tribunal for Rwanda*, Cheltenham: Edward Elgar, 2016.

Osborn, Frederick, 'Races and the Future of Man', in Osborne, Richard (ed), *The Biological and Social Meaning of Race*, San Francisco: W.H. Freeman & Co., 1971.

Osborne, Richard, 'The History and Nature of Race Classification', in Osborne, Richard (ed), *The Biological and Social Meaning of Race*, San Francisco: W.H. Freeman & Co., 1971.

Parker, Karen, Neylon, Lyn Beth, '*Jus Cogens*: Compelling the Law of Human Rights', *Hastings International and Comparative Law Review*, Volume 12, 1988–1989, pp. 411–463.

Paul, Angela, *Kritische Analyse und Reformvorschlag zu Art. II Genozidkonvention* [Critical Analysis and Suggestions for Reforms of Art. II Genocide Convention], Berlin: Springer Verlag, 2008.

Pictet, Jean, et al., *Commentary on the Additional Protocols of 8 June 1977 to the Geneva Conventions of 12 August 1949*, Leiden: Martinus Nijhoff, 1987.

Pocar, Fausto, 'Persecution as a Crime Under International Criminal Law', *Journal of National Security Law and Policy*, Volume 2, 2008, pp. 355–365.

Porter, Jack Nusan, 'What is Genocide? Notes Towards a Definition', in Porter, Jack Nusan (ed), *Genocide and Human Rights: A Global Anthology*, Lanham: University Press of America, 1982.

Powell, John, Menendian, Stephen, 'The Problem of Othering: Towards Inclusiveness and Belonging', *Othering & Belonging*, No 1, Summer 2016, pp. 14–39.

Proctor, Robert, 'From *Anthropologie* to *Rassenkunde* in the German Anthropological Tradition', in Stocking, George (ed), *Bones, Bodies, Behavior: Essays on Biological Anthropology*, Madison: University of Wisconsin Press, 1988.

———, 'Nazi Doctor, Racial Medicine, and Human Experimentation', in Annas, George, Grodin, Michael (eds), *The Nazi Doctors and the Nuremberg Code: Human Rights in Human Experimentation*, New York: Oxford University Press, 1992.

Prunier, Gérard, *The Rwandan Crisis: History of a Genocide*, London: Hurst & Company, 1997.

Quayle, Peter, 'Unimaginable Evil: The Legislative Limitations of the Genocide Convention', *International Criminal Law Review*, Volume 5, 2005, pp. 363–372.

Quigley, John, *The Genocide Convention: An International Law Analysis*, Aldershot: Ashgate, 2006.

Quillian Lincoln, 'Prejudice as a Response to Perceived Group Threat: Population Composition and Anti-Immigrant and Racial Prejudice in Europe', *American Sociological Review,* Volume 60, 1995, pp. 586–611.

Rafter, Nicole, *The Crime of All Crimes: Toward a Criminology of Genocide*, New York: New York University Press, 2016.

Rapley, Mark, '"How to do X without doing Y": Accomplishing Discrimination without "Being Racist" – "Doing Equity"', in Augoustinos, Martha, Reynolds, Katherine (eds), *Understanding Prejudice, Racism, and Social Conflict*, London: Sage Publications, 2001.

Ratner, Steven R., Abrams, Jason S., *Accountability for Human Rights Atrocities in International Law: Beyond the Nuremberg Legacy*, Oxford: Oxford University Press, 2nd edn, 2001.

Ratner, Steven R., Abrams, Jason S., Bischoff, James L., *Accountability for Human Rights Atrocities in International Law: Beyond the Nuremberg Legacy*, Oxford: Oxford University Press, 3rd edn, 2009.

Reydams, Luc, *Universal Jurisdiction: International and Municipal Legal Perspectives*, Oxford: Oxford University Press, 2003, reprinted 2005.

Reynaud-Paligot, Carole, 'Construction and Circulation of the Notion of 'Race' in the Nineteenth Century', in Bancel, Nicolas, David, Thomas, Thomas, Dominic (eds), *The Invention of Race: Scientific and Popular Representations*, Abingdon: Routledge, 2014.

Reynolds, John, 'Third World Approaches to International Law and the Ghosts of Apartheid', in Keane, David, McDermott, Yvonne (eds), *The Challenge of Human Rights: Past, Present and Future*, Cheltenham: Edward Elgar, 2012.

Rich, Paul, 'South Africa', in Sigler, Jay (ed), *International Handbook on Race and Race Relations*, New York: Greenwood Press, 1987.

Roberts, Ken, The Law of Persecution Before the International Criminal Tribunal for the Former Yugoslavia, *Leiden Journal of International Law*, Volume 15, 2002, pp. 623–639.

———, 'Striving for Definition: The Law of Persecution from Its Origins to the ICTY', in Abtahi, Hirad, Boas, Gideon (eds), *The Dynamics of International Criminal Justice: Essays in Honour of Sir Richard May*, Leiden: Brill Nijhoff, 2006, pp. 257–299.

Robertson, Geoffrey, *Crimes Against Humanity: The Struggle for Global Justice*, London: Penguin Books, 3rd edn, 2006.

Robinson, Darryl, 'The Identity Crisis of International Criminal Law', *Leiden Journal of International Law*, Volume 21, No 4, 2008, pp. 925–963.

Robinson, Darryl, MacNeil, Gillian, 'The Tribunals and the Renaissance of International Criminal Law: Three Themes', *American Journal of International Law*, Volume 110, No 2, 2016, pp. 191–211.

Romero-Trillo, Jesús, 'The Identity Narratives', in Zartman, I. William, Anstey, Mark, Meerts, Paul (eds), *The Slippery Slope to Genocide*, Oxford: Oxford University Press, 2012.

Roth, Paul, 'The Politics of Definition', in Rittner, Carol, Roth, John, Smith, James (eds), *Will Genocide Ever End?*, St. Paul: Paragon, 2002.

Rothenberg, Daniel, '"Let Justice Judge": An Interview with Judge Baltasar Garzón and Analysis of His Ideas', *Human Rights Quarterly*, Volume 24, 2002, pp. 924–973.

Sadat, Leila Nadya, 'Crimes Against Humanity in the Modern Age', *The American Journal of International Law*, Volume 107, 2013, pp. 334–377.

Safferling, Christoph, 'The Special Intent Requirement in the Crime of Genocide', in Safferling, Christoph, Conze, Eckart (eds), *The Genocide Convention Sixty Years After Its Adoption*, The Hague: TMC Asser Press, 2010.

Sands, Philippe, *East West Street: On the Origins of Genocide and Crimes against Humanity*, London: Weidenfeld & Nicolson, 2016.

Savage, Rowan, 'Modern Genocidal Dehumanization: A New Model', 47 *Patterns of Prejudice*, Volume 47, No 2, 2013, pp. 139–161.

Schabas, William, 'Atrocity Crimes (Genocide, Crimes against Humanity, War Crimes)', in Schabas, William (ed), *The Cambridge Companion to International Criminal Law*, Cambridge: Cambridge University Press, 2016.

———, 'Commentary on *The Prosecutor v Akayesu*', in Klip, André, Sluiter, Göran (eds), *Annotated Leading Cases of International Criminal Tribunals: Volume II: The International Criminal Tribunal for Rwanda 1994–1999*, Antwerp: Intersentia, 1999.

———, 'The Contribution of the Eichmann Trial to International Law', *Leiden Journal of International Law*, Volume 26, No 03, 2013, pp. 667–699.

———, 'Defining Genocide', in Constantinides, Aristotle, Zaikos, Nikos (eds), *The Diversity of International Law: Essays in Honour of Professor Kalliopi K. Koufa*, Leiden: Martinus Nijhoff, 2009.

———, 'Genocide', in Triffterer, Otto, Ambos, Kai (eds), *The Rome Statute of the International Criminal Court: A Commentary*, München: Verlag C.H. Beck, 3rd edn, 2016.

———, 'Genocide, Crimes against Humanity, and Darfur: The Commission of Inquiry's Findings on Genocide', *Cardozo Law Review*, Volume 27, No 4, 2005–2006, pp. 1703–1721.

———, *Genocide in International Law: The Crime of Crimes*, Cambridge: Cambridge University Press, 1st edn, 2000.

———, *Genocide in International Law: The Crime of Crimes*, Cambridge: Cambridge University Press, 2nd edn, 2009.

———, 'Genocide Law in a Time of Transition: Recent Developments in the Law of Genocide', *Rutgers Law Review*, Volume 61, No 1, 2008–2009, pp. 161–192.

———, 'Groups Protected by the Genocide Convention: Conflicting Interpretations from the International Criminal Tribunal for Rwanda', *International Law Students Association Journal of International and Comparative Law*, Volume 6, 2000, pp. 375–387.

———, 'Has Genocide Been Committed in Darfur? The State Plan or Policy Element in the Crime of Genocide', in Henham, Ralph, Behrens, Paul (eds), *The Criminal Law of Genocide: International, Comparative and Contextual Aspects*, Aldershot: Ashgate, 2007.

———, 'Interpreting the Statutes of the *ad hoc* Tribunals', in Vohrah, Lal Chand *et al.* (eds), *Man's Inhumanity to Man: Essays on International Law in Honour of Antonio Cassese*, The Hague: Kluwer Law International, 2003.

———, *The International Criminal Court: A Commentary on the Rome Statute*, Oxford: Oxford University Press, 2nd edn, 2016.

———, *An Introduction to the International Criminal Court*, Cambridge: Cambridge University Press, 4th edn, 2011.

———, 'Judicial Activism and the Crime of Genocide', in Darcy, Shane, Powderly, Joseph (eds), *Judicial Creativity at the International Criminal Tribunal*, Oxford: Oxford University Press, 2010.

———, 'The Law and Genocide', in Bloxham, Donald, Moses, Dirk (eds), *The Oxford Handbook of Genocide Studies*, Oxford University Press, 2010/2013.

———, 'National Courts Finally Begin to Prosecute Genocide, the 'Crime of Crimes', *Journal of International Criminal Justice*, Volume 1, 2003, pp. 39–63.

———, 'The "Odious Scourge": Evolving Interpretations of the Crime of Genocide', *Genocide Studies and Prevention: An International Journal*, Volume 1, Number 2, 2006, pp. 93–106.

———, 'Synergy or Fragmentation? International Criminal Law and the European Convention on Human Rights', *Journal of International Criminal Justice*, Volume 9, 2011, pp. 609–632.

———, *The UN International Criminal Tribunals: The Former Yugoslavia, Rwanda and Sierra Leone*, Cambridge: Cambridge University Press, 2006.

———, *Unimaginable Atrocities – Justice, Politics, and Rights at the War Crimes Tribunals*, Oxford: Oxford University Press, 2012.

———, 'Was Genocide Committed in Bosnia and Herzegovina? First Judgment of the International Criminal Tribunal for the Former Yugoslavia', *Fordham International Law Journal*, Volume 25, No 1, 2001, pp. 23–53.

Schiller, Barry, 'Life in a Symbolic Universe: Comments on the Genocide Convention and International Law', *Southwestern University Law Review*, Volume 9, 1977, pp. 47–83.

Schmid, Evelyne, *Taking Economic, Social and Cultural Rights Seriously in International Criminal Law*, Cambridge: Cambridge University Press, 2015.

Schuster, Matthias, 'The Crime of Genocide Applied in Practice: Selected Aspects of the Jurisprudence of the *ad hoc* Tribunals' Appeals Chambers', in Safferling, Christoph, Conze, Eckart (eds), *The Genocide Convention Sixty Years After Its Adoption*, The Hague: TMC Asser Press, 2010.

Schwelb, Egon, 'Crimes against Humanity', in Lauterpacht, Hersch (ed), *The British Yearbook of International Law*, London: Oxford University Press, 1946.

———, 'The International Convention on the Elimination of All Forms of Racial Discrimination', *International and Comparative Law Quarterly*, Volume 15, 1966, pp. 996–1068.

Searle, John, *The Construction of Social Reality*, London: Penguin Books, 1996.

Selbmann, Frank, 'The 1979 Trial of the People's Revolutionary Tribunal and Implications for ECCC', in Meisenberg, Simon, Stegmiller, Ignaz (eds), *The Extraordinary Chambers in the Courts of Cambodia: Assessing Their Contribution to International Criminal Law*, The Hague: TMC Asser Press, 2016.

Shah, Sonali, 'The Oversight of the Last Great International Institutions of the Twentieth Century: The International Criminal Court's Definition of Genocide', *Emory International Law Review*, Volume 16, 2002, pp. 351–389.

Shahabuddeen, Mohamed, 'Does the Principle of Legality Stand in the Way of Progressive Development of Law?', *Journal of International Criminal Justice*, Volume 2, 2004, pp. 1007–1017.

———, *International Criminal Justice at the Yugoslav Tribunal: A Judge's Recollection*, Oxford: Oxford University Press, 2012.

Shaw, Malcolm, 'Genocide and International Law', in Dinstein, Yoram, Tabory, Mala (eds), *International Law at a Time of Perplexity: Essays in Honour of Shabtai Rosenne*, Dordrecht: Martinus Nijhoff Publishers, 1989.

Shaw, Martin, 'Sociology and Genocide', in Donald Bloxham, Dirk Moses (eds), *The Oxford Handbook of Genocide Studies*, Oxford: Oxford University Press, 2010/2013.

Slye, Ronald, 'Apartheid as a Crime Against Humanity: A Submission to the South African Truth and Reconciliation Commission', *Michigan Journal of International Law*, Volume 20, 1999, pp. 267–300.

Slye, Ronald, van Schaack, Beth, *International Criminal Law: The Essentials*, Austin: Wolters Kluwer, 2009.

Smeulers, Alette, Grünfeld, Fred, *International Crimes and other Gross Human Rights Violations: A Multi- and Interdisciplinary Textbook*, Leiden: Martinus Nijhoff, 2011.

Smeulers, Alette, Hoex, Lotte, 'Studying Microdynamics of the Rwandan Genocide', *British Journal of Criminology*, Volume 50, 2010, pp. 435–454.

Smith, Anthony, *The Ethnic Origins of Nations*, Oxford: Blackwell, 1986, reprinted 1993.

Smith, David Livingstone, *Less Than Human: Why We Demean, Enslave, and Exterminate Others*, New York: St. Martin's Press, 2011.

Smith, Peter Scharff, 'Dehumanization, Social Contact and Techniques of Othering: Combining the Lessons from Holocaust Studies and Prison Research', in Eriksson, Anna (ed), *Punishing the Other: The Social Production of Immorality Revisited*, London: Routledge, 2016.

Spinner, Jeff, *The Boundaries of Citizenship: Race, Ethnicity, and Nationality in the Liberal State*, Baltimore: John Hopkins University Press, 1994.

Stahn, Carsten, *A Critical Introduction to International Criminal Law*, Cambridge: Cambridge University Press, 2018.

Stanton, Gregory, 'Blue Scarves and Yellow Stars: Classification and Symbolization in the Cambodian Genocide', *Occasional Paper of the Montreal Institute for Genocide Studies*, April 1989, www.genocidewatch.org/images/AboutGen89BlueScarvesandYellowStars.pdf.

———, 'Could the Rwandan Genocide Have Been Prevented?', *Journal of Genocide Research*, Volume 6, Number 2, 2004, pp. 211–228.
———, *Countries at Risk Report 2012*, Washington: Genocide Watch, 2012.
———, *The Eight Stages of Genocide* (1996), www.genocidewatch.org/aboutgenocide/8stagesofgenocide.html.
———, *The Ten Stages of Genocide* (2013), www.genocidewatch.org/genocide/tenstagesofgenocide.html.
Staub, Ervin, 'The Roots and Prevention of Genocide and Related Mass Violence', in Zartman, I. William, Anstey, Mark, Meerts, Paul (eds), *The Slippery Slope to Genocide: Reducing Identity Conflict and Preventing Mass Murder*, Oxford: Oxford University Press, 2012.
Straus, Scott, 'Contested Meanings and Conflicting Imperatives: A Conceptual Analysis of Genocide', *Journal of Genocide Research*, Volume 3, 2001, pp. 349–375.
———, *The Order of Genocide: Race, Power, and War in Rwanda*, Ithaca: Cornell University Press, 2006.
Stultz, Newell, 'Evolution of the United Nations Anti-Apartheid Regime', *Human Rights Quarterly*, Volume 13, 1991, pp. 1–23.
Sullam, Simon Levis, 'The Italian Executioner: Revisiting the Role of Italians in the Holocaust', *Journal of Genocide Research*, Volume 19, No 1, 2017, pp. 22–38.
Sundquist, Christian, 'The Meaning of Race in the DNA Era: Science, History and the Law', *Temple Journal of Science, Technology and Environmental Law*, Volume 27, 2008, pp. *231–265.*
Sunga, Lyal S., *The Emerging System of International Criminal Law: Developments in Codification and Implementation*, The Hague: Kluwer Law International, 1997.
Sussman, Robert Wald, *The Myth of Race: The Troubling Persistence of an Unscientific Idea*, Cambridge: Harvard University Press, 2014.
Swaak-Goldman, Olivia, 'The Crime of Persecution in International Criminal Law', *Leiden Journal of International Law*, Volume 11, 1998, pp. 145–154.
———, 'Persecution', in Kirk McDonald, Gabrielle, Swaak-Goldman, Olivia (eds), *Substantive and Procedural Aspects of International Criminal Law: The Experience of International and National Courts, Volume I*, The Hague: Kluwer Law International, 2000.
Szpak, Agnieszka, 'National, Ethnic, Racial, and Religious Groups Protected against Genocide in the Jurisprudence of the Ad Hoc International Criminal Tribunals', *The European Journal of International Law*, Volume 23, No 1, 2012, pp. 155–173.
Tajfel, Henri, *Human Groups and Social Categories: Studies in Social Psychology*, Cambridge: Cambridge University Press, 1981.
Talmon, Stefan, 'Determining Customary International Law: The ICJ's Methodology between Induction, Deduction and Assertion', *European Journal of International Law*, Volume 26, 2016, pp. 417–443.
Tams, Christian, Berster, Lars, Schiffbauer, Björn, *Convention on the Prevention and Punishment of the Crime of Genocide: A Commentary*, München: C.H.Beck, 2014.
Tang, Hua et al., 'Genetic Structure, Self-Identified Race/Ethnicity, and Confounding in Case-Control Association Studies', *American Journal of Human Genetics*, Volume 76, 2005, pp. 268–275.
Taulbee, James Larry, *International Crime and Punishment: A Guide to the Issues*, Santa Barbara: ABC Clio, 2009.

Taylor, Christopher, *Sacrifice as Terror: The Rwandan Genocide of 1994*, Oxford: Berg, 1999.

Taylor, Paul, *Race: A Philosophical Introduction*, Cambridge: Polity Press, 2nd edn, 2013.

Temoney, Kate, 'The 1994 Rwandan Genocide: The Religion/Genocide Nexus, Sexual Violence, and the Future of Genocide Studies', *Genocide Studies and Prevention: An International Journal*, Volume 10, No 3, 2016.

Thirlway, Hugh, *The Sources of International Law*, Oxford: Oxford University Press, 2014.

Thornberry, Patrick, *International Law and the Rights of Minorities*, Oxford: Clarendon Press, 1991, reprinted 1992.

Tochilovsky, Vladimir, *Jurisprudence of the International Criminal Courts and the European Court of Human Rights: Procedure and Evidence*, Leiden: Martinus Nijhoff, 2008.

———, *The Law and Jurisprudence of the International Criminal Tribunals and Courts: Procedure and Human Rights Aspects*, Cambridge: Intersentia, 2nd edn, 2014.

Todorov, Tzvetan, 'Critical Response: "Race", Writing, and Culture (translated by Mack, Loulou)', *Critical Inquiry*, Volume 13, No 1, 1986, pp. 171–181.

Tomuschat, Christian, 'Universal Criminal Jurisdiction with Respect to the Crime of Genocide, Crimes against Humanity and War Crimes', in Institute of International Law, *Yearbook, Volume 71, Session of Krakow – First Part*, Paris: A. Pedone, 2005.

Triffterer, Otto, 'Genocide, Its Particular Intent to Destroy in Whole or in Part the Group as Such', *Leiden Journal of international Law*, Volume 14, No 2, 2001, pp. 399–408.

van den Herik, Larissa, 'Accountability Through Fact-Finding: Appraising Inquiry in the Context of Srebrenica', *Netherlands International Law Review*, Volume 62, 2015, pp. 295–311.

———, *The Contribution of the Rwanda Tribunal to the Development of International Law*, Leiden: Martinus Nijhoff Publishers, 2005.

———, 'The Schism between the Legal and the Social Concept of Genocide in Light of the Responsibility to Protect', in Henham, Ralph, Behrens, Paul (eds), *The Criminal Law of Genocide: International, Comparative and Contextual Aspects*, Aldershot: Ashgate, 2007.

———, 'Using Custom to Reconceptualize Crimes Against Humanity', in Darcy, Shane, Powderly, Joseph (eds), *Judicial Creativity at the International Criminal Tribunal*, Oxford: Oxford University Press, 2010.

van der Vyver, Johan, 'Apartheid', in Shelton, Dinah (ed), *Encyclopedia of Genocide and Crimes Against Humanity*, Farmington Hills: Thomson Gale, 2005.

———, 'Prosecution and Punishment of the Crime of Genocide', *Fordham International Law Journal*, Volume 23, 2000, pp. 286–356.

van Schaack, Beth, 'Darfur and the Rhetoric of Genocide', *Whittier Law Review*, Volume 26, 2005, pp. 1101–1141.

———, 'The Definition of Crimes Against Humanity: Resolving the Incoherence', *Columbia Journal of Transnational Law*, Volume 37, 1998–1999, pp. 787–850.

Vasiliev, Sergey, 'International Criminal Tribunals in the Shadow of Strasbourg and Politics of Cross-Fertilization', *Nordic Journal of International Law*, Volume 84, No 3, 2015, pp. 371–403.

Verdeja, Ernesto, 'Genocide: Debating Definitions', in Lupel, Adam, Verdeja, Ernesto (eds), *Responding to Genocide: The Politics of International Action*, Boulder: Lynne Rienner Publishers, 2013.

Verdirame, Guglielmo, 'The Genocide Definition in the Jurisprudence of the Ad Hoc Tribunals', *International and Comparative Law Quarterly*, Volume 49, 2000, pp. 578–598.

Vest, Hans, *Genozid durch organisatorische Machtapparate* [Genocide by means of organisational power structures], Baden-Baden: Nomos Verlagsgesellschaft, 2002.

———, 'A Structure-Based Concept of Genocidal Intent', *Journal of International Criminal Justice*, Volume 5, 2007, pp. 781–797.

Vianney-Liaud, Mélanie, 'Legal Constraints in the Interpretation of Genocide', in Meisenberg, Simon, Stegmiller, Ignaz (eds), *The Extraordinary Chambers in the Courts of Cambodia: Assessing Their Contribution to International Criminal Law*, The Hague: TMC Asser Press, 2016.

Vierdag, EW, *The Concept of Discrimination in International Law: With Special Reference to Human Rights*, The Hague: Martinus Nijhoff, 1973.

Villiger, Mark, *Commentary on the 1969 Vienna Convention on the Law of Treaties*, Leiden: Martinus Nijhoff, 2009.

von Hebel, Herman, Robinson, Darryl, 'Crimes within the Jurisdiction of the Court', in Lee, Roy S. (ed), *The International Criminal Court – The Making of the Rome Statute; Issues, Negotiations, Results*, The Hague: Kluwer Law International, 1999.

Vrdoljak, Ana Filipa, 'Genocide and Restitution: Ensuring Each Group's Contribution to Humanity', *European Journal of International Law*, Volume 22, 2011, pp. 17–47.

Wacquant, Loïc, 'For an Analytic of Racial Domination', *Political Power and Social Theory*, Volume 11, 1997, pp. 221–234.

Wagner, Markus, 'The ICC and its Jurisdiction: Myths, Misperceptions and Realities', in von Bogdandy, Armin, Wolfrum, Rüdiger (eds), *Max Planck Yearbook of United Nations Law*, Volume 7, Leiden: Martinus Nijhoff, 2003.

Wald, Patricia, 'Genocide and Crimes against Humanity', *Washington University Global Studies Law Review*, Volume 6, 2007, pp. 621–633.

Weatherall, Thomas, Jus Cogens*: International Law and Social Contract*, Cambridge: Cambridge University Press, 2015.

Weber, Max, *Grundriss der Sozialökonomik, III. Abteilung: Wirtschaft und Gesellschaft* [Economy and Society], Tübingen: Verlag von J.C.B. Mohr (Paul Siebeck), 1922.

Weiss-Wendt, Anton, Yeomans, Rory, 'The Holocaust and Historiographical Debates on Racial Science', in Weiss-Wendt, Anton, Yeomans, Rory (eds), *Racial Science in Hitler's New Europe, 1938–1945*, Lincoln: University of Nebraska Press, 2013.

Weitz, Eric, *A Century of Genocide: Utopias of Race and Nation*, Princeton: Princeton University Press, 2003.

Werfel, Franz, *Die vierzig Tage des Musa Dagh*, Berlin: Paul Zsolnay Verlag, 1933.

Werle, Gerhard, 'General Principles of International Criminal Law', in Cassese, Antonio (ed), *The Oxford Companion to International Criminal Justice*, Oxford: Oxford University Press, 2009.

Werle, Gerhard, Jessberger Florian, *Principles of International Criminal Law*, Oxford: Oxford University Press, 3rd edn, 2014.

Werther, Steffen, '"Nordic-Germanic" Dreams and National Realities: A Case Study of the Danish Region of Sønderylland, 1933–1945', in Weiss-Wendt, Anton,

Yeomans, Rory (eds), *Racial Science in Hitler's New Europe, 1938–1945*, Lincoln: University of Nebraska Press, 2013.

Wielenga, Cori, 'Genocide and Identity: Stereotyping, 'Othering' and Violence in Rwanda', 2011, www.genocidescholars.org/sites/default/files/document%09%5Bcurrent-page%3A1%5D/documents/IAGS%202011%20CORI%20Wielenga.pdf.

Wilson, Edward, *The Social Conquest of Earth*, New York: Liveright Publishing Corporation, 2012.

Wilson, Richard Ashby, 'Crimes against Humanity and the Conundrum of Race and Ethnicity at the International Criminal Tribunal for Rwanda', in Feldman, Ilana, Ticktin, Miriam (eds), *In the Name of Humanity: The Government of Threat and Care*, Durham: Duke University Press, 2010.

———, 'Expert Evidence on Trial: Social Researchers in the International Criminal Courtroom', *American Ethnologist*, Volume 43, No 4, November 2016, pp. 730–744.

———, 'Propaganda and History in International Criminal Trials', *Journal of International Criminal Justice*, Volume 14, 2016, pp. 519–541.

Wolff, Elisabetta Cassina, 'Biological Racism and Antisemitism as Intellectual Constructions in Italian Fascism: The Case of *Telesio Interlandi* and *La difesa della razza*', in Weiss-Wendt, Anton, Yeomans, Rory (eds), *Racial Science in Hitler's New Europe, 1938–1945*, Lincoln: University of Nebraska Press, 2013.

Wouters, Jan, Verhoeven, Sten, 'The Domestic Prosecution of Genocide', in Behrens, Paul, Henham, Ralph (eds), *Elements of Genocide*, Abingdon: Routledge, 2013.

Young, Rebecca, 'How Do We Know Them When We See Them? The Subjective Evolution in the Identification of Victim Groups for the Purpose of Genocide', *International Criminal Law Review*, Volume 10, 2010, pp. 1–22.

———, '"Internationally Recognized Human Rights" before the International Criminal Court', *International and Comparative Law Quarterly*, Volume 60, No 1, January 2011, pp. 189–208.

Yudell, Michael, *Race Unmasked: Biology and Race in the Twentieth Century*, New York: Columbia University Press, 2014.

Zahar, Alexander, 'Apartheid as an International Crime', in Cassese, Antonio (ed), *The Oxford Companion to International Criminal Justice*, Oxford: Oxford University Press, 2009.

Zahar, Alexander, Sluiter, Göran, *International Criminal Law: A Critical Introduction*, Oxford: Oxford University Press, 2008.

Zartman, I. William, Anstey, Mark, 'The Problem: Preventing Identity Conflicts and Genocide', in Zartman, I. William, Anstey, Mark, Meerts Paul (eds), *The Slippery Slope to Genocide: Reducing Identity Conflicts and Preventing Mass Murder*, Oxford: Oxford University Press, 2012.

Zeegers, Krit, *International Criminal Tribunals and Human Rights Law: Adherence and Contextualization*, The Hague: Asser Press, 2016.

Index

For Product Safety Concerns and Information please contact our EU
representative GPSR@taylorandfrancis.com
Taylor & Francis Verlag GmbH, Kaufingerstraße 24, 80331 München, Germany

www.ingramcontent.com/pod-product-compliance
Ingram Content Group UK Ltd.
Pitfield, Milton Keynes, MK11 3LW, UK
UKHW022012180926
475701UK00003B/332
* 9 7 8 1 0 3 2 0 8 9 1 4 0 *